RELEASED

# European Labor
# Relations

# European Labor Relations

## Text and Cases

**Thomas Kennedy**
Harvard University

**LexingtonBooks**
D.C. Heath and Company
Lexington, Massachusetts
Toronto

**Library of Congress Cataloging in Publication Data**

Kennedy, Thomas, 1912-
    European labor relations.

    1. Industrial relations—Europe—Case studies. I. Title.
HD8376.5.K46          331'.094          78-14155
ISBN 0-669-02663-8

Fourth printing, May 1983

Published simultaneously in Canada

Printed in the United States of America

International Standard Book Number: 0-669-02663-8

Library of Congress Catalog Card Number: 78-14155

*To My Wife, Ruth*

# Contents

List of Figures and Tables     xi

Preface and Acknowledgments     xiii

**Chapter 1**     **Labor Relations in Great Britain**     1

Introduction     1
The Union Movement     2
Employers' Associations     5
Legislation and Agencies     6
Collective Bargaining     7
Legislated Employee Protection and Benefits     14
Absenteeism     17
Worker Participation     18
Profit Sharing and Employee Ownership     19
Case 1     Barrett Cycle Company (A)     23
    Barrett Cycle Company (B)     33
Case 2     M-S Limited (A)     35
    M-S Limited (B)     42
    M-S Limited (C)     44

**Chapter 2**     **Labor Relations in France**     45

Introduction     45
The Union Movement     46
Employers' Associations     48
Collective Bargaining     48
Legislated Employee Protection and Benefits     52
Absenteeism     56
Worker Participation     57
Profit Sharing and Employee Ownership     59
Case 3     Poncet Mine (A)     63
    Poncet Mine (B)     72
Case 4     Bouclier Copper Company (A)     75
    Bouclier Copper Company (B)     81
    Bouclier Copper Company (C)     82

**Chapter 3**     **Labor Relations in Italy**     85

Introduction     85
The Union Movement     86

Employers' Associations                                    90
Collective Bargaining                                      91
Legislated Employee Protection and Benefits                96
Collective Bargaining by Managers                         100
Absenteeism                                               101
Worker Participation                                      102
Case 5      Barachim                                      105

**Chapter 4      Labor Relations in the Netherlands        117**

Introduction                                              117
The Union Movement                                        118
Employers' Associations                                   122
Collective Bargaining                                     122
Legislated Employee Protection and Benefits               126
Absenteeism                                               128
Worker Participation                                      128
Profit Sharing and Employee Ownership                     133
Case 6      Hobbema and van Rijn, N.V. (A)                137
            Hobbema and van Rijn, N.V. (B-1)              147
            Hobbema and van Rijn, N.V. (B-2)              150
            Hobbema and van Rijn, N.V. (B-3)              151
            Hobbema and van Rijn, N.V. (B-4)              153
            Hobbema and van Rijn, N.V. (B-5)              154
            Hobbema and van Rijn, N.V. (C)                155
Case 7      Europa Food Industries B.V.                   157

**Chapter 5      Labor Relations in West Germany           173**

Introduction                                              173
The Union Movement                                        174
Employers' Associations                                   177
Collective Bargaining                                     178
Legislated Employee Protection and Benefits               181
Absenteeism                                               185
Worker Participation                                      185
Profit Sharing and Employee Ownership                     195
Appendix 5A: Functions and Authority of the
      Works Council                                       197
Case 8      Pickardt-Rhine International A.G. (A)          203
            Pickardt-Rhine International A.G. (B)          215
            Pickardt-Rhine International A.G. (C)          217
Case 9      Fischer Electric A.G.                         219

**Chapter 6**     **Labor Relations in Sweden**                                     233

Introduction                                                                               233
The Union Movement                                                                 234
Employers' Associations                                                            239
Collective Bargaining                                                               239
The Legislation of the Seventies                                               245
The Decrease in Management Authority                                   246
Legislated Employee Protection and Benefits                          247
Absenteeism                                                                            251
Worker Participation                                                               251
Profit Sharing and Employee Ownership                                  252
Case 10     Dagens Nyheters                                                     257
Case 11     Homeland Manufacturing Company                       287

**Chapter 7**     **Labor Relations in the United States**                        295

Introduction                                                                               295
The Union Movement                                                                 296
Employee Rights                                                                       297
Union Recognition                                                                     298
Employer Rights                                                                        299
Contract Negotiations                                                               299
Grievance and Arbitration Procedures                                      300
Strikes and Lockouts                                                                301
Absenteeism                                                                            302
Worker Participation                                                               302
Case 12     First National Bank of Lake City                           305
Case 13     Wilson Distributors Company (A)                          321
                     Wilson Distributors Company (B)                          327
                     Wilson Distributors Company (C)                          328

**Chapter 8**     **Transnational Labor Relations**                                329

Multinational Conglomerates versus National
     Industrial Unions                                                                 329
The Threat to Union Bargaining Power                                    330
Labor's Response—International Trade
     Secretariats                                                                        331
International Trade Secretariats' Aid and
     Support for National Unions                                               333
The International Trade Secretariat's Goal:
     Transnational Bargaining                                                     337

Barriers to the International Trade Secretariats'
        Progress                                                    339
The Threat to Union Political Power                                 342
The Union Response in the Political Arena                           342
Restrictive National Legislation                                   342
Regulation of Multinational Conglomerates by
        International Organizations                                 343
Guidelines of the Organization of Economic
        Cooperation and Development                                 348
Summary                                                            352
Case 14      Belgian Royal Airways                                  357
Case 15      Meert International                                    367

**Chapter 9      Some Major Issues in European Labor Relations      377**

Employee Representation on Company Boards                           377
Works Councils                                                     380
Asset Formation and Employee Ownership                             384
Dismissals                                                         386
Absenteeism                                                        388
Rights and Benefits for Women Employees                            391

**Statistical Appendix**                                            397

**Index**                                                           407

**About the Author**                                                429

# List of Figures and Tables

**Figures**

| | | |
|---|---|---:|
| 2-1 | Selection of Plant and Company Employee Representatives | 58 |
| 4-1 | Works Council | 130 |
| 4-2 | Board Appointments | 132 |
| 5-1 | Supervisory Board Membership in West Germany | 187 |

**Tables**

| | | |
|---|---|---:|
| 5-1 | Supervisory Board Membership | 190 |
| 9-1 | Sick Pay Provisions | 389 |
| 9-2 | Maternity Protection and Benefits Acts in Six Western European Countries | 392 |
| A-1 | Population | 399 |
| A-2 | Gross National Product | 399 |
| A-3 | Consumer Price Index | 399 |
| A-4 | Unemployment Rates | 400 |
| A-5 | Average Hourly Compensation for Production Workers in Manufacturing | 401 |
| A-6 | Output | 401 |
| A-7 | Productivity | 402 |
| A-8 | Unit Labor Costs in Local Currencies | 402 |
| A-9 | Unit Labor Costs in U.S. Dollars | 402 |
| A-10 | Unemployment Benefit Systems | 403 |
| A-11 | Estimated Union Membership | 404 |
| A-12 | Days Lost through Industrial Disputes | 405 |
| A-13 | Sickness Absenteeism—Industrial Workers, 1973 | 406 |

# Preface and Acknowledgments

Labor relations in Western Europe can be classified into three major types: the British system, the southern continental system, and the northern continental system. This study includes texts and cases in each of these three areas. Within the three major areas, however, each country in Western Europe has its own distinct legislation, institutions, customs, and practices in labor relations. I regret that time has not permitted me to prepare texts and cases for all of the Western European countries. The study has been limited to a chapter on each of six countries: Great Britain, France, Italy, the Netherlands, West Germany, and Sweden. I hope the study can be expanded at some future time to include the other Western European countries.

Because European managers and labor leaders have exhibited great interest in the U.S. labor-relations system, I have included a note and two cases on it. There is no attempt in this chapter on U.S. labor relations to be definitive. Instead, the purpose is to provide Europeans with the broad elements of U.S. labor relations, especially those elements which are different from the elements of the European systems.

In chapter 8, I present text material and two cases on multinational collective bargaining, a subject that has assumed increasing importance in Europe as labor leaders there have moved to develop means to deal more effectively with what they see as the growing threat of multinational corporations. In this chapter, I discuss both the economic and the political devices through which the unions are attempting to control multinational companies.

Finally, in chapter 9 I discuss six issues which, together with multinational bargaining, are among the major topics of debate in European labor relations: employee representatives on company boards, works councils, asset formation and employee ownership, dismissals, absenteeism, and rights and benefits for women employees.

All thirteen cases in this book are real. The incidents actually occurred in a European or a U.S. company. The facts were carefully checked by analyzing written records and by conducting lengthy discussions with those who participated in the actions. Finally, the written cases were approved by management as a true record of what actually occurred. All but one of the cases, however, have been heavily disguised to protect the identity of the companies, unions, and individuals.

This book grew out of my experience in developing and teaching a course in Switzerland, on European labor relations, first for the Senior Management Program (SMP) of the Harvard Business School and later for the Top Management Program (TMP) of the newspaper industry. The experience began in the spring of 1976 with six months of study and case writing in various Western European countries. Since then, I have taught the European labor course seven times: in the fall of 1976, spring of 1977, fall of 1977 and spring of 1978 to the SMPs, and in the fall of 1978, spring of 1979, and winter of 1979 to the TMPs. At each of these sessions, the SMP and TMP participants, many of whom had had experience in labor relations in one or more of the European countries, made suggestions that greatly improved the material, and they also provided leads for new cases in their own and other companies. I am extremely grateful to them for these contributions. In a very real sense, this book represents their joint effort, for which I served as researcher, writer, and editor.

Two of the cases were not written by me or under my supervision. One of the Dutch cases, Hobbema and Van Rijn, was written by Professor Dwight Ladd, and one of the international cases, Belgian Royal Airways, was written by James H. Leonhard under the supervision of Professor Francis Aguilar. I am indebted to these gentlemen for permitting these cases to be printed in this book. Two case writers worked under my direction during the school year 1976-1977. Leroy B. Fraser wrote four of the cases: Pickardt-Rhine, Fischer Electric, Europa Food Industries, and Dagens Nyheters. Yaakov Keren wrote Ponce Mine and Bouclier Copper. Also, one of the U.S. cases was written by Michael J. Jedel under my direction at an earlier time. I appreciate the work that each of these men did. It was a pleasure to work with them.

I was told when I undertook the project that I would find European managers reluctant to permit me to write cases concerning their experiences in labor relations. This did not prove to be true. I received excellent cooperation, and for this I am grateful to the many European executives who gave so generously of their valuable time. I would like to refer to each one of them by name but to do so would break the disguises of the cases. In developing the chapters on labor relations in the various countries, I also received excellent cooperation from labor leaders, government officials, and professors. I am most grateful to all of them.

Space does not permit me to name all of those who have helped in this project. However, I would like to give special thanks to Lawrence Fouraker, dean of the Harvard Business School, who made it possible for me to spend two and one-half years in this challenging task and to John Baitsell, corporate labor relations manager of Mobil Oil Company; to John Mac-Arthur and Bruce Scott, professors at the Harvard Business School, for their special efforts in opening doors for me at a number of European companies where I was able to write cases; to Professor John Stamm of Babson College, who generously agreed to read a number of the chapters and offered very constructive criticism and suggestions; and, finally, to my wife,

Ruth who accompanied me on most of the case-writing trips and who has read all the material and has made many corrections and suggestions that have greatly improved it.

**European Labor
Relations**

# 1 Labor Relations in Great Britain

## Introduction

The population of Great Britain in 1978 was 56 million which was the third largest in Western Europe, exceeded only by West Germany and Italy. Yet during the 1970-1978 period, British population increased only 0.72%—the lowest rate of growth of all the countries in this study. In the seventies, British population was surpassed by Italian population, and if the trend continues, France will also have a larger population than Britain in the eighties (see table A-1).*

The gross national product of Great Britain in 1976 was $234 billion which was smaller than that of the United States, France, or West Germany but larger than that of Italy, the Netherlands, or Sweden. However, the gross national product per person in Great Britain was only $4,180—less than that of any of the other countries except Italy. Moreover, the gross national product per person during the period 1970-1976 grew at a rate of only 1.7% per year which, although equal to the U.S. rate, was lower than that of any of the other five European countries studied (see table A-2).

Consumer prices in Great Britain during the period 1970-1978 Increased 170%, the highest of all the countries studied (see table A-3). During the same period, unemployment averaged 4.3% which was also higher than the rate in the other European countries, but lower than that of the United States (see table A-4).

Great Britain's average hourly compensation for production workers in manufacturing in 1978 was $4.58; the lowest of all the countries. During the 1970-1978 period, the average hourly compensation increased 180%—lower than the increase in any of the other European countries but higher than in the United States. In terms of local purchasing power, compensation for British workers increased only 27% which, although almost twice as high as the increase in the United States, was much lower than that of the other European countries (see table A-5).

Output in manufacturing in Great Britain increased an average of 2.3% per year during the period 1960-1978 and only 0.7% per year during 1970-1978. The rates of increase were the lowest of any country in the study (see table A-6). Productivity as measured by percentage change in

---

*Tables A-1 through A-13 referred to in this chapter are in the statistical appendix at the end of the book.

output per hour increased 3.2% per year during the period 1960-1978 and 1.8% during 1970-1978. The rate of increase in productivity during the 1960-1978 period was lower than in any of the countries except in the United States, and the rate during 1970-1978 was lower than in any of the countries including the United States (see table A-7).

Unit labor costs in terms of British currency increased 7.9% per year during the period 1960-1978 and 15.8% during 1970-1978. In both of these periods, the increase was greater than in any of the other countries (see table A-8). In U.S. dollars, the increases in unit labor costs were 5.4% per year during the period 1960-1978 and 10.8% per year during 1970-1978. These figures were lower than those of the other European countries, but in the 1970-1977 period, the increase was greater than that of the United States or Italy (see table A-9).

## The Union Movement

There are 274 certified independent trade unions in Great Britain with approximately 12 million members who make up about 50% of the work force.[1] Many of the unions are quite small, and there is a strong trend toward merger and amalgamation.[2] As a result, over half of the membership is now concentrated in the following large unions:

1. TGWU        Transport and General Workers Union (Britain's largest union—over 2 million members)
2. AUEW        Amalgamated Union of Engineering Workers
3. NUGMW       National Union of General and Municipal Workers
4. EPTU        Electrical and Plumbing Trades Union
5. ASTMS       Association of Scientific, Technical, and Managerial Staffs
6. NUPE        National Union of Public Employees
7. NUM         National Union of Mineworkers
8. NUR         National Union of Railway Workers

Between 1963 and 1974, the density of union membership increased from 42.7% to 50.4%. White-collar employees, including professionals and supervisory employees, are increasingly represented by unions, and the division between union and non-union personnel occurs much higher up in the hierarchies of British companies than in U.S. companies where even foremen are seldom union members. However, since 1948 the unions have made substantial gains in both the manual and white-collar groups, from 51% to 58% in the former and from 30% to 39% in the latter.[3] As a percent of the workforce, union membership in Britain is twice as large as in the United States or France, but considerably smaller than in some continental countries (see table A-11).

*The Trades Union Congress (TUC)*

One hundred and fifty-eight of the certified unions with about 10 million members are affiliated with the Trades Union Congress (TUC).[4] The TUC is a confederation in which the national unions have jealously guarded their autonomy and strongly resisted centralized control. As a result, the TUC has little or no power over the activities of its affiliates. The TUC does not engage in collective bargaining, but it does wield significant political influence.

*Structure*

In the analysis of trade unions, three categories are generally used: craft, industrial, and general. A craft union is one that accepts into membership all workers with a particular skill, such as electricians or patternmakers, regardless of the industry in which they work. An industrial union is one that accepts into membership all workers in a particular industry regardless of the craft at which they work. A general union cuts across both craft and industry lines and accepts into membership a variety of skilled and unskilled workers in various industries. British unions do not lend themselves to an easy classification into these three categories. The TGWU and the NUGMW claim to be general unions, but in some industries they organize only the operators and laborers, leaving the skilled maintenance workers to their separate unions. The National Union of Mineworkers comes closest to being an industrial union. However, most British unions spill over into the boundaries of all three categories. As Clegg has written, "There is no other trade union movement with so complex a structure."[5]

*Jurisdictional and Demarcation Disputes*

As a result of the complex structure of the union movement, most British plants are subject to multi-unionism. In the late 1960s, the royal commission found that four-fifths of the union stewards came from plants where more than one union represented manual workers, and nearly one-third came from plants where more than one union competed for the same workers. One automobile plant has twenty-two different unions. A 1968 study of several companies showed an average of 7.4 unions per plant.[6] As a result, British industry is subject to demarcation and jurisdictional disputes, with management caught in the middle of inter-union struggles. However, this problem appears to be less troublesome than it was some years ago. The merging of unions has eliminated some points of friction and the TUC has developed an internal mechanism (The Bridlington procedure) whereby all TUC affiliates must submit such disputes to conciliation and, if necessary, binding awards by the TUC disputes committee. The committee handles sixty to seventy cases per year. Although the awards are not legally binding, they have been seriously challenged only twice since World War II. In recent years, inter-union difficulties have accounted for less than 5% of all strikes in Britain.[7]

## Closed Shop

A closed-shop agreement is one in which the company and the union agree that an employee must be a member of the union in order to work at the plant. The British distinguish between a pre-entry and a post-entry closed shop, In the former type, an employee must be a member of the union in order to be hired by the company. In the latter, members or nonmembers can be hired, but they must join the union and remain in good standing after becoming employed. Under the Trade Union and Labor Relations Act (1974), the closed shop in all its forms, including the pre-entry and the post-entry shop, is now permitted. This is in contrast to the situation in the rest of Western Europe, where the law gives employees the freedom to join or not to join a union.

In Britain as in the United States, however, the only way a union can obtain a formal closed shop is through an agreement with an employer. The employer is free to reject the closed-shop demand, in which case the union is free to strike.

Although closed-shop agreements are spreading and are common in the coal, maritime, waterfront, printing, power, railway, and trucking industries, the great majority of workers are not covered by them. However, actual closed-shop situations are much more prevalent than the formal agreements indicate. In 1974, McCarthy found that two out of five British workers had no choice but to join a union, although at that time only 750 thousand were covered by formal closed-shop agreements.[8]

## Checkoff

The payment of union dues through payroll deduction, although legal, is not widespread in Britain. In 1968, the royal commission estimated that only 20% of union dues were collected by this means, mainly in the public services and nationalized industries. In private industry, the task of collecting dues usually falls on the shop stewards, but check-off provisions appear to be growing.

## Employee Rights

Under the current labor laws, workers are protected against discrimination because of union membership or activity. If an employee believes discrimination has been practiced against him, he can appeal to an industrial tribunal whch may award him compensatory damages. In case of discharge for union membership or activity, a tribunal may recommend reinstatement and provide interim relief in the form of wages until a final settlement is reached. However, where the closed shop is in effect, employees who refuse to join, except for those who are members of religious groups that prohibit joining, have no protection against being dismissed.

The 1974 labor laws also provided workers with a right to claim before an industrial tribunal that they had been arbitrarily excluded from union membership. In the 1976 amendments, this provision was repealed. The TUC has set up an independent review body to hear such complaints. Moreover, a worker may bring a suit under common law rights, but is not likely to do so.

## Politics

The trade union movement has an exceptionally strong affiliation with and strong influence on the Labor party. Most of the unions have a political fund from which members must contract out if they do not want part of their union dues to be used for political purposes.[9] The unions provide 90% of the Labor party's funds and control four-fifths of the votes at the party's annual conferences.[10] Through the Labor party, the unions exercise heavy influence on national legislation. Many of the Labor party members of parliament are subsidized by unions.[11] The last Labor party prime minister, Callaghan, and two-thirds of his cabinet members were former union officials.

## Ideology

It is difficult to generalize regarding the ideology of the British labor movement. Although in the past the union movement supported democratic socialism and the nationalization of coal, steel, electric power, railways, and airlines, there appears to be less interest in further nationalization. Some unions, such as the bank employees union, now actually oppose nationalization of their own industries.

## Employer's Associations

British companies are organized into employer's associations to deal with the labor unions. There are over a thousand such associations. In the past, the major collective bargaining negotiations were carried on between the associations and unions or groups of unions. Some associations offer financial indemnity to members involved in stoppages, provided they have followed the association's guidance.

The largest employers' association is the Engineering Employers' Federation (EEF) which represents 5,600 member firms. The EEF, in addition to negotiating with a confederation of unions in the engineering field, maintains a procedure under which disputes may be settled during the life of the contracts. The EEF also carries on extensive educational, training, and lobbying activities.

The central spokesman for business in Britain is the Confederation of British Industries (CBI). It has as members over two hundred associations and 13,000 individual companies. Although the CBI does not engage directly in collective bargaining, it does present industry's position on labor matters to the public and to parliament, and attempts to keep up a constructive relationship with the TUC, especially through the Advisory Conciliation and Arbitration Service and other government agencies on which both organizations are represented.

## Legislation and Agencies

There have been so many new laws, repeals of old laws, amendments to laws, and codes of practices in the labor field in Britain in recent years that management has had difficulty keeping abreast of them. The most important acts have been:

| | |
|---|---|
| 1963 | The Contracts of Employment Act |
| 1965 | The Redundancy Payments Act |
| 1969 | The Redundancy Rebates Act |
| 1971 | The Industrial Relations Act (repealed in 1974) |
| 1972 | The Contracts of Employment Act (reenacted) |
| 1974 | The Trade Union and Labor Relations Act (TULRA) |
| 1974 | The Health and Safety at Work Act |
| 1975 | The Employment Protection Act (EPA) |
| 1975 | The Social Security Pensions Act (SSPA) |
| 1975 | Amendments to TULRA |

Under these various acts, several government agencies have been established to interpret and administer the laws. The most important of these agencies with respect to collective bargaining are listed here.

1. *ACAS*—The Advisory Conciliation and Arbitration Service was established by the Employment Protection Act (EPA) in 1975. It consists of a chairman and a council of 9 members, 3 of whom are nominated by the TUC and 3 by the CBI. In addition to offering advice, conciliation, and arbitration, the ACAS has responsibility in disputes over trade union recognition, disclosure of information for collective bargaining, equal pay, sex

discrimination, and racial discrimination. Moreover, since January 1, 1977, when Schedule 11 of the EPA became effecive, it has had the additional responsibility of hearing claims by unions that the wages of certain employers are below those set forth in a national industry agreement; or if no industry agreement exists, below the wages being paid generally by employers in the industry in the district. Finally, it has been given the task of preparing codes of practice to serve as guides to managements and unions in interpreting and applying the laws. Three such codes have been published.

2. *CAC*—The Central Arbitration Committee was also established by the EPA in 1975. At the end of 1977, the CAC consisted of a chairman, 4 deputy chairmen, and 63 "side" members chosen from management or labor. Each case is usually heard by an ad hoc committee consisting of a neutral chairman and one member each from the labor and management panels. It issues final and binding decisions in recognition, disclosure, and Schedule 11 cases that the ACAS has not been able to solve through conciliation. It also will arrange for arbitration of any dispute if requested to do so by both labor and management.

3. *Certification Officer*—This officer decides which trade unions are independent of management control, and issues certifications to that effect which are necessary if a union is to avail itself of the advantages under the TULRA and EPA.

4. *Industrial Tribunals*—First established in 1964, the tribunals consist of a chairman who is a lawyer and two lay members with labor relations experience. The recent labor legislation provides that workers may file with tribunals complaints against employers on numerous issues, including claims of unfair dismissals. Likewise, unions may file complaints on several issues, including failure of employers to follow the rules regarding redundancies.


## Collective Bargaining

### Union Recognition

Sections 11-16 of the EPA (1975) which became effective February 1, 1976, provide that if an employer refuses to recognize and bargain with a certified independent union or refuses to extend the area or scope of recognition to other employees or other items, the union may appeal the matter to the ACAS. The ACAS will seek to conciliate, but if conciliation is unsuccessful, it may hold an election or seek by other means to determine if the employees wish to be represented by the union. The ACAS will then make a recommendation. If it recommends recognition but the employer continues to refuse to recognize and deal with the union, the union may appeal to the Central Arbitration Committee and make a claim for terms and conditions of employment which may then be awarded by the CAC and become part of the contracts of employment of the individual workers concerned. However, neither the ACAS nor CAC has the power to force an employer to recognize and bargain with a union.

During the first two years of operation of sections 11-16, that is, from February 1, 1976, to February 1, 1978, the unions referred 1,072 recognition cases to the ACAS. Action was taken on 560 of these cases. Recognition was granted in 321 or 57%, either as a result of conciliation or following a recommendation by the ACAS. By the end of 1977, only seven cases had been appealed by the unions to the CAC. However, the CAC expected that the volume of such cases would increase.

*Multiple Recognition*

The exclusive recognition concept whereby management is required by law to recognize and bargain with one union only for a particular group of employees is not part of the British labor law system. Even if Union A can demonstrate that it has the support of 70% of the skilled workers in a plant, there is no legal procedure whereby it can be certified as the sole bargaining agent for all the skilled workers. If Union B has the support of the remaining 30%, it is free to try to force management to recognize and bargain also. However, in most plants, management recognizes and deals only with one union for each particular group of workers. It is likely also that the ACAS, by recommending recognition of only majority unions will have a salutary influence in this respect.

*Government Restraints*

Free collective bargaining over wages and related economic matters has not been possible in Britain for more than a decade. Since 1966, with the exception of one year (1971), bargaining has never been technically free from government wage restraints in one form or another. The restraints have not always been effective, but they have interfered with free collective bargaining and, during the last few years under the Labor government, they seem to have been quite effective in preventing leapfrog bargaining and in damping down inflation. On July 21, 1978, the government announced a new wage-increase guideline of 5% to become effective August 1 for the following twelve months. The guidelines permitted wage increases above 5% only if the excess was offset by higher productivity. Companies that granted higher increases were subject to sanctions, such as withdrawal of government contracts and financial aid. To the extent that the controls were effective, collective bargaining, especially at the industry level in the private sector, was less significant in wage matters, but at the same time, the scope of bargaining was extended into many new nonwage matters.

*Levels of Bargaining*

The usual pattern of collective bargaining in Britain consists of three or four levels.

1. *Industry-wide bargaining* occurs when a basic national agreement is negotiated between an industry employers' association and a national union or group of unions. (In the engineering industry, thirty-four unions have combined into the Confederation of Shipbuilding and Engineering Unions to bargain with the Engineering Employers' Federation representing over 5,600 firms and employing over two million workers.) The national agreements deal with two major areas—procedure and substantive issues. The procedural part of the agreement sets forth a series of negotiation steps (usually three) which the union must follow in an attempt to settle any dispute before it is free to strike. The national agreements formerly were quite limited regarding substantive issues, usually only dealing with: 1. minimum wage rates, 2. the normal work week, 3. overtime, 4. holidays, 5. shift premiums, and 6. apprenticeship. However, as a result of the recent wage freezes, the scope of national bargaining in many industries has been expanded to include many fringe benefits. Actually, national bargaining usually results not in a single agreement, but instead in a series of agreements with different termination dates. (In the engineering industry, there is an Engineering Handbook of National Agreements that has more than 300 pages.) However, the unions are free at any time to raise new claims on matters not covered by the existing agreements, and wage agreements usually do not specify a fixed period of time. Thus, the national agreements are neither closed-end ones, nor are they set for fixed terms, with the result that there tends to be continuous bargaining.

2. *Regional bargaining* occurs in some but not all industries. Where it does occur, the district employers' association negotiates with the union or unions. Regional wage rates may be agreed upon and added to the national minima. Likewise, certain work rules may be established. However, this level of collective bargaining has become less significant in recent years as subjects formerly negotiated here have been moved into either national or local bargaining spheres.

3. *Company bargaining.* Some companies negotiate directly with unions either in place of or in addition to industry-wide negotiations. When

negotiations take the place of industry-wide bargaining, they tend to cover many of the subjects industry negotiations would cover, plus matters that are especially related to the company and its employees. Where company bargaining occurs in addition to industry bargaining, it tends to concentrate on special company problems.

4. *Local bargaining* occurs at the plant level between the local plant management and the shop stewards, frequently organized into a stewards' council. Local agreements usually cover supplementary wage rates, piecework prices, bonus payments, allowances, merit money, and overtime arrangements. Issues of discipline, safety, redundancy, health, and welfare also are normally handled at the local level by the management and the shop stewards. Often the local bargaining is very informal, resulting only in an oral understanding. In recent years, local bargaining has grown in significance, and as a result management's unilateral authority in the plant has diminished.[12]

### Dispute Procedures

Although a British labor agreement does not guarantee labor peace for a fixed period, usually it does contain a dispute procedure that must be exhausted before an official strike over wages or a change in the agreement can occur. In the engineering industry, the procedure consists of six steps. While these six steps are being implemented, the status quo must be maintained. The unions are not free to strike, but likewise management is not free to make changes. Although this procedure has been reasonably effective, it has not prevented some unauthorized strikes and slowdowns. Also, management at times has felt that the unions have used the procedure to delay necessary changes. At the end of the procedure, there is no final and binding award. Instead, management is free to put its decision into effect and the union is free to strike.

The agreements generally contain a grievance procedure for disputes concerning the meaning of the terms of the agreement, and for disputes about discipline and discharge of employees. However, the grievance procedure ends in a final proposal which the union is free to accept or reject by striking. There is often no final and binding arbitration of grievances. As a result, the discipline or discharge of an employee, especially if he is a shop steward, sometimes results in a wildcat strike. (It is estimated that 10% of all British strikes have such an origin.) However, the great majority of grievances are settled in the established procedures without strikes. The EPA (1975) also provides that an employee who is terminated may appeal to a tribunal where management must defend its action. The tribunal may order a money award, and since April 1, 1978, may also order rehiring or reinstatement.

*Information for Bargaining*

Sections 17-21 of the EPA state that management must provide a recognized independent union with financial and other information without which the union would be materially impeded in its efforts to bargain effectively. Confidential information is specifically excluded. The ACAS issued a code of practice on this subject effective August 27, 1977, which lists the following as examples of types of information that must be supplied: pay and benefits; policies on hiring, redundancy, and promotion; manpower; performance; and cost structure, profits, transfer prices, and other financial data. A union can file a complaint claiming that an employer has refused to disclose the required information. The ACAS will attempt to conciliate the matter, but if conciliation fails, the CAC may hear the disputants and order the employer to provide the information that it deems necessary for effective bargaining. If the employer continues to refuse to supply the information, the CAC may establish the terms and conditions of the employees. The CAC order becomes an effective part of the employment contracts between the employer and his employees.

*Paid Time Off for Shop Stewards*

Effective April, 1978, (under the EPA, 1975) stewards and other working representatives of unions are given the right to reasonable time off with pay to carry out their industrial relations duties and to undergo training in industrial relations. In addition, they have the right to a reasonable amount of time off without pay to take part in the activities of their unions. The ACAS has issued a code of practice on this issue which does not fix specific amounts of time but recommends that managements and unions should work out details.

*Labor Agreements*

Labor agreements are not legally enforceable in Great Britain. In 1969 when the Ford Motor Company sought an injunction against unions that were supporting a strike while a valid labor agreement was still in effect, the judge ruled that an injunction could not be granted because collective bargaining agreements in Britain are "binding in honor only."

In the Industrial Relations Act of 1971 which was passed by the Conservative government, it was provided that every written labor agreement would be legally binding unless the parties inserted a disclaimer clause. The provision was ineffective, however, because unions refused to sign contracts without a disclaimer clause.

When the Labor party came to power, it reversed the provision. The TULRA (1974) provides that a collective agreement is not intended to be legally enforceable unless it contains a provision to that effect. Few, if any, agreements are likely to be made that provide for legal enforceability.

On the other hand, an individual employment contract, even if only oral, is fully enforceable by law. Under the Contracts of Employment Act (1972), an employer is required to give an employee a written statement of the main terms of employment no later than thirteen weeks after he has been hired.

*Extension of Agreement Terms*

Under Schedule 11 of the EPA, a union (or an employers' association) may file a claim with the ACAS that an employer's wages are below those set forth in the national industry agreement, or if no industry agreement exists, below the wages being paid generally by employers in the industry in the district. When such a claim is filed, the ACAS must attempt to conciliate it. If conciliation fails, the matter may be referred to the CAC. The CAC may order the employer to observe the national agreement terms or the district terms, as the case may be. The CAC order becomes an effective part of the employment contract between the employer and his employees.

In addition to Schedule 11 claims forwarded to the CAC by the ACAS, cases under the Fair Wages Resolution are forwarded to the CAC by the employment secretary. The Fair Wages Resolution states that employers who are performing work for the government must provide wages and conditions no less favorable than those of the national labor contract in the industry, or if such a contract does not exist, no less than are generally paid by employers in the industry in the district.

In 1977, a total of 1,124 Schedule 11 claims were filed with the ACAS, 742 of which were sent on to the CAC. In addition, the CAC received 230 Fair Wage Resolution claims, for a total of 972 cases. Schedule 11 and Fair Wage Resolution claims accounted for approximately 95% of all the cases filed with the CAC in 1977. There was considerable criticism that this procedure was being used to circumvent the government wage restraints.[13]

*Conciliation, Mediation, and Arbitration*

The ACAS provides conciliation, mediation, and arbitration services in both individual and collective labor disputes. The services are voluntary. They are provided only if both parties to the dispute are willing to accept them.

Under recent labor legislation, British workers have the right to complain to an industrial tribunal on many matters. However, such complaints are first referred to the ACAS for conciliation. The ACAS conciliators have been quite successful in these cases, with the result that the workload of the tribunals has been considerably reduced. At the request of the parties, the ACAS conciliators may become involved also in collective labor disputes. In 1977, the ACAS received 3,299 requests for conciliation from unions and managements. In 74% of these cases, conciliation was successful.

An ACAS conciliator does not impose or recommend a settlement but simply tries to help the parties arrive at their own solutions. On the other hand, a mediator usually recommends a solution, and an arbitrator or arbitration board imposes a solution. Arbitration awards are not legally binding in Britain, but such awards are normally implemented by the parties. Although ACAS personnel do not serve as mediators or arbitrators, the service does maintain a list of competent mediators and arbitrators and aids the parties in setting up the mediation or arbitration procedure best suited to their needs. Moreover, the mediators' and arbitrators' fees and expenses are paid by the ACAS. In 1977, the ACAS aided management and labor in setting up 287 arbitration and 31 mediation procedures.

## Strikes

Over the ten-year-period 1967 through 1976, there were 425 days lost because of strikes per 1,000 employees per year in Britain. There were less strike losses in Britain than in the United States, but considerably more than in the continental countries, except Italy. Britain's losses were approximately fifteen times those of Germany's (see table A-12). However, far more emphasis has been placed on these differences than is warranted. Actually, a very insignificant number of workdays were lost as a result of strikes in Britain—not 5% or 1%; but rather, only 2/10 of 1%. Admittedly, this was fifteen times the losses in West Germany, but it was still very small. It is like saying fifteen grains of sand are larger than one grain of sand—neither is a very significant amount. Far more time was lost in Britain as a result of unemployment, absenteeism, or even tea breaks than was lost as a result of strikes.

Most strikes in Britain are unofficial, that is, they are not authorized by national union leaders. During the period 1970 through 1976, only 25% of the strikes were official. The leaders hesitate to authorize strikes because the union must then pay strike benefits, and when strike benefits are paid, the striking employees and their families receive less in unemployment and social security benefits.

Strike losses in Britain have been concentrated in a few industries. Over a four-year period, 44% of the time lost was in four industries (coal, automobile, dock, and shipbuilding) which employed only 8% of the working population.[14] During the five-year period 1971-1975, in any one year over 97% of British manufacturing plants were free from stoppages.[15] It is not a problem of widespread industrial stoppages, but rather a concentration of stoppages in a relatively small number of establishments. One type of industrial action that has been developed very effectively in Britain is the work-to-the-rule strike under which employees continue to work but refuse overtime, and follow every rule so scrupulously that production is greatly reduced.

In the winter of 1978-1979, numerous strikes were called by British unions to try to force managements to grant increases above the 5% guideline set by the Labor government. The secondary picketing that accompanied these strikes, especially in the trucking industry, seriously disrupted British industry and inconvenienced much of the public. The inability of the Labor government to control or limit the strikes was a major cause of its fall in March, 1979, and its defeat by the Conservatives in the election that followed in May, 1979.

### Proposed Labor Law Reform

The Conservative government of Margaret Thatcher that took office in 1979 did not propose a far-reaching labor reform bill such as was enacted by the previous Conservative government in the early seventies. The new government recommended changes in only three areas: picketing, closed shop, and secret ballots. Under the proposed legislation: secondary picketing would be prohibited; a closed-shop agreement still would be permitted, but only after an overwhelming majority of the workers had voted for it by secret ballot and it would not apply to existing nonmembers or to employees with "a deeply held conviction" against membership; a worker who was expelled from a union would have the right to appeal the expulsion to the courts; and secret elections for union officials, changes in union rules, and the calling and ending of strikes would be funded by the government.

### Legislated Employee Protection and Benefits

#### Effect on Collective Bargaining

The labor legislation sponsored by the Labor government, under pressure from the TUC, in recent years has had as one of its major objectives the expansion of collective bargaining. This was clearly one of the basic thrusts of both the TULRA and the EPA. For example, when the ACAS was created by the latter legislation, it was specifically given the overall task "to encourage the extension and the development . . . of collective bargaining."

However, the union movement and the government have not been content to rely solely on collective bargaining to provide protection and benefits for workers. For many years, workers, along with the general public in Britain, have been protected by a vast network of social security benefits, including medical and hospital care, sick pay, and retirement pay. The British system has been referred to as giving "cradle to the grave" protection. During the 1970s, further protection and benefits, some of which are dicussed here, have been provided directly to workers through the TULRA, EPA, and other legislation.

It is significant that to the extent that protection and benefits have been provided directly by legislation, the scope of collective bargaining has been limited. Some very important issues that might have been subjects for collective bargaining instead have been incorporated into legislation. It will be interesting to see to what extent Britain will continue this policy of favoring direct legislation in the future and how it will affect collective bargaining. Will the scope of bargaining be kept very narrow because of the broad protection and benefits provided by legislation, or will the legislation merely provide a foundation upon which much more elaborate labor agreement structures will be built?

*Unfair Dismissals*

The TULRA and EPA protect employees against unfair dismissals. If requested to do so, an employer must give the employee a written reason. The employee may then appeal to an industrial tribunal. Before the tribunal, the burden is on the employer to show that there was substantial reason and just cause for discharge. If the tribunal decides the dismissal was unfair but that reinstatement or reengagement is not desirable, it may order a money award up to a maximum of £7,600. Effective April 1, 1978, the tribunals were given the power to order reinstatment in addition to money awards to employees who were found to have been unfairly dismissed. Prior to that date, the tribunals only had the power to recommend reinstatement plus additional money awards if management refused to follow its recommendation.

In June 1977, the ACAS issued a code of practice on this subject which recommends a system of corrective and progressive discipline in which oral and written warnings would precede more severe penalties, including dismissal. It recommends also that a special grievance procedure be worked out with the union for discipline and discharge cases. Although these recommendations are not legally enforceable, they can be used as evidence before a tribunal.

In 1975, 30,000 dismissals were appealed to the tribunals which found 38% to be unfair. In 1976, there were 38,000 appeals and 36% were upheld. However, the tribunals have ordered reinstatement in only a very few cases, and the money awards have been small. In 1978, the median award was running at £408, with 55% less than £400 and only 1.8% £3,000 or more. As one writer has stated, "in practice—the 'right not to be dismissed' as it is termed in U.K. law is in a very real sense a misnomer. . . . In Britain there is simply a right to be compensated for unfair dismissal . . . and the compensation is not likely to be very large."[16]

## Redundancies

Under the EPA, an employer is required to consult with the union prior to a layoff "at the earliest possible opportunity" but not less than ninety days prior to the first dismissal when a hundred employees are involved over a ninety-day period, or not less than sixty days prior when ten or more employees are to be laid off over a thirty-day period. If such notice is not given, an industrial tribunal may award protective wages for the period. In addition, the employer must give the employees notice prior to termination. The notice required varies with length of service—one week for employees with three weeks of service, two weeks for employees with two years of service, and then one additional week for each year of service, up to a maximum of twelve weeks.

An employee who is made redundant receives a lump-sum payment under the Redundancy Act (1965) as follows: for each year of employment from age 18 to 22—one half week's pay, for each year of employment from age 22 to 41—one week's pay, for each year of employment from age 41 to 65—one and a half week's pay, with a limit of £100 per week for 30 weeks or £3,000. The Redundancy Rebate Act (1969) provides that an employer may claim 50% rebate of these amounts from a fund that is financed from social security contributions.

## Pay for Short Work Weeks

Sections 22-28 of the EPA provide for guaranteed payments to be made to an employee who is laid off for a full day or more. The employee is entitled to a maximum of £6.60 per day for a period of five days in each quarter. Eligibility is lost if the employee refuses suitable alternative work or if the layoff is the result of a trade dispute involving his employer or an associated employer.

## Equal Pay and Equal Opportunities

The Equal Pay Act was passed in 1970 but did not become fully effective until December 29, 1975. It provides that a female employee must be paid the same rate as is paid to a male employee for the same or similar work. In 1975, the provisions for equality were extended by the Equal Opportunity Act which prohibits discrimination in hiring, promotion, transfer, training or other benefits, facilities, or services because of sex or marriage. Discrimination against males is also prohibited. The act established an Equal Opportunities Commission which is primarily an educational and investigatory body to promote equal opportunity, although it may seek injunctions to prevent employers from continuing discriminatory practices. Complaints of violation of the act are referred to the ACAS, which received 367 such complaints in 1976. If the issue is not conciliated by the ACAS, it can go to an industrial tribunal which may award damages up to a maximum of £5,200. Furthermore, if the tribunal recommends action to eliminate the discrimination and the employer refused to comply, the award may be increased. In 1977, 56% of the cases referred to the ACAS went forward to a tribunal for hearing.

In 1976, a Race Discrimination Act, modeled after the 1975 Equal Opportunity Act, made it illegal also for employers to discriminate against employees because of color, race, nationality, or ethnic or national origin.


*Maternity Protection and Pay*

The Employment Protection Act provides that an employee may not be dismissed because of pregnancy unless she is unable to perform her job or do available alternative work or is prevented from doing so by law. Moreover, a mother has the right to return to her job or a similar one at any time up to twenty-nine weeks after the birth of the child. A female employee working in a British plant or office is entitled to six weeks of maternity pay provided she has two years of service, works until eleven weeks before the expected birth, and gives her employer three weeks notice. The maternity pay together with social security amounts to about nine-tenths of the employee's regular pay. The employer recovers the payments from the maternity pay fund to which each employer contributes 0.05% of his wage bill. An employee may appeal to an industrial tribunal if she feels her pregnancy or maternity rights have been violated. Failure to continue to employ a pregnant woman or failure to reemploy a woman after childbirth is treated as an unfair dismissal and the onus of proof is on the employer.


**Absenteeism**

Absenteeism is lower in Great Britain than in any of the other European countries in this study, but higher than in the United States or Japan. A study by the Swedish employers' association indicated that in 1973, sickness absenteeism was 5% in Britain compared with 10% in Sweden, 4% in the United States, and 3% in Japan (see table A-13).

Britain's better absentee record may be partly a result of the fact that its national sick pay plan is less liberal than the ones on the continent. Whereas the sick pay plan provides 90% of earnings in Sweden and 100% of earnings in West Germany, the benefits are considerably lower in Britain. In 1974, the British plan paid a flat benefit of £8.60 per week plus earnings-related benefits equal to 33.3% between £10 and £30 per week, and 15% between £30 and £42 per week. In addition, there were family supplements. The benefits were paid after a three-day waiting period.

Although absenteeism is lower than in the continental countries, losses because of absenteeism are a serious drain on the British economy. In 1976, British employees lost 350 million man days of work as a result of "certified sickness" absences alone; that is, absences of three days or more covered by doctors' certificates. Only 6 million man days were lost in strikes by British workers during the same year.

## Worker Participation

Worker participation in company decision making either through works councils or board representation has not been as important in Britain as in Germany, the Netherlands, and the Scandinavian countries. However, during the fifties many plants did have employee representation committees. These bodies possessed advisory power only. In recent years, as the power of the shop stewards has increased and local bargaining has expanded, the number and effectiveness of such committees have greatly decreased.

Since 1967, the British Steel Corporation (BSC) has been experimenting with a type of worker director system. Although no worker directors sit on the main board, two sit on each of the six divisional boards. The worker directors are appointed through the unions with final screening by the general manager. However, a recent study reports that there is general agreement that the worker directors have not significantly affected the policies and actions of the BSC.[17]

In December, 1975, the government appointed a committee with Lord Bullock as chairman to examine and report on employee representation on boards of directors. The committee's charge was not to determine if such representation was desirable, but instead to decide "how it could best be achieved." After extensive study of the problem, the committee in January, 1977, issued what has become known as the Bullock report[18] which recommended that employee board representation be required if: 1. a company had two thousand or more employees, 2. a union with 20% or more of the company's employees as members proposed it, and 3. a majority of the employees voted for it. The committee further recommended that there should be a single tripartite board (as opposed to the two-tier system in West

Germany) composed of an equal number of employee and owner representatives, plus a smaller number of neutral members chosen by the first two
groups. The employee representatives would be chosen in secret elections
where only union members would vote and where the candidates would be
nominated by the unions and need not be employees of the company.

Through the CBI and other employer organizations, management
strongly opposed the adoption of the Bullock proposals into law. Labor was
not united in its support, and several top union leaders openly expressed
their opposition. As a result, the government did not issue a white paper on
the matter until May, 1978.

The white paper is a watered-down version of the Bullock report.
Although it supports employee representation on company boards, it places
immediate emphasis on the establishment of a joint representation council
(JRC) in each company with over five hundred employees. The JRC would
be composed of representatives of all the independent unions that negotiate
with the employer. The board of the company would be required to discuss
company strategy with the JRC before decisions were made.

Employee representation on a company board would occur only if
desired by the JRC in a company with over two thousand employees, after
the JRC had been in operation for three or four years. The JRC could then
demand an election on the matter and, if a majority of all the employees
voted for representation on the board, it would be required. There would be
a two-tier board system consisting of a policy board and a management
board, with one-third employee representation on the policy board, and the
remaining two-thirds composed of owner representatives. There would be
no neutral members. The policy board would elect the members of the
management board. The Labor government did not exclude parity representation as "an ultimate outcome" but proposed one-third representation as a
reasonable first step. It recognized as "a clear dilemma" the problem of
whether election of employee representatives should be through the union
structure or open to all employees including non-union employees.
Although the government appeared to favor the union structure, it did not
put forward a fixed position on this issue. However, it did state that funds
would be made available to educate and train employee board representatives regardless of how they might be chosen.


**Profit Sharing and Employee Ownership**

Until now, there has been no law in Britain that would encourage or require
companies to adopt profit sharing. Nevertheless, some companies, including three banks (Barclays, National Westminster, and Williams and
Glyn) have adopted profit-sharing plans, and 100 or more other companies,

including BICC, RACAL Electronics, and BOC, have adopted share-savings plans. However, none of these plans has been negotiated with unions, and unions are not involved in any administration. Likewise, none envisages employee or union participation in company control through stock ownership.

In 1977, the TUC issued a statement opposing schemes of profit sharing and co-ownership but indicated that it would favor a form of capital sharing based on a national fund administered through the trade union movement. In September, 1977, the Liberal party announced that it had reached an agreement with the Labor party to proceed with a bill on profit sharing. The Conservative party has also mentioned profit sharing in its proposals for labor relation reform. Early in 1978, Inland Revenue published a consultative document setting forth three proposed plans whereby profit sharing might be made more attractive through tax relief. It is possible, therefore, that a profit-sharing bill will be proposed sometime in the future, but it is unlikely that the Conservative government will sponsor a scheme that will permit the unions to play a major role or will enable unions or employees to participate in company control through stock ownership.

## Notes

1. Under the Trade Union and Labor Relations Act (1974, revised 1976), if a union wishes to avail itself of the advantages of the legislation, it must be certified as an independent union which means it must be free from domination or financial support by an employer. As of January 1978, 274 unions had been certified, 30 applications had been refused, 3 had been withdrawn, and 1 had lapsed. ("Trade Union Certification," *Employment Gazette* 86 [1], 1978:7).

2. Lord Bullock, *Report of the Committee of Inquiry on Industrial Democracy* (London: Her Majesty's Stationery Office, 1977), p. 16.

3. Ibid., p. 11.

4. "Trade Union Certification," p. 7.

5. Hugh A. Clegg, *The System of Industrial Relations in Great Britain* (London: Basil and Blackwell, 1970), p. 57.

6. Seyfarth, Shaw, Fairweather, and Geraldson, *Labor Relations and the Law in the United Kingdom and the United States* (Ann Arbor: University of Michigan, 1968), p. 19.

7. Clive Jenkins and Barrie Sherman, *Collective Bargaining* (London: Routledge and Kegan Paul, Ltd., 1977), p. 36.

8. W.E.J. McCarthy, *The Closed Shop in Great Britain* (London: Blackwell, 1964), pp. 30-34.

9. Roger W. Rideout, *Principles of Labour Law* (London: Sweet and Maxwell, 1976), pp. 265-69.

10. Margaret Stewart, *Trade Unions in Europe* (Epping, Essex, Great Britain: Gower Press, 1974), p. 182.

11. Jenkins and Sherman, *Collective Bargaining*, p. 14.

12. Kevin Hawkins, *British Industrial Relations* (London: Barrie and Jenkins, Ltd., 1976), p. 120.

13. P.B. Beaumont, "Arbitration and Extension of Terms in Britain," *The Arbitration Journal* 34 (2), 1979:33.

14. Clegg, *System of Industrial Relations*, p. 318.

15. "Trade Union Certification," pp. 9-10.

16. *European Industrial Relations Review*, No. 57, Oct. 1978, p. 15.

17. Peter Brennan et al., *The Worker Directors* (London: Hutchison of London, 1976).

18. Bullock, *Report of the Committee*.

# Case 1
# Barrett Cycle Company
# (A)

## Background

In 1891 Edward Barrett, with the help of a few workmen, began to construct bicycles in a small shop in the town of Folcroft about thirty miles east of Manchester, England. Barrett was not only an expert craftsman, but also a very good manager. Under his leadership the business grew rapidly. As time went on, he developed a number of new products including the famous Barrett motorcycles.

When each of Edward Barrett's three sons finished their schooling, they entered the business. Following the founder's death in 1941, John became the general manager. John, like his father, exhibited excellent business ability and the company prospered under his leadership, adding a number of products including power lawn mowers.

However, in 1968, John who had been in poor health for several years, decided to retire. The three brothers then determined that the best interests of the family would be served by selling the business. A sale was arranged with one of Britain's leading multi-industry companies. Soon afterward, the two other brothers retired. Although some members of the third generation of the Barrett family remained active in the business after 1968, the actual control passed to a general manager and other executives appointed by the owning company.

By 1972, the company employed 3,000 workers, including 2,500 on the hourly payroll and 500 on the weekly staff payroll. Most of the hourly paid workers had been represented for many years by two general unions, the Transport and General Workers' Union (TGWU) and the Amalgamated Union of Engineering Workers (AUEW).[1] These two general unions did not represent separate and distinct groups of jobs within the plant. Instead, any employee other than certain craft workers could be represented by either one of these general unions. Moreover, since the contract with the two unions did not require union membership, a sizable number of the employees were members of neither of the unions. Thus, on a particular machine some operators might be members of the TGWU, others members of the AUEW, and others members of neither. However, the chief stewards of the two unions, who were paid by the company and spent their full time on industrial relations matters, were on friendly terms and there was no competition between the two unions for membership. Moreover, the two unions did not attempt to outdo each other but instead always presented joint demands to the company. In addition to the two general unions, the company had recognized three craft unions: the electricians union, the sheet metal workers union, and the patternmakers union. A demarcation agreement had been worked out between the company and the five unions whereby each type of job was represented either by only one of the craft unions or by the general unions.

The company was a member of the Engineering Employers' Federation which represented 5,700 fims who employed over 2 million workers. The federation negotiated national agreements with the major unions in the field. These national agreements covered only major issues and basic wage rates. The Barrett Company and other member firms of the federation negotiated local plant contracts with the unions which supplemented and added to the national agreements, including additions to the basic wages.

Under family ownership and control, there was a great deal of benevolent paternalism at Barrett. It became known as the best place to work in the area and the relationships between the company and the unions were very good. Management was of the opinion that the current plant union leaders, although very independent, were intelligent, reasonable, and capable. In turn, the union leaders spoke of the integrity of the Barrett management and the company's sincere concern for the welfare of its workers.

However, the contracts between the company and the unions were not closed for a fixed period of time. Thus, a union was free to present new demands at any time and after exhausting the negotiating procedure of the contract was legally free to strike. As a result, it was not unusual for the company to have one or two strikes by small groups of workers each year. In addition, over the years there had been several longer and more general strikes over major issues. Although such strikes were troublesome, the total production loss as a result of strikes over the years had been insignificant.

Prior to the sale of the company in 1968, only the draftsmen among the weekly salary employees were represented by a union. However, soon after the change of ownership, the clerks became unionized. Then early in 1972, a number of foremen, inspectors, production engineers, technicians, and stores employees joined the ASTMS (Association of Scientific, Technical, and Managerial Staffs Union). The group that the ASTMS claimed to represent included about 180 employees, five of whom were women. Management was not happy with this new development but agreed to recognize the ASTMS, apply the federation contract to these employees, and bargain with the union on local matters.

The original local demands of the ASTMS were extensive and extreme, including a £6 per week general increase. Management was of the opinion that the salaries of ASTMS members were already very liberal and that any sizable increase would cause dissension among the other workers and unions in the plant. Therefore, the company refused to grant the £6 increase.

As a result, the union membership replaced the original leaders with a new group that promised more militant action. Management became convinced that the new leadership was intent on showing the union's power and that strike action was inevitable unless the company acceded to very unreasonable demands.

## The Equal-Pay Issue

On June 28, 1972, at the request of the ASTMS local leaders, a meeting was held to discuss a number of matters including equal pay for women.[2] The meeting was attended by the three members of the union's executive committee and by two representatives of management. The discussion of the equal-pay issue follows:

**Wilkins (union):** The female employees of our union are paid only 90% of the male rates, whereas the hourly paid female employees are paid 95%. We were told our female members also would be at 95% as of January 1 of this year. It is already April.

**Parvis (company):** What we work out with the hourly workers unions is entirely separate. The company never agreed to a 95% rate for your members and we are not prepared to increase the rate at this time.

**Wilkins (union):** If the company insists on not paying the 95% the union will make it an issue for negotiation and demand a works conference.

**Parvis (company):** Our position remains the same.

## Works Conference

On September 30, a works conference on the female pay issue was held at the plant. Mr. Green, a district official, represented the union. He stated that:

1. The forewomen were doing grade 1 foreman work but receiving only 90% of the grade 1 foreman rate,
2. Mrs. Glass, a technical assistant, also was being paid at 90% of the male rate,
3. In the plant negotiations last year the company had agreed to 95% and the union was now asking the company to honor its promise retroactive to January 1.

The company replied that:

1. No promise had ever been made to pay 95%,
2. Only 2 forewomen and one technical assistant were involved,
3. The forewomen were being paid 98% of the rate of grade 2 which was their proper classification. Even if they were considered grade 1, they were receiving 93%,
4. The female technical assistant was getting 97% of the grade 2 male rate which was the proper classification. Even if her job were classified as grade 1, she was receiving 90%,
5. Regardless of the classifications, the amount being paid by the company to these female employees was in excess both of those required by the Equal Pay Act and of those being paid by most other employers.

No agreement was reached.

## Executive Level Meeting

The union then appealed the matter to the central conference level where an industrial relations officer of the Manchester branch of the Employers' Federation served as chairman. Two meetings were held at this level—one in early February, 1973, and one in early March, 1973, but no agreement was reached. The union had now exhausted the settlement procedure and was free to strike.

## Strike Notice

On May 24, 1973, the union secretary sent a notice to the company which read in part:

> At a union meeting held last night, the members voted unanimously to take industrial action in support of the 95% rate for female employees. The group will withdraw its labor for one day on June 22 and this will be followed by a strike on June 26 to continue until agreement is reached. We regret this action is necessary because of management's dictatorial attitude.

Management learned later that the union meeting at which the strike vote had been taken had been very poorly attended and that the radical left-wing group had been in complete control. It was informed that many of the foremen and other ASTMS members were surprised by the action and opposed to it. Management was informed further that before the June 22 deadline, the union majority would vote down the strike action. Although management received word indirectly that the union leadership would be willing to engage in further discussion of the issue with the hope of avoiding a strike, the company decided not to take the initiative in calling a meeting.

**One-day Strike**

On June 22, the one-day strike occurred as scheduled. Of the 180 employees represented by the ASTMS, only four reported for work. However, employees represented by the other unions crossed the picket lines, and production was not noticeably affected.

Management learned later that at a union meeting held the evening before the strike, an attempt was made by some members to have a new vote on the strike action but that the chairman had ruled the motion out of order, saying that the issue had been decided earlier and that the only matter left to be determined was how it was to be effectuated.


**Meeting of June 23**

On the day following the one-day strike, the union requested a meeting with management. The union claimed again and the management denied again that the 95% had been promised. The union asked if the company was prepared now to grant the 95%. The company declared it was not even willing to discuss the question under duress. The union then asked if the company would grant the 95% if the union withdrew the strike notice. The company replied that it was not prepared to grant it now but would be willing to negotiate the matter at the next regular negotiations which would occur in six weeks. The union then asked if the company would now agree to pay the 95% in six weeks and negotiate on retroactivity at that time. The company refused whereupon the union stated that the strike action as indicated in the notice would begin on June 26 unless the company changed its position.


**One-week Strike**

On June 26, the employees represented by the ASTMS again failed to report for work and set up picket lines around the plant. However, the non-union employees and members of the other unions crossed the picket lines. Management representatives replaced the foremen and other ASTMS members where necessary, and production proceeded much as usual.

Prior to the strike, the district officer of the union informed the employees that they would receive strike pay equal to 90% of their wages. At the end of the first week of the strike, the striking employees received the strike pay. However, the national union indicated it would not pay in this situation, and local funds could not support more than the first week's pay. It was clear by the end of the week that there would be no further strike pay.

Friday evening, a union meeting that was well attended was held in the community hall. Despite strong urging by the local union leaders that the strike be continued, the members voted by a large majority to return to work on Monday.

## Aftermath

Following the return to work, the union requested a meeting which was held on July 4, 1973. The union proposed that since the duress was removed the company should now pay the 95%. The company refused.

On August 8 the company met again with the union committee and informed it that the company's policy would be to move progressively toward achieving equal pay by July, 1975, (six months before the legal requirement) as follows:

> July 1973—90%
> Jan. 1974—93.5%
> July 1974—95%
> Jan. 1975—97.5%
> July 1975—100%

The union committee again requested the 95% immediately and when it was denied, asked that it be given the opportunity to discuss the matter with the general manager. The company representatives stated they would pass on the request to the general manager. The union did not pursue the matter further.

## The Redundancy Issue

During all of 1972 and the first eight months of 1973, the company's sales and production were considerably below normal. During this eighteen-month period, management decreased the number of hourly paid workers by 303. This decrease was carried out in cooperation with the unions that represented the hourly paid employees. Despite this reduction, the company continued to operate at a loss.

Prior to August, 1973, the company had not moved to decrease the number of staff employees. However, at that time management decided that the situation required also a cut in the size of the staff. The general manager, Haydn Evans, informed Dwight Crane, the general manager of personnel, that he should work with the production manager in drawing up a plant procedure to cut the staff force. As a result of a series of meetings, it was decided that the following cuts could and should be made in the staff group that was represented by the ASTMS:

Production engineering            2
Foremen                          12
Work study                        6
Quality control inspection        5
Stores                            3

Total                            28

Crane then met with Parvis, the assistant personnel director, and Butters, the work manager and the three agreed that the criteria for determining who would be released would be length of service, qualifications, and experience, with length of service being the determining factor unless the other two factors were compelling. Crane asked Parvis to work with Butters in drawing up the list.

One week later, Parvis and Butters met with Crane and presented him with a proposed list. Crane was surprised and disturbed with what he saw.

**Crane:** This is going to cause a bloody racket! All three members of the union's executive committee: Burns, Kent, and even the Chairman, Wilkins, are on the list. All together you have six members out of the eleven of the full union committee. It will certainly look like we're taking revenge against them because of the strike action. The union will play that up.

**Parvis:** Bill and I recognize that the union will not like it but we have followed very objectively the criteria which we agreed on. We haven't played any favorites. This is the way the chips fall.

**Crane:** It's clear you didn't always follow length of service. Burns, who is a time study engineer and a member of the union's executive committee, is on the list but he has a lot more seniority than Blakey who was hired only six months ago. How can we possibly justify that? I thought we agreed to give a lot of weight to length of service.

**Parvis:** We have followed length of service except in a very few cases where the qualifications and experience of the junior men were clearly superior. Blakey is one of those exceptions. He was hired specifically because of his expertise in electrical matters. He has a lot of knowledge and experience with electrical distribution. Burns can't do that work nearly as well as Blakey. I can assure you no one is on the list because of the strike. We didn't consider that at all.

**Crane:** Well, it sure doesn't look that way. You have Kent on the list too. How can you justify sending him out? He has over twenty years of service. A lot of the people who will remain have a lot less. How will we ever convince anyone that Kent, who is a member of the executive committee and who we all know was one of the most active supporters of the strike, is not being sacked for that reason?

**Parvis:**     It's true Kent has over twenty years of service in the plant but he's the lowest man in service in his grade. We considered grade service not plant service in every case and on that basis, Kent has to go. We didn't discriminate against him in any way. Do you think we should give special treatment to the union leaders?

**Crane:**      No, but I had no idea it would turn out this way. It's bound to cause a lot of bitterness in the ASTMS group. I wish you would go over it again very carefully. If we go this way, we have to be very sure, especially where long service employees are involved: Let's meet again on it next week.

At the meeting the next week, Parvis and Butters presented the same list of names and vigorously defended their choices. In every case, they insisted, the selection was made solely on the basis of the criteria of length of service, experience, and qualifications.

Crane asked them to go over the material once more and make a final report to him the following week. Parvis and Butters again reviewed each case carefully and again reported to Crane that fairness and equity required that the three members of the union executive committee and three other members of the full committee be made redundant. Crane wondered what he should do.

After careful consideration of the alternatives, Crane decided to recommend to top management that the company proceed with the layoff according to the list prepared by Parvis and Butters. Top management gave its support to his recommendation.

On September 8, 1973, Crane met with the executive committee of the union:

**Crane (company):**     I have called you to give you some very distasteful facts. Our order books, as you know, are down and the company has been losing money for some time. We are overstaffed. During the past eighteen months we have cut the hourly paid group by about 300. We will now have to declare a redundancy of about thirty of your people.

**Wilkins (union):**     Will the company consider volunteers?

**Crane (company):**     Yes, but the company's interest must be taken into account.

Crane then presented a list of the jobs that would be eliminated, but not a list of the names of the workers. He said the names would be given to the committee after the workers had been notified.

On September 15, Crane again met with the executive committee and gave them the list of the names of the employees who had been declared redundant. After the list was reviewed, the following discussion occurred:

| | |
|---|---|
| **Burns (union):** | We don't recognize the need for this redundancy. All these men are really needed in the plant. |
| **Wilkins (union):** | This is purely and simply a shake-out of the union leadership! There is no reasonable justification for it! Some men with long service are on the list, and men with much less service who are not active in the union are not on it. |
| **Crane (company):** | There has been no discrimination. We followed objective criteria. We regret it's this way but any other way would be unfair. |
| **Burns (union):** | Will those laid offs now be given the first opportunity when and if the company needs men? |
| **Crane (company):** | The company will have to consider each case on its merits. |
| **Burns (union):** | There is no sincerity in the company. This is shameful discrimination against the union. |
| **Wilkins (union):** | We do not accept this. We will register a "failure to agree." |

Following a Works Conference Meeting at the plant at which no agreement was reached, the union requested a central conference meeting which was held at the Engineering Employers' Federation Office in Birmingham on October 1. John Bratton of the EEF served as chairman and the union was represented by its regional chairman, Johnson, and two full time union officials, Condon and Wherry, as well as the local union's executive committee. The following are excerpts from the record of the meeting:

| | |
|---|---|
| **Johnson (union):** | We agree there is a manning problem but the position of the company is a clear case of victimization. It's an inhuman approach. We ask the company to withdraw the list and instead use volunteers. |
| **Condon (union):** | This is a bloody attack on the trade union movement! The company has selected every member on the executive committee and allowed some non-union men with less seniority to stay on. |
| **Johnson (union):** | The men have been selected arbitrarily. There are more human ways to do this. We see this as an attack on union representatives in all plants in this region. We can't agree to it. |
| **Wherry (union):** | The national union supports our position. |
| **Bratton (employers' federation):** | Do you take the position that elected union representatives are in a privileged position? |

| | |
|---|---|
| **Johnson (union):** | We take the position that "last in-first out" is not the best way. We want the company to withdraw the list and ask for volunteers. |
| **Bratton (employers' federation):** | No, the company will not agree to withdraw the list but we will agree to send out a letter asking for volunteers and we will decrease the list to the extent that the volunteers make it possible to do so. |
| **Johnson (union):** | We appreciate the offer to send a letter asking for volunteers but that's not enough. The list must be withdrawn and some time allowed. If the list is not withdrawn, believe me when I say a much more difficult situation will arise. |
| **Bratton (employers' federation):** | We cannot agree to withdraw the list. |
| **Johnson (union):** | Then a dispute continues to exist and the union has exhausted the procedure required before strike action. |

Following the central conference meeting, Crane wondered what action, if any, the company should take. The union had exhausted the contract procedure and was now free to strike on the issue. Crane recognized that in this instance the union leadership had a much stronger issue than the equal pay matter. He wondered if it was worth risking a strike or if the company's interests would be served better by accomplishing the redundancy entirely by volunteers and attritions.

## Notes

1. At the time that the Barrett Company recognized TGWU and AUEW as representatives of its employees, there was no legislation that specifically required the company to do so. However, the Employment Protection Act of 1975 now provides that the Advisory Conciliation and Arbitration service (ACAS) may recommend that a union be recognized by an employer. If the employer then refuses to negotiate, the recognized union may complain to the Central Arbitration Committee (CAC) which may make an enforceable award of terms and conditions of employment for the employees concerned.

2. In 1970, parliament had passed the Equal Pay Act which provided that by December, 1975, women had to be paid equal pay for comparable work. Prior to this time Barrett, along with many other British firms, had paid women less than men for comparable work.

# Barrett Cycle Company (B)

On September 22, a meeting of the ASTMS membership was held to consider strike action on the redundancy issue. It was very well attended. The three members of the executive committee unanimously recommended strike action. However, after a long and at times bitter discussion the membership voted not to strike.

In July the union members elected a new executive committee. Several months later at an informal meeting attended by a national officer of the union and representatives of the company, the new members of the executive committee indicated that they were very satisfied with their relationship with management.

Only one of the employees who was dismissed appealed to an industrial tribunal. George Burns, a time study engineer and a former member of the union executive committee, claimed he had been unfairly dismissed because of trade union activity at the same time that a less senior man, Blakey, had been retained. Both Parvis and Butters who had prepared the redundancy lists for the company testified at the hearing. The tribunal in deciding unanimously for the company against Burns' plea wrote:

> We are satisfied that Mr. Parvis and Mr. Butters are witnesses of truth and we accept their evidence. We appreciate the reasons for the suspicions of ASTMS, but it appears to us that they are suspicions only, and are not substantiated by evidence. We consider that the selection of the applicant for redundancy was fair and had nothing whatever to do with his union activities. We consider that the reason for the selection for redundancy of the applicant rather than Mr. Blakey is reasonable and genuine.

# Case 2
# M-S Limited (A)

**Background**

M-S Ltd. which manufactured small, high-quality electric switches and other small electrical products was located in Bankdown, a medium-sized community near Newcastle, England. In 1976 the company had 500 employees, 300 of whom were manual workers. From 1923 when it was founded by John Brewer who held the patents to its early products until 1965, it was a family concern. However, in 1963 it was acquired by Imperial Electric Products, Inc. (IEPI), one of Britain's major electrical manufacturing companies. Following the acquisition, Brewer retired. The management team that had served under him continued, but as time passed more and more of the executives were appointees of IEPI. The emphasis under the new management was on production and profitability. Employee relations which had been a special concern of Brewer were no longer given high priority.

Bankdown's primary industry was coal mining which accounted for 70% of its employment. It had a long history of militant left-wing unionism. It was not surprising, therefore, that a large majority of the manual workers at M-S joined unions early in the company's history. For a number of years the manual workers were represented by several unions, including the foundry workers union and the Amalgamated Union of Engineering Workers (AUEW). However, in 1966 the foundry workers union was merged into AUEW at the national level and following that date all manual workers at M-S were represented only by the AUEW. Originally the company's designers and draftsmen were represented by a separate union, Draftsmen and Allied Technicians Association, but in 1971 it also was merged at the national level into AUEW becoming a separate negotiating unit, the Technical and Supervisory Section (TASS) of AUEW. Following the acquisition of the company by IEPI in 1965, the clerical workers became represented by the Association of Professional Executive Clerical and Computer Staff (APEX) and the charge hands, foremen, supervisors, service engineers, sales engineers, and laboratory staff became represented by the Association of Scientific, Technical, and Managerial Staffs (ASTMS).

There were a number of intra-union and inter-union rivalries at M-S which caused serious difficulties. Despite the fact that the foundry workers union had been merged into AUEW nationally, the local foundry group retained its identity and there was continuous conflict between it and the engineering section of the union. Likewise, TASS although a part of AUEW retained its separate identity and negotiated its own contracts both at the national level with the federation and at the local level with M-S.

After the office and staff employees became unionized, disputes arose over lines of demarcation between TASS, APEX, and ASTMS. A particularly bitter dispute had arisen recently between AUEW and ASTMS as a result of instructions from the national AUEW leadership to the M-S local that workers who became foremen should retain their membership in AUEW. The ASTMS had always viewed foremen as within its jurisdiction and indeed had represented them at M-S for a number of years.

M-S was a member of the Engineering Employers' Federation which represented 5,700 firms who employed over two million workers. The federation negotiated national agreements with the major unions in the field, including AUEW, TASS, APEX, and ASTMS. However, these national agreements covered only major issues, including the basic wage structure. M-S and other member firms of the federation negotiated local plant agreements with the union which supplemented the national agreements, including additions to the basic wages. The labor agreements were open ended. A union was free to raise a new demand at any time and after exhausting the settlement procedure of the agreement was free to strike.

**The 1975 Strikes**

Two strikes in 1975 were especially costly to the company. One strike involved demands of the foundry employees for higher pay and better working conditions. The company believed that the demands were extremely unreasonable. It was of the opinion that both wages and working conditions in its foundry were equal to or superior to those in other foundries in the area or in the industry. Moreover, it believed that to grant the foundry section's demands would create serious inequities within the plant, especially vis-à-vis the engineering section. Therefore, the company refused to grant the demands whereupon the AUEW, after having exhausted the settlement procedures of the agreement, called a strike of its three hundred members which included both the foundry and the engineering sections. The strike lasted for ten weeks at which time the company acceded to the foundry workers original demands.

Later in 1975 the engineers section of AUEW demanded an increase. The company was not opposed to granting an increase to the engineers but the foundry section insisted that any increase granted to the engineers must also be given to them. However, the engineers stated that if the increase was given also to the foundry, they, the engineers, would strike. The company finally worked out a compromise which the AUEW agreed to. However, the foundry section breached the agreement and went on strike. This time the company stood its ground but the strike lasted for ten weeks before the members finally voted to return to work on the terms agreed upon before the strike.

## The Closed-Shop Issue

A closed-shop agreement is one in which the company and the union agree that an employee must be a paid-up member of the union in order to continue to work at the plant. Under the Industrial Relations Act of 1971 which was passed by a Conservative government, it was illegal for a company and a union to negotiate a closed shop. However, in 1974 the Labor government repealed the 1971 act, and companies and unions were free to negotiate such clauses.

In 1975, 97% of the hourly-paid workers at M-S were dues-paying members of the AUEW. From time to time, friction had developed in the plant between the members and the small group of nonmembers who were called "free riders." In December, 1975, the AUEW indicated to the company that it wished to negotiate a closed shop for all hourly-paid employees. After a number of negotiating sessions during which the union leadership indicated a willingness to accept certain management proposals in return for the closed shop, the company agreed to a post-entry closed shop arrangement whereby management was free to hire union or non-union employees but after the probationary period the workers had to become and remain dues-paying members of the union. The agreement was reached on January 10, 1976, to become effective March 1, 1976.

Immediately following the signing by the company and AUEW of the closed-shop agreement for hourly-paid employees, the three staff unions (TASS, APEX, and ASTMS) notified management that they also wished to negotiate closed-shop provisions. The company indicated its willingness to negotiate such provisions provided an agreement could be reached first on the sphere of influence of each of the three unions. After a number of discussions the three unions were able to agree on clear lines of demarcation between their spheres which were satisfactory also to the company.

However, the sphere of influence of the ASTMS remained unclear because of its dispute with the AUEW over employees who were promoted to foremen. The company feared that negotiation of a closed shop with the ASTMS under these conditions would provoke an extremely strong reaction from the AUEW. On the other hand, the ASTMS, seeing its long-term position threatened by the new AUEW attitude regarding foremen, aggressively pressed the company for a closed-shop agreement which would include the foremen.

The company, caught in the middle by the conflict, called a conference of the two unions on February 3 for the purpose of trying to work out an arrangement. The conference was not successful. The AUEW insisted on the right to retain in its membership workers who were promoted to foremen. The ASTMS insisted that all foremen remain within its jurisdiction. Following the unsuccessful conference, the company on February 5 addressed a letter to the unions which stated:

The Company views with extreme concern the possible consequences of the present dispute, which they emphasize is essentially based on a conflict between the two Unions. They are accordingly not prepared to make any decision which implies acceptance of either Union's standpoint.

The Company is willing to sign and implement the recognition and negotiating arrangements provided for in the draft agreement with ASTMS. The Company however is not prepared, in the absence of agreement between the two Unions, to sign the closed shop provisions of the draft agreement.

The Company urges the two Unions:

(a)  to reconsider their positions, and
(b)  to seek to utilize any available external machinery for resolving their differences, including discussions involving, as appropriate, the Executives of the Unions, the TUC and the ACAS.

The Company wishes it to be known that if the two Unions are prepared to refer the present dispute to arbitration, the Company will accept the findings of such arbitration.

### Work-to-the-Rule and Overtime Ban

On February 10, 1976, the company received the following letter from the secretary of the ASTMS:

A motion was passed at the Group Meeting this morning that the following action will be taken following the Management's decision to allow the AUEW a right of veto on an ASTMS agreement.

1.  ASTMS will implement their Closed Shop Agreement.
2.  ASTMS will implement an immediate work to the rule which will involve among other things production staff working a forty-hour week and nonproduction staff working a thirty-seven-hour week.

This action has official backing from the ASTMS National Executive.

The "work-to-the-rule" action resulted in considerable inconvenience to the company. The ASTMS members refused to answer telephones, refused to take orders from anyone except their immediate superiors, and in other ways made life difficult for management. However, the refusal to work overtime created a much more serious problem because of a flextime working schedule agreement that management had signed with the AUEW.

### The Flextime Issue

Under the flextime agreement, hourly-paid employees worked a standard eight-hour day but were permitted to start work at any time between 7:00 and 9:00 A.M. which resulted in quitting times from 4:00 P.M. to 6:00

P.M. Because of safety requirements and also to allocate the work, supervisors had to be present at all times when manual workers were on the job. However, the supervisors were not on a flextime schedule but instead worked a regular 8:00 A.M. to 5:00 P.M. shift each day with one hour for lunch. Therefore, in order to have supervisors on hand from 7:00 A.M. to 6:00 P.M., the company had developed a rotating overtime system whereby a certain number of the supervisors worked overtime each day. The supervisors liked the system because they received more than forty hours of pay each week, and the additional hours were paid at time and one-half.

If the supervisors who were members of the ASTMS refused to work overtime, there would be no supervision in the plant for the workers from 7:00 to 8:00 A.M. and from 5:00 to 6:00 P.M. The company decided, therefore, that if the supervisors were permitted to refuse overtime it could not continue to operate under the flextime schedule. However, the flextime schedule was a part of its written agreement with the AUEW.

The company recognized that it faced a very difficult dilemma. There were some in management who recommended a showdown with the ASTMS. They argued that the ASTMS action constituted a breach of its contract and, therefore, the company had a legal right to suspend employees who followed the union's "work-to-the-rule" and overtime ban. Others argued that it would be better to tolerate the ASTMS action and simply discontinue the flextime schedule. The managing director was convinced finally that the latter approach was the wiser under all the circumstances. As a result, on Friday, February 13, the following notice was posted on the three plant bulletin boards.

### HOURS OF WORK

Until further notice Supervision is only available during dayshift, from 8:00 A.M.-5:00 P.M., and therefore, with immediate effect, flextime will be suspended and AUEW hours of work during dayshift will be confined to 8:00 A.M.-5:00 P.M., Monday/Friday.

W.R. Embick
Plant Manager

## A Discipline Problem

A few hours after the notices were posted James Poppins, the AUEW senior steward, wrote in large letters across the bottom of each of these with a heavy black marker the following messsage:

FLEXTIME WILL OPERATE TOMORROW AS PER AUEW AGREEMENT WITH MANAGEMENT.

J. Poppins
Senior Steward

When the plant manager, William Embick, saw what Poppins had written he called him into his office and informed him that he was being suspended immediately for countermanding an order of management and that severe disciplinary action would be taken against him the next workday. Embick then attempted to get in touch with Brandon, the regional full-time representative of the union,[1] and when he was unable to do so had the following letter delivered to Brandon's office:

13 February 1976

Dear Mr. Brandon,

Earlier today I tried unsuccessfully on several occasions to contact you on the telephone to advise you of a serious situation that has arisen. A Management written instruction has been countermanded in writing by Mr. J. Poppins (Shop steward of AUEW). On the basis of the facts available to us it is our intention to take severe disciplinary action and this we propose to do at 9:00 A.M. on Monday, 16 February 1976.

Yours sincerely,
W.R. Embick

The following Monday a conference was held in the plant manager's office attended by: Embick, the plant manager; Carlson, the personnel director; Carl Brandon, the regional full-time union representative; and Poppins. Embick stated that Poppins had openly countermanded his orders, which was a serious offense and that the company intended to discharge him. Brandon pleaded with the company not to take such drastic action, pointing out that in his opinion the company itself had violated the agreement first by posting the notice. He said the men in the plant were in a very angry mood and that he could not guarantee that they would remain at work if Poppins were discharged. After the discussion the plant manager wrote Poppins the following letter with a copy to Brandon:

16 February 1976

Dear Mr. Poppins,

I confirm, following our meeting this morning that, as a result of your countermanding a Management instruction last Friday, you have been dismissed from M-S for gross industrial misconduct.

Sincerely,

W.R. Embick
Plant Manager

The disciplinary procedure in effect at the company provided that an employee who was not satisfied with the decision of the plant manager had the right to appeal to the managing director.[2] Poppins exercised his right under this provision and immediately appealed. Three days later on February 19 the managing director, John Mahon, scheduled a hearing at 10:00 A.M. in his office which was attended by Embick, the plant manager, Carlson, the personnel director, Brandon, the regional union representative, and Poppins. Embick and Carlson argued that Poppins's action in openly countermanding a management order clearly warranted discharge. Brandon argued that the company had breached its agreement with the AUEW by posting the notice and that Poppins's statement was in compliance with the agreement. Brandon warned again that the men in the plant were in a very angry mood and that he could not be responsible for their action if in his words "the company insists on sacking Poppins for doing his duty." After hearing both sides Mahon said he wished to have some time to think over the matter. He asked them to return to his office at 3:00 P.M. at which time he would give them his decision.

### Notes

1. The industrial relations code of practice which became effective February 28, 1972, provided that "no disciplinary action should be taken against a shop steward until the circumstances of the case have been discussed with a full-time official of the union concerned."

2. The industrial relations code of practice stated that the disciplinary procedure should "provide for the right of appeal, wherever practicable, to a level of management not previously involved."

# M-S Limited (B)

## The 1976 Strike

At 3:00 P.M. on February 19, 1976, Mahon handed to Poppins and Brandon, the union representative, a signed statement in which he upheld Poppins's discharge "for the serious offense of openly countermanding an order of management." As soon as Mahon's decision became known in the shop, all the hourly paid workers immediately stopped production, marched out of the plant, and set up picket lines.

The next day the draftsmen who were members of TASS, a section of AUEW, refused to cross the picket line. However, the office workers who were represented by APEX reported for work as did those employees represented by ASTMS, including the foremen. The company was able to ship some products from inventory in area warehouses but there was no production at the plant. Although the foremen and supervisors reported for work they refused to man the machines left idle by the strikers.

The picket lines at the plant were very effective. Any AUEW member who refused to picket was dismissed from the union which meant that under the closed shop agreement he would not be able to work in the plant when the strike was over. The strike received strong support from the national leaders of the union who declared it an "official strike" which made the strikers eligible for strike benefits of £5 per week from the national union. (Normal pay when working was £55 to £65 per week.)

During the next four weeks despite numerous meetings between the AUEW representatives and management, at times attended by government mediators, no agreement could be reached. The union insisted that Poppins be fully reinstated, an action which management refused to take. On March 19 when the strike was one-month-old, the managing director sent the following letter to each employee:

19 March 1976

TO ALL EMPLOYEES

Dear Employee,

I am once again taking the unusual step of writing to you in view of the serious situation now facing our Company.

When we were facing industrial action last year I told you of my fears for the future. At that time our trading position was being weakened, our customers were becoming disillusioned and our competitive position was being undermined.

During the course of the present year my fears have been realized. Last month's orders were half those needed to keep the factory running at the required level. The present strike is further weakening our trading position. We are now in a very grave situation.

I now wish you to know that our Company will have to be reorgnized. This will mean manning reductions. We will be discussing this with your Union representatives. These changes are essential to keep the business in operation.

I would finally state that a speedy return to normal working is essential in the interests of us all.

Yours sincerely,
John Mahon
Managing Director

Following receipt of the above letter the union held a meeting and the membership voted overwhelmingly to continue the strike until Poppins was reinstated.

Under British labor law Poppins had the right to appeal Mahon's decision to an industrial tribunal.[1] Poppins delayed such an appeal, however, until May 14, just a few days before the three-month limit on such appeals. By this time the strike had been in effect for over twelve weeks. Poppins' decision to appeal led to a resumption of negotiations. The union indicated its willingness to return to work immediately if the company would agree to reinstate or reengage Poppins if the tribunal so recommended.

**Note**

1. The Employment Protection Act of 1975 provided that an employee who believed he had been unfairly dismissed could appeal to an industrial tribunal. The industrial tribunal could recommend reinstatement or reengagement of the employee, or it could order compensation in lieu of reinstatement or reengagement as follows: a *basic award* equal to redundancy pay up to a maximum of £2,400 plus a *compensatory award* up to a maximum of £5,200. If the tribunal recommended reinstatement or reengagement and the company refused, the tribunal in addition to the above monetary awards could order an *additional award* of thirteen to twenty-six weeks pay which could be from twenty-six to fifty-two weeks if the tribunal found that the dismissal was a result of union activities or racial or sexual bias.

# M-S Limited (C)

The company refused to commit itself in advance of a tribunal decision and as a result the strike continued. However, the pressure on both sides to reach an agremeent had become very great and after three more weeks of strike on June 10, 1976, an agreement finally was reached which provided:

1. no change in the company's position regarding reinstatement of Poppins,
2. a lump sum payment of £125 to each striker,
3. in return for the lump sum payment certain concessions on work rules.

Following the strike settlement Poppins pursued his appeal before the tribunal. However, before a decision could be handed down, an out-of-court settlement was reached whereby he withdrew his demand for reinstatement in return for a lump-sum payment of £3,500.

Immediately after the AUEW members returned to work the company negotiated a closed-shop agreement with ASTMS which covered foremen and supervisors as well as other ASTMS members. ASTMS then withdrew its work-to-the-rule action and overtime ban and the company reinstated the flextime schedule. AUEW took no action to oppose the company's closed-shop agreement with ASTMS.

During the strike, the company had declared a redundancy of fifty staff jobs which was worked out with APEX and ASTMS. Following the strike, seventy manual jobs were declared redundant. However, all of these redundancies were accomplished by attrition and volunteers in cooperation with the AUEW.

# 2 Labor Relations in France

## Introduction

The population of France in 1978 was 53 million, the fourth largest in Western Europe, exceeded only by West Germany, Italy, and Great Britain. During the period 1970-1978, French population increased 4.94%, surpassed only by the Netherlands and Italy among the European countries in this study. If the trend continues, France's population will exceed Britain's in the eighties and will be the third largest in Western Europe (see table A-1).*

The gross national product of France in 1976 was $356 billion—second only to West Germany in Western Europe. The gross national product per person in that year was $6,730 which was the third highest in Europe, exceeded only by Sweden and West Germay. Moreover, the gross national product per person during the 1970-1976 period grew at a rate of 3.3% per year, the highest rate of any of the seven countries in the study (see table A-2).

Consumer prices in France during 1970-1978 increased 100%. This growth was greater than in West Germany, the Netherlands, Sweden, or the United States but less than in Italy and Great Britain (see table A-3). During the same period, unemployment averaged 3.7%—higher than in the other European countries (except Great Britain) but considerably lower than in the United States (see table A-4).

In 1978, the average hourly compensation for production workers in manufacturing in France was $7.69 which was lower than in the Netherlands, Sweden, West Germany, and the United States but higher than in Italy or Great Britain. During the period 1970-1978, the average hourly compensation increased 275%, a greater increase than occurred in all the countries except the Netherlands and West Germany. In terms of local purchasing power, French workers' compensation during 1970-1978 increased 53%, which was exceeded only in West Germany and Italy (see table A-5).

Output in manufacturing in France increased an average of 5.7% per year during the period 1960-1978 and 4.4% per year during 1970-1978. During the latter period, the rate of increase was the highest of any of the seven countries in this study (see table A-6). Productivity, as measured by percentage change

*Tables A-1 through A-13 referred to in this chapter are in the statistical appendix at the end of the book.

in output per hour in manufacturing, increased 5.6% per year during the 1960-1978 period, the rate of increase in productivity, although less than in West Germany or the Netherlands, was more than twice as high as in the United States (see table A-7).

Unit labor costs in terms of French currency increased 5.4% per year during the period 1960-1978 and 10.2% per year during 1970-1978 (see table A-8). In terms of U.S. dollars, the increases in unit labor costs were 5.7% per year during 1960-1978 and 12.6% per year during 1970-1978. The increase in unit labor costs in terms of U.S. dollars during the 1970-1978 period, although lower than in the Netherlands, West Germany, and Sweden, was over twice as high as in the United States (see Table A-9).

## The Union Movement

Under French law, the worker's right to belong to the union of his choice is protected. It is illegal for management to discriminate against workers because of union membership or union activities. However, there are a great many claims of discrimination in the form of physical assaults, isolation, layoffs, and such, filed with the Ministry of Labor each year.[1]

### Structure

The labor movement in France is divided into five federations which were originally based on political and religious affiliation. The federations with their estimated memberships are:

CGT  —  Confédération Générale du Travail                          1,500,000
CFDT —  Confédération Française Démocratique du Travail    600,000
FO    —  Confédération Générale du Travail—Force
              Ouvrière                                                            500,000
CGC  —  Confédération Générale des Cadres                          200,000
CFTC —  Confédération Française des Travailleurs Chrétiens  100,000

The CGT, the oldest and largest of the federations, is closely tied to the French Communist party. Some of its leaders are also leaders of that party and its philosophy is strongly Marxist and anticapitalist. The CFDT was the former Catholic trade union federation, but in 1964 it severed all connection with the church and has adopted a strong anticapitalist position. In recent years, the CGT and CFDT have worked closely together. The FO was formed in 1947 by a group of noncommunists who broke away from the CGT. Although its philosophy is socialist, it strongly supports collective bargaining. The CFTC is made up of unions that retained their ties with the Catholic church when the CFDT adopted its new position in 1964.[2] The CGC consists of unions of executives, foremen, salesmen, technicians, draftsmen, and senior clerical workers. It is generally more conservative than the other federations.

Each federation consists of many affiliated industrial unions, which usually cover wide areas. Thus, within the CGT there is one large industrial union covering all metalworking companies. In each industry, there are usually five such unions—one affiliated with each federation. In addition to the unions affiliated with the federations, there are a few important independent unions such as the FEN (the teachers' union, which is the largest union in France—90% of all teachers are members), and the police union.

Plural unionism rather than exclusive representation is the legal principle in France. Exclusive representation was proposed by the Popular Front government in 1936, but under it the CGT would have controlled all employee representation and collective bargaining. As a result, the other unions and management opposed it, and the law as enacted provides for plural unionism, including proportional representations on factory committees.

The French labor movement is highly centralized. The federations have strong control over the affiliated unions. Most of the unions are run from Paris offices with weak local organizations. At the district and plant levels, the unions usually have no paid representatives, but instead must rely on enthusiastic militants to do the work without pay. Workers are frequently unfamiliar with the name of their union, and refer to themselves as being members of the CGT or one of the other federations.[3]

*Membership and Dues*

It is estimated that the total membership in French unions does not exceed 3.8 million or approximately 23% of the work force, making France the most under-unionized of the countries in this study (see table A-11). Dues in French unions are very low, averaging only about one hour's pay per month. They are collected by union secretaries who sell stamps. It is estimated that not more than 10% of the workers are fully paid-up members. As a result, the unions and the federations are financially weak and severely understaffed. The CGT has only five full-time organizers.[4]

*Closed Shop and Check-Off*

Both the closed shop and the check-off of union dues are illegal. The French constitution guarantees workers the right to join or not join a union, and a 1956 law provides that "no employer shall deduct union dues from the wages of his employees. . . ."

*Ideology*

The ideology of the French labor movement is strongly anticapitalist. The chief federations have heavily supported government ownership of major industrial and financial institutions. As one student of French labor relations has stated, "the hallmark of French trade unionism is its fundamentalist revolutionary anti-capitalism."[5]

*Politics*

There is no single labor party to which the labor movement is attached as in Great Britain. However, the CGT, the largest federation, is closely allied to the Communist party (PCF). The general secretaries of the CGT have always been members of the political bureau of the PCF and, at all levels of the CGT, small groups of PCF members have controlled the federation and its actions. The situation is one in which the party controls the federation rather than vice versa as in Britain where the unions control the Labor party. The CGT-FO has opposed any political domination but has maintained cordial relations with and has generally supported the Socialist party. The CFDT claims that it is not allied with any party but also generally supports the Socialist party and its programs. The federations frequently call brief political strikes in support of, or in opposition to, legislation that is under consideration by the national assembly.[6]

## Employers' Associations

In order to deal effectively with the unions, French enterprises, many of which are small (97% have less than 100 employees), have developed strong employers' associations. In each industry, the employers are organized into regional and national organizations. The national associations in turn are affiliated with Conseil National du Patronat Française (CNPF) which is known as "Patronat."[7]

## Collective Bargaining

*Levels of Bargaining*

Although there are a few notable exceptions, French companies do not negotiate directly with the unions. Instead, labor negotiations are handled exclusively by the employers' associations. There are three levels of association bargaining: nationwide, industry-wide, and regional. Nationwide negotiations take place between Patronat and the union federations. In recent years, these negotiations have become increasingly important. They have not been concerned with wages but have resulted in nationwide agreements on such matters as pensions, unemployment benefits, termination pay, vocational training, working conditions, and hours of work.[8] In each industry, industry-wide negotiations occur between the employers' association (usually affiliated with Patronat) and the industry unions (usually one union from each of the federations). The agreements resulting from negotiations normally hold for one year. They set forth the minimum wage rates and the general conditions that must be observed by all companies in the industry association. Regional negotiations, which occur between the regional employers' association of an industry and the industry unions, usually take place after the industry-wide negotiations. The agreements negotiated at this level supplement the industry-wide agreements.

Company negotiations are unusual in France, but there are some companies, such as Renault, that do negotiate contracts directly with the unions. Patronat has strongly opposed this type of bargaining, arguing that it allows the unions to play one company against another, and generally weakens the bargaining power of management. Plant negotiations have been strongly resisted by French management and are not widespread, though they appear to be growing. Where they occur, the usual result is to increase the wages established in the industry and regional agreements, and to supplement those contracts in ways beneficial to the employees.

### Scope of Bargaining

The role of collective bargaining in France is limited by two factors: the scope of employee benefits required by law, and the significance of the individual employment contract. The extent and generosity of the employee benefits established by law are among the highest in the European Economic Community (EEC). They include pay for: vacations (four weeks), holidays (eleven), sick leave, maternity leave, hospital and medical care, death, retirement, severance unemployment, and size of family. As a result, the scope of bargaining is severely limited.

The individual employment contract (usually oral) remains the primary agreement regulating the employment relationship in France. It sets the nature of the job, the working conditions, and the actual wages to be paid. The French worker is free to negotiate for himself wages that are above the minima established in the collective agreements. Actual wages often far exceed the collective contract minima, especially in prosperous firms during periods of full employment. Thus, the importance of collective bargaining is reduced.[9]

*Conciliation, Mediation, and Arbitration*

Conciliation is required by law in France. The legislation provides that unless there is a procedure for conciliation in the labor agreement, the employers and the unions must accept conciliation by a tripartite commission of nine members appointed by the government. If conciliation is not successful, the chairman of the commission may initiate mediation and, if the parties are unable to agree on a mediator, appointment may be made by the Minister of Labor. The mediator may hold hearings and make a recommendation which, if not accepted by the parties in forty-eight hours, may be publicized by the Minister of Labor unless both parties request him not to do so. The original draft of the law also imposed compulsory arbitration, but both management and labor strongly objected to the arbitration provisions and they were deleted.

It is not clear in the law whether conciliation is required before or only after a strike occurs. In any event, the government has not enforced the law, and its provisions are rarely used by the French management and unions.[10]

*The Labor Agreement*

The usual practice in France has been to negotiate a one-year agreement. However, the law provides that, unless otherwise stated, an agreement remains in effect after its expiration date until the parties reach a new agreement. As a result, the agreement serves as an underpinning for negotiations which occur intermittently rather than during a specific period close to the contract termination date.[11]

French labor agreements are legally enforceable, and workers or unions who break an agreement by an illegal strike may be sued for damages.[12] However, the labor agreements do not prohibit strikes. Although some agreements do contain so-called no-strike clauses, these merely provide for a period of notice or exhaustion of a conciliation procedure before a legal strike may occur.[13] The unions view the agreements, which they prefer to call "statements," as no more than short-term compromises that can be reopened as soon as the balance of power shifts in their favor. Thus, French labor agreements, like British labor agreements, are essentially open-ended.[14]

*Grievance Procedure*

In the day-to-day handling of worker problems within a plant, the unions play only a minor role. Under a 1968 law, they have the right to appoint shop representatives (*délégués syndicaux*) but such representatives may act as observers only. The actual discussion of employee problems and grievances with management is carried out by a committee of workers elected by the workers (*délégués du personnel*). Only the unions have the right to nominate candidates for the *délégués du personnel* on the first ballot. However, if the unions fail to nominate candidates or if less than one-half the employees vote in the first ballot, a second election must be held in which non-unionists may be candidates. The election is set up according to a complicated proportional representation system to prevent the CGT from obtaining complete control over the committee. Once the election is completed, the management has to deal only with this one committee on personnel matters, although the committee usually is composed of representatives from the various unions. *Délégués du personnel* cannot be dismissed without the approval of the labor inspector.

French law requires that the grievance procedure have at least the following three levels of representation: foremen, *délégués du personnel*, and a labor court. Many labor contracts provide for additional steps to be taken prior to going to the labor court. However, an employee is always free to appeal directly to a labor court if he so desires.

*Strikes*

The right to strike in France is a carefully guarded constitutional provision. During a strike, the employee's rights under his employment contract are merely suspended. However, if the employee engaged in serious misconduct (*faute lourde*) during the strike, the employment contract may be breached. The lockout is generally recognized as illegal unless the employer can prove that there is no work available for the employees who are willing to work.[15]

In addition to effecting walkouts, French unions have been especially adept at developing the following types of strikes to meet special conditions:

*bottleneck strike* (grève bouchon)—a small group of workers in a key operation are able to stop the production of the entire plant,

*rotating strike* (grève tournante)—groups of workers take turns striking (Since the employer is not free to lockout, he must continue to pay the non-striking workers),

*slowdown strike* (grève perlée)—may be illegal but French law is not clear on this point,

*work-to-the-rule strike* (grève du zèle)—production is slowed down by strict application of all work rules,

*warning strike* (bras croisés)—is very short, usually only a few minutes, and serves to warn the employer that the workers are unhappy, *political strike* (grève politique)—protests some government action or proposed legislation (not protected by law and therefore usually disguised as an economic strike),

*occupational strike or sit-in* (grève sur le tas)—usually but not always has been declared illegal by the French courts.

Most French strikes are of short duration, lasting only a few hours or a few days. The unions are not financially able to pay large strike benefits, and employees cannot afford to stay out for a long time. Although strikes are particularly bothersome to French management because of the large number of them and the difficulty of predicting when they will occur, the actual production loss is quite small. During the ten-year-period 1967-1976, only 210 days were lost because of strikes per year per 1,000 employees, or approximately 1/10 of 1% of France's total production—less than the strike losses in Italy, the United States, or Great Britain (see table A-12).

## Legislated Employee Protection and Benefits

The French government and the unions have not been content to rely on collective bargaining to protect workers' rights and provide them with benefits. Instead, a vast network of social security provisions offer protection to the general public, including workers. Moreover, certain protections and benefits have been legislated specifically for workers. As indicated earlier, to the extent that such matters have been covered by legislation, the scope of collective bargaining has been reduced. In France, however, employee protections and benefits frequently have been negotiated by Patronat and the unions first, and then adopted into law with their support. Thus, many of the labor laws constitute the extension of labor agreements to cover the entire economy. Some of the most important legislated employee rights and benefits are discussed here.

### Minimum Wage

A minimum wage law, the *Salaire Minimum de Croissance* (SMIC) first became effective in France in 1950. It applies to all workers in industry, commerce, the professions, agriculture, and marine work. Originally it provided for area wage differentials and a lower rate for agricultural workers. In 1968, however, the differentials were eliminated, and now there is one minimum wage for all employees covered by the law. The SMIC is adjusted every two months to the national retail price index. As of April 1, 1979, the SMIC was 11.60 francs (about $2.73) per hour. Failure to pay the SMIC subjects employers to a fine which can be as high as 360 francs per employee.[16]

*Overtime*

The forty-hour week is applicable in all French industries but there is a considerable amount of overtime. In January, 1973, the average work week was 43.8 hours. The extra hours are paid at the regular rate. There is no premium pay for overtime except for Sunday work. However, such overtime is completely voluntary, and overtime work usually is not permitted if some employees at the plant are on layoff. A 1975 law provides for a period of rest equal to 20% of all hours worked over forty-two in any one week. The rest must accumulate to eight hours, and then the worker is given a day off at his convenience. Thus, in reality the new law provides a 20% premium for overtime work but gives it in rest instead of in pay.

*Shift Work*

In 1976, the French government published a report on shift work by a research team headed by Professor Alain Wisner. Wisner and his associates found that shift work was very detrimental to the health and famiy life of French workers and recommended that it be severely limited. After much discussion of the issue, the government enacted a new decree in June, 1977, which provides that new shift operations may be undertaken only after consultation with the works council and approval by the employment office. Moreover, employees on new shifts must be given at least fourteen hours of rest beginning on Saturday evening. Finally, shift workers must be given special medical examinations and surveillance.

*Mensualization*

In 1964, President Pompidou initiated a campaign in which he urged management to pay manual workers a monthly salary. By the end of 1977, it was estimated that 84% of French manual workers were being paid in this manner. The change to salary payment was frequently accompanied by the elimination of certain benefit distinctions between manual and white-collar workers. In December, 1977, Patronat reached a national agreement with the FO and CFTC whereby the remaining manual workers would receive monthly salaries. In addition, the agreement gave manual workers certain other benefits that formerly were only available to white-collar workers. One of these was improved sick pay provision. The sick pay improvements are available, however, only if the employee obtains a medical certificate from his own physician and is willing also to submit to an examination by another physician. Two unions, the CGT and CFDT, refused to sign the new agreement because of the provision requiring a medical examination. Nevertheless, on January 20, 1978, the government enacted the new mensualization agreement into law, making it applicable to all sectors of industry, effective as of October 1, 1978.[17]

*Dismissals*

A law passed in 1973 provides that any dismissal may be challenged in the courts on the basis that it is not for "real and serious" reasons. The law recognizes four types of offenses that may result in dismissal:

1. *Flagrant Misconduct* (faute lourde) includes theft, fighting, insults to supervisors, major breach of professional obligations, and other very serious offenses. Such conduct justifies immediate dismissal and the employee loses all rights to severance pay and holiday pay.

2. *Gross Misconduct* (faute grave) includes offenses that are serious, but less serious than those considered to be flagrant misconduct. It is a matter of degree, and the line between the two is not very clear. Gross misconduct also warrants immediate dismissal. However, if the offense is judged to be gross but not flagrant misconduct, the dismissed employee loses severance pay, but not holiday pay.

3. *Real and Serious Reasons* (des causes réelles et sérieuses). The term "real" has been interpreted to mean that the employer must put forward concrete and precise reasons, not just general statements, as the basis for the termination. The term "serious" has been interpreted to mean that the conduct of the employee has been such as to make continuation of the employment relationship at least difficult and might involve real harm to the enterprise. (It has been found also that a series of minor incidents may add up to "real and serious reasons.") For this type of offense, immediate dismissal is not warranted, but rather, the employer must follow the due notice procedure to be discussed later. An employee discharged for "real and serious reasons" is eligible for both severance pay and holiday pay.

4. *Minor Reasons* (faute légère) include lateness, absenteeism, or other such offenses that the courts judge to be less serious in nature than those included under the other three categories, and, therefore, not cause for dismissal. The courts may order the reinstatement of the employee and/or at least six months' salary plus severance pay and holiday pay.

Except in cases involving flagrant or gross misconduct, the law provides that the employer may not summarily dismiss an employee, but instead, must pursue the following procedure:

1. The employer must invite the employee to discuss the proposed disciplinary action (At the meeting, the employee may be accompanied by another employee of his choice).
2. The employer must send a letter to the employee twenty-four hours later.
3. The employee may then demand the reasons in writing.
4. The employer must give notice of one month to an employee with six months to two years of service, and two months to an employee with more than two years of service. (Pay may be given in lieu of notice.)[18]

*Redundancies*

French law requires that before an individual or a group of workers may be laid off, the employer must first supply the economic, financial, production, and other data about the employment situation to the works council, and then consult with them regarding the layoff. The employer must then secure the approval of the regional department of labor. If approval is withheld, the employer may appeal to a joint industry committee which will advise the labor department. The whole process may involve weeks or months, during which the layoff is forestalled. The impact of the law has been almost entirely on group layoffs. When an employer lays off a worker for economic reasons, often he does not seek approval of the labor department, and when he does, it is little more than a formality.

Unemployment compensation in France involves a combination of public and private systems. The private system, Union Nationale Interprofessionelle pour l'Emploi dans l'Industrie et le Commerce (UNEDIC), which was originally negotiated by the CNPF (Patronat) and the unions in 1958 and was renegotiated in 1979, provides the major share of the benefits. Prior to July, 1979, employees who were dismissed for economic reasons received from the two systems 90% of pay for a period of one year. The new agreement between Patronat and the unions which became effective July 1, 1979, is much more complicated. Some very low-paid workers may still receive 90% of pay for a full year, but for most workers the amount will be less than 90% in the first quarter (it may be as low as 75%) and will decrease each quarter (it may be as low as 60% for the fourth quarter). It is hoped that the new plan will provide dismissed workers with an increasing incentive to find new jobs. Under the 1979 agreement and an earlier 1977 agreement, workers age sixty to sixty-five who are dismissed or who retire voluntarily to make jobs available for younger workers are given 70% of pay until they reach retirement age (sixty-five).

*Maternity Protection and Pay*

A 1975 French law provides that an employer may neither refuse to hire nor dismiss a worker because of pregnancy. It provides also that a working woman is entitled to fourteen weeks of paid maternity leave, (six weeks before birth and eight weeks after birth), at 90% of basic pay up to a certain maximum. After giving birth, a mother is entitled to a leave of one year to care for the child, with the right to return to work at the end of that period. In many industries in France, benefits more favorable than those required by the law have been negotiated. Under the labor agreement covering the Paris area insurance firms, where a majority of the employees are women, a woman is entitled to twenty weeks of maternity leave at full pay.[19]

In January, 1978, Prime Minister Barre proposed a change in the law whereby maternity leave required by the law would be increased from fourteen to twenty-six weeks. Moreover, the additional twelve weeks would not have to be taken continuously, but instead, could be used to reduce working time over a four-year period after the birth.[20]

### Absenteeism

A study by the Swedish employers' association reported that in 1973, sickness absenteeism in France was 7%—higher than in West Germany, Great Britain, or the United States, but lower than in the Netherlands, Italy, or Sweden (see table A-13).

In 1977, the French government published a study on absenteeism prepared by François Heilbronner, a tax inspector at the Ministry of Economics and Finance. According to Heilbronner's report, absenteeism is a major problem in French industry, accounting for almost 100 times the number of days lost in strikes. He found that the absentee rate in 1975 was twenty-one days per employee per year or 8.3%. However, 50% of the employees were not absent during the year, with the result that the other 50% averaged forty-two days or 16.6%.

French managers have reported that they believe the increase in absenteeism during the sixties and seventies has been at least partly a result of the extension of mensualization which now covers practically all French workers. As part of the mensualization agreements, supplemental sick pay which formerly was given only to white-collar workers is now given to blue-collar workers. Management is of the opinion that blue-collar workers now take more time off because the gap between their sick pay and their pay for working is much narrower than it used to be.

Heilbronner found that 78% of those absent reported that they were sick, but he concluded that in many cases they were simply taking advantage of lax controls. Forty percent of those who reported ill were not at home when a social security inspector called.

Heilbronner recommended that:

1. all workers who report off sick be required to be at home between 10:00 A.M. and 5:00 P.M.
2. medical supervision be tightened up.
3. the waiting period for sick pay be increased from three to seven days, and
4. sick pay be classified as taxable income.

The French managers with whom we discussed the problem agree with Heilbronner that the lack of control over sick pay is the most important reason for the high rate of absenteeism. French companies are prohibited by law from conducting medical checks to determine if absent employees are eligible for basic sick benefits, which equal to 50% or more of pay, depending on family status. Such checks may be made only by doctors of the state social security system who, according to French management, have been very reluctant to deny benefits to employees. However, in 1978, despite very strong objections by the French unions, the French Supreme Court did support a company's right to check on employees before paying supplementary sick benefits. This court ruling may prove helpful in controlling absenteeism.

## Worker Participation

### Works Councils

Worker participation in company decision making either through works councils or employee representatives on boards of directors is very limited in France. French law does provide that every enterprise with fifty or more employees must establish a *comité d'entreprise*. However, in 1975 the Sudreau Commission found that less than half the companies with fifty or more employees had set up such *comités*.

The law provides that the *comité* shall be composed of employees who are elected by their fellow workers. In the first ballot, only unions may nominate candidates. However, if the unions fail to nominate candidates or if less than one-half the employees vote in the first ballot, a second ballot is held in which non-union workers may be candidates. The election involves a complicated proportional representation system to prevent the CGT from gaining complete control of the *comités*. Where the company has more than one plant, the employees elect members to a *comité d'establissment* to deal with plant matters only. The *comité d'establissment* in turn appoints members to the *comité d'enterprise* which deals with company-wide matters (see figure 2-1).

The function of the *comité d'enterprise* is purely consultative. It has no veto or codetermination authority. Management must provide it with certain information and must meet with it at least once per month to discuss such matters as safety, working conditions, production, and layoffs. The *comité* also has the responsibility of operating the firm's social activities, such as canteens and holiday facilities.

Neither French management nor French unions appear to be very happy with the *comités d'enterprise*. Many managements complain that they consume too much time and energy, and at times tend to delay important decisions. Some managements admit that they have developed techniques to

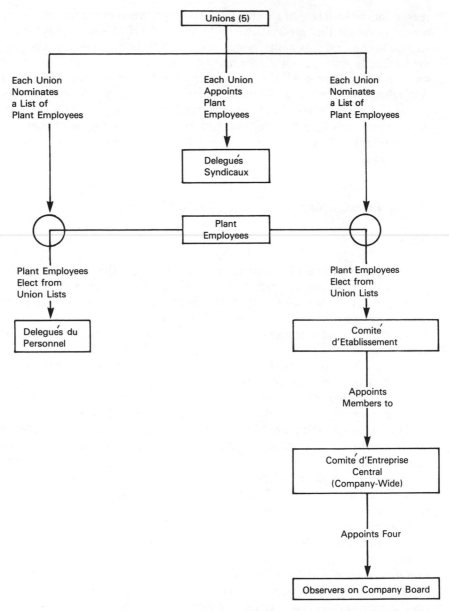

**Figure 2-1.** Selection of Plant and Company Employee Representatives

weaken the influence of the *comités*. Unions also view the *comités* as ineffective devices that have served only to fragment and weaken union influence at the local level.[21] In 1975, the Sudreau Commission recommended that those establishments with fifty or more employees that had not set up *comités d'entreprise* should be required to do so. The Sudreau Commission further recommended, however, that the *comités* should remain purely consultative.

## The Social Audit

In 1975, the Sudreau Commission recommended that workers should be provided with much more information regarding the operation of the enterprise. On July 12, 1977, the government incorporated the Sudreau proposals into the Social Audit Act which provides that each year an employer must present to his workers a report that gives adequate information regarding: employment levels; pay and fringe benefits; health and safety; training; industrial relations developments; and living conditions of the workers and their families that are related to the employment. A draft of the report must be presented to the works council and the shop stewards for their comments and suggestions at least two weeks prior to its issuance. Failure to issue such an audit to the employees, or the issuance of incomplete or erroneous information, subjects the employer to imprisonment of from two months to one year and/or a fine of from 200 to 10,000 francs. Repeated violations may be penalized by imprisonment of up to two years and fines of up to 20,000 francs. The act becomes operative progressively, beginning in 1979 with employers who have 750 employees and reaching employers with 300 employees in 1982. By 1982, the reports must also cover two years and indicate the progress that has been made in these matters over the two-year period.

## Board Observer

French workers and unions have no legal right to representation on company boards of directors. However, a *comité d'enterprise* does have the legal right to send four observers to board meetings. Where such observers have been appointed, the effect has been illusory. Standard procedure in France is to hold, prior to the board meeting, an informal meeting at which all problems are thrashed out and decisions are made. At the formal meeting that follows, votes are taken quickly with little or no discussion of the major factors that entered into the decisions[22] (see figure 2-1).

## Profit Sharing and Employee Ownership

France has two basic systems of profit sharing which operate under two different laws: the 1959 act and the 1967 act. Under the 1959 act, profit sharing is voluntary. An employer is free to negotiate with the workers' representatives a plan whereby the workers will receive a certain share of either the profits, the dividends, or the productivity increases. The company in turn is given certain tax advantages. The benefits are paid to the workers in cash each year (each quarter, if linked to productivity). Very few companies have negotiated such programs. A study in 1973 reported only 243 such agreements, covering 125,000 workers.

The 1967 act, which was sponsored by de Gaulle, is compulsory. It requires all companies with 100 or more employees to create from its profits a "special participation reserve" for its workers. The amount that the company must contribute is arrived at by a complicated formula which applies only after a 5% profit for the owners has been deducted. The remaining amount is multiplied by a factor representing capital-labor intensity and then multiplied by 50%. The resulting fund may be used in one of three ways: to buy shares in the company; to make a loan to the employer; or to be deposited in a unit trust. The details of the plan must be negotiated with the works council, union officials, or the employees who represent the union. The workers must wait five years before receiving money from the fund. In other words, profits placed in the fund in 1980 would be available (with interest or dividends) in 1985. Employers receive certain tax benefits. According to the Ministry of Labor, 4.7 million workers in 11,000 firms are covered by this legislation.

Since the 1967 act became effective, in many companies there has not been a yearly profit of over 5%, and in others the amount over 5% has been small. In 1968, only eleven of France's fifty largest companies had to share profits. In 1974, the average per worker in companies that had to share was only 400 francs. However, in some companies, sharing has been significant. In one year it was 6,415 francs per employee for Viniprix; 4,250 francs for Carrefour, and 1,700 francs for L'Oreal. The 1967 legislation has had a minimal effect on employee ownership and control of French corporations. Less than 2% of the plans provide for allocation of shares.

The unions have opposed the schemes. The CGT claims that the only beneficiaries have been the employers, because the plans have provided them with money for investment programs as well as tax benefits. According to the CGT, such plans are simply a way of conning the workers into believing they are part of management.

In the spring of 1977, the government released the Delouvier report in which the subject of profit sharing and employee shareholding was reexamined. The report, although favoring several changes that would make it easier for workers to participate in share-ownership schemes, proposed no basic changes for the 1959 and 1967 legislations.

In addition to the profit-sharing acts, there is also legislation, the 1973 Employee Shareholding Act, under which French management may permit workers to buy shares in the company. However, the effect of this legislation has not been significant. Only about twenty-five companies have adopted such stock purchase plans.

Late in 1978, the Minister of Labor proposed a bill to parliament which would require all French companies whose stock is quoted on the French stock exchange and who have paid at least two dividends in the past three years to distribute 3% of their share capital to their employees. This would be a one-time distribution, and the employees would not be entitled to sell or receive the dividends for a period of at least three years.

## Notes

1. Everett Kassalow, *Trade Unions and Industrial Relations: An International Comparison* (New York: Random House, 1969), p. 127.

2. Jean-Daniel Reynaud, "Trade Unions and Political Parties in France," *Industrial and Labor Relations Review* 28 (2), 1975:208.

3. Seyfarth, Shaw, Fairweather and Geraldson, *Labor Relations and the Law in France and the United States* (Ann Arbor: University of Michigan, 1972), p. 15.

4. Jack Barbash, *Trade Unions and National Economic Policy* (Baltimore: Johns Hopkins Press, 1972), p. 146.

5. Ibid., p. 146.

6. Reynaud, "Trade Unions and Political Parties," pp. 209-212.

7. Jean-Jacques Oechslin, "The Role of Employers' Organizations in France," *International Labor Review* 106 (5), 1972:391-413.

8. *Background Paper for Tripartite Advisory Meeting on Collective Bargaining* (Geneva: International Labor Office, 1976), p. 17.

9. Seyfarth et al., *Labor Relations*, p. 178.

10. Ibid., p. 171.

11. Yves Delamotte, "Recent Collective Bargaining Trends in France," *International Labor Review* 103 (4), 1971:354.

12. Seyfarth, et al., *Labor Relations*, pp. 21-11.

13. Ibid., p. 127.

14. *Background Paper for Meeting*, p. 13.

15. Seyfarth, et al., *Labor Relations*, pp. 148-51.

16. Ibid., p. 327.

17. "France: New Law Forces Pace on Staff Status Changes," *European Industrial Relations Review*, Vol. 49, Jan. 1978, p. 10.

18. "Individual Dismissals in France," *European Industrial Relations Review*, Vol. 45, Sept. 1977, pp. 12-13.

19. "Maternity Protection in France," *European Industrial Relations Review*, Vol. 28, Apr. 1976, pp. 14-16.

20. "France: Government's New Program," *European Industrial Review*, Vol. 49, Jan. 1978, p. 4.

21. Barbash, *Trade Unions and Economic Policy*, p. 156.

22. Seyfarth et al., *Labor Relations*, p. 200.

# Case 3
# Poncet Mine (A)

On Monday, June 12, 1972, Monsieur Jacques Minot, general manager of Region 4 of Charbonnage de France (CdF), faced the difficult problem of what action, if any, he should recommend to his superiors in Paris. Minot's difficulties had arisen from management's decision to close Poncet, the highest cost mine in the region. The unions opposed the closure and ordered a strike which on this day was very effective throughout Region 4. Moreover, the miners from Poncet had been occupying the Region's general offices at Vercon since Tuesday, June 6. Finally, the unions had called a twenty-four-hour sympathy strike for the next day at a number of the other regions of CdF.

## The French Coal Industry

In 1975, France produced 22.4 million metric tons of coal which made it the third largest producer in Western Europe, exceeded only by Western Germany's 92.4 million tons and United Kingdom's 128.7 million tons. However, in France as in the other EEC countries, coal was a declining industry. Following World War II, French coal production had increased slowly until 1958 when it reached a peak of 57.7 million tons, but since 1958 the decline had been rapid. The 1975 output was only 39% of the 1958 peak (see exhibits 3a-1 and 3a-2). This decline in production was reflected in a heavy drop in employment. In 1973, only 93,000 workers were employed in the industry compared with 197,000 in 1963 and 267,000 in 1953 (see exhibit 3a-2). Since the industry was concentrated in the north and northeast of France, the social and economic effects of the decline had a heavy impact on certain communities in those areas.

In 1946 the French government had nationalized the coal industry. The private mining companies throughout the country were purchased by the government and placed under the control of a newly created agency, Charbonnage de France, which had its headquarters in Paris. By 1975, CdF produced close to 100% of all the coal mined in France. (Some few captive mines were still operated by utilities and other companies.)

In order to administer the industry effectively, CdF divided it into producing areas, each of which was given considerable authority over actual operations within general guidelines set down by CdF. One of these areas

**Exhibit 3a-1**
**Coal Production in France: 1946-1975**
*(in thousands of metric tons)*

| Year | Amount Produced | Year | Amount Produced | Year | Amount Produced |
|------|-----------------|------|-----------------|------|-----------------|
| 1946 | 47,155 | 1956 | 55,129 | 1966 | 50,338 |
| 1947 | 45,230 | 1957 | 56,795 | 1967 | 47,624 |
| 1948 | 43,291 | 1958 | 57,721 | 1968 | 41,911 |
| 1949 | 51,199 | 1959 | 57,606 | 1969 | 40,583 |
| 1950 | 50,843 | 1960 | 55,960 | 1970 | 37,838 |
| 1951 | 52,972 | 1961 | 52,358 | 1971 | 33,899 |
| 1952 | 53,365 | 1962 | 52,359 | 1972 | 30,574 |
| 1953 | 52,588 | 1963 | 47,754 | 1973 | 26,350 |
| 1954 | 54,405 | 1964 | 53,030 | 1974 | 24,036 |
| 1955 | 55,355 | 1965 | 51,348 | 1975 | 22,414 |

Source: Monthly Bulletin of Statistics, United Nations, New York, New York.

**The Poncet Mine**

One of the mines in Region 4 was at Poncet, 32 kilometers from Vercon. Poncet had approximately 5,500 inhabitants within its town lines and another 7,000 in the surrounding area. The economy of Poncet was entirely dependent upon the mine. There were no other industries in the area. In 1970, the Poncet mine employed 1,200 workers—925 underground and 275 on the surface. Over the years since nationalization, Region 4 management had expended considerable funds at Poncet in order to provide it with efficient mining equipment. Despite these expenditures, the quality of the coal and the size of the seams at Poncet made it the least productive per man hour and the highest cost per ton facility in Region 4. (See exhibit 3a-3.)

The miners at Poncet had a choice of four different unions which they could join if they desired to do so. Each of these unions was an industrial union for miners affiliated with a separate national federation. Each federation was made up of a number of unions from other industries as well as its miners' union. The four federations were:

1. *Confédération Générale du Travail (CGT)*, the largest and most powerful of the four federations. CGT was dominated by Communists who had captured control of it after World War II. The president was a member also of the Politburo of the French Communist party. The CGT's goal was socialization of the economy.

2. *Confédération Française Démocratique du Travail (CFDT)*, the second largest of the federations. Historically closely related to the Catholic church and its social philosophy, the CFDT had asserted its independence from both the Church and the Catholic Republican party (MRP) in 1964. Following 1970 it had embraced socialism and developed a close relationship with the CGT.

**Exhibit 3a-2**
**Coal, Industry Production and Employment in France: 1946-1975**

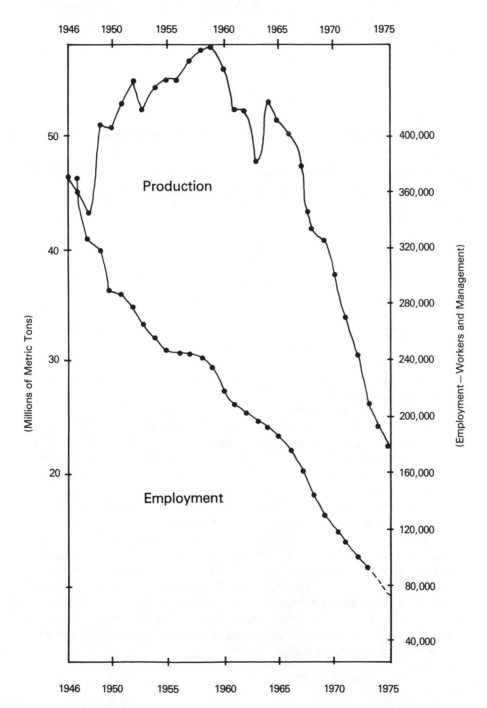

**Exhibit 3a-3**
**Employment in Region 4**

| Year | Underground French | Others | Surface & Management French | Others |
|------|------|------|------|------|
| 1960 | 11,219 | 6,557 | 10,623 | 2,325 |
| 1965 | 12,709 | 4,493 | 8,612 | 1,016 |
| 1970 | 9,698 | 2,419 | 6,938 | 803 |
| 1975 | 8,302 | 2,372 | 6,604 | 718 |

Source: Company records.

3. *Confédération Générale du Travail—Force Ouvrière (FO)*, split off from the CGT in 1947. Although its basic philosophy was socialistic, it maintained an independence in politics and emphasized collective bargaining.

4. *Confédération Française des Travailleurs Chrétiens (CFTC)*, the smallest of the four federations. It broke away from the CGT in 1919 and became closely related to the Catholic church and the Catholic Republican Party. In 1964, most of its membership split off to form the CFDT.

The workers at Poncet never referred to the name of their particular miners' union but always to the federation to which it was affiliated. Thus a miner might refer to himself as a member of the CGT or CFDT or FO or CFTC. Members of all four unions worked together on the same jobs in the mine. However, membership in a union was not compulsory and a considerable number of the miners were not dues-paying members in any of the four organizations.

Many of the engineers, supervisors, and technicians at Poncet were members of another union, Conféderation Générale des Cadres (CGC). The CGC was a moderate organization without political affiliation which had split off from the CGT in 1952. However, some of the engineers, supervisors, and technicians were members of unions affiliated with the four other federations.

The period 1946 to 1959 was a time of growth and development for the French coal industry (see exhibits 3a-1 and 3a-2). Coal was in heavy demand and CdF was happy to have the production from Poncet even though it was high cost. However, following 1959 the industry found itself with a growing amount of excess capacity, as oil and other energy sources replaced coal. CdF attempted to meet this condition by: developing new uses for coal; decreasing its manpower through attrition and later by granting bonuses and wage guarantees to miners who were willing to move to other industries; and developing new industries for its coal mining communities to absorb the manpower no longer needed in coal.[1]

In the late sixties, production capacity remained considerably in excess of demand. Costs in the industry were outrunning income, requiring heavy government subsidy.[2] In 1969, the government decided that during the sixth five-year plan 1971-1975, coal production would have to be decreased.[3] Region 4 was ordered to cut its production by several million tons during the five-year period. The pressure from the Ministry of Industry was on CdF and through CdF on Region 4 to make the cut by eliminating high-cost mines and thus keeping the required government subsidy as low as possible. Poncet with its low output per man hour and high costs per ton was a natural target for action.

### The Decision to Stop Preparatory Work

The first open move to cut production and eventually close the Poncet mine occurred on January 29, 1972. On that date a proposal was placed before the board of directors of Region 4 to discontinue the preparatory work on new areas at Poncet. This proposal was rigorously opposed by the five personnel representatives on the board who recognized that without such preparatory work, production at the mine would eventually have to stop. Despite their strong protests, the majority of the board (the vote was 9 to 5) voted in favor of the proposal.

### The Union and Community Reaction

The decision to stop the preparatory work sparked a strong reaction from the unions and the political leaders of the area. On February 3 at a meeting at the Poncet town hall, a committe for defense of the mine was created consisting of the mayor of Poncet, a number of mayors of nearby towns, and representatives from unions and professional groups. On February 5, the committee met with Minot who explained to them the reasons for closing Poncet. He also offered his assistance in developing an industrial area for the town and getting new industries to occupy it.

On February 28, representatives of the committee were received in Paris by the Minister of Industry who explained to them that coal production had to be concentrated in the more efficient mines but that every effort would be made to take care of the miners who would be displaced.

The unions that represented the miners also reacted strongly. The CGT proposed that all the unions should forget their differences and join together to fight the closing. Representatives of the CGT, CFDT, CFTC, FO, and CGC then met, formed the inter-trade union committee, and agreed upon a statement opposing the board's action in stopping the preparatory work. On March 5, 1972, at an extraordinary meeting of the

Region 4 works committee, after the general manager had explained the reasons for the need to close Poncet, the unions read a joint declaration that stated that the closing was unnecessary; would make their region an economic desert; and, would create for the area major social problems that had not been given sufficient attention.

On the morning of March 6, two of the union representatives and the secretary of the mayor of Poncet held a meeting at the entrance to the mine. They reviwed the works committee meeting and were strongly critical of management's attitude. As a result of the meeting, the miners were one hour late in reporting for work. The next day managment announced that the miners' regular pay for the previous day would be cut by one hour because of their delay in going into the mine caused by the speeches. One of the union leaders commented later, "the miners could make them pay dearly for the one-hour's pay they held back."

### One-Day Strike and Demonstration

On April 15, 1972, the unions called a one-day strike at Poncet and a one-hour sympathy strike at the other Region 4 mines. The Poncet strikers were joined by political, professional, and business leaders from Poncet and nearby towns in what was called a "dead cities" demonstration in the town square. The assembled group unanimously adopted a petition urging the board of directors of Region 4 not to close the mine.

The board was meeting that day at Vercon. At 5:30, about 200 miners from Poncet assembled at Vercon in the streets outside the buiding where the board was meeting. The board agreed to receive a committee who presented the petition. Later, some of the crowd penetrated the building and loudly insisted on talking with the chairman. However, by 7:30 the demonstration had ended without any damage to persons or property.

### The April 19 Incident

Following the decision of the Region 4 board on January 29, 1972, to stop preparation work at Poncet, management on April 19, 1972, assigned a crew of workers to disassemble the equipment that had been used in the preparatory work. At 9:00 A.M., a miners' delegate of the CGT ordered the crew to stop work. The crew followed the delegate's order and disassembly of the equipment was halted.

When management was informed of the action, it decided to have the disassembly work performed by engineers who were members of the CGC. Five engineers were sent to that part of the mine to perform the task.

However, soon after they started to work, they were seized by a union delegate and a group of nine miners who pushed them into a cul-de-sac and informed management that the engineers would be held as hostages until the decision to stop the preparation work was reversed.

A number of management meetings were held during the day at Poncet, Vercon, and Paris. It was decided to take no immediate action. The engineers were held in the cul-de-sac all day. Then at 7:30 P.M. the Ministry of Industrial and Scientific Development announced that the Minister would be willing to meet with the Poncet defense committee in Paris in the middle of May and that all disassembly work at the mine would be halted prior to that meeting. When the miners were informed of the Minister's order, the engineers were released.

Statements approving the holding of the engineers by the miners were issued by the union leaders and many of the Poncet civil leaders. The defense committee congratulated the miners. The CGT indicated it was happy with the results obtained. The CFDT stated that while it was regrettable that it was necessary to use these tactics, it was the only type of action that would have been effective and, therefore, had to be approved. However, the CGC which represented the engineers who had been held as hostages, strongly condemned the incident as "a type of action which can break the unity of action highly desirable at the current time" and went on to state "we are astonished that the local elected officials would approve such actions."

Management followed the Minister's orders not to proceed with the disassembly until he had had an opportunity to meet with the inter-union defense committee and further evaluate the situation. No disciplinary action of any kind was taken against the group of miners who had participated in the action.

On May 15, 1972, representatives of the inter-union defense committee were received by the office director of the Ministry of Industrial Development at his office in Paris. They pleaded vigorously against the closing of the mine. The director listened attentively to their pleas but made no official statement.

## Strike and Occupation

On June 5, 1972, the management of CdF agreed to meet with representatives of the defense committee at CdF headquarters in Paris. Over 300 miners and businessmen from Poncet went to Paris and demonstrated in front of the CdF offices while the meeting was in progress. CdF management listened sympathetically to the committee's pleas but confirmed once more that the closing of the mine was necessary and unavoidable.

Early on Tuesday morning, June 6, 1972, the miners who had been to Paris gathered at the Poncet mine entrance and informed the other miners of the negative results of their efforts. The miners then decided to strike and to go to Region 4 headquarters at Vercon. Arriving at Vercon, they broke down the doors and occupied the office building. When the office workers and engineers arrived for work at 8:30 A.M., they were expelled from the building. In the afternoon, the Poncet businessmen sent food and beer to the miners who were occupying the offices. Management proposed a conference to try to work out an agreement but the miners refused and continued the occupation.

By Friday, June 9, the strike had spread and 80% of Region 4 production was down. Despite proposals by CdF and Region 4 to settle the conflict, no progress was made. The occupation of the Vercon offices continued and by Monday, May 12, the strike throughout Region 4 had become fully effective. This same day the national officers of the unions, except the CGT and CFDT[4] met with the officers of CdF in Paris and signed a new agreement on salaries covering the miners in all of CdF properties including Region 4. However, twenty-four-hour sympathy strikes were called in a number of the other regions for Tuesday, June 13. The interunion committee insisted that the strike and the office occupation would be ended only if management agreed to continue preparation work at Poncet with a view to keeping the mine operating. Region 4 and CdF management met to determine what action, if any, they should take to try to resolve the conflict.

**Notes**

1. French workers who were laid off were entitled to benefits from two sources: National Unemployment Fund and the Union Nationale Interprofessionelle pour l'Emploi dans l'Industrie et le Commerce (UNIDEC). In addition, the National Employment Fund could under certain circumstances supplement the other two. Generally a worker could expect:

1. Unemployment compensation benefits as high as 80-90% of prior wage during a retraining period,
2. Moving and resettlement payments to encourage worker migration to areas of short labor supply,
3. Make-up pay for taking lower paying jobs in a depressed area (90% of former wage for six months and 75% for an added six months),
4. An allowance to workers over age 60 but under age 65 involved in a group layoff, until they could qualify for a pension at age 65 (the amount was at least equal to total unemployment compensation payable under governmental and supplemental programs).

2. Guy de Carmoy in his book *Le Dossier Européen de l'Énergie* (1971) stated that in the EEC the subsidy per ton of coal mined was $4.40 in 1965 and $8.60 in 1968. "The heaviest subsidies are granted by Belgium, $14.00 per ton, and France, $10.80 per ton. . . ."

In a speech on April 14, 1972, Georges Pompidou, President of France, stated that the continuation of the coal mining industry in its present condition had been possible only "because the State, that is to say the French people contribute 400 million Francs . . . each year."

3. See *Sixth National Plan 1971-1975, du Développement Économique et Social*, Appendix B4, p. 111. "The reduction of coal extraction is rendered unavoidable by the cost which has been levied on the economy. . . ."

4. There was nothing unusual about the CGT and CFDT refusing to sign the wage agreement. It was their custom not to sign such agreements.

# Poncet Mine (B)

## The Agreement

On June 13, 1972, the Region 4 management met with the leaders of the five unions. The miners were still on strike and the Region 4 offices continued to be occupied. After long hours of negotiation, an agreement was reached which contained the following provisions:

1. Production would be concentrated at the more efficient mines with a progressive reduction of personnel,
2. Region 4 would guarantee all employees against being laid off as a result of concentration of production,
3. Employment at Poncet would be progressively reduced up to the beginning of 1976 to make possible easy placement at other mines or in other industries,
4. CdF and Region 4 would cooperate actively in bringing about industrialization of the mining region with special emphasis on Poncet,
5. Each employee would be free to choose between movement from Poncet to one of the other mines or to a job in another industry,
6. All employees would be permitted to keep their houses at Poncet, but if they chose to move would be given new modern housing at the new location, moving expenses, and an indemnity of 900 to 1,200 francs,
7. Commuting costs from Poncet would be paid to employees who transferred to other mines,
8. To the extent that it was necessary to ensure production at Poncet up to 1976, preparation work would be done,
9. Employees who returned to work on June 14 would be given 50% of the wages they would have earned if they had not been on strike from June 6 to June 19.

The miners indicated disappointment and dissatisfaction with the agreement. They had hoped that it would have contained a provision guaranteeing continued production at Poncet. However, they left the offices and the following week production at the mines, including Poncet, returned to normal.

## Aftermath

Following the June 13, 1972 agreement, management worked closely with Poncet leaders in developing a new industrial zone for which Region 4 provided 80% of the financing. Miners were moved to other mines as they

was Region 4 with its headquarters and major mine at Vercon. Region 4 was one of the largest producing areas in CdF.
indicated a desire, and others were trained for jobs in the new factories which opened in the industrial zone. Although at times management was concerned that not enough workers were moving out, by September, 1975, the workforce had dwindled to 302.

The last day of operation, September 15, 1975, was marked by a protest march in Poncet and occupation of the mine by the remaining workers. There followed several months of protests, short sympathy strikes in the other mines, resignations by the municipal councils at Poncet and nearby towns, appeals to and speeches by national political figures, including a speech at the Poncet mine by one of the national leaders of the Socialist party.

On December 1, 1975, an incident occurred which was reminiscent of the case of the five engineers four years earlier. An attempt was made to hold Minot and one of his assistants as hostages in his office. However, Minot escaped and the plan failed.

Through this period, Region 4, CdF, and the government refused to consider continuing the operation of Poncet beyond 1975. Finally, on December 15, 1975, the workers left the property at Poncet and the struggle was over. Transfers to other mines or jobs in other industries were offered to the remaining employees and nearly all of them accepted.

# Case 4
# Bouclier Copper
# Company (A)

Bouclier Copper Company's Grand Verger plant was located on the Adour River near Bayonne, France, where it had the advantages of cheap water transportation of copper ore from Africa and South America and cheap electric power from the Pyrenees hydro-stations. Grand Verger was fully integrated. It received the ore from the boats at its own unloading docks, smelted it, refined it electrolytically, and then rolled, cast, extruded, or drew it into products which were sold both in France and abroad.

There were approximately 4,000 blue-collar workers at Grand Verger when the plant was operating at capacity. These workers had a choice of four different metalworking unions which they could join. Each of these four unions was affilaited with one of the four French labor federations; CGT, CFDT, FO, or CFTC. At Grand Verger, the CGT union was the most important, followed by the CFDT union. The other two unions, although they had some members, were not significant. However, workers were not required to be union members in order to hold their jobs and as a result, fewer than one-fourth regularly paid dues to any of the unions.

Some years ago, Grand Verger had had a labor agreement that was signed by the leaders of all the unions. In recent years, however, the CGT and CFDT which cooperated closely with each other both on a local and a national level had refused to sign an agreement (Evidently they found it difficult to maintain interest and membership in the union once an agreement had been signed.) The CGT and CFDT jointly maintained a large list of demands. If some of these demands were met by the company, new demands were added. (For a list of the demands in effect on April 1, 1976, see exhibit 4a-1.) As a result, the unions were free to strike if their immediate demands were not met.

The management at Grand Verger anticipated that the spring of 1976 might be a period of labor unrest at the plant. During 1974 and 1975, production at the plant had been low. The unions had hesitated to strike during that period knowing that the company was not in need of production. However, since the beginning of 1976, demand for the company's products had been increasing rapidly and as a result, production by April 1 was close to capacity. Management was now anxious to avoid any losses in production as a result of strikes, and the union leaders, therefore, were in a much stronger bargaining position. Moreover, spring had always been the most troublesome time of the year in labor relations at Grand Verger. By that time, if work had been steady in January, February, and March, the workers would have paid off the debts they had contracted over the

**Exhibit 4a-1**
**CFDT and CGT List of Demands, April 1, 1976**

1.  A fifth crew and reduction of hours without reduction of pay where there is continuous operation.
2.  A forty hour week for others without loss of pay.
3.  Complete revision of the job classification system.
4.  An increase in the point value in the job classification system.
5.  A general increase of 360 francs to make up for salary losses.
6.  A fifth week of paid vacation.
7.  A general bonus to make up for the losses resulting from unemployment during the past two years.
8.  One hour of trade union information per month.
9.  No more cutting of the six-month bonus because of strikes or sicknesses.[a]
10. A roof over the parking lot.
11. Free safety shoes for certain workers who do not now receive them.
12. A wage increase for the change house guards.
13. Production bonus for the change house guards.
14. Increase for the drivers and their replacements.
15. An additional truck at the smelting furnaces.
16. An increase for the masons and their helpers.

[a]Each employee received a bonus of one-half a month's salary every six months. However, the bonus was decreased by 1/150 for each day of absence and 1/20 for each day of strike.

Christmas season. It was a good time, too, to spend some days working in the garden or taking a trip up into the mountains to visit relatives and friends. Finally, the company recently had thoroughly revised the job classification system with the usual result that some groups of workers were dissatisfied with the evaluation of their jobs compared with other jobs.

One of the major operations at Grand Verger was smelting which was performed in a row of twelve furnaces in a separate building called the smelting plant. The copper ore and other materials were loaded into the furnaces by overhead cranes. The furnace men, the crane operators, and auxiliary workers were grouped together into the smelting department.

The twelve furnaces were lined with special firebricks which had to be replaced after a certain number of heats. The old bricks were removed by digging them out with a special machine which had been developed for that purpose. Then masons and their helpers were lowered down into the furnace and they relined it with new firebricks. Management tried to arrange production so that only one or two furnaces were down for relining and other repairs at any one time. The employees were performed the work associated with relining, including the masons, were not part of the smelting department, but instead, were grouped into a separate refractories department. There were forty-eight manual workers in the refractories department.

Management was aware before Monday, April 5, that the refractory masons were not satisfied with the rate they were being paid under the new job classification system. For several months they had complained through the unions that the evaluation of their job was not accurate. They insisted that certain factors had been greatly underrated and claimed they were receiving about 10% less pay than they deserved. Management had carefully reexamined the evaluation and had concluded it was accurate and that the masons were being paid properly relative to other jobs in the plant. However, the union leaders had continued to support the masons' demand and had threatened action.

## Monday, April 5, 1976

On Monday morning, April 5, at 6:30 A.M. Jacques Raison, manager of Grand Verger, received a telephone call at his home from the director of smelting operations, Robert Bonjour. Bonjour informed Raison that the employees on the first shift in the refractories department were on strike. All of them had reported as usual at 6:00 A.M. and had remained in the plant but were refusing to do any work until their demands, including a 10% increase in pay for the masons, were satisfied by the company. The smelting department had not joined in the strike action, Bonjour reported, so production on the ten operating furnaces was normal. Raison told Bonjour to call François Boulanger, director of labor relations, and arrange to have him meet with them in Raison's office at the plant in half an hour.

At Raison's office, the following communication occurred:

Raison: François, the masons claim their rate is out of line. What about it?

Boulanger: We've checked it very carefully and we can't agree with them. The rate is very fair.

Bonjour: I agree with François. The rate is fair and if we increased it we'd have complaints from all the other men in the smelting plant who would then want an increase too.

Raison: There are two furnaces down now. What about the other ten?

Bonjour: Number 8 and Number 12 will probably have to be relined early next week but unless something unforeseen occurs, we can operate ten furnaces all this week.

Raison: Every day of strike by the masons will hurt us because we can use all the production we can get now, but as long as the furnace crews and the crane operators keep working we'll not be hurting too much if it doesn't last over a week.[1]

Boulanger:     I'm sure the unions will try to get the furnace men or the crane operators or the electrolytic plant to join the masons and then escalate the whole thing into a general negotiations involving Paris headquarters. That's what they'd really like to do if the men would support them.

Bonjour:       When the furnace men walked out several years ago we had to close the whole plant down very soon because electrolytic had nothing to process and send through to rolling, casting, and extruding. If the masons can prevent us from relining, the same effect would occur here but it would take a lot longer. I don't think they'd be willing to do without pay that long. Moreover, the furnace men have special skills and there was no way to replace them. That's not true with the masons. There are lots of masons in the building industry in this area and any of them could do the relining job. As a matter of fact, J & M Construction Company which is building the new addition to the casting shop has a crew of masons who could do this job very well. Also our own foremen could do it without any trouble.

Boulanger:     Are you suggesting that we subcontract the work to J & M?

Bonjour:       It's a possibility in this case. It would serve to show the masons that their job is not so skilled and that the company is not dependent on them.

Raison:        I think we should make every effort to get the masons to go back to work before we bring in outside masons. On the other hand, I agree, we can't let our masons get away with this kind of action. I suggest the two of you talk with the men and the union delegates again and if they continue to refuse to work we'll discuss the matter further at noon and decide then what action to take.

Bonjour and Boulanger went to the refractory area and had a long discussion with the union delegates and the striking employees. Boulanger indicated that the company would be willing to reconsider their demands if they returned to work. The delegates, supported by the employees, replied that the men would not return to their work until the company agreed to their demands including an increase of 10% for the masons.

At a meeting at noon, Bonjour and Boulanger reported to Raison that the refractory employees had refused to return to work. After a discussion of the various possible alternatives, it was decided to ask the J & M Construction Company to do the relining. Arrangements were made to have the J & M masons begin work on the furnaces at 8:00 A.M. the next morning if the company's employees were still on strike at that time. The second-shift refractory workers (2:00 P.M. to 10:00 P.M.) and the third-shift refractory workers (10:00 P.M. to 6:00 A.M.) joined the strike when they reported for work.

**Tuesday, April 6, 1976**

The next morning at 6:00 A.M., the first-shift refractory workers returned to the plant but continued their strike action. At the shift change, Brandon, (the CGT delegate), and Cassell, (the CFDT delegate), addressed the smelting department employees, including the furnace men and the crane operators, urging them in Brandon's words to "join the masons in this struggle to get some action on our demands." However, the first-shift smelting department employees reported to their jobs and production got underway normally on the other ten furnaces and throughout the rest of the plant.

At 8:00 A.M., the masons from J & M entered the smelting building and began to prepare the two furnaces for relining. At 10:30 A.M., the CGT delegate Brandon and ten of the strikers who had been waiting in the change room went to the furnaces where the J & M men were working. They informed the J & M men that they were strikebreaking and urged them to leave. When the J & M men continued to work, Brandon tried to block the elevator which was carrying the bricks up to where they were working. However, he was not successful and he and the strikers then left the building.

At 11:00 A.M. a meeting was held, attended by Brandon and three of the grievants representing the employees, and Bonjour and Boulanger representing the company. Boulanger stated that management was prepared to meet with the union leaders to negotiate on the refractory workers' demands on Monday, April 12, if the men would return to work today. At the change of shifts at 2:00 P.M. Brandon met with the first- and second-shift refractory workers and asked them if they wanted to accept the company's offer or continue to strike. The workers voted to continue to strike.

During the second shift (2 P.M. to 10 P.M.), CGT and CFDT delegates spoke through megaphones in various parts of the plant urging the workers in the words of one of them "to join the struggle with your comrades in the refractory department against the management and the strikebreakers and force Mr. Cabot (Bouclier's general manager) to come down from Paris and negotiate with us." As a result, the maintenance mechanics in the smelting shop and all the employees in the casting shop joined the strike. However, the furnace men and the crane operators continued to run the furnaces, and production in the smelting plant, the electrolytic plant, and elsewhere other than in the casting shop continued to be normal.

At 3:30 P.M., a group of strikers led by two union delegates blocked the entrance to the materials elevator which was being used to take firebricks up to the J & M masons. Bonjour went to the elevator and asked the delegates and the strikers to move aside but they refused to do so. Brandon said the strikers would stay in the plant "until Cabot agrees to sit down and settle with us the many serious grievances which the Grand Verger workers have placed before the company." Bonjour reported the blocking of the elevator to Raison and Boulanger. Since the J & M masons could not get firebricks, they had to stop work.

At 4:00 P.M., Raison met with Bonjour, Boulanger, and Jean Brun, the plant labor lawyer, to discuss what action should be taken with respect to the elevator blockage. Brun informed Raison that the blockage was clearly illegal and recommended that the company have a sheriff witness it and then ask a court to take action against the union leaders who were involved. Raison followed Brun's advice. The sheriff arrived at 5:00 P.M. and observed "forty strikers blocking the elevator entrance." In the sheriff's presence, Bonjour ordered the strikers to leave but they refused to do so and continued to block the elevator door. The sheriff later wrote and signed a report detailing what he had witnessed.

At 6:00 P.M., the J & M masons left the plant. On the third shift (10:00 P.M. and 6:00 A.M.), the refractory, casting, and smelting maintenance mechanics continued the strike but production elsewhere was normal.

### Wednesday, April 7, 1976

The next morning the casting employees returned to work. However, the refractory employees and the smelting maintenance mechanics remained on strike and continued to block the materials elevator. The J & M masons waited in the parking lot to see if they could return to the furnace work. One of the CGT leaders addressed the company railroad workers urging them to join the strike. The railroad workers continued to operate the trains. The union leaders were more successful with the smelting plant electric maintenance men who stopped work at 7:30 A.M. At 11:00 A.M., the J & M masons were told that it would not be possible for them to work. They left the parking lot and returned to their homes.

At about 2:00 P.M., the sheriff again entered the refractory area and this time witnessed Bonjour order by name the two union delegates and eight masons to stop blocking the elevator. They refused to move aside as did the other fifteen strikers who were blocking the way.

### Notes

1. Under French law, the employer did not have the right to lock out employees. The burden was on the employer to show first that there was no work available for the special employees before they could be laid off without pay.

# Bouclier Copper Company (B)

Late in the afternoon of April 7, 1976, Raison discussed the situation with his advisors and made two decisions: 1. the company would take legal action against the two union delegates who were leading the blockage of the elevators and 2. the foremen would be asked to replace the masons and repair the two furnaces. At the company's request, a court in Bayonne ordered the two union delegates to appear at a hearing set for Saturday, April 10.

### Thursday, April 8

At 9:30 A.M., the foremen manned the "digger" and began to remove the old bricks from one of the furnaces. A group of ten strikers and two union delegates went to the refractory area and tried to persuade the foremen not to work but they were unsuccessful. Likewise, they were not successful in preventing the foremen from getting material to the furnaces. By 11:30 A.M., the foremen were laying bricks in one of the furnaces. At 12:00 P.M., the refractory strikers left the area and had a meeting with the maintenance mechanics in the change house. Later the refractory workers and maintenance mechanics left the plant. In the meantime, at 10:30 A.M., the CGT and CFDT delegates in the extrusion mill were successful in getting the employees there to go on strike. The second- and third-shift foremen continued to work on the relining of the two furnaces, and by 1:00 A.M. the next morning the repairs had been completed. The striking masons and other refractory workers on the third shift then went home after saying "if the foremen want to do the work, we can't stop them."

### Friday, April 9

The next morning, Friday, April 9, at 6:00 A.M., the smelting maintenance mechanics, the smelting maintenance electricians, and the extrusion mill employees returned to work. Only the refractory workers remained on strike. Brandon, the CGT delegate, then requested and was granted a meeting with management.

# Bouclier Copper Company (C)

At the meeting on April 9 between the management and the unions, the following agreement was reached:

1. *Furnace Masons*
   Able to achieve a higher point evaluation after passing a special exam (could result in an eventual increase of less than 5% for some of the masons).

2. *Furnace Mason Helpers*
   A part of the group to be promoted by selection to a higher classification (an eventual increase of less than 5% for the helpers selected.)

3. *Master Molders*
   Fifty-franc increase per month (about 2% increase).

4. *Crane Operators*
   Fifty-franc increase per month (about 2% increase).

5. *Bonus Loss as a Result of Strike*
   Decreased from 1/20 loss per day of strike to 1/150 for employees who returned to work on their next shift.

When Brandon reported the above agreement, the refractory employees returned to their jobs.

After the workers returned to their jobs, management decided not to press the legal charges against the union delegates who had blocked the use of the elevator and refused to move even when ordered to do so by name in front of an officer of the court. Likewise, no disciplinary action was taken against any of the employees who engaged in the strike except that those who participated in the elevator blocking were sent the following warning letter.

> On April 6, 1976 with some other workers you blocked the entrance to the material elevator which carries refractory bricks for the repair of the furnaces, preventing thereby the normal work in the department and exposing yourself and others to serious danger.
>
> Although in the spirit of appeasement we have dropped court action against you, we are placing you on notice that such conduct constitutes an offense which, in the future, could warrant severe disciplinary action, including discharge.

On April 13, 1976, the Grand Verger labor counsel addressed the following letter to Georges Cabot, the general manager of Bouclier in Paris:

As you ordered me last Saturday, I appeared before the tribunal in Bayonne and withdrew the charges against the strikers who had blocked use of the materials elevator.

Mr. Lyon, the lawyer for CGT, emphasized to the court that the act of obstruction had ceased before we filed for a hearing and that the filing, therefore, was solely for the purpose of putting pressure on the employees to abandon the strike. He hoped by this statement to make it more difficult for us to obtain a court order in the future if we should need one.

I replied of course that our withdrawal did not imply that we recognized as legal the occupation of the work place by strikers, but that since things had returned to normal at the plant, there was no longer any cause to proceed with the hearing.

Mr. Lyon argued also that we ought to be ordered to pay some indemnities to the defendants because of the inconveniences and loss of work which appearance before the tribunal caused them. I, of course, strongly opposed such a claim.

In conclusion, I believe that I should inform you that in case of a future strike of this kind in which equipment is occupied, it would be desirable to seek a court hearing as soon as the facts are established. Otherwise, we risk the acceptance of a practice which it would be difficult to overcome.

# 3 Labor Relations in Italy

## Introduction

The population of Italy in 1978 was 57 million, the second largest in Western Europe, exceeded only by West Germany in this study. During the period 1970-1978, Italy's population increased 5.67%, which was the third highest rate of increase, surpassed only by the Netherlands and the United States. In the seventies, Italy's population surpassed Britain's, and if the trend continues, it eventually will grow larger than West Germany's to become the highest in Europe (see table A-1).*

The gross national product of Italy in 1976 was $181 billion—smaller than that of West Germany, France, Britain, or the United States but larger than that of the Netherlands or Sweden. However, the gross national product per person in Italy in 1976 was only $3,220 which was the lowest of all the countries. Moreover, the gross national product per person during the period 1970-1976 grew at only 2% per year. Only Britain and the United States had lower rates of increase (see table A-2).

Consumer prices in Italy during the period 1970-1978 rose 165%, a greater increase than in all countries except Britain (see table A-3). During the same period, unemployment averaged 3.3%, which was higher than in West Germany and Sweden but lower than in France and Britain, and considerably lower than in the United States (see table A-4).

In 1978, the average hourly compensation for production workers in manufacturing in Italy was $6.71, the lowest of all countries except Britain. During the period 1970-1978, the average hourly compensation rate increased 261% which was higher than in Britain, Sweden, and the United States but lower than in France, West Germany, and the Netherlands. In terms of local purchasing power, Italy's worker compensation during the period 1970-1978 increased 66%, the greatest increase of all the countries (see table A-5).

Output in manufacturing in Italy increased an average of 6.2% per year during the period 1960-1978 and 4.1% per year during 1970-1978. In the 1960-1978 period, this rate of increase in output was higher than in any of the other six countries (see table A-6). Productivity in Italy as measured by percentage change in output per hour in manufacturing increased 6.2% per

---

*Tables A-1 through A-13 referred to in this chapter are in the statistical appendix at the end of the book.

year during the 1960-1978 period and 4.6% per year during 1970-1978. During the 1960-1978 period, only the Netherlands had a higher rate (see table A-7).

Unit labor costs in terms of Italian currency increased 8.7% per year during 1960-1978, and 16.3% per year during the 1970-1978 period (see table A-8). In terms of U.S. dollars, the increases in unit labor costs in Italy were 7.2% per year during 1960-1978, and 10.4% per year during the 1970-1978 period; this latter increase was lower than that of all countries except the United States (see table A-9).

## The Union Movement

### Constitutional and Legislative Guarantees

Article 39 of the Italian constitution protects the rights of unions to organize and to bargain without interference from the government or the employer. The only legal obligation of a union under the constitution is that it must register as such with the Ministry of Labor. In order to register, a union would have to provide proof of internal rules and procedures guaranteeing democratic control. Once registered, the union would be recognized as a legal personality with the right to hold property and incur liability, the right to sue, and the right to negotiate legal agreements. Moreover, registration would make it possible for a union to negotiate agreements that would have the *erga omnes* effect; that is, they would apply to all employers within the industry.[1] However, all these constitutional provisions related to registration have not been implemented because the unions, fearing that such action would be too restrictive of their freedom, have steadfastly refused to register with the Ministry of Labor. As a result, unions in Italy are simply de facto associations.

Some aspects of the constitutional guarantees have been implemented in legislation. The Statute on Workers' Rights (Law 300, 1970) in Article 14 guarantees to all workers "the right to form trade unions, to be members thereof and to perform activities related thereto, within the working premises"; in Article 26 provides that workers have "the right to collect dues and to engage in publicity and recruitment activities for their union within the workplace so long as they do not interfere with the normal work activities of the company"; and in Article 28 prohibits an employer from "placing obstacles that impair or limit a union's activities or its right to strike." If a union is of the opinion that its rights under Article 28 have been violated, it may petition the district court which must "summon the parties within two days," and if a violation is found, must issue an immediately effective decree ordering the employer "to cease all illegitimate action and to remove all obstacles."

*Structure*

In Italy the labor movement is divided into three major confederations and one minor one, all of which are based on political affiliation. The confederations in order of size are:

1. *CGIL—General Confederation of Italian Labor.* The CGIL has been closely allied with the Italian Communist party. Within this confederation there is also a Socialist minority. The CGIL was affiliated with the Communist-dominated World Federation of Trade Unions (WFTU). However, in 1977 its leadership announced that it was withdrawing from that organization.

2. *CISL—Confederation of Italian Trade Unions.* The CISL has been allied with the Christian Democratic party. It was formed in 1949 when its leaders split away from the CGIL. It is affiliated with the noncomunist International Confederation of Free Trade Unions (ICFTU). In recent years, it has moved from union management cooperation to class unionism.

3. *UIL—Union of Italian Labor.* The UIL has been allied with the Social Democratic and Republican parties although it has never been as politically oriented as the CGIL and CISL. It has strongly rejected communism and has supported collective bargaining on all matters. It is also affiliated with the ICFTU.

4. *CISNAL—National Confederation of Italian Labor.* The CISNAL is allied with neofascist groups. It has a very limited membership but in recent years has shown some strength among railroad and other public service employees.

There are no craft unions and no general unions in Italy. Instead, each of the major confederations is composed of a group of industrial unions, usually referred to as category unions. The area covered by each category union is usually quite broad. Thus, the metal-mechanical category union, FLM, which is the largest union in Italy, covers steel, automobile, shipbuilding, electrical equipment, and other metal-fabricating industries. Within each plant, the employees are usually represented by three category unions, one affiliated with the CGIL, one with the CISL, and one with the UIL.

The Italian labor movement is highly centralized. Unlike the American Federation of Labor and Congress of Industrial Organizations (AFL-CIO) in the United States or the TUC in Britain which are weak federations where the affiliated unions retain much power, the confederations in Italy have the power. The activities of the industry unions are guided strictly by the policies established by the confederations. The confederations invariably play an active role not only in lobbying for legislation and dealing with the national employers' association, but also, together with the category unions, in bargaining with industry employers' associations.

In the last decade, the Italian labor movement has been moving toward unification but is still a long way from fully achieving it. The decisions of the conventions of the three major confederations in 1969-1970 to sever their formal links with the political parties opened the road to independent and united action. The confederations and their unions almost always succeed in developing joint demands and tactics before negotiating with management, and if negotiations are not successful, in jointly supporting strike action. In 1972 the confederations did agree to merge, but this was later revoked because of strong opposition within the CISL and UIL. However, a federation of confederations has been established with a common executive board and a joint secretariat. Strong pressure for one unified confederation is now coming from the metal-mechanical workers who in 1975 merged their three separate organizations (FIOM, FIM, and UILM) into one union, the FLM, which is the largest and strongest in Italy. The CGIL strongly favors unification and its move to divorce itself from the WFTU will probably make a merger easier.

In addition to the unions affiliated with the confederations, there are several autonomous unions, for example, unions for bank employees, doctors, lawyers, and high-school teachers. One of the important autonomous organizations is the National Federation of Managers of Industrial Enterprises (FNDAI), which has never engaged in a strike and generally conducts itself more like an association than a union. The Italian constitution gives managers and executives the right to belong to and be represented by an organization, and many of them do belong to the FNDAI. One plant manager informed us that everyone in his plant except himself was represented by a union, including his employee relations director. (Actually, the manager could have been a member of the FNDAI.) The FNDAI has negotiated a national multi-industry agreement with the central employers' association, the Italian Confederation of Industrial Employers (Confindustria), which provides minimum standards for managers and executives regarding vacations, transfers, social insurance, and severance pay.[2]

### The Closed Shop and Check-off

Article 39 of the constitution guarantees to individuals the right to join or not to join a union. Thus, the closed shop is illegal in Italy. (The CISL and UIL have strongly opposed the closed shop, because under an exclusive bargaining and closed-shop arrangement their membership would be largely eliminated by the CGIL.) Instead, as indicated previously, there is plural unionism in most plants—some employees are represented by a CGIL union, others by a CISL or UIL union, and frequently a majority are members of no union.

As indicated earlier, workers have the right under Article 26 of Law 300 to collect dues for their unions within the plant. Article 26 also provides that a union may bargain a check-off as part of a labor agreement. It provides further that, even where there is no agreement between the union and the company on the issue, an employer must check off union dues if requested to do so by an employee. Since the passage of the 1970 act, the number of employees covered by the check-off has grown but is still a small percentage of all Italian workers.

### Membership

Total union membership in Italy has been estimated at 4.3 million or 34% of the working population (see table A-11). However, actual dues-paying members may be a lot fewer. In one major industrial plant that has a dues check-off, we found that only 14% of the employees has agreed to have the dues deducted from their pay. Italian management reports that such a low figure is not unusual, although in some industries it is much higher.

### Financial Status

The dues of Italian unions are very low, but even so, a great majority of workers do not pay them. As a result, despite some growth of the check-off since the passage of the 1970 law, Italian unions remain financially weak. None of the confederations or their category unions has a strike fund. It has been claimed that in the past, the major unions received direct financial aid from the political parties that they supported.

### Unions and Politics

The most important political organization in Italy is the Christian Democratic party followed by the Communist party. Together these two parties now receive 70 to 80% of the votes. However, since World War II no party has been able to secure a majority, with the result that all the governments have been coalitions. In February, 1979, a Christian Democratic government that had the support of the Communists fell when that support was removed. Unstable coalitions in which the Communists will play an important role appear to be inevitable in the near future. In addition to their role in the national government, the Communists hold many important political positions. The president of the senate is a Communist, as are many of the local judges, and the mayors of several leading cities, including Rome.

The CGIL, which contains more than one-half of the union members in Italy, is dominated by Communists. Its general secretary, Luciano Lama, is an active member of the Communist party and prior to 1969, served also as a Communist deputy in parliament.

During the fifties and sixties, the goals and strategies of the unions followed closely those of the political parties to which they were attached and from which they received financial support. In the late sixties, strong pressure developed among the leaders of the key national unions to break the ties with the political parties. As a result, all three of the major confederations at their 1969-1970 conventions affirmed their independence from political parties and insisted that their officers not be members of parliament or communal councils or on the executive bodies of the political parties. Since that time, the unions have been less tied to the goals and strategies of competing parties and instead, have developed joint economic and political goals. However, as indicated earlier, attempts to form a unified labor movement have not been successful.

## Employers' Associations

An Italian employer is free to bargain directly with the labor unions or he may decide to have an employers' association perform that function for him. The great majority of the employers have chosen the latter method. There are over one hundred national industrial employers' associations and over one hundred regional employers' associations that are affiliated with Confindustria. In addition, the commercial employers' groups and the agricultural employers' groups are each affiliated with separate confederations—Conforcommercio and Confagricoltura.

Although Confindustria once represented both private and government-owned industries, it now represents only the former. Some years ago, it was decided that it was not proper for the government-owned industries to be governed by rules established by Confindustria. As a result, the government-owned companies established a separate association called Intersind; and the National Hydrocarbon Corporation (ENI), which operates the government-owned petrochemical industry, established its own association, the ASAP. Each of these government-owned employers' associations bargains separately with the unions and at times has set patterns that were later followed by the private employers' associations affiliated with Confindustria.

Prior to 1970, Confindustria was dominated by the owners of small and medium-sized companies that were strongly opposed to unions and especially to union activity at the plant level. However, in 1970 the confederation was reorganized in a manner that gave more power and influence to the

larger, more progressive companies. A new general manager was appointed
and new policies were adopted. Then, in 1974, Giovanni Agnelli of the Fiat
Company was elected president and took the lead in trying to establish a
better relationship with the unions. Confindustria now does not oppose
decentralized bargaining but instead argues for "articulated bargaining;"
that is, that each level of bargaining should have clearly defined jurisdiction
over certain matters and that bargaining over the same matter should not
take place at different levels. Guido Carli, who was formerly governor of
the Bank of Italy, is now president of Confindustria.

## Collective Bargaining

### Levels of Bargaining

There are currently five levels of bargaining in Italy:

1. *Bargaining at the Government Level.* In recent years, direct bargaining between the government and the Union confederations on matters of
social reform, such as housing, health, and transportation, has become very
significant. The government has described the dealings with the unions as
"consultations" but in reality they have been negotiations. To a considerable extent, the trade unions have taken over the role of the political
parties in what has become known as the reform strategy. Often these
negotiations in turn have affected the terms of the agreements with the industry employers' associations, such as when the unions supported Confindustria's efforts to make the government take over a part of the social
security costs, thus relieving the employers of this direct burden.

2. *Bargaining with Confindustria.* From time to time, the union confederations and Confindustria, Intersind, or the ASAP bargain on major
nationwide issues. In 1953, it was at this level, rather than by legislation or
industry agreements, that the internal commissions (employee works councils with advisory powers only) were established. Similar agreements have
been reached on several other issues including geographical wage differentials (eliminated in 1969), equal pay for women, cost of living adjustments
(1951 and 1975), and procedures regarding dismissals and the reduction of
the work force.

3. *Bargaining at the Industry Level.* The most important level of
bargaining in Italy has been and continues to be between the national
category unions and the industry employers' associations. During the fifties
collective bargaining was almost entirely at this level and was limited
generally to minimum wages and a few basic working conditions. In recent
years, the scope of industry bargaining has been greatly expanded to include
such matters as job classifications, incentives, bonuses, holidays, vacations,

pensions, seniority increases, marriage leave, meal subsidies, transportation, working conditions, health and safety, promotions, temporary assignments, transfers, termination notice, severance pay, subcontracting, and checkoff. For example, the 1975 agreement between the private petroleum companies and their national unions included seventy-five printed pages covering many of the above matters plus a fifty-nine page appendix on job classifications.

4. *Bargaining at the Company Level.* The most important innovation in Italian labor relations during the sixties and seventies has been the development of company and plant bargaining. During the fifties there was no bargaining at the level of the enterprise. Rather, it was left to the individual employer to apply or improve upon the minima established by industry bargaining. The company and the plant were viewed as personal inviolable property in which management rights were supreme, and the employers both directly and through Confindustria strongly opposed the attempts of the unions to gain a foothold at the company and plant levels. The internal commissions that were established in the plants as a result of an agreement between Confindustria and the union confederations in 1953 were advisory only and possessed no right to bargain on any matter.

In 1962 however, managers of the government-owned sectors of Italian industry, reached an agreement with the unions called the Protocol of Intentions. This agreement stated that industry contracts could be supplemented by local bargaining on certain specified matters—piece rates, job classifications, and output bonuses. (Even under this agreement, no local bargaining structure was recognized, but instead, the bargaining on local matters was carried out with the local management by the provincial trade union leaders.) The move by the IRI and ENI became a pattern which was followed later in the sixties by the private industry sector. By 1970, it was estimated that there were 4,400 local labor contracts in effect. This system was referred to as articulated bargaining because there was an attempt made to set precise boundaries on the jurisdiction of each level of bargaining.

The Statute on Workers' Rights (1970) provides in Article 19 for the formation in each enterprise with over fifteen employees "of trade unions within the company" and states that "trade union representation may be formed . . . by the workers of each operational unit." (In reality, the law was simply stating what had already occurred in many companies.) Under the law, employees in a particular work unit, for example, a machine shop, elect from their own members a delegate or a number of delegates depending on the size of the work unit. (In one plant with seven hundred employees, thirty-three such delegates are elected.) In turn, the delegates choose several of their members to make up a factory council, called the Consiglio di Fabbrica (CDF). The size of the CDF varies with the number of employees in the plant as follows: 3 for up to 100 employees, 6 for 101 to

250 employees, 9 for 251 to 600 employees, 12 for more than 600 employees. Under the law, members of the CDF are protected from discriminatory discharge or layoff.

In a company with more than one plant, the factory councils appoint delegates to a company council. (In some conglomerate companies that are involved in production in several industry divisions, the factory councils may appoint delegates to an industrial division council.) The factory councils and the company councils have the right not only to advise and consult with management at their respective level, but also to bargain on certain specific matters. For example, the 1972 labor agreement between the petroleum industry and the petroleum workers unions stated that:

> the regulations governing the following shall be negotiated at the company level, within the limits prescribed by the respective articles of this Contract:
>
> | Article  4 | Employee Classification |
> | --- | --- |
> | Article  6 | Training |
> | Article  7 | Student Worker |
> | Article 23 | Easter Bonus |
> | Article 26 | Production Yield Bonus |
> | Article 29 | Special Agreement Allowance |
> | Article 32 | Transportation Allowance |
> | Article 33 | Disposability Allowance |
> | Article 34 | Allowance for Oil Exploration Personnel |
> | Article 37 | Travel Allowance |
> | Article 63 | Company Benefit Plans |

5. *Bargaining at the Plant Level.* As indicated earlier, where the company has more than one plant, the factory councils elect delegates to a company council which then bargains at the company level. However, in such cases the factory council still has the right to bargain at the local plant level on matters (such as working conditions) that affect the workers in that particular plant. In a company that has only one plant, the factory council also takes over all the bargaining functions described earlier that are performed by a company council in a multi-plant company.

The collective bargaining process in Italy is very unsettled, and major changes probably will continue to take place. Articulated bargaining has not been entirely successful. The lines of jurisdiction between the various levels is not clear, and there is often an attempt to bargain the same item at more than one level. As one authority has stated:

> The present bargaining pattern can thus be described as an uncoordinated, multi-tiered system ranging from what are virtually political negotiations with the Government at the top to informal bargaining by workers' delegates at the bottom.[3]

*Labor Agreements*

Apart from the fact that no-strike clauses are probably unenforceable, it is generally accepted that collective bargaining agreements are legally enforceable in Italy on the employers' associations, employers, and unions that are party to them.[4] On the other hand, some Italian legal authorities point out that as a result of the unenforceability of any no-strike clause and the fact that under the law a contract does not prevent unions from bringing forth new claims at any time, the contracts really are open-ended and there is "continuous bargaining."[5] This has led some Italian legal authorities to conclude that the Italian labor agreement is no longer a contract.

*Mediation*

There is no compulsory mediation or arbitration in Italy and there is no official mediation service. However, the Ministry of Labor and Social Security provides mediation services both locally and nationally. Either party may request mediation help. When the government mediator proposes a settlement, it is usually accepted, since refusal to accept may have unwelcome political consequences. The system is subject to much political influence. The Minister of Labor's sympathy for the union positions has been so marked that employers have charged him with dictating terms and pressuring Intersind to reach agreements that then set patterns for the private sector.

*Strikes*

Article 40 of the 1948 Italian constitution specifically protects the right to strike. The constitutional guarantees in this respect are so sweeping that it is very doubtful that a no-strike clause in a labor agreement is legally enforceable. As a result, many contracts contain no such clauses.

On the other hand, the constitution is silent with respect to a lockout by an employer, and Italian authorities differ as to whether such action is legal or illegal.[6] In any event, it is a weapon that Italian employers have been reluctant to use. Although employers do have a legal right to operate during a strike, picketing is likely to be so effective and often so violent that in practice, they usually are prevented from operating.

Workers on strike are not eligible for unemployment benefits, and Italian unions do not pay strike benefits. Likewise, Italian employers' associations do not maintain strike funds and thus do not give financial assistance to employers.

There are no recognition strikes in Italy because any union that represents employees has the right under the law to be recognized and to bargain. Likewise, there are no jurisdictional strikes because there are no craft unions and no right of a particular union to claim particular work. There are, however, many short (usually one-day) political strikes which until recently were thought to be illegal but, nevertheless, were a fact of industrial life in Italy. A recent decision of the constitutional court provides that such strikes are not illegal, but rather, are protected by the constitution.

Not only political but all types of strikes in Italy tend to be of very short duration. Nevertheless, during the ten-year period 1967-1976, Italian employees lost an average of one and one-half days of work per year as a result of strikes, which represented about 0.64% of the total working time. This was by far the highest of any of the seven countries in this study, being over forty times as high as in West Germany and even two and one-half times as high as in the United States (see table A-12). It is easy, however, to overemphasize strike losses. During the ten-year period, considerably less than 1% of Italian production was lost because of strikes, compared with 8% or more resulting from sickness absenteeism (compare tables A-12 and A-13).

## Grievance Procedure

Under the 1953 agreement between Confindustria and the union confederations, the internal commissions were given the primary role in handling grievances and complaints. The customary steps in the grievance procedure were: 1. the internal commission and the plant manager, 2. the union and the industry employers' association, 3. the local court. In recent years, the internal commissions have been replaced by the factory councils. There are no special labor courts in Italy; instead, the regular local tribunals or magistrates are used. Very few companies and unions have agreed to an arbitration step in the procedure. However, the employee always has the right to appeal to the court, either before or after exhausting the other steps in the procedure.

## Cost-of-Living Adjustments

In 1951, Confindustria and the union confederations reached an agreement to adjust wages every three months based on changes in the cost of living. In 1975, this agreement was changed so as to nationally unify the wage escalation clause over a period of two years. Under the new agreement, the cost-of-living increases eventually will be given as a fixed amount of lire to each employee rather than as a percentage of wage rates. The result will be that the lire differentials will be maintained while the real wage differentials will be narrowed. However, automatic cost-of-living adjustments have been frozen for high-income employees. An employee with a salary of from 6 million to 8 million lire per year receives half of any adjustment in cash and half in five-year government bonds which pay 14% interest. An employee with a salary of 8 million lire or more receives 100% of any adjustment in government bonds. The cost-of-living agreement, although enabling low- and middle-income Italian workers to temporarily catch up with past infla- tion, has at the same time been an important factor in causing more infla- tion.

*Extra-month Bonuses*

Under a 1946 agreement between Confindustria and the union confedera- tions, hourly-paid Italian workers receive a Christmas bonus of two hun- dred hours of pay and salaried workers receive another month's check. In addition to this legally required thirteenth-month bonus, a second or fourteenth-month bonus is now paid in nearly all of the quasi-government agencies and in commerce and the service industries, usually at Easter time. There is a tendency for this Easter bonus to spread to other sectors of the economy. The national labor contracts covering the employees of banks and insurance companies actually provide for three months of bonus in ad- dition to the Christmas bonus, for a total of sixteen months of pay.[7]

## Legislated Employee Protection and Benefits

*Hiring*

The law in Italy requires that hiring of unemployed workers be accom- plished through the government employment offices in each locality. Private employment agencies are prohibited, and employers are subject to prosecution for failure to use the public placement agencies. Companies report that most hiring of unskilled blue-collar workers and low-level white- collar workers is done through these government agencies, although a com- pany may employ directly a worker who is not unemployed, that is, has a job with another firm. The company informs the agency of its needs and the agency chooses the workers and sends them to the company. The company must keep these workers for at least the probationary period, unless it has a very good reason not to do so. However, companies report that, in practice, they are able to directly hire skilled blue-collar workers and higher-level white-collar employees, such as engineers and accountants. The law requires also that in each company some employees must be from the ranks of the handicapped. These employees also are supplied to the companies by the government employment agencies.

In the summer of 1978, a court in Milan found that Gaetano Cortes, president of Alfa Romeo, one of Italy's largest automobile companies, was guilty of violating Article 8 of the workers' statute because the company had employed private detectives to check on the political and trade union activities of job applicants. The court found that the company's action was illegal also because it conflicted with the legally established function of the state employment service. Cortes was sentenced to a prison sentence of one month and ten days which was held in abeyance pending appeal.

### Unfair Dismissals

In 1965, Confindustria and the union confederations reached an agreement on a special grievance procedure to be followed in case an employee was dismissed. This procedure was later embodied in Act 604 (1966). It provides that:

1.  an employee may be dismissed only for justified reasons and must be given written notice for five days before he is dismissed,
2.  the onus of proof is on the employer,
3.  the employee may demand a meeting of the union and the employers' organization,
4.  the employee may demand a hearing before a board of arbitration which must render a decision in fifteen days,
5.  the employee may appeal to the courts, either instead of, or in addition to the arbitration board.

Under this act, the arbitration board or the courts could recommend rehiring and could order damages up to fourteen months' pay if the employee was not rehired, but the company could not be forced to rehire the dismissed employee. This was changed in Law 300 (1970). Under the new law, an employee who has been improperly dismissed must be reinstated and "shall have the right to compensation for damages suffered . . . which shall be not less than five months' pay."

Companies report that under the provisions of the law it is almost impossible to discharge an employee. Such cases always go to the court where the burden of proof is on management, and the magistrates are generally very pro-labor. Only dishonesty and serious misdemeanors are recognized as "just cause."

*Temporary Layoffs and Short-time Work*

Under the 1975 labor law, an employer must inform and consult with the trade union representative in the company regarding any layoff or short-time work that is anticipated. A worker who is laid off or placed on a short-work schedule is eligible for 80% of his normal pay up to a minimum of forty hours per week for a period of six months. The payments are made from the central wage guarantee fund (CIG) which is financed by an employers' contribution of 1% of payroll, except in the building trade where the contribution is 3%. In some cases the CIG payments, coupled with income from one or more unreported jobs, enable workers to earn more than when they were employed full time.[8]

*Redundancies*

It is very difficult to terminate employees in Italy. In terminating 20% of the work force or five hundred employees, the employer must notify the union which can delay the action for twenty-five days if it is the result of economic conditions, or forty days if it is the result of technological change. Permanently dismissed employees as well as those temporarily laid off are eligible for 80% of their pay for a period of six months, payable by the CIG. Despite these payment provisions, companies have found that in practice it is extremely difficult to terminate any sizeable group of employees because the plant is immediately occupied and work is impossible until a solution satisfactory to the employees is worked out. Some companies have been able to buy themselves out of such difficulties by giving "golden handshakes" to departing employees.

*Subcontracting*

One of the ways in which Italian companies have tried to achieve a degree of flexibility under the conditions that make it very difficult to layoff employees is by subcontracting. It is reported that one company, by making extensive use of subcontracting, has built fifteen turnkey plants with a labor force of only fifty employees and that another company with 1,400 employees at times has had an equal number in its subcontracting force.[9]

Because of the use of subcontracting to avoid hiring of regular employees and also because of certain abuses of the practice, Italian unions have moved to repress it. As a result of union pressure, Law 1369 was passed in 1960 which provides among other things that it is forbidden to subcontract: 1. mere working services, or 2. piecework by workers taken on and paid by intermediaries, or 3. work in which the subcontractor uses equipment or machinery supplied by the employer. Moreover, employees of the subcontractor must receive pay and social benefits and other conditions not inferior to those paid to the regular employees of the company.

Many companies in recent years have discovered, however, that subcontracting does not relieve them of the obligation to provide permanent employment, because an attempt to decrease or to discontinue the work of the subcontractors also results in an occupation of the plant. In one case, the subcontractors' employees occupied a plant for eighteen days. Attempts by the management to get a court order to have them removed was not successful. The company finally worked out an arrangement under which it agreed to continue to use the services of the contractors, and the contractors in turn guaranteed employment to their workers. In another instance, a company's attempt to transfer to another bus company a contract to provide transportation for its employees to and from its plant was met by the employees of the original bus company blocking the entrance to the plant with their vehicles. Appeals to the police to open the road were not successful, and the issue was finally settled only when permanent jobs were offered to the original bus drivers.

## Equal Pay and Equal Opportunities

The Italian constitution requires equal pay for men and women for the same or similar work. On December 18, 1977, a new Anti-Discrimination Act became effective. In addition to requiring equal pay for equal work, it prohibits discrimination because of sex, marital status, or pregnancy with respect to hiring, training, promotion, and career development. It provides, moreover, that promotion opportunities shall not be prejudiced by maternity leaves and that women may opt to retire at age sixty instead of at age fifty-five. (The statutory retirement age had been fifty-five for women and sixty for men.) An employee or a union representative may file a claim with a court that the provisions of the law have been violated. The judge may order the employer to discontinue the discrimination. Failure to comply with the order can result in a fine of 80,000 lire or three months in jail. Failure to comply with certain sections of the act, including the equal pay provisions, may result in fines up to one million lire. However, since the act establishes no commission to interpret and seek enforcement of its provisions, it is not clear how effective it will be.

## Maternity Protection and Pay

The Act for the Protection of Working Mothers (1971) provides that:

1. a woman may not be dismissed because of pregnancy,
2. a woman is entitled to an eight-week leave prior to childbirth and a twelve-week leave following childbirth at 80% of pay,

3. a mother is entitled to up to six months leave during the first year following birth to care for the infant at 30% of pay,
4. during all of the above periods the worker retains her job rights.

Although these benefits are paid through the government sickness insurance agency, INAM, a large percentage of the cost is paid by the employer. A recent study by the University of Milan indicates that the heavy costs have deterred employers from hiring women.

*Vacations and Holidays*

The law requires that workers be granted a minimum of three weeks of vacation with pay. The labor agreements then provide additional paid vacation depending on years of service. The petroleum industry contract has the following scale:

| | |
|---|---|
| 1 to 2 years of service | 15 days |
| 3 to 10 years of service | 20 days |
| 11 to 18 years of service | 23 days |
| over 18 years of service | 27 days |

In addition, until 1977, Italian workers were paid for seventeen public holidays. However, in January, 1977, the union confederations and Confindustria reached an agreement whereby the number of holidays was decreased from seventeen to ten.

## Collective Bargaining by Managers (Dirigenti)

Much of the legislation just discussed does not apply to employees in managerial positions. Article 2095 of the 1942 civil code, although not defining managers precisely, indicates that they are similar to employers and, therefore, not part of the employee group covered by the various labor or employment laws. In order to protect their interests, Italian managerial employees are organized into unions that are affiliated with the National Confederation for Managers (CIDA) which has negotiated four national agreements (for private industry, commerce, agriculture, and public corporations) as well as supplementary agreements with many major companies. Some 95,000 managerial employees are protected by these various agreements which often provide benefits far superior to those given to other workers. For example, under the CIDA private industry agreement, a *dirigenti*, in case of dismissal, must be given a notice period of seven months for two years of service and one-half month for each additional year of service. If the *dirigenti* believes the dismissal to be unjustified, he has the right to appeal to an arbitration board which, although it does not have the right to reinstate, can order compensation. The length-of-service bonus provision is also much more generous under the CIDA agreement, providing for an annual bonus of one month's pay for each year of service for the first eight years and a one-half month bonus for each additional year of service.[10]

## Absenteeism

Absenteeism is a major problem in Italian industry. *Business Europe* reported recently that, in a survey of twenty multinational companies with plants in Italy, absenteeism was listed as one of the two most difficult problems of doing business in that country. (Restrictions on hiring and firing was the other problem.) A study of sickness absenteeism by the Swedish employers' association found that in 1973, sickness absenteeism was 8% which was the highest of any country in the survey except Sweden (see table A-13). Confindustria has reported that in 1977, the Italian industrial workers were absent an average of 27 days and that more than half of this amount was from certified sick leave. Fiat has reported that an average of 20,000 or 11% of its 183,000 workers are absent from work each day. Although the percentage of time lost as a result of strikes during the 1967-1976 period was much higher in Italy than in any of the other countries in this study, the loss resulting from absenteeism was ten or twelve times the loss resulting from strikes (compare tables A-12 and A-13).

Under Italian sick pay legislation, an ill worker is entitled to 50% of earnings for the first twenty-one days and 66.6% of earnings thereafter for a maximum of six months per year. In addition, under a standard provision in all labor agreements, employers pay full wages for the first three days of absences resulting from sickness. Finally, in many industries the labor agreement provides for much more liberal sick pay benefits. For example, the agreement in the petroleum industry provides full pay for six months for employees with five years of seniority and full pay for one year for employees with over fifteen years of seniority. As a result, many Italian workers suffer no loss of pay when they report off because of sickness.

A considerable part of the absence that is paid for as sickness is believed to be simply the result of workers taking advantage of a system in which the difference between sick pay and pay for work provides no incentive to work and in which the controls are very lax. Under Article 5 of Law 300 (workers' charter), an employer is not permitted to make medical checks on employees to determine their eligibility for sick pay. Such checks may be made only by doctors employed by the state agency, INAM. However, the agency has been severely understaffed and its doctors have been reluctant to deny sick pay to workers.

The top union leaders agree with management that absenteeism is out of control in Italian industry and results in serious losses to the economy. In the January, 1977 labor negotiations, the unions agreed to a series of provisions that had as their purpose the decreasing of the absentee rate. Among other things, they called for major improvements in INAM, the agency that administers the sick pay benefits. To date, however, the agreement appears to have had little or no effect on the absentee rate. It is doubtful that the changes will prove effective so long as many workers are eligible for 100% of pay for absences because of sickness.

## Worker Participation

Article 46 of the Italian constitution provides for worker participation. It states:

> In order to improve the economic and social conditions of employees, and in harmony with production requirements, the Republic recognizes the right of employees to participate in the management of undertakings, in accordance with the procedure and to the extent laid down by law.

However, following its ratification in 1947, thi. provision of the constitution remained unimplemented by legislation for many years.

### Works Councils

When a form of worker participation was first developed it was by way of collective bargaining. In 1953, Confindustria and the union confederations agreed to the establishment of internal commissions at the plant level. In 1966, the 1953 agreement was renewed and expanded. The 1966 agreement called for commissions of from three to twenty-one members depending on the size of the work force. The commissioners were employees elected by their fellow workers from slates of candidates proposed by the unions, although non-union employees could also be candidates. The commissions were purely advisory and consultative. They had no powers of veto or codetermination.

The functions of internal commissions included: making sure that the company observed the provisions of the national agreement and social legislation, including health and safety rules; participating in the settlement of grievances; advising and consulting on plant rules, vacation periods, work schedules, wage systems, and similar matters; operating the suggestion system; and playing a role in the administration of insurance welfare, and culture and recreation programs. However, under the 1966 agreement, the commissions were specifically excluded from matters that were subject to collective bargaining by the unions and the employers' association.

Although the 1966 agreement between Confindustria and the union confederations establishing the internal commissions is still in effect, the commissions have practically disappeared. After passage of the Statute on Workers' Rights in 1970, they were replaced by factory councils (CDFs). (CDFs were described earlier under the sections dealing with company and plant bargaining.) In addition to their collective bargaining function, the CDFs have taken over the consultative and advisory functions previously performed by the internal commissions.

### Employee Representation on Company Boards

In Italy, a limited liability company (Societa per Azioni) has a single board structure which consists of a council of administrators (Consiglio d'amministrazione) whose members are elected by the shareholders. Under the law, the council has extensive authority with few restrictions on its power to manage the company. In practice, however, in most large and medium-sized companies the council delegates much of its authority to an executive committee or an administrator. There is also a shareholders' committee which has a broad auditing function but practically no decision-making authority except to refer matters to the general meeting.[11]

Italian workers and their unions are not represented on the councils of administrators and are not likely to be so represented in the near future. Italian unions, like American unions, have been and continue to be opposed to such representation. The unions prefer a conflictual or dialectic role to one of participation in the making of major corporate decisions. Membership of employees or union officials on the councils of administrators would, in their opinion, result in a conflict of interest. They are satisfied that the workers' best interest is served through collective bargaining and socialization rather than by cooperative participation with private management. This attitude of the Italian unions runs counter to the position of the Commission of the European Communities which in its Green Paper in 1975 stated that the two-tier board system with employee participation in the supervisory board is a major objective of the European Economic Community (EEC).[12]

### Participation through Collective Bargaining

Although opposing representation on company boards, Italian unions are insisting on more control over company strategic decisions through the expansion of the scope of collective bargaining. For example, in 1974 they negotiated with several major private companies, including Fiat, Alpha Romeo, and Montedison, "development agreements" whereby managements consented to make major investments in the south and other depressed areas of the country. In 1976, the unions increased the number of companies and industries covered by such agreements.[13] The FLM, the largest union in Italy, has moved forward rapidly in this area by negotiating agreements with the major firms in the industry. These agreements require that the companies inform its employee union representatives of plans and consult with them before taking action on such matters as product innovation, technological changes, and subcontracting.[14]

## Notes

1. Mario Galloti, *Labor Relations in Italy* (Rome: American Embassy, 1975), p. 3.

2. Seyfarth, Shaw, Fairweather, and Geraldson, *Labor Relations and the Law in Italy and the United States* (Ann Arbor: University of Michigan, 1970), p. 305.

3. Gino Guigni, "Recent Trends in Collective Bargaining in Italy," *Collective Bargaining in Industrialized Market Economies* (Geneva: International Labor Office, 1973), p. 294.

4. Seyfarth et al., *Labor and the Law*, p. 70.

5. Pietro Merli Brandini, "Italy: Creating a New Industrial Relations System from the Bottom," in *Worker Militancy and Its Consequences 1965-1973*, ed. Solomon Barkin (New York: Praeger Publishers, 1975), p. 103.

6. Seyfarth, et al., *Labor and the Law*, p. 89.

7. Galloti, Labor Relations in Italy, p. 17.

8. "Italy: Compensation for Lay-offs and Short-time Working," *European Industrial Relations Review*, December, 1977, No. 48, pp. 22-24.

9. "Companies in Italy Assess the Current Labor Climate," *Business Europe*, March 18, 1977, p. 84.

10. "Managerial Rights, Italian Style," *European Industrial Relations Review*, No. 53, May, 1978, pp. 25-26.

11. European Communities Commission, *Employee Participation and Company Structure in the European Community* (Luxembourg, 1975), pp. 82-85.

12. Ibid., p. 78.

13. "Italy: Developments in Industrial Democracy," *European Industrial Relations Review*, March, 1978, No. 51, pp. 22-23.

14. "Italy: Industrial Democracy: A Union Assessment," *European Industrial Relations Review*, June, 1978, No. 54, pp. 17-18.

# Case 5
# Barichim

Barichim (Bari Petrochemical Co., Inc.) was organized in Italy in the middle thirties. Prior to World War II, the company was relatively small and produced a limited number of petrochemical products. During the war, the company's plant was almost completely destroyed. In the postwar period, it constructed a new and much larger plant near Bari on the east coast of Italy and moved into production of a much larger line of petrochemicals. Although its sole plant was at Bari, headquarters of the company was in Rome.

During the fifties and sixties, the company continued to expand and modernize its facilities. By December, 1977, it had 850 regular company employees, only 108 of whom were in maintenance, and over 420 contract employees all of whom were in maintenance of one type or another.

## Unions at Barichim

There were in Italy three major confederations of unions: CGIL, CSIL, and UIL. Originally, these three confederations were closely tied to political parties and ideologies: CGIL to the Communists, CSIL to the Christian Democrats and UIL to a lesser extent to the Social Democrats and the Republicans. Since the late sixties, however, the unions had moved to become more independent of the parties and had made some movement toward developing a common labor movement. Each confederation was composed of a group of industrial or category unions. For example, in the chemical industry, there was a union affiliated with the CGIL, one affiliated with the CSIL, and one affiliated with the UIL.

The closed shop was illegal in Italy and there was no provision for exclusive representation by one union within a plant. As a result, workers at Barichim were free to join the union of their choice or no union at all. The CGIL union represented the largest group of the company's unionized workers, but the CSIL and UIL affiliates also had members. In each department of the plant, there were members of each of the three chemical workers' unions. The company recognized and bargained with representatives of each of the three unions.

Each of the three unions had requested the company to permit a check-off of union dues, a request that the law required the company to respect. However, in the plant less than 15% of the employees had agreed to have their union dues checked off.

**Plant-Level Employee Representation**

In 1953, Confindustria, the organization that represents all the industrial employers' associations in Italy, and the three union confederations agreed that internal commissions made up of employees elected by employees should be established in each plant. The 1953 agreement was later modified by a 1966 agreement which is still in effect between Confindustria and the union confederations. Under the agreement, the company established an internal commission at the plant which was operative for many years. The commission's function was purely advisory. It had no power to bargain or to codetermine. However, it did serve as a communication device between the personnel department and the employees.

In 1970, the statute on workers' rights (Law 300) provided for trade union representation at the plant level. Following passage of this law, the chemical workers' union appointed a three-man (one from each union) committee to represent the employees in the plant. The committee that was called the RSA (*rappresentanze sindicali azienda*) replaced the internal commission as the representative body for the employees.

More recently under the 1976 industry agreement, the chemical industry employers' association and the national unions had agreed to the establishment of factory councils (CDFs) in the plants. At Barichim the CDF had replaced the RSA. Under this arrangement, each group of workers elect one or more delegates who form a plant committee. There were thirty-eight such delegates in the Barichim plant. These thirty-eight delegates then chose a council of twelve employees (the CDF) which met directly with the plant manager. Unlike the internal commission which had only the power to advise, the CDF had the power to negotiate in certain specific areas.

**Collective Bargaining**

Collective bargaining in the chemical industry was highly centralized. The major companies that employed 500,000 workers were represented by an employers' association which bargained an industry-wide contract with the representatives of the three chemical workers union every three years. The latest national agreement was signed in July, 1976.

Until the sixties, the national agreements were limited to wage rates and a few major working conditions. However, during the sixties and seventies the scope of the bargaining was greatly expanded. The 1976 agreement consisted of eighty-four printed pages plus a forty-nine-page appendix on job classifications.

The most significant change in labor relations at the plant in recent years has been the growth of local bargaining. Whereas prior to 1960 the manager's word was law, now his actions were subject to challenge by the CDF. The CDF had not only the power to advise, but also the power to bargain. The national labor agreement provided that:

> the following shall be negotiated at the company level, within the limits prescribed by the respective articles of this Contract:

| | |
|---|---|
| Article  4 | Employee Classifications |
| Article  6 | Training |
| Article  7 | Student Worker |
| Article 23 | Easter Bonus |
| Article 26 | Production Yield Bonus |
| Article 29 | Special Agreement Allowance |
| Article 32 | Transportation Allowance |
| Article 33 | Disposability Allowance |
| Article 34 | Allowance for Oil Exploration Personnel |
| Article 37 | Travel Allowance |
| Article 63 | Company Benefit Plans |

## Contracting Out of Work

Until 1960, the company had done much of its maintenance work with its own employees. At one time it had over four hundred men in its own maintenance department. However, following 1960, management adopted a policy of decreasing its own maintenance group and contracting out maintenance work as much as possible. The decision to move to subcontracting was made for two reasons: lower costs and manpower flexibility.

The contracting companies were relatively small units that were owned and operated by men who had formerly worked in the trade for one of the major companies in the area or for one of the other contractors. What happened was that a couple of brothers or friends would open a small shop in Bari and then expand by taking on contract work at the big plants in the area. The major mechanical contractors, for example, employed anywhere from fifty to three hundred workers and each had contracts with from four to ten plants.

During the sixties and early seventies, Barichim was able to have work performed by the contractors for as much as 30% below its own total labor costs. The contractors were able to do the work at the lower prices and still make a profit for several reasons. First, their basic labor rates were lower. They were not tied to the chemical industry contract rates. Second, their fringe costs or social benefit costs were also lower. They were not bound by the fringe benefits of the chemical industry contract and moreover, they often avoided payment of social security taxes. Finally, they gave their workers no subsidized cafeterias or free transportation services which Barichim provided for its own employees.

In addition to lower labor costs, the contractors enabled the company to retain flexibility of manpower in the face of developing labor law in Italy which made it more and more difficult for the company to dismiss employees who were no longer needed. When the company needed more maintenance workers, the contractors provided a ready pool, and when the workers were no longer needed, the company could simply discontinue the contract. Under these conditions, it was the contractors and not Barichim that had to deal with the provisions of the new labor laws. In many cases, the contractors simply ignored the laws.

The decrease in the size of the company's own maintenance department from over 400 to 108 by 1974 was accomplished during a period when the amount of maintenance work was actually increasing. None of the company's maintenance employees was terminated, although a number were moved to production jobs, and also as men retired or left the company voluntarily, they were not replaced. By 1974, management was still in the process of decreasing its own maintenance group. It expected that eventually it would be decreased considerably below one hundred.

In the late sixties, the company was engaged in a major modernization and expansion program. During that period, it had as many as 35 contractors with over 900 workers on the property. However, by 1974 the expansion program had been completed and the outside contractors who now numbered only 27 with 540 men were used primarily for maintenance work. Prior to 1974, the company had experienced no difficulty in decreasing the number of contractors and contract workers as the construction program tapered off.

The twenty-seven contractors with which the company had contracts in 1974 were:

|                           | Number of Contractors | Number of Workers |
|---------------------------|:---------------------:|:-----------------:|
| Mechanical                | 8                     | 230               |
| Electrical and instrument | 5                     | 54                |
| Civil                     | 3                     | 57                |
| Painting                  | 2                     | 22                |
| Cleaning                  | 2                     | 66                |
| Insulation                | 2                     | 20                |
| Material handling         | 2                     | 22                |
| Transportation            | 1                     | 31                |
| Cafeteria                 | 1                     | 25                |
| Security                  | 1                     | 13                |
| Total                     | 27                    | 540               |

## Union Opposition to Contracting Out

In 1973, the unions in the Bari area had mounted a campaign to force the companies in the region to eliminate subcontracting and to hire directly employees to perform maintenance and other work. Numerous strikes occurred at other plants in the area as the unions pursued this objective. Barichim was not immune. The problem was made more difficult by the fact that the plant had a number of projects programmed which it could not get permission to build. As a result, contract workers had to be laid off. During 1973, the company had numerous short strikes, almost all of which resulted from this problem.

## The 1974 Strike

Prior to 1974, the plant management had negotiated contracts with the various contractors. However, in 1974 the plant manager, Alberto Pivari, was informed by the company headquarters in Rome that all contracting had to be done by bidding with at least three bids for any sizeable job. When the contracts with the eight mechanical contractors were about to run out, Pivari informed them that there were certain major maintenance jobs that he wished to have performed and asked them to bid on them. The eight mechanical contractors were very suspicious of the new procedure. They thought it would result in lower income and less work for them. Although Pivari assured them that under the new arrangement there would still be plenty of work for all eight of them, they were not convinced. The mechanical contractors refused to bid and told their workers that the new procedure would mean that some of the firms would not be successful in the bidding and as a result would have to lay off their workers.

The unions (CGIL, CSIL, and UIL) then called an in-plant meeting of the 540 contract workers. The contractors and the union officials informed the men that the new bid procedure would result in some of them losing their jobs. Together it was decided that the contractors would not bid on the maintenance work and that the workers would strike. The 540 contract workers then occupied the plant and placed picket lines at its entrances. The unions indicated that the strike would continue until the company guaranteed employment to the 540 employees of the contractors. The company refused to return to the old contract negotiation procedure or to guarantee employment.

The day following the occupation of the plant, Pivari appealed to the police department, asking that the workers be removed from the plant and protection be given to the company's regular employees so that they could come through the picket line. The police chief informed the company that he could not take such action without a court order.

The company's lawyers then appealed to the local court for an order requiring the striking workers to leave the plant. The unions' lawyers opposed the order, claiming that the contract workers had a right to strike where they worked. The court took the matter under advisement.

The company was able to make arrangements with other chemical companies to keep its customers supplied. As a result, it did not lose its market. However, the cost to the company of having the plant stand idle was very high because labor costs which were eliminated by the strike were only a small percentage of total costs, whereas capital costs were very high. Nevertheless, management decided to wait out the strike.

The occupation of the plant went on for three weeks. It was clear by that time that neither the police nor the courts would take action against the strikers. There was also no indication that the 540 workers would leave the plant unless their demands were met. Management was concerned also by the fact that its own 850 employees were unable to work and had been without pay for three weeks. A review of the situation was conducted in Rome, following which the general manager informed Pivari that the company did not wish the strike to continue and that he should take whatever steps were necessary to bring it to an end.

### Negotiations and Settlement

Pivari wondered how he could get negotiations under way without revealing his weak position. He believed that any direct contact with the contractors or the union leaders would be viewed by them as a sign of surrender. He decided that the best thing to do was to contact the regional labor commissioner. Instead of revealing his own need for a quick settlement, Pivari took the position with the commissioner that he had been informed that the men were tired of the strike and the contractors and the union officials were anxious to negotiate a reasonable settlement but were afraid to ask for negotiations because it would expose their weak position. The commissioner agreed to contact the contractors and the union leaders who indicated a willingness to meet with management. A meeting was then set up by the commissioner in his office in downtown Bari.

The negotiations were complicated by the fact that the workers were ostensibly bargaining with the contractors and only the contractors with the company. The unions demanded a 25% increase in pay plus a free cafeteria and a guarantee of employment for all of the 540 contract workers. In turn, the contractors demanded of the company an increase in rates which would enable them to pay the 25% increase and a guarantee of enough work to keep the 540 employees on the job. Finally, the union demanded of the company that it give its own 850 employees full pay for the three-week period during which the strike had prevented them from working.

The negotiations continued all that day with the help of the commissioner. Late that night, he announced that the following agreements had been reached.

1. A contract between the contractors and the union which include:
   a. a 15% increase in pay for the contract workers,
   b. a guarantee of full employment to all of the 540 contract workers,
   c. a cafeteria for contract workers in which meals would be highly subsidized;

2. A contract between the company and the contractors which included:
   a. an increase in the contractors' fees from 2,500 lire to 3,000 lire per man hour,
   b. a guarantee that current contractors would be given priority in maintenance and construction work.

In addition, the company committed itself to providing sufficient work in the future to the contractors so that they could continue to employ the 540 workers. It also gave a letter of intent to the commissioner in which it indicated that it would give priority to these contract workers when regular company jobs became available. Finally, the company agreed to reimburse all of its own employees for the three weeks of pay they had lost as a result of the strike.

**Problems since the 1974 Strike**

In October, 1975, the contract workers went on strike for one day and presented three demands:

1. a 20% increase in pay,
2. that work on the cafeteria be expedited,
3. that a list of the names of the 540 contract workers who had been guaranteed jobs be made available.

The Company recognized that the contract workers were underpaid and an agreement was quickly reached to increase their wages by 10% accompanied by a corresponding increase in fees for the contractors. The company also agreed to speed up the cafeteria construction. A list of the names of the 540 workers who had been guaranteed jobs was given to the regional labor commissioner.

As the company completed its expansion and modernization program and as demand for its products dropped because of the generally depressed conditions in Italy, it found it difficult to provide enough work to the contractors to enable them to keep their forces fully occupied. When this occurred, the contractors accused the company of violating the 1974 agreement. Some contractors moved some of their workers temporarily from the plant to their own shops and laid off some of their shop people. However, in the winter of 1976 the main mechanical contractor sued the company for damages of $700,000, claiming violation of the 1974 agreement. By the end of 1977, no decision had been rendered by the courts.

In the spring of 1977, four of the maintenance contractors claimed that they were no longer able to keep all of the men employed with the contracts provided to them by the company. As a result, they informed eighteen of their workers that they would be suspended but would receive unemployment compensation equal to 90% of their pay. The union leaders strongly opposed the layoff, claiming that the agreement guaranteeing employment was being violated. Although the plant was permitted to operate, all the maintenance men went on strike and the union threatened to again close the plant unless the company took quick action to revoke the layoffs. The company again sought the aid of the regional labor director and other government officials. An agreement was worked out whereby the government agreed to help the contractors secure additional work elsewhere so that they would not have to lay off the eighteen men, and the company agreed to increase its rates to the contractors.

## The Bus Blockade

The company provided free bus service to the plant for its employees from various points in and around Bari. The company had always contracted out this operation to a private bus company. In September, 1977, when the contract with the bus company ran out, management requested bids from it and several other bus companies. It received four bids, two of which were considerably lower than the bid of the bus company that had held the contract. One of the lower bids was actually 42% below that of the current contractor. The company investigated the equipment and finances of the low bidder and was convinced that it was competent to provide the same service as the current operator. It then signed a contract with the low bidder.

The owner of the bus company that had had the earlier contract called the drivers together and explained to them that he had lost the bid and, therefore, would have to terminate twenty-eight of them. The drivers then met alone and decided to take action. They seized the buses, drove them to the plant gates, and parked them bumper to bumper in such a way that no traffic could enter or leave. When asked to remove them by the plant guards, they refused to do so and also refused to get out of the drivers' seats so that someone else could move them. They then sent a representative to talk with Alberto Pivari, the plant manager. Pivari explained to the representative that he had followed regular business practice in giving the contract to the lowest bidder. He said he was sorry that the drivers had been dismissed by the bus company but that there was nothing he could do about it. He suggested that their dispute was with the bus company and not with him. He pointed out that the action they had taken was completely illegal and unless they stopped it, he would have to ask the police to take action.

The representative took Pivari's message back to the drivers and after some discussion with them returned to inform Pivari that the men had decided to continue the blockade until they had jobs. However, he stated that the jobs didn't have to be driving buses. They would be very happy to accept jobs in the plant if Pivari would guarantee permanent work to them.

Pivari had a meeting with the plant union representatives. He pointed out to them that unless the blockade was stopped, the plant would have to be closed and all the employees placed on layoff. He urged them to use their influence to cause the bus drivers to leave. Several hours later, one of the union men informed him that there was nothing they could do to stop the blockade.

Pivari then called the police. He explained the situation to the chief and asked him to take action. The chief said he would send some officers to the scene immediately. Ten minutes later a police car arrived and Pivari, from his office, could see the officers talking with the leader of the bus drivers. However, the drivers did not remove the buses and the police did not appear to be ready to cause them to do so. Pivari called the chief of police again but was unable to contact him. Pivari then called the local governor, explained the situation to him and asked that the police be ordered to clear the road. The chief of police later called Pivari and said he had told his men on the scene to order the drivers to leave but they had refused to do so. He said it would take him some time to get together a force large enough to remove them but that he would do so.

Within two hours at about 11:00 P.M., about thirty helmeted and armed policemen had arrived at the road leading to the plant gates. The chief then spoke over a loudspeaker and warned the drivers that if they did not stop the blockade within ten minutes, he would have to remove them from the buses and arrest them. The drivers replied through their leader that they were simply protecting their jobs and that any attempt to remove them could only lead to violence. Several of the drivers turned their buses toward the police group, switched on their lights, and reved up the motors as if ready to drive down on them. In addition, several of the drivers moved their buses inside the company gates and began driving them recklessly around the property, threatening to crash them into the chemical equipment. Pivari was very fearful that a spark from the exhausts or a crash would set off a series of explosions, resulting in serious loss of life and property.

At the end of half an hour, the drivers had not removed the buses and the police had taken no action. The chief then came to Pivari's office and the two discussed the situation. The chief stated that he had enough men at the scene to remove the drivers. However, he indicated that because of the attitude of the drivers and the fact that they had control of the buses, he thought this could be accomplished only at the cost of some bloodshed and the danger of considerable loss of life and property.

Pivari and the chief decided that under the circumstances it was better for the police not to take the offensive and attempt to remove the drivers from their buses but instead simply to stand guard so as to prevent any harm to the company's personnel and property. It was hoped that in time the drivers would get tired and hungry and leave of their own free will. The chief pointed out that the leader of the drivers had told him that the men did not really want to continue the blockade, but were simply protecting their jobs and would leave immediately if the company would offer them work, so that they could support their families.

Pivari then called the prefect and discussed the situation with him. The prefect arranged to have the leader of the drivers, the owners of the two bus companies, and Pivari meet in his office with him. It was clear from the beginning that the prefect had no intention of using force to remove the blockade but instead expected the parties to work out an agreement. The negotiations were difficult. After three days, during which the drivers continued to blockade the plant, the company, under heavy pressure from the prefect, arranged with the outside contractors to guarantee ten of the drivers permanent jobs in the plant. The successful bidder agreed to hire ten of them, and the loser agreed to continue the remaining eight in his employment. As soon as this information was communicated to the drivers, they ended the blockade and drove the buses back to the garage.

### The Situation in December, 1977

Following 1974, whenever openings had occurred in the regular work force, the company had given top priority to the men on the contractors' guaranteed employment list. Between 1974 and December, 1977, eighty-five of these men had been hired as regular company workers. In addition, the company had attempted to get some of them permanent jobs with other employers in the area but that effort had not been very successful. Some had also left voluntarily for various reasons. However, in December, 1977, there were still 420 contract workers, including the ten former bus drivers, who were on the guaranteed employment list. In addition, the company had 108 men in its own maintenance department for a total of 528 employees to do the maintenance work.

By December, 1977, however, demand for the company's products had dropped to the point where the plant was operating at only 70% of capacity. At that level of production, management estimated that it needed ony 300 maintenance workers. Even if production were to be increased to full capacity, management estimated that it would need no more than 400 employees in maintenance work.

At the current level of production, the plant was operating at a heavy loss and Pivari was under strong pressure from headquarters in Rome to cut costs. In the old days, costs could have been quickly reduced by declaring redundant many of the maintenance employees. As Pivari worked on his 1978 production and cost forecasts, he wondered if there was any way he could cut the labor force costs and still maintain production and labor peace. He noted that contracting out was no longer a bargain for the company. The cost of contract labor was, if anything, higher now than the cost of hiring employees directly. He wondered also what long-run policies and programs he might adopt that would enable him to avoid excessive labor costs in the future.

# 4 Labor Relations in the Netherlands

## Introduction

The population of the Netherlands in 1978 was 14 million. Only Sweden of the seven countries in this study had a smaller population. However, during the period 1970-1978, Dutch population increased 6.98% which was far higher than in any of the European countries and even slightly higher than in the United States (see table A-1).*

The gross national product of the Netherlands in 1976 was $92 billion, smaller than in all the other countries except Sweden. Its gross national product per person that year was $6,650 which, although it was more than double that of Italy's, was lower than the figure in all the other countries except Great Britain. However, the per capita gross national product during the 1970-1976 period grew at a rate of 2.6% per year, the highest rate of all countries except France (see table A-2).

Consumer prices in the Netherlands during the period 1970-1978 rose 83%—a lower increase than in all the other countries except West Germany and the United States (see table A-3).

The average hourly compensation for production workers in manufacturing in the Netherlands in 1978 was $11.44; the highest of the seven countries. During the period 1970-1978, the average compensation for Dutch production in manufacturing in terms of U.S. dollars increased 365% which was also the highest increase of all the countries. In terms of local purchasing power, Dutch worker compensation increased 52% in the period 1970-1978 which, although less than in West Germany and Italy, was three times the increase in the United States (see table A-5).

Output in manufacturing in the Netherlands increased an average of 5.4% per year during the period 1960-1977 and 2.3% per year during 1970-1977. Only France and Italy had output increases larger than the Netherlands in the 1960-1977 period (see table A-6). Productivity, as measured by percentage change in output per hour in manufacturing, increased 7.4% per year during the 1960-1977 period and 6.4% per year during 1970-1977. In both periods, these were the highest increases of all the countries (see table A-7).

Unit labor costs in terms of Dutch currency increased 5.7% per year

---

*Tables A-1 through A-13 referred to in this chapter are in the statistical appendix at the end of the book.

117

during the 1960-1977 period and 8.3% per year during 1970-1977. In the latter period, Dutch unit labor costs increased more rapidly than in West Germany or the United States but less rapidly than in the other four European countries (see table A-8). In terms of U.S. dollars, the increase in unit labor costs in the Netherlands was 8.3% per year in the period 1960-1977 and 14.8% per year during 1970-1977. In the long period, 1960-1977, the increase in the Netherlands' labor costs was exceeded only slightly by that of West Germany's, and in 1970-1977, it was higher than that of all the countries and almost two and one-half times as high as the increase in the United States (see table A-9).

## The Union Movement

### Structure

Dutch society has been divided into three blocks or "pillars" on a religious and ideological basis: Catholic (40%), Protestant (35%), and Socialist-Humanist (25%). The pillar to which one belongs influences strongly one's social, economic, and political activities. However, in recent years there has been a tendency for the barriers between the pillars to be less rigid.

The three-way split in Dutch society was carried over into the union movement. Until 1976, there were three separate union confederations: Socialists (NVV) with 704,000 members in 15 unions; Catholics (NKV) with 350,000 members in 9 unions; and Protestants (CNV) with 230,000 members in 13 unions. However, in 1976, the NVV and NKV combined to form the Netherlands Trade Union Federation (FNV) with over one million members.

In the past, and to a considerable extent even today, the Dutch union movement has been highly centralized with much of the power and authority residing in the officers of the confederations. In this respect, it has differed greatly from the U.S. and British labor movements where the AFL-CIO and the TUC are weak federations in which the central organization has little authority over the affiliated unions.

The national unions that are affiliated with the FNV and CNV are industrial. In the past, each industry has had three unions: one Socialist, one Catholic, and one Protestant. Thus, in the major Dutch companies, employees have been represented by each of three different unions. As a result of the merger of the NVV and NKV, the number will probably be reduced to two in the future. In recent years, the national unions have been gaining power and authority at the expense of the confederations. This change has been a result of several factors, including the growing significance of industry bargaining as compared with national bargaining, and the decrease in the number of national unions and the increase in their size. Before the FNV merger, two unions had more than one-half of the NVV membership, and one union had over one-third of the NKV membership.

The local unions operate on a geographic rather than a company or plant basis. They have had very little local autonomy and a high degree of direction from the national unions. Few locals have full-time officials. The national unions have district representatives who serve as the link between the local and national union officials. The district representatives rather than the local officials handle grievances. As yet, there has been little development of union structure at the company or plant level. There is no counterpart of the U.S. plant local or the English shop steward committee. However, there is more and more pressure for a union presence on the shop floor; and in some firms, especially in the metal industries, some progress has been made in this direction. Employers are strongly opposed to a role for unions in the individual enterprise. Most employers, although accepting the legitimacy of unions as spokesmen for the workers at the level of the economy or the industry will not tolerate a formal union presence in their plants.[1]

*Cooperation*

Although one might expect that there would have been strong rivalry among the union movements, such has not been the case. In 1945, the three groups adopted the same dues and benefits schedules and agreed not to compete for membership. In 1958, they established the union consultation board (RO) through which they have worked together over the years to present a united front in dealing with employers, the government, and the public. In 1967 and again in 1971, the three confederations formulated joint action programs which set forth their views on social, economic, and labor policies.

*Amalgamation*

As cooperation among the three organizations progressed, pressure developed to merge them into one single federation. It was hoped also that eventually the affiliated unions in the NVV, CNV, and NKV would merge. Since the number of category unions in each of the federations was already in the process of being decreased by mergers, the sponsors of the merger of the federations envisaged a highly compact movement of one federation with only six or so affiliated national unions.

A committee made up of representatives from each of the federations was set up to work on plans for consolidation. However, it became apparent as the discussions proceeded that the CNV, the Protestant federation, was not prepared to go as far as the other two in giving up its independence. As a result, in 1975 the CNV withdrew from the discussions. However, the representatives of the NVV and NKV continued to meet; and effective January 1, 1976, they agreed to merge into the FNV. (The Catholic and Socialist groups were not always so cooperative. As recently as 1954, the Dutch Catholic bishops issued a pastoral letter forbidding Catholics to join the NVV unions.) Three of the NVV affiliated unions are already in the process of merging with their corresponding NKV affiliated unions, and it is expected that within a few years there will be only one FNV union in each category.

As a result of NKV's merger with NVV, the NKV unions representing civil servants and executive grade employees with 40,000 members have withdrawn from the NKV and joined the CNV. Moreover, the RO has been discontinued and no substitute vehicle for cooperation between the FNV and CNV has been established. Finally, on certain proposed labor legislation, the FNV and CNV have adopted different positions. It is not clear, therefore, as to what extent and through what mechanism labor cooperation may be achieved in the future.

### Closed Shop and Check-Off

The closed shop is not illegal and is practiced in some trades, such as printing and diamond cutting, but is not widespread. Likewise, the check-off of unions dues, although not illegal, is not widely practiced. Instead, Dutch unions employ messengers (*bodes*) who collect the dues at the members' homes and receive a percentage for their service. The unions have tried to encourage membership by negotiating higher wages and benefits for union members only and the company payment of union dues. Generally, these attempts have not been successful. However, since 1966 many employers have been paying a small amount (10 florin) per year per union member to the union. Although the amount is not significant, an important precedent has been established.

### Membership

About 40% of eligible employees are union members, a figure that has not changed since 1957 (see table A-11). About 20% of the union members are in independent unions, including those which represent white-collar, professional, and staff employees—although the large federations also compete for membership in these areas. An important development in recent years has been the rapid growth of two unions for higher staff and supervisory employees, the BLHP and NCHP, which have frequently been in conflict with the other unions in their attempt to retain salary differentials and special benefit rights for their membership.

Unions are also important in the Dutch armed forces: 80% of the officers and enlisted men are unionized. Of the eleven unions that bargain for military personnel, the Union of Dutch Conscripts claims a membership of 30,000 of the 54,000. It has been successful not only in gaining pay raises and better living conditions for its members, but also in eliminating short haircuts, reveille, and saluting (except on ceremonial occasions).[2]

## Leadership

Top union officials are not directly nominated or elected by the union membership but rather, are coopted by the existing leaders, subject only to ratification by the membership or their representatives. Thus, the system is not very democratic, but it has resulted in bringing in, at the top, independent leaders with good education and technical training. One student of Dutch labor relations views this method of selection as an important factor which in the past has contributed "to the ability of union leaders to exercise wage restraint."[3]

## Ideology

There is no major Communist power center in the Dutch labor movement. In fact in 1977 the NVV, the socialist organization, supported dissident groups in Poland and Czechoslovakia and denounced the oppression of opposition in East European countries.

In its official policy statements, however, the NVV has always favored socialization. More recently, it has been joined in this respect by the NKV. In a statement in 1977 after the NVV and NKV had merged into the FNV, the Catholic labor leaders stated that they favored the socialization of the production process and that the mere factor of capital was no basis for a voice within the enterprise. However, the CNV, the smaller Protestant federation, still strongly rejects the doctrine and practice of the class struggle in any form.

Despite the stated policy of the major federations, Dutch unions, in practice, have not pressed for nationalization of industry. Rather, during the postwar period they constituted the model of "responsible unionism," working amicably together with management and the government to prevent inflation and maintain labor peace and stability. Following the reconstruction period, they were content to share in the prosperity without seeking to change the system. However, in recent years, as there has been less to share and as unemployment has increased, the movement has become much more militant and critical of the free enterprise system. Viewing this trend, Dr. M. Albrecht, an executive of Hoogovens, one of Holland's leading industrial companies, stated in 1975 that continued support for the capitalist system by the labor movement can be expected only if "we find solutions to the social problem."[4]

### Politics

In recent years, the unions have moved to be more and more independent of the churches and the political parties with which they were originally closely associated. The unions give no direct financial aid to the parties. Their chief contributions in recent years have been votes, facilities, and expertise. However, union leaders are often very active in party politics. Some years ago, a survey found that thirteen members of the Lower House of Parliament were union officials and six were former union officials.[5]

## Employers' Associations

In each industry, Dutch companies have developed strong employers' associations to deal with the unions. Since most companies bargain through the industry association rather than directly with the union, the associations are very important in the industrial relations structure. In the past, there were three associations in each industry—a Catholic, a Protestant, and a nonconfessional association. The industry associations, in turn, were united into three employer confederations: Catholic (NKVW), Protestant (VPCW), and nonconfessional (VNO). However, in 1970 the NKVW and VPCW united to form one Christian employers' federation (NCW). Moreover, most of the employers who maintain membership in the NCW are also members now of the VNO which claims to represent 80% of Dutch industry. The VNO and NCW work closely together in dealing with the unions and the government. In 1976, for example, they made a joint presentation to parliament opposing changes in the works council law.

## Collective Bargaining

### National or Economy-Wide Bargaining

Collective bargaining in Holland has been highly centralized. There are two important levels of bargaining: national and industry. National or economy-wide bargaining occurs between the representatives of the union confederations FNV and CNV representing the workers, and representatives of the employers' confederations VNO and NCW representing management, with guidance and support from the government.

One of the key institutions that affects national bargaining is the Social and Economic Council (SER). The SER consists of 45 members: 15 representing the union confederations; 15 representing the employers' confederations; and 15 independent experts appointed by the government. The SER conducts studies and advises the government on all major economic and labor matters. Each year, with the assistance of the central planning bureau, SER produces a report in which it recommends the level of wage increases that is appropriate for the coming year if excess inflation is to be avoided.

A second key institution is the Foundation of Labor. Established immediately after World War II, it includes all the major interest groups: industry, labor, small business, and agriculture. Many of its major functions were taken over by the SER when the latter was established in 1950. Prior to that time, the foundation played a major role in the formulation of economic and social policy for the nation. The foundation still plays an important role in national bargaining. After the foundation receives the guidelines recommended by the SER, it attempts to reach an agreement on the level of wage increase that the unions and the employers' associations will be permitted to bargain.

During the period of reconstruction following the war and during the period of growth and prosperity that followed the reconstruction, labor relations in Holland were very harmonious. Working through the foundation, labor and management leaders, with the aid of the government, were able to reach agreements on the allowable wage increases. Inflation were restrained, losses resulting from strikes were negligible, and the Dutch labor movement was proclaimed as the outstanding example of "responsible unionism."

More recently, however, as prosperity has faded, unemployment has risen, and increases in real wages have not been possible, the harmonious system has broken down. In 1977, agreement could not be reached on continuation of the automatic cost-of-living clause and the union federations' demand for a 2% wage increase. The unions developed a "spearhead plan" which involved strikes in a small number of selected firms. Although only 36,000 workers were involved, the plan was successful in paralyzing major sectors of the economy. After three weeks of what was reported as "the worst labor unrest in Holland since World War II," peace was restored by a compromise (the Hague Protocol) in which the automatic cost-of-living adjustment was continued, management agreed to supply the unions with more financial and economic data, and the wage demand was referred to industry bargaining.

It is not clear now what role national bargaining with the help of the SER and the Foundation of Labor will play in the future. There are those who believe that the era of harmonious relations is being replaced by one of confrontation and an increasing demand for fundamental redistribution of income, knowledge, and power. In this kind of an atmosphere the SER and the foundation may prove ineffective, but new institutions have not yet been developed and the transition may be difficult.[6]

*Industry Bargaining*

The labor contracts in Holland are bargained at the industry level with representatives of two or three national unions on one side of the table and representatives of the industry employers' association on the other side. (There are only a few companies, such as Philips and Hoogovens, that bargain directly with the unions.) In recent years, industry bargaining has assumed greater importance as the national guidelines have become less rigid, the scope of bargaining has expanded, and the power has moved from the union confederations to some of the large national unions.

Industry bargaining results in one of two types of agreements: one with standard conditions, which cannot be changed at the company or plant level; or one with minimum conditions, which may be improved at the local level. Once a contract has been signed by the employers and the national unions, the government may extend its terms to cover all other companies within the industry.

*Local Bargaining*

In the past, the Dutch unions have had little influence at the plant level. As indicated earlier, the local union structure has been very weak. Moreover, Dutch employers have insisted on the right to run the shop without interference. Discussion of local issues has been limited to the works councils (which will be discussed later). There has been no local bargaining with the unions and no union grievance procedure to protect employees against unfair dismissals or other unfair action.

More recently, however, this condition has been changing. In 1964, the Dutch metalworkers' union began a program in which local shop stewards (*kaderledens*) would represent the union at the plant level, and this concept has now been spreading to other industries. Indicative of the growing importance of local bargaining is the fact that in 1977, the SER issued an unanimous opinion favoring a set of rules that would require management to provide trade unions with facilities in the work place. The unions are now pressing to have this opinion translated into legislation which, in addition to providing union bulletin boards and meeting rooms in the plant, would give the stewards special protection against dismissal, and give full-time union officials the legal right to enter the plant. One interesting issue that must now be faced is the relationship between the works councils and the shop stewards. The Minister of Social Affairs has requested the SER to issue an opinion on this matter, but so far the SER has avoided the issue.

### The Collective Agreement

A collective bargaining agreement is legally enforceable in the Netherlands. A worker, a union, or an employer may take a complaint of contract violation directly to the courts. However, this procedure is seldom used. Instead, the contracts provide a grievance procedure that consists of several steps and usually provides for arbitration as the terminal point. In practice, arbitration is almost never used, but rather, agreement is achieved by the company and the union. Under the authority given to it in a 1945 law, the board of mediation frequently extends a labor agreement to cover all the enterprises in an industry. The 1945 law provides also that when a labor agreement terminates, its terms are automatically extended on a month-to-month basis until a new agreement is reached.

### Strikes

For some years, there has been a question as to whether strikes are legal in the Netherlands. In 1960, the High Court ruled that workers on strike were guilty of nonperformance of their employment contracts. Therefore, a union that called or supported a strike was guilty of inducing breach of contract, and both the striking workers and the union could be enjoined. Moreover, the employer could sue the union and the workers for damages. However, the court added that circumstances could arise where "according to prevailing tenets of justice it cannot in fairness be required of employees that they continue at work . . . In such a case one cannot speak of nonperformance on the part of employees." The court did not specify the circumstances that might justify a strike.[7] However, during the labor unrest in the spring of 1977, the court did declare that a strike in the food industry was illegal. In order to clarify the situation, the SER has proposed legislation that would make strikes legal if conducted by a legitimate labor organization.

Over the years, the strike record in the Netherlands has been exceptionally good. During the ten-year period 1967-1976, the days lost through industrial stoppages averaged only 30 per 1,000 employees or about 1/100 of 1% of the working time. This was the lowest rate in any of the seven countries included in this study (see table A-12). Both management and union representatives have indicated that the low incidence of conflict has been a result of factors other than the questionable legal status of strikes. In view of the breakdown of the harmonious relationship and the flurry of strikes in 1977, there is some question as to whether this good record will continue in the future. Dutch unions have accumulated substantial strike funds over the years from which they stand ready to pay large benefits if they decide to use the strike weapon.

## Legislated Employee Protection and Benefits

### Unfair Dismissals

A Dutch employer may not dismiss an employee without special permission from the district employment office. In 1975, out of 80,411 employer requests for dismissal, only 46,135 were granted. Even after permission is granted, the employee is entitled to a period of notice of one week for each year of service up to a maximum of thirteen weeks, plus an additional week for every year of employment after age 45 with a maximum of thirteen weeks, for a total maximum of twenty-six weeks.

An exception is made if the dismissal is for "urgent cause" which is defined as persistent insubordination, theft, sabotage, and such. If the employee believes he has been unfairly dismissed, he may appeal to the courts which may order indemnity payments or reinstatement. However, appeals to the courts are unusual. In most cases, an agreement is worked out with the aid of an industry committee made up of union and management representatives.[8] Rather than dismiss an employee, some companies now agree to have him declared unable to work for physical reasons which enables him to draw up to as much as 100% of his pay from the national health plan (WAO) until retirement at age 65.

### Redundancies

Employees have the right to terminate employees for lack of work. Such terminations, however, must be approved by the district employment office, and employees so terminated are entitled to up to a maximum of twenty-six weeks of notification as described previously with respect to dismissals. Moreover, the SER has established guidelines that must be followed by employers in terminating employees because of mergers or plant closings.

The employer must hold prior discussions with the unions and must provide the terminated employees with retraining, termination pay, and aids in relocation. Failure to follow these guidelines can result in cancellation of a merger.[9]

*Labor Placement Law*

In 1979, the unions were pressing for a Labor Placement Law (APO) to guarantee existing employment and encourage new employment. Under the proposal: it would become much more difficult for employers to declare employees redundant; all overtime would be banned; every vacancy would be immediately filled by the local employment office; private employment agencies would be banned; every company would be assigned a minimum quota of workers, and any increased cost would be covered by state wage subsidies.

*Equal Pay and Equal Opportunity*

In 1975, the Dutch government enacted an Equal Pay Act that establishes the right of men and women "to claim equal pay for work of equal value." The act created the equal pay committee composed of two nominees of employers' associations, two nominees of unions, and a civil servant as chairman. Employees may complain to the committee which has no power to take a matter to court but which is empowered to issue a report that may be used by the employee in a court appeal.

In July, 1978, an EEC directive requiring equal opportunities for women became effective thoroughout the European Economic Community including the Netherlands, and later the Dutch government proposed an equal opportunities law that would give statutory support to the EEC directive. Under the new law, discrimination in hiring, promotion, training, working conditions, and dismissals because of sex, marital, or family status would be illegal. An equal opportunities committee consisting of the same membership as the equal pay committee would be established. Enforcement of the provisions of the act would be through the regular courts. Individual grievants could complain to the courts which could award damages and order reinstatement. However, by the summer of 1979, the equal opportunities legislation had not been passed, with the result that some Dutch women were threatening to appeal to the European Court for enforcement of the EEC directive. Moreover, as a result of the displacement of several married women in early 1979 because they were not "breadwinners," the Dutch parliament passed an emergency measure that outlaws dismissals based solely on sex, marital, or family status. It is expected that these factors will put pressure on the parliament to move to adoption of the Equal Opportunities Act.

## Maternity Protection and Benefits

Under Dutch law, women are provided with twelve weeks of maternity leave at full pay—six weeks before and six weeks after childbirth. The pay is provided from the national health insurance system to which the workers and the employers contribute. During a maternity leave, an employee's employment contract remains in effect, giving her a legal right to return to her job at the end of the maternity leave period. An August, 1976 law provides also that employees may not be dismissed at any time because of marriage, pregnancy or confinement.

## Absenteeism

Absenteeism because of claimed sickness in the Netherlands is the third highest of the seven countries studied exceeded only by Italy and Sweden. A study of absenteeism in 1973 by the Swedish employers' association indicates that in the Netherlands the average in that year was 8% compared with only 6.5% in Germany, 5% in Britain and 4% in the United States (see table A-13). The high rate in the Netherlands is evidently a result of its very liberal sick pay plan under which workers are paid; 80% of their full wages even for one day of sickness.

## Worker Participation

### Works Councils

In 1950, the first works council law was passed in the Netherlands. It required every employer with twenty-five or more employees to establish a council that was purely advisory. The council was composed of employees elected by their fellow employees, plus the general manager who served as chairman. However, the law contained no penalties, and as a result, less than 50% of the companies covered by it set up works councils.

In 1971 another works council act replaced the 1950 act. Under the 1971 law, firms with one hundred or more employees were subject to penalties for failure to establish works councils and as a result there was general compliance with it. Under the 1971 act the council possessed not only consultative rights but also had codetermination rights over a small number of issues.

The 1971 act was subject to strong criticism from FNV, which argued that: the works councils should be composed of employees only; the consultative and codetermination rights under the law were too limited; the escape clause (paragraph 25), which permitted management to take action without consultation with the council in situations where "the major interests of the firm militate against such consultation," should be eliminated; and work council candidates and members were not given sufficient protection against adverse action by management.

In 1979 FNV was successful in securing the passage of a revised Works Councils Act which became effective September 1, 1979. Under the new act the general manager is no longer a member of the council. Instead membership is limited to employees elected by employees. The chairman of the council is also an employee elected to that position by the other council members. Lists of candidates for the council may be proposed by the unions or by groups of non-union employees. The candidates on each list must represent a cross section of the various categories of employees. The number of council members varies from 7 to 25 depending on the size of the plant or office. Members are elected for a period of two years. The costs of the council, including the time spent on it by the council members, are paid by the employer. (See figure 4-1).

The new law provides strong job security for council numbers. They may not be dismissed except for four reasons: where the employee is guilty of gross misconduct such as theft, or other behavior which warrants summary dismissal; where there is a serious lack of cooperation on the part of the employee, rendering continued employment untenable; where there is a collective redundancy; or where the termination is by mutual agreement.

As under the 1971 law, the unions' role under the new law is limited to their right to propose lists of candidates. There are no union representatives on the council and union officials have no right to attend council meetings.

Although the manager is no longer a member of the council, a "joint meeting" must be held when requested by either the council or the employer. At least six "joint meetings" must be held each year.

Under the 1971 act, the works council had codetermination rights with respect only to work rules; pension, profit sharing or saving schemes; working hours and holiday arrangements; and safety and health measures. Under the 1979 act, codetermination rights have been expanded to include: wage scales; training; rating systems; welfare services; shop floor consultations; and grievance procedures. If the council and the employer are not able to agree on any of these matters they can be referred to the trade commission of the industry. Such trade commissions have been set up by the SER and consist of not less than six members, one-half appointed by employers' organizations and one-half appointed by the unions. The trade commission may appoint a neutral chairman and give him a vote if it desires

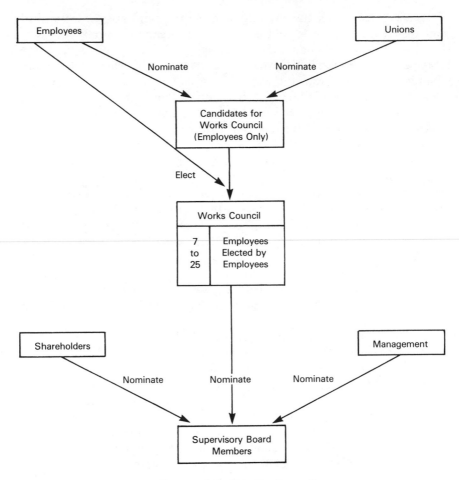

**Figure 4-1.** Works Council

to do so. Decisions of the trade commission may be appealed to the Minister of Social Affairs.

The new act also extends the area over which the council has prior consultation rights and eliminates the escape clause. Management must now consult with the council before taking action on the following matters: establishment of new undertakings; closure of a firm or division; substantial reduction, expansion, or other changes in activities; major changes in organization; move to another location; withdrawing or entering into permanent ties with other firms; seeking advice from outside experts; taking on temporary workers; and appointment or dismissal of a manager who would have the power to deal with the council in a "joint meeting."

The new law provides also for a period of waiting if the council rejects management's decision regarding a matter of which it must be consulted. The employer may not implement his decision for one month from the time the council was notified. During this one-month period the council may appeal to the Amsterdam Court of Justice which must decide "whether the employer could reasonably have arrived at the decision in question after weighing all interests involved." Thus, even on matters where the council is given only consultative rights, management does not have the final authority. There is one exception. The one-month's delay and court appeal do not apply to the appointment or dismissal of a manager. The works council must simply be consulted on this issue.

Under the law Dutch management must also provide the works council with the following information: a report every six months on the general activities of the firm; an annual financial report; and reports on future prospects of the firm, including long-run budgets as they are developed.

The new law has strong support from the major labor federation, the FNV, which views it as a "definite step on the road to industrial democracy." However, the employers' association, VNO, opposes it as leading "towards greater polarization of approach as between workers and the employer."[10]

### Employee Influence on the Board

In 1971, a new Company Structure Act was passed, which applies to a public company that has one hundred or more employees, capital plus reserves of 10 million Dfl, and a works council. Such a company must now have a two-tier board system—a supervisory board (*raad van commissarissen*) and a management board (*direktie*). The new law does not require either employee or union representatives on the supervisory board. In fact, it specifically excludes from the supervisory board: employees of the company, officials of unions that represent employees of the company, and managers of the company. However, members of the supervisory board may be nominated by the works council as well as by the shareholders and management. Appointments to the supervisory board are made by the board members themselves; that is, new members are co-opted. However, the works council (also the shareholders) may veto any candidate on two possible grounds: 1. the candidate is unqualified, or 2. his appointment would cause the board to be unbalanced. The supervisory board may appeal a veto to the SER which makes a recommendation to the Minister of Social Affairs who has the power to make a final decision (see figure 4-2).

A holding company with more than 50% of its employees outside of Holland is exempt from these provisions of the act. Although such companies must have works councils if they have over one hundred employees,

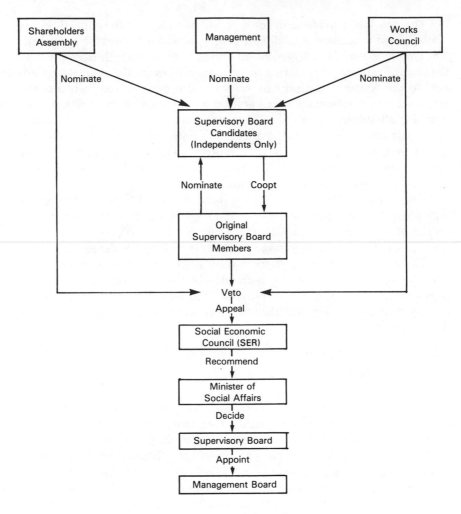

**Figure 4-2.** Board Appointments

these councils do not have the right to nominate or veto candidates for their boards.

The supervisory board appoints the members of the management board and checks on the annual account. In addition, the management board must get the supervisory board's approval on:

1. increasing or decreasing the number of shares
2. capital participation in another firm
3. a major investment
4. amendment of the Articles of Association

5.  dissolution of the company
6.  termination of a significant number of employees
7.  radical changes in the working conditions for a significant number of employees

Within these constraints, the management board has the authority to make the decisions necessary for the day-to-day operation of the company.

Although there have been several instances in which works councils have opposed candidates for supervisory boards, Dutch management has not found the provisions of the Company Structure Act difficult to live with. One manager expressed the opinion that, "We believe our employees will be reasonable in helping us to secure a competent board and we are certain that we shall be able to work out our differences without the necessity of ever having to appeal to the SER."

On the other hand, in May 1977, the FNV issued a statement criticizing the present Company Structure Act. Although it opposed the appointment of trade union officials to the supervisory board or the direct election of supervisory board members by employees, it strongly urged that the works council should appoint one-half of the supervisory board members, the shareholders should appoint an equal number, and together they should choose one or more independent members.

**Profit Sharing and Employee Ownership**

Some Dutch firms have profit sharing plans, and the Foundation of Labor has issued a statement that such plans should be based on an agreement with the unions. However, at present there is no law that requires profit sharing. Moreover, the profit-sharing plans that do exist are not such as will result in eventual ownership and control of the companies by the workers or their representatives. A 1965 Company Savings Act provides for statutory voluntary profit sharing. A 1970 act permits nonstatutory voluntary profit sharing, and a bill now under consideration would establish compulsory profit sharing.

*Statutory Voluntary Plans*

The 1965 act permits companies to establish three types of savings plans:

1.  *bonus-savings plans*, under which a worker may agree to have up to 750 guilders per year tax free deducted from his pay for four years and invested in company shares or a savings bank. (The amount of bonus added by the employer varies with the nature of the plan. Under the so-called fixed bonus plan, an employer is obligated to add 25% to each deposit made by the worker.)

2. *profit-sharing plans*, under which the employer agrees to invest for the worker in company shares or a savings bank a percentage of the company's profits up to 750 guilders per year tax free which becomes available to the worker only after seven years.

3. *wage savings plans*, under which the employer and the union may negotiate a compulsory deduction of up to 2% of pay which is placed in a jointly administered fund and is available to workers only after seven years.

If an employee desires to use the money from any of these plans for paying off a mortgage on his home, it will be released immediately. In 1973, 38% of Dutch workers were participating in bonus-savings or profit-sharing plans. However, the only major wage saving plan was in the graphics industry, where 20,000 workers were involved.[11]

### Nonstatutory Voluntary Plans

In 1970, the legal restraints of the 1965 law were removed and since then, a variety of new plans have been adopted. In 1976, over 9,000 Dutch companies had nonstatutory plans of which 52% were profit-related. About 43% of the 170 Dutch collective bargaining agreements now include some sort of provision in this area. Unilever, Akzo, and KLM are among the large companies that now have profit-sharing plans.

### Compulsory Profit Sharing (VAD)

In 1964, the three union federations jointly published a compulsory "capital growth sharing plan" which has become known as the VAD. The original VAD proposal provided for a national fund to be financed by the "excess profits" of enterprises and managed entirely by trade union representatives. The majority of the fund's income (75%) would be used for collective rather than for individual employee benefits. The ultimate result would be a redistribution of Dutch wealth and control of Dutch business by the unions.

Wim Kok, chairman of the Netherlands Trade Union Federation, has stated:

> The accent lies either on the promotion of the acquisition of private property by the worker, or the apportionment of part of the capital growth of the enterprise to the collectivity of the workers, with equal rights for all workers regardless of the financial results of the enterprise they work for. . . . The basic idea . . . is that, in principle, participation in the capital growth is expressed in the transfer of title deeds and does not lead to money grants, at least not for a long time. There are diverse opinions about whether the possession of these title deeds should encompass rights of codetermination. I think they should.[12]

As would be expected, Dutch management and owners were fiercely opposed to the original VAD plan, and although the unions received strong help from the Labor party, they were not able to receive majority support for it in the Dutch parliament. In July, 1977, the split over VAD was a major factor in preventing the formation of a new coalition government. At that time, Queen Juliana appointed Willem Albeda, professor at Erasmus University, Rotterdam, to attempt to mediate the issue. With Professor Albeda's help, the Labor party, the Christian Democratic party, and the D '66 Center party agreed on a compromise solution which provided that: compulsory profit sharing would be required only of companies with gross annual profits of over 200,000 guilders per year; workers would receive 20% of the gross profits starting January 1, 1978, and the percentage would be raised 1% each year to a maximum of 23%; one-half of the money would be used to buy shares for the workers in the companies to which the plan applied, and one-half would be paid to the national pension plan so that all workers would benefit; and the companies would be given special tax concessions.

However, the 1977 compromise was never enacted into law. Instead, in 1978 the government introduced a new bill which provides that:

1. a company with pre-tax profits of 100,000 guilders would have to set aside 24% of its excess profits (it is estimated that over 2,000 companies would meet the 100,000-guilder requirement),

2. 12% of the excess profits would be given to the company's employees in the form of cash and other benefits,

3. 12% of the excess profits would be paid into a national fund administered by twelve trade union and eight government appointees,

4. the money in the national fund would be used to finance early retirement schemes and to improve pension arrangements for all Dutch employees.[13]

It is significant that the 1978 proposed legislation does not provide for participation in company decision making by employees or their union representatives through stock ownership. However, the unions would have control over the administration of half of the amount of the excess profits tax. Changes in this 1978 proposal may result from a study made by a special parliamentary committee.

## Notes

1. Jack Barbash, *Trade Unions and National Economic Policy* (Baltimore: Johns Hopkins Press, 1972), p. 66.

2. Bowen, Northrup, "This is an Army, Well It has Arms, Marches—Sort of," *Wall Street Journal*, October 1, 1974, p. 1.

3. John Windmuller, *Labor Relations in the Netherlands* (Ithaca, New York: Cornell University Press, 1969), p. 221.

4. M. Albrecht, *Industrial Relations as a Balancing Factor Between Employers and Trade Unions*, Speech to American Chamber of Commerce, Rotterdam, January 23, 1975.

5. Windmuller, *Labor Relations*, p. 230.

6. J.T.M. Andriessen, "Developments in the Dutch Industrial Relations System," *Industrial Relations Journal* 7 (2), 1976:53.

7. Windmuller, *Labor Relations*, p. 322.

8. "Individual Dismissal in the Netherlands," *European Industrial Relations Review*, No. 41, May, 1976, pp. 12-13.

9. Bram Peper, "The Netherlands: From an Ordered Harmonic to a Bargaining Relationship," in *Worker Militancy and its Consequences*, ed. Solomon Barkin (New York: Praeger Publishers, 1975), p. 141.

10. "Netherlands: Works Councils, the New Formula," *European Industrial Relations Review*, Vol. 54, June, 1978, p. 12.

11. "Savings and Profit Sharing Schemes in the Netherlands," *European Industrial Relations Review*, Vol. 45, September, 1977, p. 14.

12. Wim Kok, *Labor Relations in Europe*, Speech to European Management Forum, Davos, Switzerland, February 1, 1977, p. 5.

13. "Netherlands: From Economic Democracy to Profit Sharing," *European Industrial Relations Review*, Vol. 53, May, 1978, p. 11.

# Case 6
# Hobbema & van Rijn, N.V. (A)

## Functioning of a Central Workers' Council

In October, 1974, Dirk van Berkel, chairman of the management board of Hobbema & van Rijn, N.V., was reviewing his experiences in dealing with the central workers' council which had been functioning in the company since January, 1974. Mr. van Berkel was concerned about several general issues that appeared to be involved in working with such a council, and with a very specific issue that was emerging. This latter involved the sale of the company's Amersfoort division, which was currently being negotiated by management, and which would have to be presented to the central workers' council for the latter's "advice" before final consummation. Dirk van Berkel anticipated that this issue could cause a good deal of difficulty in the months ahead, and that it could well have a good deal of influence on future functioning of the Council.

Hobbema & van Rijn, N.V., was engaged in the layout design and furnishing of offices—primarily for business, government, and institutions, such as schools and hospitals. The company had a large staff of designers, architects, decorators, and such, whose services were available on a contract or consulting basis. The company also manufactured certain lines of office furniture and equipment—primarily filing cabinets and other stamped metal items. These were sold directly to institutional clients and through a number of retail shops that the company operated in major Dutch cities. These shops sold a complete line of office supplies. In addition to the Dutch operations, the company had sales offices and design staffs in West Germany, Belgium, Switzerland, and the United Kingdom. In 1973, total company sales were about Dfl. 285,000,000 and profits were Dfl. 9,700,000. (For comparative purposes, these were equal, in January 1975, to about U.S. $112 million and U.S. $3.5 million, respectively.)

Contract sales and design work accounted for about 50% of sales, manufacturing for about 35%, and retail shops for about 15%. In terms of employees, between 45% and 50% were employed in manufacturing operations. The company had some 3,400 employees working in sixty separate operating units. Overall, about 60% of the employees were in managerial, professional, or clerical positions, with the remainder being production and maintenance workers. About 50% of the total work force was unionized. For management purposes, the sixty operating units were grouped into ten divisions, such as retail stores and commercial contract sales. The Amersfoort division which manufactured filing cabinets and similar items was one of the ten divisions. It employed about 650 people and accounted for about one-half of the company's manufacturing turnover.

## General Approach to the Council

The underlying issues that concerned Mr. van Berkel were centered around a conflict between his views of the roles of business and of management on the one hand, and the purpose of a workers' council on the other. The Dutch government had first passed a law calling for worker participation in management in 1956, but that law was permissive rather than mandatory, and under it, very few workers' councils were established. In 1971, the government enacted a new law that made such workers' councils mandatory in all concerns employing at least one hundred people. The law stated that the workers' councils were to be established "in the interest of the correct functioning of the enterprise in all its objectives, and in behalf of the consultation with, and representation of the persons employed in the enterprise." During the debate over the law, there was a good deal of conflict over whether the councils should function as pressure groups for workers or as broadly based supervisory boards. The ambiguous language of the law made it clear that the conflict over purpose was not resolved. In effect, companies and their councils were left with the task of setting their own direction, and in his opening remarks to the central workers' councils, Mr. van Berkel addressed this problem directly:

> I regret that I cannot give you a watertight formula for the task of the Council. The law under which we have been established, describes a two-fold function. On the one hand, we must contribute to the successful functioning of Hobbema & van Rijn. On the other hand, the Council is charged with being the representative of the workers in Hobbema & van Rijn. From our preliminary discussions, I have the distinct impression that for you, the second function weighs much more heavily than the first, and in the circumstances I regard this as extremely desirable for Hobbema & van Rijn. Nevertheless, I must ask for your understanding that as your chairman and as a member of the management of Hobbema & van Rijn, I see my task as one of maintaining equity among all groups—employees, investors, management, customers, suppliers, Dutch society—that are essential to the successful functioning of Hobbema & van Rijn. It is clear that an area of tension exists, but that will merely give a greater challenge to us in our discussion.

The basic idea of a workers' council did not entirely fit this view of the enterprise. While it did give workers a status within the company more or less equal to that of investors, it also gave them a rather special status as compared with the other groups. On the other hand, Dirk van Berkel and his colleagues in top management had entirely rejected the traditional view that workers were simply suppliers of labor, believing, as he put in his opening remarks to the council, "that employees are joint players of leading roles in the game called enterprise." These somewhat conflicting views could lead Dirk van Berkel to attempt to minimize the role of the council, or to attempt to make it into an important force in the company. Based on his experience with the council since January, he felt that he could have considerable influence over the direction the council took.

Beyond these basic questions of approach and attitude, Mr. van Berkel faced an important tactical question. The Amersfoort division had been losing money for some time, and a potential buyer for it had been found. If the sale were neogitated, the law required that the matter be referred to the workers' council for its advice to managment. The council could not veto such a sale, but could have a good deal of influence over workers' response to it. Two members of the council were employees of the Amersfoort division (see exhibit 6a-1). Since the possible sale had thus far been discussed only by a few members of top management, there was a distinct possibility that supervisors in the division would learn of the impending sale from subordinates. On the other hand, Mr. van Berkel realized that if the matter were carefully handled, the two employees could be very helpful in disarming opposition to the sale in the division. It was also possible, of course, that the two members would attempt to forestall or sabotage the sale. Mr. van Berkel recalled the recent instance where workers in AKZO, the large Dutch chemical combine, had effectively blocked the closing of a plant even though the union involved had initially agreed to the closing.

**Makeup of the Council**

The central workers' council at Hobbema & van Rijn consisted of Mr. van Berkel who was its chairman by law and nineteen members elected by employees. (Everyone except the three members of the management board was considered to be an employee.) The number of members was specified by law and was based on the number of employees in the company, though councils were never larger than twenty-five. Members of the central workers' council were elected by local councils from among their own members. (The law required that every division or branch of a company with more than one hundred employees must have its own workers' council, though if there were several divisions in the same community, they could have a single joint council. There were twelve local councils in Hobbema & van Rijn which were somewhat smaller than the central workers' council, ranging in size from five to eleven members. For the most part, their devel-

**Exhibit 6a-1**
**Members of the Central Workers' Council**

| Member | Position | Salary Index | Age | Joined Company |
|--------|----------|-------------|-----|---------------|
| J.F.B. | Machine operator | 100 | 42 | 1965 |
| P.J.E. | Draftsman | 140 | 42 | 1956 |
| P.L.B. | Manager, accounting department | 400 | 53 | 1948 |
| J.S. | Draftsman | 140 | 44 | 1945 |
| G.B. | Sales clerk | 175 | 41 | 1955 |
| M.A.R.[a] | Designer | 300 | 35 | 1972 |
| M.S. | Foreman | 150 | 52 | 1960 |
| K.J.S.[b,c] | Blueprint maker | 175 | 39 | 1966 |
| W.J.C.[c] | Maintenance manager | 200 | 47 | 1953 |
| H.J. | Designer | 200 | 34 | 1963 |
| M.A.M.[a] | Chief acountant | 300 | 37 | 1957 |
| P.J.W.C. | Architect | 300 | 34 | 1971 |
| H.J.K.S. | Order clerk | 175 | 61 | 1967 |
| D.P.S. | Accountant | 200 | 44 | 1972 |
| G.V.O. | Decorator | 200 | 35 | 1964 |
| M.H. | Assistant decorator | 175 | 39 | 1971 |
| L.A.B. | Chief accountant | 250 | 57 | 1946 |
| M.P. | Foreman | 150 | 31 | 1969 |
| G.M.V. | Clerk | 175 | 25 | 1972 |

[a]Female
[b]Secretary of council
[c]Members from Amersfoort division

opment had followed the pattern of the central workers' council described in this case, though as might be expected, they tended to concentrate on local matters.) Representation on the central council reflected the relative size of the divisions. All persons who had been employees for at least one year were eligible to vote in the election of local council members. Unions with members in a company or division had the right to nominate candidates, and candidates could also be nominated by at least thirty non-union employees. Council members, who had to have been employees for at least three years, were elected for three-year terms and were eligible for reelection. Exhibit 6a-1 shows the members of the Hobbema & van Rijn central workers' council, where they worked, and their relative status in the company.

The law required that the manager of the company or his representative be the chairman of the council, a stipulation that had continued to be a matter of controversy. The Socialist unions were advocating a shift to an elected chairman not from management, while the Christian unions were advocating that the councils be changed into something like the German supervisory boards with an outside or neutral chairman.

## Council Procedures

The law required that each workers' council meet at least six times a year, and that council members be furnished with annual and semi-annual financial reports. Hobbema & van Rijn actually planned to have seven or eight meetings a year, and Mr. van Berkel gave council members quarterly financial reports for each division within the company. The company annual budget was also discussed with the council though the law did not require it. The workers' council had a secretary elected from among its members, and a four-member agenda committee of which Mr. van Berkel was chairman. The agenda committee met at least once before each council meeting. In addition, the elected members (everyone except the chairman) met together at least once before each formal meeting. Council meetings generally took about one-half day. Mr. van Berkel estimated that each meeting required about two days of his time, a good deal of which was involved in preparation, since he felt it necessary to try to be prepared to deal with any issues that might come up. Council members were reimbursed for any expenses in travelling to and from meetings. They received their regular pay while attending meetings, but were not compensated for any overtime involved. Mr. van Berkel said complaints had been received from the supervisor of the council secretary to the effect that the secretary's work took so much time that he was no longer able to do his regular job properly.

## Information

Early operation of the workers' council had raised several issues in connection with information. Under the law, all information given to the council was supposed to be confidential unless it was agreed to disseminate it. Mr. van Berkel stated that thus far there had been no unauthorized leaks of company information, though he added that most of the information given to the council was no longer "hot."

A somewhat more difficult issue had to do with the relationship between the workers' council and the regular formal channels of communication within the company. Mr. van Berkel observed that since he seriously tried to involve the council in company decisions, it was virtually impossible in the give-and-take of discussion for him to avoid referring to facts and opinions that had not been made public in the company. This meant that council members might be in possession of information not yet known by their superiors, a possibility not without serious consequences for established relationships within the company. This problem had been part of Mr. van Berkel's concern about the upcoming discussion in the council of the possible sale of the Amersfoort division.

Finally, there was a problem of communication between the workers' councils and the rest of the employees they represented. An agenda for each council meeting was posted on all official notice boards throughout the company, and official summaries of each meeting were similarly made available. At Mr. van Berkel's urging, council members from two of the operating companies arranged plant meetings in their units to discuss the agenda of the council. Attendance at these meetings, however, was very small.


## Relationship between Council and Unions

The law that mandated the creation of workers' councils made special provisions for unions in the election of members and, in effect, protected any prior rights of unions under collective bargaining agreements. At the same time, the councils were given very extensive powers under the law and a potential for conflict between councils and unions was present. As a general rule, Dutch unions had not been enthusiastic supporters of the establishment of workers' councils. They felt that if the councils developed into effectively functioning bodies under management chairmanship, their influence with workers would be undermined. They were further concerned about the possibilities of open conflict between two groups representing workers. Mr. van Berkel described one instance where just such a conflict had developed.

Early in 1974, Hobbema & van Rijn decided to discontinue one of its minor product lines, a move that would eliminate the jobs of about seventy-five employees. About thirty-five of these could be given comparable jobs elsewhere in the company, but the remainder would have to be let go. Hobbema & van Rijn prepared a "social plan" required by union agreements in such cases, which provided that if these latter employees had to take jobs at lower pay, Hobbema & van Rijn would make up the difference on a sliding scale ranging from six months for workers under 29 years old to five years for workers over 60. The unions involved had agreed to this social plan, but just before the discontinuance was to take place, the elected members asked to have the matter put on the agenda of the central workers' council. The plant manager who negotiated the agreement with the union was entirely opposed to discussion by the central workers' council on the grounds that the agreement might be upset. Council members felt equally strongly that this was precisely the sort of question with which the council should deal. In legal terms, discussion with the local workers' council was required, but it was not at all clear that this issue had to be brought before the central workers' council, and Mr. van Berkel was rather sure that it did not. However, because he felt that the council should develop as a collaborative and significant part of the organization, he decided to accept the question as an agenda item, but only for purposes of "advice" to management and not for "consent" by the council. Council members agreed to this format, and, after discussion, accepted the decision already negotiated. However, the council did insist on publication of a special report on its deliberations and conclusion. Mr. van Berkel felt that this was a reflection of the council members' desire to establish some visibility and importance vis-à-vis the unions and the local council.


## Council Business

After several meetings of the workers' council in 1974, it had not become clear with what kinds of issues the council would concern itself. In his role as chairman, and given his knowledge of company affairs, Mr. van Berkel really controlled the agenda and observed, late in 1974, that he had been more concerned with getting things on the agenda than with keeping things off. (A summary of the agenda of the first few meetings of the Hobbema & van Rijn workers' council is included as exhibit 6a-2.) On the whole, Mr. van Berkel felt that the workers' council did not really get at important issues, but tended to focus on trivial things or on matters that came up accidentally, and to do so without much systematic analysis. For example, the first issue that the council wanted to discuss was payment for members of the board of directors. (Annual compensation of Hobbema & van Rijn board members amounted to about Dfl. 20,000. Total operating expenses were Dfl. 263,000,000.) On another occasion, council members questioned the policy governing use of company cars. This had been recently studied by management but the council insisted on studying it for themselves anyway, assigning the task to one member. That member eventually reported that there was no really good policy so that the present company policy, developed by management, should be left undisturbed.

One of the statutory rights of the Dutch workers' council is approval of appointments to the company's board of directors. Under Dutch law, shareholders of public companies do not elect board members. In effect, board members appoint their own successors, though shareholders do have the right to appeal appointments through the courts. If appointments are made without approval of the workers' council, the latter also has the right of appeal to the courts. Dutch law also requires that directors of public companies must retire at age 72. Just prior to the first meeting of the Hobbema & van Rijn workers' council the board chairman reached that age. On behalf of the board, Mr. van Berkel proposed as new chairman a former university professor who was widely regarded as a very able man, but who had been an active member of one of the right-wing political parties. This, not surprisingly, made his candidacy very unpalatable to the workers' council. Because of the recognized ability of the nominee, Mr. van Berkel was

**Exhibit 6a-2**
**Agenda of Workers' Council Meetings**

| Topic | Initiated by | Disposition |
|---|---|---|
| *First meeting* | | |
| 1.  Appointment of secretary | Routine | Done |
| 2.  Preparation of by-laws (largely by statute) | Routine | Done |
| 3.  Communication between council and rest of organization | Van Berkel | Not resolved, but see text of case for steps taken |
| 4.  Appointment of board chairman | Statute | See text of case |
| 5.  Payment of travel expenses and overtime for council meetings | Council member | See text of case |
| 6.  Training for council members | Van Berkel | Not resolved |
| *Second meeting* | | |
| 1.  Training for council members | Van Berkel | Not resolved |
| 2.  Introduction of Hay system for management compensation | Van Berkel | Information only |
| 3.  Request for employee discount on purchases from company | Council member | Referred to local councils |
| 4.  Elect agenda committee | Statute | Done |
| 5.  Make up of board of directors | Van Berkel | Paper presented primarily for information |
| 6.  Policy for use of company cars | Council member | See text of case |
| *Third meeting* | | |
| 1.  Retroactivity of extra pay for statutory holidays | Council member | Extra pay had been agreed to by company but held up by temporary government wage freeze. Company agreed to retroactivity when freeze lifted. |
| 2.  Group insurance for private cars of employees | Council member | Investigation showed that there was no benefit, but council made report to all company, showing its initiative. |
| 3.  Announce takeover of a small retail store | Van Berkel | Council members wanted to consider such issues before decision, but agreed that it would be too difficult in light of negotiations involved. |
| 4.  Presentation of annual report and budget | Statute | Two weeks before publication. New board chairman present for discussion at request of council. |
| *Fourth meeting* | | |
| 1.  Report from council member present by invitation at shareholders' meeting | Council member | Information only |
| 2.  Pension fund direction | Council member | Law requires pension fund directors to be 3 from management and 3 from employees participating in fund. Law also gives "responsibility" for pension matters to council. Conflict resolved by having council member be one of participant directors. |
| 3.  Product line discontinuance | Council member | See text |

anxious to have him appointed, and so he proposed a compromise to the council. He pointed out to them that because of the mandatory retirement age, several other board seats would soon become vacant. He proposed that the next board vacancy would be filled by a nominee of the workers' council with the provision that the appointee would function as a regular board member and not as a designated representative of the workers. The workers' council quite readily accepted Mr. van Berkel's proposal and the issue was resolved. However, Dirk van Berkel realized as a result of the discussions that his colleagues on the council had very little idea of the functions of a director nor any idea of whom to select—even though the law permitted them to do so.

Mr. van Berkel felt that this general failure to probe into more significant issues reflected a lack of sophistication and experience on the part of most council members. All of the council members had gone through one of the three-day training programs sponsored by the Dutch unions. These programs involved instruction in such things as financial statements, organization structure, company law, and so on, and devoted about an equal amount of time to the techniques of participating in and conducting meetings. The training programs were put on for the members of specific councils and there was a good deal of emphasis on group dynamics and team building. Because the manager chairman of each council was also a member, the union programs had agreed to include him for the last evening and final day of the program.

**Future Possibilities**

After four meetings of the workers' council of Hobbema & van Rijn, Dirk van Berkel felt that the institution had been introduced into the company without major difficulty, and that its impact had thus far been quite limited. From the point of view of management, it meant that greater care had to be exercised in making decisions and publishing them, and Mr. van Berkel felt that the upcoming discussion of the proposed sale of the Amersfoort division would put that care to the test. It did not appear to Mr. van Berkel that the council had as yet contributed much to the quality of decision making in Hobbema & van Rijn, though he felt that this might be the case as members became more knowledgeable and experienced.

Mr. van Berkel's concerns about the workers' council encompassed three different time dimensions. In the immediate short run was the discussion of the potentially touchy issue of the sale of the Amersfoort division. The outcome of this could have an influence on the somewhat longer-run question of whether to try to minimize the role of the council or to try to make it into a positive and important force in the company. In the still longer run, Mr. van Berkel felt that the powers of the council would increase—partly because of the greater strength resulting from experience, but mostly because the

Dutch government was actively pushing to expand those powers. He foresaw that the distance between members of the council and their constituents would increase and that the council would become increasingly like a parliament. He felt this tendency would be an inevitable result of increasing council activity. As noted previously the supervisor of one council member had already complained about time away from the job, and Mr. van Berkel felt that eventually council membership would be a full-time job. The inevitable result of this, van Berkel felt, would be to make the council increasingly political and that the ambiguity of purpose contained in the law would willy-nilly be resolved in favor of political bargaining as opposed to collaboration. Mr. van Berkel was anxious that his dealing with the council in the near future would not accelerate this trend.

# Hobbema & van Rijn, N.V. (B-1)

On the afternoon of November 14, 1974, Dirk van Berkel, chairman of the management board of Hobbema & van Rijn, N.V., was reviewing his preparation for a meeting of the central workers' council of the company which was to take place the next morning. The meeting had two items of business: an interview with a nominee for the company's board of directors, and consideration of the proposed sale of the Amersfoort division to another company. The latter question would be the first item discussed, and Mr. van Berkel anticipated a good deal of controversy over it. As required by agreement, the unions had been informed on November 7, of the company's intention to sell the division.

The Amersfoort division of Hobbema & van Rijn had been acquired by a previous management several years prior to 1974, and had operated at a loss since then. The division, which manufactured filing cabinets and other stamped metal items, had considerable excess capacity, a situation that was made worse in 1974 by the decision to discontinue a line of metal desk-top items that the plant had manufactured. It was apparent to both management and workers that continuation of the operation would require a significant reduction in the size of the work force. In these circumstances, the management of Hobbema & van Rijn was delighted to be approached with an offer to buy the Amersfoort division. The offer came from a relatively large company that manufactured a wide range of stamped metal cabinets and housings for such things as machinery and furnaces. The potential buyer operated throughout the EEC. The offer was at a price attractive to Hobbema & van Rijn, and while it did not include any guarantees that jobs would not be eliminated, the buyer did believe that because of his much broader market, he could utilize the facilities more effectively than could Hobbema & van Rijn, thus minimizing the number of necessary layoffs. The buyer also agreed to maintain the same employment conditions for those employees who were kept on.

As soon as the buyer and Hobbema & van Rijn reached general agreement on the terms of the takeover, management reported that fact to the unions in the Amersfoort plant as was required by labor agreements. This was done on November 7, and at the same time management, with the agreement of the unions, called a special meeting for November 8, of the central workers' council of Hobbema & van Rijn. Under the law, a matter such as this had to be brought before the workers' council for its "advice," though the council did not have the legal right to veto the sale. There was, however, some difficulty over the questions of jurisdiction. Since the sale of such a major division would affect the entire company, the law gave jurisdiction to the central workers' council. However, the workers' council of the Amersfoort division argued that since they were the ones who would be sold, they should be able to advise management. The central workers' council asserted that the function of the local council was to provide information and judgments, and that this could be done through the two members of the central workers' council who were representatives of the Amersfoort workers' council. Management attempted to resolve this issue by agreeing to accept advice from both councils, and the Amersfoort council countered this with a proposal that, on this matter, the two councils meet jointly. The Amersfoort council feared that if they gave negative advice while the central workers' council gave positive advice, management could go ahead with the sale and could state that it did so with worker approval. Because it wanted to preserve its position in such an eventuality, the central workers' council rejected the proposal for joint meetings, and since the law supported its position, joint meetings were not held. Management's commitment to accept advice from both councils remained in effect.

Dirk van Berkel was a chairman of the central workers' council and was the member of management most directly involved in the sale. However, he had no official relationship with the Amersfoort workers' council whose chairman was Jan Sonneveldt, manager of the Amersfoort division. Mr. Sonneveldt reported to, but was not a part of, top manageme of Hobbema & van Rijn.

At the meeting on November 8, the central workers' council heard Dirk van Berkel outline the plans for the sale, and describe management's reasons for believing that it was good for the company as a whole. While most council members seemed initially to understand management's position, Mr. van Berkel felt that the open and strident hostility of the two members from Amersfoort tended to diminish the support of the other members for the sale, and the council decided to exercise its right to present formal questions to management about the latter's views on the sale. These questions were drafted. The elected members of the workers' councils had the legal right to meet separately in order to draw up these questions, but they specifically asked Mr. van Berkel to assist them. He, of course, was put into the somewhat unique position of helping to frame questions that he would have to answer.

The first of these questions to be presented to management concerned finances. The workers asked about the general financial position of the new owner, about how he would finance the purchase and what would be his likely financial position after the takeover. The second question concerned the commercial future of Amersfoort under the new management. The workers' council wanted to know how the buyer saw the future of his business in Europe and specifically how the Amersfoort division would share in it. Finally, the workers' council asked about social policy—specifically about working conditions, pension rights, and promotion and retention policies.

Mr. van Berkel had the controller of the company and the prospective buyer prepare the details of the answers to these questions. In response to a question from the controller, Mr. van Berkel suggested that he approach the financial question from a more or less neutral stand, that he take neither the role of the buyer nor of the seller. In its own prior thinking, of course, Hobbema & van Rijn management had thought only as sellers—sellers who were anxious to get rid of a poorly performing division. The data that had been prepared for Mr. van Berkel did not, he felt, provide a basis for very reassuring answers to the members of the workers' council. For one thing, it was not at all clear from the financial statements that the buyer did have the financial resources necessary to purchase and integrate the Amersfoort division into his own company. Further, Mr. van Berkel felt that the information on commercial prospects provided by the purchaser was obviously optimistic as well as extremely offhand and superficial. It indicated, he felt, that the management of the buyer did not take the ability of the workers' council very seriously. While Mr. van Berkel wished that the answers to the questions posed by the central workers' council offered more convincing support for management's position, he retained his conviction that most members of the central workers' council did accept the validity of the argument that Hobbema & van Rijn would be better off without the ailing division. It was with these somewhat conflicting thoughts that he contemplated his strategy for the meeting next morning.

# Hobbema & van Rijn, N.V. (B-2)

On the morning of November 15, 1975, Dirk van Berkel convened a formal meeting of the central workers' council of Hobbema & van Rijn, N.V. The first item to be discussed by the council was management's proposal to sell the Amersfoort division and specifically to discuss management's answers to several questions about possible impact of the sale on Amersfoort employees which the council had submitted some days earlier.

As management's answers were reviewed, it appeared to Mr. van Berkel that the central workers' council (with the exception of the two members form the Amesfoort division) generally accepted management's conclusion that Hobbema & van Rijn would be strengthened by divestiture of the Amersfoort division. The two members from the Amersfoort division indicated opposition because they had not been convinced by management's analysis of the financial strength of the purchaser, nor about how the Amersfoort division would fit into and fare within the purchaser's European operations. They feared that the profitable parts of the operation might be transferred elsewhere and the balance eventually shut down.

As the discussion went on, the opposition of the Amersfoort group became more open and more strident, and Dirk van Berkel felt that the initial support for the sale was slipping away and that the members of the central workers' council were moving toward a negative position based on support of fellow workers. He concluded that if the meeting took a formal vote, it would result in the central workers' council advising management against the sale.

However, before a vote could be proposed, the discussion had to be adjourned so that the central workers' council could interview the candidate for the board of directors. The Amersfoort representatives announced that their council was going to prepare its own advice to management. (Though not required by law to do so, management had agreed to receive that advice.) The central workers' council then agreed to postpone further discussion of the proposed sale until the Amersfoort workers' council had prepared its advice. It seemed likely that this would take several weeks.

# Hobbema & van Rijn, N.V. (B-3)

On December 2, 1974, the Amersfoort Workers' council presented its advice to management in the form of a sixty-five page printed and bound report. (The report was sent to the board of directors, the management board, the central workers' council, and to the Minister of Social Welfare in the Dutch cabinet.) The elected members of the council had exercised their legal right to meet without the chairman, Jan Sonneveldt, being present, and as a result, no one in management really knew what to expect from the report. Mr. Sonneveldt's position was extremely difficult. He was not a part of and could not speak for top management. Furthermore, he would continue as plant manager if the sale were made, and hence did not wish to alienate his fellow workers. As a result, the elected council members felt that they were neither getting a hearing with those who counted nor getting very convincing answers to their questions.

The report was a rather thorough-going condemnation of the proposed sale and of the management of Hobbema & van Rijn. It reviewed the uncertainties about the purchaser's financial strength and about his market prospects, and pointed out that these uncertainties had not been diminished by the discussions that council members had had with the management board of the purchasing company. In short, the report constituted a negative advice to management, though at one point it did suggest that the workers might look somewhat more favorably on a partial sale which would leave Hobbema & van Rijn with a 49% interest in the division.

The central workers' council scheduled a meeting for December 10 to discuss its own position in light of the advice from the Amersfoort workers' council. The hostile tone of the Amersfoort report influenced the central workers' council which demanded that the meeting not be held in the usual meeting place in company headquarters, but on "neutral" ground. Thus, the meeting was held at the Holiday Inn in Leiden, and at the time of the meeting, all of the members of the Amersfoort workers' council were present and demanding to be heard. The central workers' council refused to admit their colleagues from Amersfoort, either as participants or as observers, arguing that the two Amersfoort members could adequately present the point of view of the others. The latter remained in the motel throughout the meeting.

The meeting went on for several hours, and especially as a result of the aggressiveness of the two Amersfoort members, backed up by the aggressive tone of their report, the meeting moved steadily away from support of management's position. A draft of an advice to management which was essentially negative in tone was slowly put together, but since the meeting had been going on for several hours, it was decided to adjourn temporarily. The meeting was officially adjourned until the next afternoon, this time to be held in the usual meeting place in company headquarters, but to be held without the chairman, Dirk van Berkel.

As he left the meeting, Dirk van Berkel sensed that things were going rather badly. He felt quite certain that without some new inputs, the adjourned meeting would produce a negative advice, and that in that event, the sale would collapse. The buyer would withdraw, and even if he did not, the unions that had initially accepted the sale would now oppose it. Mr. van Berkel realized that he really had to deal with both councils, and wondered if the partial sale referred to in the report of the Amersfoort council provided a basis for negotiating with that group. In the case of the central workers' council, he wondered if the members were not operating on the assumption that management would go through with the sale whatever advice they gave, and thus felt that they could show support for fellow workers without losing anything. These thoughts ran through Dirk van Berkel's mind as he headed for what promised to be a long evening of discussion with his colleagues on the management board.

# Hobbema & van Rijn, N.V. (B-4)

During the evening on December 10, Dirk van Berkel and his colleagues on the management board took stock of the situation and reached several decisions. To counteract the possibility that the central workers' council was reaching a decision without any feeling of responsibility for the outcome, it was agreed that before the meeting of the elected members scheduled for the next afternoon, van Berkel would inform them that management would regard negative advice from the council as a veto.

The management board also considered the idea that many of the difficulties had occurred because van Berkel had never had any face-to-face contact with the Amersfoort workers' council. He and his colleagues agreed that he should meet with them as soon as possible. This was arranged by having Jan Sonneveldt suggest to his council that they discuss the situation with van Berkel. Members of the council accepted this suggestion and a meeting was arranged for the morning of December 11 in Amersfoort.

Finally, the management board agreed that in the meeting with the Amersfoort council, van Berkel should attempt to explore the possibility of a compromise built on a partial sale. It was agreed that a retention of a 49% interest was out of the question, and that a 20% interest was most suitable. However, Dirk van Berkel was authorized to accept a deal based on Hobbema & van Rijn retaining, for a relatively short period of years, a 40% interest in the division. It was understood, of course, that if such a compromise were reached, it would have to be approved by the board of directors.

# Hobbema & van Rijn, N.V. (B-5)

Dirk van Berkel met with the Amersfoort workers' council on the morning of December 11, and was immediately met with an ultimatum that the workers would go on strike if the sale of the division were approved. After this initial hostile outburst, van Berkel referred to the suggestion of a partial sale which had been included in the council's report to management. He explained that the 51% sale proposed in the report would not interest management because the result would really be a joint venture rather than a sale. However, he did indicate that Hobbema & van Rijn would consider retaining a smaller participation, and after some discussion back and forth, a 60% sale with the remaining 40% to be sold in equal annual installments over five years beginning in 1977 was proposed by van Berkel.

The Amersfoort council countered this with qualifications that the sale of the additional 8% in any year could be made only if the Amersfoort division (not the whole of the purchasing company) had operated at a profit, and that Hobbema & van Rijn could sell to a third party only after five years and only if the purchaser had not used his option. Finally, the Amersfoort council insisted that the new company agree to maintain labor conditions on the same basis as those held under Hobbema & van Rijn.

A written statement was prepared in which Mr. van Berkel agreed to try to get approval from the board of directors for this arrangement, and if the board approved, the council agreed to give a positive advice to management. The meeting ended with the signing of this agreement about half an hour after it began.

Because the Amersfoort members of the central workers' council were unable to reach company headquarters in time for the afternoon meeting of that group, it was postponed until the morning of December 12. However, during the afternoon of December 11, Mr. van Berkel met informally with the other members and told them that their negative advice would be considered as a veto.

On the morning of December 12, the central workers' council met to decide on its advice to management. At the beginning of the meeting, they were informed by Mr. van Berkel about the 60-40 compromise plan. The council had previously arranged to have expert opinion from the manager and controller of the Amersfoort division and from the controller of Hobbema & van Rijn. These men were questioned both about the sale in general and about the 60-40 arrangement. After due deliberation, the council voted to give management advice approving the sale on the 60-40 basis.

# Hobbema & van Rijn, N.V. (C)

Dirk van Berkel did not have an entirely easy time selling the compromise to his board of directors. Opposition came especially from the chairman (see Hobbema & van Rijn [A]) and from one other member. Two objections were raised. The first was that Hobbema & van Rijn was somewhat at the mercy of the purchaser who could shift all of his unprofitable business to the Amersfoort plant. The second was that for accounting purposes, the 40% interest should really be written down to a very nominal value, an action that would wipe out a substantial proportion of 1974 reported profits. However, after considerable discussion, the board approved the terms of the sale.

In reviewing the development of the Amersfoort situation, van Berkel felt that, on balance, the result was beneficial for all concerned, and better than it would have been if management had handled it alone. He believed that the results provided better protection for the Amersfoort personnel. Within Hobbema & van Rijn, he believed that employees' morale was fostered because employees felt that they had not been manipulated; that they had fought for a voice in decision making and had an impact on a decision that directly affected them. He agreed that in a purely financial sense, Hobbema & van Rijn would probably have been better off with a straight unencumbered sale, but that this was more than offset by the other factors.

He also felt that the affair had left some scars that probably could have been avoided. He asserted that he should have intervened personally with the Amersfoort council before feelings had become so aroused. He did observe that his slowness in intervening was partly attributable to a deficiency in the law governing workers' councils. Some of the difficulty might have been avoided if there were legal provisions for combining the two councils in such cases. This would have kept him in touch with the local council, and possibly have diminished the rivalry between the two councils.

# Case 7
# Europa Food
# Industries B.V.

## Introduction

On June 6, 1975, Peter Staaterman, general manager of the marketing division for Europa Food Industries B.V. (EFI), was preparing to implement a major reorganization of his company's marketing staff in both Belgium and the Netherlands. The reorganization called for a 17% reduction in the division's manpower, from 228 to 190 employees by September 1, 1975. Two days earlier, on June 4, Staaterman had met with Derk van Rijn, employee relations manager of EFI's Dutch operations, and Hendrick Vermeer, EFI's general counsel. Both van Rijn and Vermeer had urged Staaterman to reconsider the implementation plan, arguing that in their opinion it was contrary to the company's expressed policies and would result in a deterioration of relations with the works council and the employees. In view of their criticisms, Staaterman was reviewing the plan.

## The Company

Europa Food Industries B.V. was a subsidiary of the American Food Products Corporation of New York. American Foods had established itself in the European market shortly after the end of World War II. Initially, its efforts were focused on markets for corn oil, corn meal, and other corn products. In the late 1950s, it had expanded its U.S. product line by acquiring small one-product companies. In the early 1960s, it had begun to follow a similar strategy in Europe. EFI was one of its first acquisitions in Europe.

Prior to the acquisition, EFI had been in the business of manufacturing and marketing detergents and cleaners. At the time of the acquisition in 1962, EFI was selling one brand of laundry detergent and two types of household cleaners to retail stores in the Netherlands. Industrial strength cleaners were sold by the EFI marketing group both to Dutch and Belgian industrial customers. The company also sold some of its products in bulk through distributors in other European countries.

In the first three to four years following the acquisition, American Foods did little to change the traditional patterns of business at EFI. By 1966, however, American Foods had completed a series of acquisitions on the Continent and had begun the process of integrating the marketing and production operations of its European companies.

157

The EFI product line began to grow. The first major expansion was in the area of food products, followed several years later by additions to the industrial product line. By 1970, EFI was selling three basic types of products: food products (vegetable oils, corn and corn meal products, margarine), soaps, cleaners and detergents (for both industrial and retail markets), and special chemical products. Total sales in 1974 were DFL 877 million.

EFI continued to produce only cleaners and detergents. Other products were imported from other American Foods subsidiaries in the EEC and United States. The EFI plant near Utrecht had been expanded several times in the last ten years and was able to supply detergents and cleaning products to other American Foods subsidiaries throughout Europe.

Although production was done on a regional basis, marketing operations for all products were controlled on a country-to-country basis. The only exception to this was in the case of EFI where the Dutch subsidiary controlled the marketing of all products in the Netherlands, Belgium, and Luxembourg.

The EFI marketing organization was divided into two groups. The Dutch market was covered by the marketing group in Amsterdam, while the marketing for Belgium and Luxembourg was done by a similar group in Brussels. Both of these organizations reported to Staaterman, general manager of EFI's marketing division in Amsterdam.

In 1971, a major change occurred in the management of the regional headquarters in Brussels. American Foods' top management in New York had been disappointed by the growth in European sales and profits between 1967 and 1970. As a result, several top executives in the Brussels headquarters were replaced. A new vice-president for European marketing was transferred in from New York, and he very quickly began to reorganize the marketing operations of all the European companies.

At EFI, the marketing department was restructured around the concept of product managers, and the sales force was expanded. The marketing department was then upgraded to become the marketing division and a general manager for the division was brought in from the United States. The concept behind the reorganization and expansion was that with a better organized, more efficiently run marketing group, EFI sales would grow rapidly. In 1971, the division was consciously overstaffed so that people in the division would be fully prepared to handle the expected growth in sales.

## Industrial Relations at EFI

EFI employed approximately 750 people; of these about 450 worked at the plant near Utrecht, and the remainder were split between the head office in Amsterdam and the marketing office in Brussels.

## Union Relations

Roughly 50% of the plant workers were unionized. These employees belonged to one of three industrial unions, each of which was a member of one of three large Dutch labor federations. Employees at the head office and Brussels office were not unionized, although there had recently been a move by some of EFI's Dutch managers to form a quasi-union group, the Organization of Higher Personnel (VHP).

Each year the company negotiated a contract with the three chemical workers' unions. Although all three unions were present for the negotiations, they all spoke through a single negotiator, and the contract that resulted from these negotiations was signed by all three unions. The company had willingly accepted the pattern established by the unions in negotiation with the food industry employers' association. Negotiations had been friendly and constructive. The company had never had a strike or even a threat of a strike.

## Employee Relations

The relationship between the company and its employees had always been good. However, in recent years management had become somewhat alarmed by the rising militancy of a small group of the young workers at the Utrecht plant. This group had organized itself within the plant and claimed to be the voice of all unionized employees. They published a newsletter in which they made demands on the company and argued the righteousness of their cause. Management's outward reaction to the group was one of indifference. As long as the members of the group did their jobs and did not prevent others from doing theirs, management thought they should be free to express themselves in any way they might wish. Management was concerned, however, that over the last few years this group had been able to gain control over the blue-collar seats on the plant works council. This success had given the group a more legitimate avenue for pressuring the company to give in to their demands.

Relations with the non-union employees in the Amsterdam head office had also undergone a slight change in recent years. Many of EFI's middle managers and other salaried individuals had become disgruntled over the narrowing differences between the annual incomes of blue- and white-collar employees. The wage increase guidelines handed down by the government over the years had tended to favor blue-collar workers and employees at the lower end of the salary scale. The result had been a gradual "pancaking" of the overall salary scale. To protest the pancaking of the wage scales and to more effectively represent their views to the company and the government, a number of managers and professional employees had formed a VHP at EFI.

*The EFI Works Council*

Under a 1971 law, a Dutch company with one hundred or more employees was required to have a works council. Because EFI operated in the Netherlands from two locations, it had two councils. The Utrecht council had eleven members, the Amsterdam council had nine members. As allowed under the law, the general manager appointed the chairman of both councils. As EFI's chief executive was American he had decided to appoint high-ranking Dutch managers to these positions. The two councils could have demanded the creation also of a central works council but they had not done so.

The Utrecht council was the more active and militant of the two EFI works councils. This was partially because the militant union group mentioned earlier had been able to secure control of the blue-collar seats on the works council. The other reason for apparent differences between the two councils was that the VHP group at Utrecht controlled three of the five white-collar seats. On the other hand, at Amsterdam there was no union representing the head office employees and the VHP was not so active. (See exhibit 7-1 for a list of the members on both EFI works councils.)

When the works councils were formed in 1971, management had stated that it welcomed this avenue of communication with its employees, would keep the councils fully informed, and seek their advice on all matters that might affect the interests of the employees. The relationship had been good. On only one occasion did management find itself in serious conflict with one of the works councils. In 1973, the Utrecht council was dissatisfied with the information on salaries given to it and, when management refused to provide it with the rates paid to specific individuals, the council appealed to the industry committee. However, the industry committee, which was made up of half union and half management representatives, upheld the company's position and the works council did not carry the dispute further. Although preparation for and serving as chairman of the council meetings took a considerable amount of time and energy for the two company representatives, the company believed that in general, it was time and energy well spent.

*EFI Workers and the Supervisory Board*

The 1971 Dutch corporation law required that companies with one hundred or more employees and capital including resources of ten million guilders had to have a two-tier board system—a supervisory board and a management board. Dutch workers did not have the right to elect representatives to either of the boards but works councils did have the right to nominate candidates for the supervisory board and to veto any candidate.

**Exhibit 7-1**
**Membership of Works Councils at Europa Food Industries**

| Members | Male/Female | Age | Job Title | Years at EFI |
|---------|-------------|-----|-----------|--------------|
| Amsterdam | | | | |
| 1 | M | 45 | Accountant | 12 |
| 2 | M | 37 | Product manager | 8 |
| 3 | F | 33 | Secretary | 7 |
| 4 | M | 29 | Salesman | 4 |
| 5 | F | 45 | Secretary | 13 |
| 6 | M | 52 | Product group manager | 25 |
| 7 | M | 36 | Salesman | 10 |
| 8 | M | 41 | Marketing operations manager | 15 |
| 9 | F | 40 | Payroll administrator | 17 |
| Chairman | M | 39 | Employee relations manager | 9 |
| Utrecht | | | | |
| 1 | M | 27 | Process technician | 5 |
| 2 | M | 34 | Production line supervisor | 7 |
| 3 | M | 40 | Shop foreman | 12 |
| 4 | M | 52 | Production superintendent | 25 |
| 5 | F | 39 | Secretary | 15 |
| 6 | M | 29 | Quality control engineer | 5 |
| 7 | M | 33 | Production-line worker | 4 |
| 8 | M | 33 | Machine operator | 7 |
| 9 | M | 38 | Accountant | 18 |
| 10 | M | 41 | Personnel manager | 17 |
| 11 | M | 36 | Maintenance foreman | 6 |
| Chairman | M | 44 | Labor relations manager | 16 |

EFI had a six-man supervisory board. Three were Americans who were employed by the European headquarters of American Food Products. The three others were Dutch, one a businessman, one a lawyer, and one a local political officeholder who had formerly been a union leader. All of the board members in the past had been proposed by the management and in each case had been approved by the works council following interviews. Management was happy to have the former labor leader on the board. It believed that his presence gave the workers confidence that their interests would not be neglected.

**Reorganization of the Marketing Division**

When the financial results for fiscal year 1974 became available in early October 1974,[1] it was obvious that sales forecasts made in previous years were in error. In three of the last four years, EFI had failed to meet its sales growth targets.

In 1970 and 1971, the company had reorganized and expanded its marketing and sales staffs in anticipation of substantial growth in EFI's markets. But, by the end of fiscal year 1974, the market results indicated that management's decision to expand the marketing division had been ill-advised. The anticipated market growth had not materialized. Although sales were still growing, they were not growing at the rates previously forecasted. Profits were also signficiantly below anticipated levels.

American Foods regional headquarters had closely watched EFI sales and profit figures over the last eighteen months. Finally, in November, 1974, at the behest of corporate headquarters in New York, the president of the European region ordered EFI to initiate a cost-cutting program throughout the company. The directive also specified that EFI was to undertake a study with the aim of eliminating the redundancies that had developed in the marketing division. The EFI general manager, Alex Thompson, was told to reduce the number of personnel in the marketing division to 190 or below by the beginning of fiscal year 1976. These instructions were received by Thompson at the annual European operations review meeting held in Brussels in mid-November. Thompson recalled the event as follows:

> At the end of a very complete review of EFI fiscal year 1974 (FY 74) successes and failures, I was told by the Vice President for International Operations that our profit performance was unsatisfactory. In FY 74 EFI's pretax earnings on sales was just over 6%. I was told that by the end of FY 76 the ratio should be not less than 10%.
>
> The Vice President of European Operations then directed that we plan and execute during FY 75 a major cost reduction program. I was told that the sales to marketing expense ratio of our company was the lowest in Europe and that I was to "get the fat" out of the Marketing Division. Based on sales to marketing expense ratios of other American Foods subs in Europe, we should cut our Marketing force to below 190 people.
>
> I'd sat through these meetings before, but always on the other side of the table.[2] From where I was seated, it wasn't a very comfortable experience to say the least.
>
> Our plan for the overall cost cutting and the reorganization of the Marketing Division was to be presented to the regional office in February. Needless to say, upon my arrival back in Amsterdam it was the first thing on the agenda.

The plan for the reorganization and reduction of marketing personnel was developed in December and January. While the general cost reduction planning effort received wide publicity within the company, the reorganization of the marketing division was done in secret. Thompson involved only a very select group in this effort. "The Marketing Project" planning group consisted of the following people:

Mr. Thompson, EFI general manager

Mr. Staaterman, general manager—marketing divisions

Mr. van Osten, marketing manager—the Netherlands

Mr. duBois, marketing manager—Belgium and Luxembourg

Mr. van Rijn, employee relations manager—the Netherlands

Mr. Leclergue, employee relations manager—Belgium

Several other individuals assisted this group in the analysis and preparation of the plan. Among these were EFI's general counsel, the general counsel at the regional office in Brussels, and one manager from each of the marketing and employee relations departments in Amsterdam and Brussels. These twelve men and Thompson's secretary were the only people in EFI who knew of the project. Thompson's goal in keeping "The marketing Project" secret was to prevent a serious deterioration in the morale of the marketing division. It would not be until April or May that the individuals who would be released would be precisely identified. Rather than have everyone in the division worried about their job security, Thompson directed that the group's work be conducted in the strictest confidence.

The general plan for the personnel reduction was completed in early February and presented to the top management at the Brussels regional office. The plan was approved and forwarded to the international division in New York for final approval. In early March, Thompson received word that the plan had been approved by the vice president for international operations. He was instructed to proceed with the plan's implementation.

In the plan submitted for approval, the general restructuring of the marketing division was outlined with provision for the reduction in manpower as required. The division would go from a total of 228 employees to 190. In the new organization, the administrative personnel that had formerly worked in each of the product group areas was consolidated into two units and placed under the control of the marketing managers of Belgium and the Netherlands. The number of personnel in the new consolidated groups was roughly 25% smaller than the number employed under the old structure. The field sales force was cut back from 109 to 92, approximately 16%. Technical service personnel assigned to the product groups was reduced in number from 17 to 8, and the head office technical service group which was increased from 10 to 12 picked up the bulk of the responsibilities previously handled at the product group level. In all, the new reorganization called for the elimination of 38 jobs, 21 in Belgium and 17 in the Netherlands. Forty-three people were to be transferred within the organization. Exhibits 7-2 and 7-3 show the division's organizational structure and

**Exhibit 7-2**
**Marketing Division prior to Reorganization**

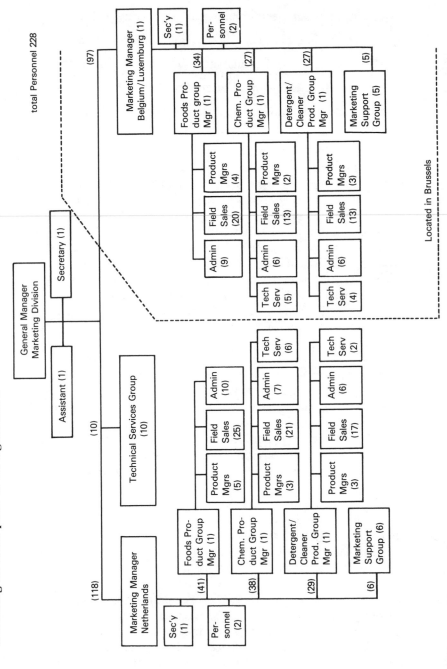

**Exhibit 7-3**
**Marketing Division after Reorganization**

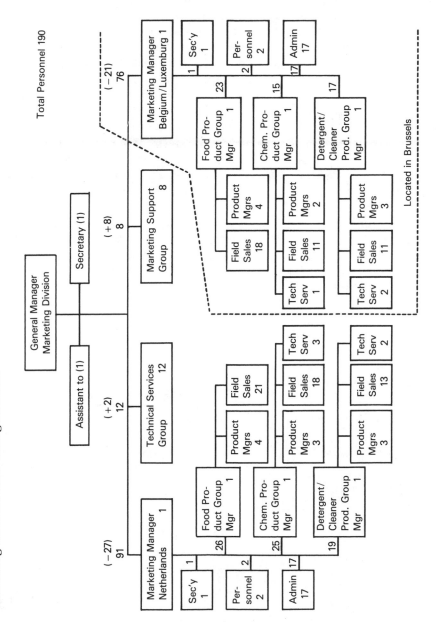

manning prior to and following the reorganization. Exhibits 7-4 and 7-5 show the number and types of positions eliminated and the transfers that resulted from the reorganization.

In the weeks following the approval of the plan, the planning group set about identifying those individuals who would be released or transferred. Great care was taken to review both the professional records and the personal situations of those selected for release. Where possible, the planning group attempted to designate certain individuals for early retirement rather than dismissal. The group also attempted to identify individuals who would have less difficulty finding other employment. The group made confidential approaches to other companies in the industry that were thought to be in a position to hire some of EFI's redundant personnel. A detailed "social plan" was developed which outlined the severance compensation arrangements to be made in each individual case.

While the labor law of both Belgium and the Netherlands made termination compensation mandatory, release of employees in Belgian law was fairly straightforward. Each employee released from the Brussels marketing office would receive a lump sum of two to three years base pay. Because the age profile of the people terminated from the Brussels operation was higher, the cost of the settlements would be much higher for the Belgian employees than it would be for those released from the Amsterdam office. The absolute cost of the severance pay for Dutch employees would be lower;

**Exhibit 7-4**
**Redundant Personnel**

| Personnel Divisions | Number of Redundancies in Approved Plan | Redundant Personnel Remaining As of 1 March | As of 1 May |
|---|---|---|---|
| Amsterdam | | | |
| Product managers | 1 | 1 | 0 |
| Field sales | 11 | 8 | 5 |
| Administration | 6 | 4 | 2 |
| Technical service | 2 | 1 | 1 |
| Marketing support | 1 | 0 | 0 |
| Total | 21 | 14 | 8 |
| Brussels | | | |
| Product managers | 0 | 0 | 0 |
| Field sales | 6 | 5 | 5 |
| Administration | 4 | 4 | 3 |
| Technical service | 5 | 5 | 5 |
| Marketing support | 2 | 2 | 2 |
| Total | 17 | 16 | 15 |
| Total Redundancies | 38 | 30 | 23 |

**Exhibit 7-5**
**Personnel Transfers**

| Personnel Divisions | From/To | Number of Transfers |
|---|---|---|
| Amsterdam | | |
| Administration | From product group administration To marketing department | 17 |
| Technical service | From product group To marke†ing division | 1 |
| Marketing support | From marketing department To marketing division | 5 |
| Brussels | | |
| Administration | From product group To marketing department | 17 |
| Technical service | From product group To marketing division (Amsterdam) | 1 |
| Marketing support | From marketing department To marketing division | 3 |

however, from a legal perspective the termination of the Dutch group was much more complicated.

By early May, the tentative lists of redundant personnel had been drawn up. Staaterman then prepared a time schedule for the remainder of the period up to the time when the new reorganization was scheduled to take place. The time schedule appears as exhibit 7-6. Briefly, the schedule called for the plan to be fully implemented and the new organization in place and operating by September 1, 1975. Redundant personnel would be terminated August 1. The employees to be terminated would be informed of their status during the first week in July. The schedule called for all the managers in the division down to the level of the product groups to meet during the afternoon of June 27 in the town of Tilburg in the south of the Netherlands. During the meeting, the overall plan would be presented. The new organization charts would show the structural changes that would occur, and the total number of redundancies would be revealed. The managers would be told the dates of termination, transfer of personnel, and the date the new organization would go into effect.

At the conclusion of the meeting, each product group manager would be given an envelope containing the new organizational chart for his unit. The chart would indicate the number and title of the positions in his group but not the individuals assigned to each position. On a second sheet of paper, he would be given the names of the people presently in his group.

**Exhibit 7-6**
**Timetable for Implementation of 1975 Marketing Project**

| Date | Action |
|------|--------|
| May 23 | Review of semi-final organizational charts with names of incumbents and lists of redundant personnel. |
| May 26-28 | Preparation of new office layouts. Eventual reevaluations and salary actions. |
| June 2-6 | Review and approval in principle of new office layouts and evaluations/salary actions. |
| June 9-19 | Preparation of all necessary papers for works council and marketing division meetings; individual sessions—redundant employees. Review preparations for office moves. |
| | Confidential discussions of lay-off terms with director of Amsterdam labor office. |
| | Invitations for marketing division meeting to all marketing and product group managers. |
| | Written invitation to Amsterdam works council members on June 18 (obligatory minimum period is 7 days prior to meeting). |
| June 20 | Final review of all write-ups, charts, lists, and so on, and arrangements/procedures for works council and marketing division meetings. |
| June 25 | Individual sessions with candidates for new/changed positions. |
| June 27 | A.M.   Works council meeting in Amsterdam. |
| | Noon   Information to union delegates and secretaries. |
| | P.M.   Marketing division meeting in Tilburg. |
| June 30 | A.M.   Works council meeting in Amsterdam. |
| | P.M.   Release of circular letter in Belgium and the Netherlands. |
| July 2-4 | Individual sessions with product group managers on possible revisions in lists of redundant personnel, transfers, office allocations, and so on. |
| August 1 | Release of redundant personnel. |
| August 15 | Effect transfers and begin office reorganizations. |
| September 3 | New organization in effect. |

The list was subdivided into three categories: retain, transferred, and terminated. He was free to put those in the retain category into the blank slots on his new organization chart. Those classified transferred would be moved out of his group to other positions in the division. Those terminated would have to be informed as quickly as possible. The managers would be instructed not to open these envelopes until the conclusion of the session that evening. The meeting would then adjourn for dinner. A very nice meal was planned with hopes that a good dinner would take some of the sting out of receiving the bad news.

**The Role of the Works Council**

Within the planning group, there had not been much discussion of the role that the works councils should play in the development and implementation of the marketing reorganization plan. Since all the employees who would be directly affected were represented by the Amsterdam council, it was concluded that the company would have to deal with it and not with the Utrecht council on this matter.

The lawyers on the committee had advised that the parts of the works council law that were applicable to the situation were section (1) and (5) of paragraph 25. Section (1) provided that:

> Unless there are major interests of the undertaking or of the interested parties directly involved in the undertaking that militate against such consultation, the employer shall give the works council an opportunity to state its views on any decision to be taken by himself or another person involved in the undertaking in connection with:
>
> (c) substantial reduction . . . in the activities of the undertaking;
>
> (d) major changes in the organization of the undertaking.

Section (5) provided that:

> Where a decision is likely to entail the dismissal of a considerable proportion of the staff, the employer shall, after consultation with the leaders of the workers' organization . . . set a date on which the works council is to be consulted concerning the relevant decision or notified of such decision and consulted on its implementation.

The lawyers advised that the "escape provision" of section (1)—the provision that exempted the company from the necessity of consultation with the works council if the interests of the company militated against such consultation—could be defended in this case and, therefore, it was not necessary to consult with the council regarding the development of the reorganization plan. However, they advised that under section (5), the company clearly had a responsibility to "consult" with the council regarding the "implementation" of the plan. It was a matter of consultation and not codetermination. The act did require codetermination of certain matters that were set forth in paragraph 27 of the act, but none of these matters were involved in the reorganization plan. Thus, although it was necessary to discuss the implementation of the plan with the Amsterdam council, it was not necessary to reach an agreement with them. Following consultation, even if the council disagreed concerning the whole plan of implementation or certain points of it, the company would be free to proceed.

Van Rijn, employee relations director of EFI's Dutch operations, argued that the council should be given an opportunity to carefully analyze the reorganization plan and to make suggestions regarding it. He pointed out that this was the first major issue that had arisen with the Amsterdam council since it had been formed and that to deal with it in a perfunctory manner on this important issue would be contrary to statements made by management regarding the role of the works councils at EFI. On more than one occasion, top management officials had stated that they viewed the works council as an important means of improving communications between management and the employees. The works council had been told that it would be given an active voice in advising the company on matters that affected the employees. Now was the opportunity, van Rijn argued, to show that the company was sincere. To do otherwise, he stated, would be to convince the council and the employees that the council did not really provide them with a means of effective participation. Vermeer, EFI's general counsel, supported van Rijn's position, pointing out that in his opinion, "consultation" as required by the law involved more than just informing the council of a plan of action that the company had no intention of altering. Any meaningful consultation, he argued, required that the council be given time to adequately study the company's proposal and to develop alternatives that the company had a right to reject but only after it had seriously considered them.

The position put forth by van Rijn and Vermeer was opposed by Thompson. Thompson's position was that the plan had been developed and subsequently approved by first regional and then corporate headquarters. His instructions were to execute the plan as it stood. He reasoned that if management gave the works council the opportunity to debate the proposed action, they would be opening a "Pandora's box." If the works council were brought into the decision making, it was almost certain that the implementation of the reorganization would be delayed. Thompson stated that he had made a commitment to have the new organization operating by September 1, and that was precisely what he intended to do.

It was decided finally that the Amsterdam works council would be informed on Friday morning, June 27. The following Monday, another meeting of the works council would be held at which time the council would be given an opportunity to state its views and to advise the company on the implementation of the plan.

Van Rijn and Vermeer were not happy with the decision reached by Thompson regarding the way in which the works council would be involved. As a result, they had asked for a meeting on June 4 with Staaterman. At that meeting, they had urged Staaterman to try to persuade Thompson to change the tactics that would be used in dealing with the works council. It was their opinion that certain aspects of the implementation should appear to be open ended and that the council instead of being given a plan that was set in concrete should be "asked for advice." The council should be made to feel, they said, that the management valued its advice and cooperation, especially in a matter that so vitally affected a number of the employees.

## The Problem

On June 6, as Staaterman reconsidered the problem, he realized that he had very little time to make a decision. The date the time schedule had set for "informing" the works council was only three weeks away. Four weeks after that the first people would be released, and four weeks after that the reorganization would take place. If he decided to recommend to his boss that the works council be given an opportunity to really "advise" management, the works council would have to be told of the reorganization in the next few days. Otherwise, the remainder of the time table could be upset.

Before he could do anything, however, he would have to clear it with Thompson, the EFI general manager. Staaterman knew that Thompson would strongly resist a change in the plan at this late date. He was reluctant, therefore, to recommend a change unless he could thoroughly substantiate the reasons for it. Staaterman knew that the plan in its present form had been reviewed and approved in both Brussels and New York. At EFI, anything carrying the headquarter's stamp of approval was tough to change. However, after listening to van Rijn and Vermeer, Staaterman felt as if they might have a good point. In the rush to get the reorganization planned, they had hardly enough time to think clearly about the short-term impacts on the company-works council relationship, let alone the long-term effects their actions might have. Because of a death in his family, van Rijn had not been able to attend most of the discussions on the tactics they planned to employ. The points he was making now might be correct. If so, perhaps they should rethink the approach they would take in dealing with the works council.

On the other hand, Staaterman believed that bringing the council into the process at this late stage would almost certainly result in some delays in getting things implemented, delays that Thompson had said he would not tolerate. Staaterman realized the pressure his boss was under and knew that "come hell or highwater" they would have to have a marketing division with only 190 people in it on September 1.

Staaterman was troubled. Was there a better way to go about the process of informing the works council? A way of bringing them into the process without risking inordinate delays in the final implementation of the plan? What were the short-term and long-term risks of proceeding as planned?

Some of these questions had never been asked of the planning group. In the rush to get the plan prepared and approved in the time Thompson had been given, there had been precious few moments to think about the company-works council relationship. The plan was in motion and it would be hard to stop, but if things went as planned, they might also be hard to live with. Workers' democracy was becoming one huge headache, Staaterman thought. Things were much simpler in the United States where one didn't have works councils to deal with.

**Notes**

1. EFI's fiscal year ended August 31 each year.
2. Thompson had been transferred to his present position from the international division of American Foods in New York in July, 1973.

# 5 Labor Relations in West Germany

## Introduction

The population of West Germany in 1978 was 61 million, the largest in Western Europe. During the period 1970-1978, West German population increased less than 1%. Of the seven countries, only in Great Britain did population increase more slowly than in West Germany (see table A-1).*

The gross national product of West Germany in 1976 was $462 billion, which was larger than in any of the other European countries. Its gross national product per person in the same year was $7,510, higher only in Sweden and the United States. The gross national product per person grew at the rate of 2.0% per year in West Germany during the 1970-1976 period. It was a lower rate of growth than in France, the Netherlands, or Sweden but was higher than in Great Britain or the United States (see table A-2).

Consumer prices in West Germany during the period 1970-1978 increased only 50% which was the lowest of all the countries (see table A-3). During this same period, unemployment averaged only 2.1% in West Germany—also the lowest of the European countries and about one-third the rate in the United States (see table A-4).

West Germany's average hourly compensation for production workers in manufacturing in 1978 was $9.90 which, although lower than in the Netherlands and Sweden, was higher than in the United States and considerably higher than in France, Italy, or Great Britain. During the period 1970-1978, the average hourly compensation of West German workers increased 330%, a rate exceeded only in the Netherlands in this study. In terms of local purchasing power, West Germany's worker compensation increased 58% during the period 1970-1978 which was higher than in any of the other countries except Italy. (See table A-5).

Output in manufacturing in West Germany increased an average of 4.6% per year during the period 1960-1978 and 2.5% per year during 1970-1978. During the more recent period, 1970-1978, the increase was lower than in some countries, but greater than in Great Britain, the Netherlands, and Sweden (see table A-6). Productivity as measured by percentage change in output per hour in manufacturing increased 5.5% per year during the 1960-1978 period and 5.4% per year during 1970-1978. In

*Tables A-1 through A-13 referred to in this chapter are in the statistical appendix at the end of the book.

173

the 1970-1978 period, only the Netherlands had a higher rate of productivity increase (see table A-7).

Unit labor costs in terms of West German currency increased 4.7% per year during 1960-1978 and 5.9% per year during the 1970-1978 period. In the more recent period, 1970-1978, the increase per year in unit labor costs in West Germany was less than in any of the other six countries. Over the longer period, 1960-1978, the increase per year in unit labor costs was lower only in the United States (see table A-8). In terms of U.S. dollars, the average increase in unit labor costs in West Germany was 8.8% per year during 1960-1978 and 13.5% per year during the period 1970-1978. During the latter period, these costs in West Germany increased more rapidly than in Great Britain, France, or Italy but less rapidly than in the Netherlands or Sweden. During the same period, the increase in unit labor costs in West Germany was more than double that in the United States (see table A-9).

**The Union Movement**

*Structure*

Manual or blue-collar workers in West Germany are organized into sixteen industrial unions, each of which will accept into membership all the workers in the industry regardless of their skill or craft. Industries are broadly defined by the union movement. For example, IG Metall, the largest West German union with a membership of over two million, includes in its jurisdiction not only basic iron and steel, but also automobile and many other types of production involving metalworking. The entire construction industry is covered by only one union. There are no craft unions and no general unions—only industrial unions. As a result, inter-union demarcation and jurisdictional disputes are rare.

The sixteen unions are joined together in the German Confederation of Labor (DGB). Each of the sixteen unions retains considerable autonomy. The DGB does not interfere with their internal policies or operations, although it frequently proposes guidelines and models, which are usually followed. The unions give strong financial support to the DGB, 12% of all union dues being forwarded to its treasury. The DGB does not engage directly in collective bargaining with industry. However, it does play a very active role in the development of national economic and social benefits policies and carries on extensive educational and research programs. It is also very active in lobbying for legislation that it considers favorable to the unions and their members. Union membership in the DGB unions is not confined to blue-collar workers, but also includes white-collar workers, such as clerks and typists, and also foremen and supervisors. Membership often extends upward to quite high levels in the company organization.

In addition to the DGB, there is a separate white-collar union, the DAG, with 500,000 members. (The DAG might have remained within the DGB had it not been for the strong insistence on industrial unionism within the latter.) There is also a separate union of high-level tenured civil service employees, the DBB, with 700,000 members, and a police union with 100,000 members. Regular nontenured government employees are members of the OETV, an affiliate of the DGB.

Although West German unions are strong at the national level, they are weak at the plant level. There is no counterpart in West Germany that corresponds to the strong union locals in the United States or the vigorous shop steward movement in Britain. West German unions have no legal right to represent workers locally. Instead, such power of representation is reserved to the works council which consists entirely of employees of the plant. However, 90% of works council members are also union members, and unions have referred to the works councils as "our strong arm within the plant." IG Metall and some of the other unions have tried, in recent years, to strengthen the position of the union steward in plant matters, and have succeeded in some plants, but this has been resisted strongly by managements that prefer to deal with works councils.

*Membership*

Total union membership in West Germany in 1975 was approximately 8.6 million or 38% of the working population. In recent years, the percentage has declined somewhat as growth in union membership has not kept pace with the increase in the work force. The percentage is smaller than in Sweden, Great Britain, or the Netherlands. It is, however, considerably higher than in France or the United States (see table A-11). A poll in 1966 indicated that 92% of the West German workers believed that unions are beneficial and necessary.

*Closed Shop and Check-off*

The right of unionization is guaranteed by the freedom of association clause of the German constitution (Article 9, section 3). However, employees also have the right not to join a union. In other words, the closed shop, under which employees are required to join a union, is illegal. The courts have ruled that compulsory union membership would constitute an infringement of the constitutional right of freedom of association. In 1960, the union of construction workers proposed to negotiate an "agency shop" under which employees would not have to join the union but would have to pay to the union an amount equal to the union dues. Not only the employers' association, but also the DGB opposed it as a violation of the constitution, and it was not pressed by the union. In 1967, the federal labor court ruled that labor agreements may not make any differentiation between union members and nonmembers. Union dues in West Germany are higher than in Britain or France, the standard being up to 2% of one's monthly salary. Although the check-off system is legal, it is not widespread. Where it is used, it must be the result of an agreement between the employees and the company.

### Financial Status

West German unions are financially very strong. Although union strike benefits are high (IG Metall pays 55% to 75% of wages), there have been very few strikes, and union salaries and expenses are kept at a very moderate level. The result is that every year, the unions tend to end up with surpluses that are invested and, in turn, produce more surpluses. West German unions have become big business. Their annual income is over 100 million deutsche marks.[1] Together with the cooperative movement, they own the fourth largest bank and the second largest insurance company in the country. In addition, they operate West Germany's largest housing development and rental company, a chain of over 5,000 stores, a book and record publishing company, a travel agency, an auto club, and several factories producing household goods.[2]

### Ideology

At its founding in Munich in 1949, the DGB was strongly anticapitalist and favored nationalization of all basic industry. However, at its Düsseldorf convention in 1963, the DGB reversed its policy and moved to cooperate with capitalism and free enterprise. Most of the West German unions do not now favor extension of socialization and government control, which they see as being in conflict with their goal of free collective bargaining by autonomous unions. The current ideology of the German labor movement may be described as neocapitalism.[3]

### Politics

Under the Collective Bargaining Agreement Act of 1949, as modified in 1952, unions are required to be independent of political and religious organizations. They are not permitted to contribute funds directly to any political party. During the immediate postwar period, the DGB rallied behind Adenauer and the Christian Democratic party (CPD) in support of the European Coal and Steel Community which the Social Democratic party (SPD) opposed. In return, Adenauer and the CPD in 1951 supported parity codetermination in the coal, iron, and steel industries. In 1952, however, when the CPD refused to back parity codetermination in other industries, the DGB moved its support to the SPD, where it has remained. The SPD, although more to the left than the CPD, is no longer Marxist but instead, a welfare state party that has abandoned the class struggle and nationalization of industry. Although not contributing funds directly to the SPD, the unions do provide it with heavy support during election periods in the form of staff and clerical help, vehicles, office equipment, and so on. It has been said that at such times, many union offices are almost totally mobilized for the use of the SPD.[4]

Approximately one-half of the deputies in the Bundestag are union members and in 1975, twelve of the seventeen federal cabinet members had close ties with the union movement.[5] (The former Minister of Defense had been president of the construction workers' union.) Moreover, the unions have the right to appoint officials to many government boards and agencies, such as the labor courts, and the social security, post office, and railroad boards. Through these elective and appointive positions in the government and as a result of extensive and effective lobbying, the DGB and its affiliated unions strongly affect the nature of legislation and its administration. To a considerable extent the West German union movement has used the political process rather than collective bargaining to achieve major social goals. At the same time, its political involvement has caused the leadership to take more responsible and conservative positions in collective bargaining in order to enable the government to achieve economic stability and avoid heavy inflation.

### Employers' Associations

Just as the German constitution gives the workers the right to form unions, it also gives employers the right to form employers' associations (Article 9, section 3). Employers' associations are protected and controlled under the Collective Bargaining Agreement Act (1949 and 1952).[6] It is estimated that there are eight hundred such associations, most of which are affiliated with the BDA, the national employers' association. The BDA itself does not engage in bargaining but does lay down broad guidelines and offers advice and assistance to its member associations. The BDA and its affiliates carry on extensive educational, research, and lobbying activities. Some associations also maintain funds to provide benefits to employers during strikes or lockouts.

## Collective Bargaining

### Union Recognition

In West Germany, there is no legal mechanism, such as an election, for determining under what conditions an employer must recognize and deal with a union. Since most bargaining is at the industry association level, and the associations do recognize and bargain, the issue has not been significant. However, at least one company, Melitta, did operate on a non-union basis and refused to recognize a union or bargain either directly or through an association.

### Levels of Bargaining

In West Germany, collective bargaining between unions and management is limited almost entirely to one level. There is very little national bargaining, very little company bargaining (a few major companies do bargain directly rather than through an association), and no local bargaining. The general practice is to have bargaining at the state level between an industry employers' association and the industry union. Under West German law, the union and the employers' association have the power to agree on a new contract without referring it to the employees and the employers for ratification. Within each industry, collective bargaining usually follows a pattern. Once an agreement is reached in one state, it becomes the basis for settlement in all the other states. As pointed out earlier, at the local plant level the union structure is usually very weak or nonexistent, and bargaining at that level does not occur between management and the union. The power of representation at the plant level is reserved for the works council, which is not part of the union structure.

### Scope of Bargaining

The scope of West German collective bargaining; that is, the number of issues covered by it, tends to be limited for two reasons: the breadth of the social legislation and the fact that many issues are placed by law in the jurisdiction of the works councils. Many fringe benefits that could be collective bargaining issues are covered instead by social legislation, and many local plant matters are settled by the employers with the works councils. The state-wide industry agreements are limited to minimum wage standards and a few other major matters. There are usually two contracts: the "tariff" which sets minimum wages, usually for a period of one year; and the "mantel" which establishes the structure and criteria of the job classification system, as well as working hours, supplemental payments, vacation days, and such, and usually has a duration of two or three years.

The wage rates negotiated in the labor contracts are minimal rates. Each company is free to pay higher rates and usually does. In an economy that had full employment for many years, the result was a serious wage drift. In a study in an oil-refining plant, we found actual wages were 20% above the contract rates. It is reported that plant averages of 10% to 20% above the contract are not uncommon. In many industries, the contract scale has become the minimum, which is seldom paid. During the years of full employment, the union leaders felt that their attempts to cooperate with the government to prevent inflation were frustrated and their prestige with the workers undermined by management's granting of wages considerably above the negotiated rates.

*Conciliation and Mediation*

In West Germany, the parties have been very successful in reaching agreements without receiving outside help or resorting to strike action. Private conciliation and mediation machinery has been established by many associations and unions to aid them if they reach an impasse. In 1954, the DGB and the BDA jointly adopted a model conciliation agreement which they now recommend to their constituents. The IG Metall and metal industry association machinery provides for a twenty-two-day cooling-off period during which conciliation is actively pursued. In the few cases where collective bargaining and private conciliation machinery have broken down and a strike has threatened, the government has appointed a cabinet minister or a senior civil servant to serve as mediator. This type of high-level mediation has been very successful.

*Labor Agreements*

As stated earlier, it is the practice in West Germany to negotiate state-wide labor agreements for each industry. Agreements that cover the entire country or agreements that are negotiated for a specific company are exceptional.[7] Usually two agreements are negotiated in the state for each industry—a tariff agreement and a mantel agreement. The tariff agreement, which sets the minimum wages only, is normally a one-year contract. The mantel agreement, which covers matters other than basic wages, usually lasts for two or more years. It is estimated that each year there are more than 8,000 tariff agreements negotiated in the various states.

Once a labor agreement is signed by the union and the employers' association, it is legally enforceable. Moreover, it is assumed to include "the peace obligation" whether or not a no-strike, no-lockout clause is specifically written into it.[8] If it can be proved that a contract has been violated, the labor courts stand ready to award damages to the aggrieved party or parties. In 1958, IG Metall, the metalworkers' union, was ordered to pay $25 million for breaking a contract. However, in that case the employers' association agreed not to collect in return for an arbitration agreement.

*Labor Courts*

In West Germany, claims that labor agreements have been violated are not heard by general courts, but rather, by special courts that hear only labor cases. The Labor Courts Act of 1953 established a special system of labor courts that consists of 113 local courts, one state court for each state, and one federal court. Each local labor court is composed of one professional judge, one lay member appointed by the unions, and one lay member appointed by the employers. The labor courts have jurisdiction not only over the meaning of labor agreements, but also over the interpretation of labor legislation. Complaints may be brought by individuals as well as by collective groups. The courts first attempt conciliation, which is successful in about one-third of the cases. Only if conciliation fails is a formal decision rendered. In 1975, the local labor courts heard over 387,000 cases, an increase of 83% since 1969.[9] The state and federal courts hear only appeals from the local courts.

*Strikes and Lockouts*

Under West German law, employees have the right to strike provided: the agreement has expired; the aim of the strike is economic protection or improvement of the employees; peaceful means of settlement have been exhausted; and the strike has been authorized by the national union. Sympathy strikes and political strikes are illegal, and intimidation by pickets makes any strike illegal. Recognition strikes are legal but are rare, because it is most unusual for West German management to refuse to deal with a union. The DGB rules require that before a strike may be called, the national union must approve it and 75% of the employees must vote for it in a secret election.[10] (The chemical workers' union is the only DGB affiliate that does not require a membership vote before a strike. Since 1963, it has permitted its national officers to call strikes without secret votes.)[11] Employees taking part in an illegal strike may be discharged by the employer, expelled by the union, and fined by the labor court.

Employers do not have to pay workers who are on strike or other workers who are laid off because they cannot be used efficiently as a result of a strike by others. Moreover, workers on strike are not eligible for unemployment benefits and do not receive other benefits, such as sick pay and government health insurance, unless they pay the premiums themselves. On the other hand, the unions pay very high strike benefits. IG Metall pays 55 to 75% of the striker's former pay depending on his family status and years of union membership. As pointed out earlier, the West German unions are financially very strong and, therefore, would be capable of supporting long strikes.

Lockouts are also legal and have been used effectively at times by West German employers.[12] Because labor negotiations usually cover an entire industry in a state, a lockout can be quite a massive reaction. In 1978, when the printers' unions struct in six newspaper companies, the industry responded with a lockout in all the newspaper firms in the country.

Although employees have the right to strike and employers have the right to lock out, these weapons have been used very sparingly. West Germany has had an enviable record of industrial peace since World War II. During the ten-year period 1967-1976, days lost by strikes and lockouts in mining, manufacturing, construction, and transportation were only 35 per 1,000 employees per year. Of the seven countries included in this study, only the Netherlands had a lower rate. The rate was 12 times higher in Britain and 17 times higher in the United States. The rates in Britain and the United States were in themselves quite low, constituting only 2/10 and 3/10 of 1% of the working time, but in West Germany the loss of working time resulting from strikes and lockouts was at the remarkably low rate of less than 2/100 of 1% (see table A-12).

However, during the winter of 1978-1979, West Germany did have a major strike. IG Metall called out 100,000 steelworkers in the country's 19 major steel-producing plants. The major issue was working hours. The union demanded that the work week be cut from 40 hours to 35 hours to create more jobs. The strike lasted for 44 days. In the settlement, the companies agreed to more vacation time, and there was an unwritten understanding to move toward a shorter work week. It is too early to predict whether this marks the beginning of a more militant approach by West German workers and unions. It may be significant, however, that 46% of the workers voted to continue the strike rather than to accept the agreement recommended by their union leaders.

## Legislated Employee Protection and Benefits

It was pointed out earlier in this chapter that the scope of collective bargaining in West Germany is quite narrow for several reasons, one of which is the breadth of West German social legislation. Many issues that are important subjects for collective bargaining in the United States are covered primarily by legislation in West Germany. The West German labor movement, which has had strong political influence, has frequently found it easier and more effective to secure protection and benefits for workers through legislation rather than through collective agreements. To the extent that the legislature route has been followed, the scope of collective bargaining has been narrowed. It is not clear at this point whether the West German labor movement will continue to rely heavily on legislation or in the future will direct its attention more toward collective bargaining, perhaps using the legislation as a floor upon which to build a more elaborate collectively-bargained structure of worker protection and benefits.

## Dismissals

The Protection Against Dismissal Act (1969) provides that West German workers who are over 18 years of age and have 6 months of service may be dismissed only after due notice, after consultation with the works council, and for causes that are not "socially unwarranted." The amount of notice that must be given varies with length of service as follows:

| | |
|---|---|
| up to 5 years' service | 2 weeks' notice |
| 5 to 10 years' service | 1 month notice |
| 10 to 20 years' service | 2 months' notice |
| over 20 years' service | 3 months' notice |

However, notice does not have to be given if dismissal is a result of gross misconduct, such as refusal to work, violence, fraud, theft, or revealing business secrets.

The dismissed employee may seek the help of his works council and at the same time may appeal to the local labor court. The burden of proof is on the employer to show that the dismissal was not socially unwarranted. The court must first try to conciliate the dispute, but if conciliation is not successful, it will render a decision. The court may order that the worker be continued in his job until a decision is made. The court may order the company to compensate the worker up to a maximum of 12 months' pay. (However, the maximum may be increased for aged and long-service employees; for example, up to a maximum of 18 months' pay for an employee aged 55 with over 20 years of service.) However, unlike the American arbitrators, West German courts do not order reinstatement of employees who have been unjustly dismissed.

## Redundancies

The 1969 act applies to redundancies as well as to terminations for other reasons. In redundancy cases, the labor courts have not interfered with management's right to decide whether discontinuance of certain jobs is necessary. However, the courts have been concerned whether management has fully considered the possibility of alternative jobs for the redundant workers and also whether management has given sufficient weight to "social factors" such as age, family status, and length of service when selecting the workers to be declared redundant. In cases of redundancy, management must give the same periods of notice and must consult with the works council as in termination for other causes. Likewise, if the court finds that management's actions proved to be socially unwarranted, it may order that the employees be compensated as in cases of dismissal for other causes.

In 1978, a law reform commission issued a proposed new comprehensive West German labor code that would include the basic provisions of the 1969 Protection Against Dismissal Act but would increase the periods of notice and require the employer to provide a worker with written reasons for dismissal. Under the proposed law, the required notice periods would be increased as follows:

| | |
|---|---|
| After 5 years' service | 3 months' notice |
| After 8 years' service | 4 months' notice |
| After 10 years' service | 5 months' notice |
| After 12 years' service | 6 months' notice |
| After 15 years' service | 9 months' notice[13] |

## Vacations and Bonuses

The Federal Vacation Act (1963) requires that employees with 6 months or more of service be granted paid vacations as follows:

| | |
|---|---|
| Under 18 years | 15 working days |
| 18-35 years | 18 working days |
| over 35 years | 24 working days |

However, a 1977 government survey found that 87% of the workers covered by industry-level collective agreements received 4 weeks (20 days) paid vacation and 36% received 5 weeks (25 days). The same survey found that 98% of the workers received either a year-end or vacation bonus or both and that for 57% of the workers, the total bonus was equal to 90% or more of a full month's pay. In addition to paid vacation, West German workers received 11 paid public holidays. In July, 1976, *Business Europe* reported that the West German workers "get more time off with pay than any other worker in Europe" and that the cost to the employer (including bonuses) is greater than in any other European country.[14] The VW company estimated that, because of vacations, holidays, and sick leave differences, the average worker in its United States plant would spend 35 to 40 more days on the assembly line each year than those in its West German factory.[15]

## Maternity Benefits

The Act for the Protection of Women (1972) provides that employees are entitled to: fourteen weeks of maternity leave at full pay—six weeks before confinement and eight weeks after confinement (payable from the sickness insurance fund to which both the employees and the employers contribute); free hospital and medical care, including drugs; and a lump sum of 50 to 100 deutsche marks to cover incidentals. The act provides further that: an employer may not dismiss an employee during pregnancy and for four months following confinement; pregnant workers may not be employed on noisy, heavy, or tiring jobs or, from the fifth month of pregnancy, on jobs that require constant standing; the employer must provide pregnant workers with periodic short breaks to avoid fatigue; and after childbirth, mothers are entitled to two paid one-half-hour periods per day to feed the child.

## Equal Pay and Equal Opportunities

There are no separate statutes in West Germany that provide for equal pay or equal opportunities for women. However, the federal constitution of 1949 does state that "men and women shall have equal rights" and "no one shall be prejudiced or favored because of their sex." In 1959, a federal labor court interpreted these words of the constitution to mean that women are entitled to equal pay for equal work. The 1972 Works Council Act provides that "the employer and the Works Council must ensure that . . . discrimination . . . on grounds of sex does not occur." Finally, West Germany, as a member of the European Community, is bound by the treaty of Rome (1957) which provides that "Each member state shall . . . ensure and subsequently maintain the application of the principle of equal remuneration for equal work as between men and women workers" and by a directive of the European Community council (effective in the summer of 1978) which provides that "there shall be no discrimination whatsoever between men and women on grounds of sex in the conditions of work, including selection criteria for access to all jobs or posts, whatever the branch of activity, at all levels of the professional hierarchy." Thus, West German women, who make up about 30% of the work force, would appear to have ample protection with respect to equal pay and equal opportunities, although, as just stated, there are no separate statutes on these subjects. In reality, however, there are few women in skilled or high-level jobs in West Germany, evidently primarily because they lack the basic training and education that are required.[16]

## Absenteeism

West German industry has a high rate of absenteeism. A U.S. study in the late sixties found that absenteeism in West Germany was higher than in Belgium, France, Britain, or the United States. A more recent study by the Swedish employers' association indicates that absenteeism resulting from claimed illness in West Germany in 1973 was about 6.5%. This was lower than in Sweden, Italy, Holland, or France but 50% higher than in the United States (see table A-13). The major cause of the higher rate in West Germany appears to be the liberal national sick pay plan which, since 1970, has paid 100% of wages in the case of absence because of claimed illness for a period of six weeks, including the first day; and then pays 75% for an indefinite period, limited only to 78 weeks during a three-year period for the same illness.

## Worker Participation

### Labor Representatives on the Board

West Germany has been the world pioneer in worker participation which has taken two major forms: labor directors on company boards and works councils.

In order to understand labor representation on company boards, it is necessary first to examine West Germany company structure. Under West German law, each company has a two-tier board system consisting of a supervisory board and a management board. The supervisory board usually meets not more than four times per year. Membership on it is not a full-time job. It deals only with broad economic and financial issues, but it does appoint the members of the management board. The management board consists of full-time members who actually carry on the day-to-day operation of the company. Labor representatives are elected to the supervisory board, but not to the management board.

There are three major laws under which labor representatives are elected to the supervisory boards. (A fourth law that was passed in 1956 applies to holding companies that have more than one-half of their sales in coal, iron, and steel.)

1. *The 1951 law applies only to coal, iron, and steel companies with more than 1,000 employees.* It provides for parity representation; that is, the labor board members are equal in number and power to the shareholder board members. In addition, there is one neutral member chosen jointly by the labor and shareholder members. The neutral member serves as chairman and casts the deciding vote in case of a tie. A typical board consists of eleven members—five labor representatives, five shareholder representatives, and the neutral chairman selected by the other ten. The five labor members are elected by the employees, two of whom are nominated by the works council and must be employees of the company, and three of whom are nominated by the union and need not be (and usually are not) employees of the company. One of the shareholder representatives and one of the labor representatives nominated by the union must be independent. In addition to its other duties, the supervisory board chooses a management board which includes a labor director. The labor director must have the approval of the labor members of the supervisory board (see figure 5-1). In 1951, this act applied to 151 coal, iron, and steel companies; but as a result of the decline in the industries and the consolidation of firms, by 1969 it covered only 51.

2. *The 1952 law applies to companies with 500 to 2,000 employees in industries other than coal, iron, and steel.* It provides that one-third of the members of the supervisory board of such companies shall be labor representatives. Thus, it does not provide for parity representation. All the labor representatives are nominated and elected by the employees and must be employees of the company. There is an exception: if the size of the board requires more than two labor members, the others need not be employees and in fact, usually are union officials. The supervisory board elects the management board by majority vote, and the labor director does not need the approval of the labor members (see figure 5-1).

3. *The 1976 law applies to companies with over 2,000 employees in industries other than coal, iron, and steel.* This law covers approximately 670 companies with over 6 million employees. The board, which consists of an equal number of shareholder and labor representatives, varies in size depending on the size of the company (see table 5-1). Among the employees on the board there must be at least one blue-collar, one white-collar, and one "leading employee." Section 5, paragraph 3 of the Works Constitution Act describes a leading employee as a person who: 1. is authorized to independently hire and dismiss personnel, or 2. has the power of attorney or

1. Coal, Iron and Steel Industry (1951 Law)

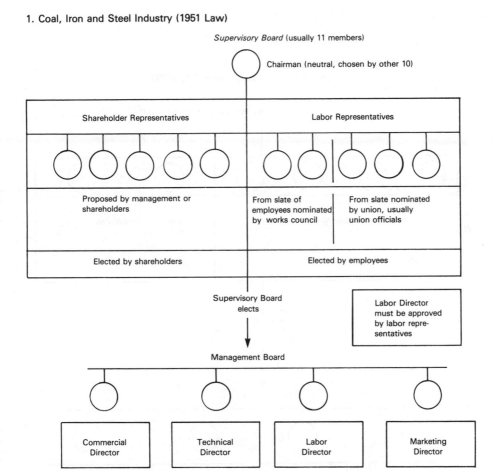

**Figure 5-1.** Supervisory Board Membership in West Germany

2. Companies Other Than Iron, Coal, and Steel with 500 to 2,000
Employees (1952 Law)

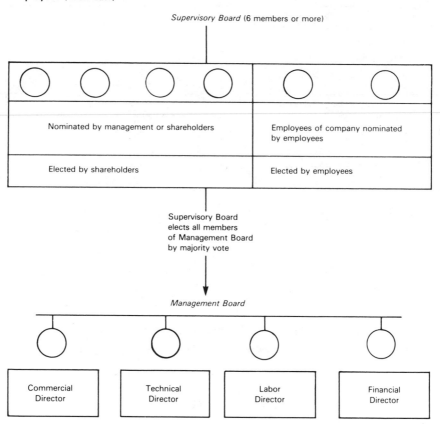

Figure 5-1 *(continued)*

### 3. Companies other than Coal, Iron, Steel with more than 2,000 Employees (1976 Law)

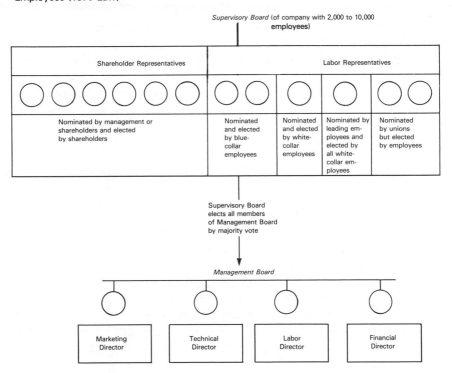

**Figure 5-1** *(continued)*

**Table 5-1**
**Supervisory Board Membership**

| Number of Employees | Board Total | Shareholder Representatives | Employees Nominated by Employees | Union Nominees | Total Labor Representatives |
|---|---|---|---|---|---|
| Up to 10,000 | 12 | 6 | 4 | 2 | 6 |
| 10,000 to 20,000 | 16 | 8 | 6 | 2 | 8 |
| Over 20,000 | 20 | 10 | 7 | 3 | 10 |

power to sign, or 3. because of his special experience and knowledge, performs (principally on his own responsibility) tasks regularly assigned to him because of his importance to the existence and development of the plant.

The employee members are nominated and elected by their fellow workers in their own group. Thus, the blue-collar members must be nominated and elected by blue-collar workers. The union nominees who need not be and usually are not employees of the company must nevertheless be elected by the employees. The chairman must be elected by the board from its own members by a two-thirds majority, but if no member can receive this majority, then the shareholder members acting alone may elect the chairman. This is important because if an issue before the board results in a tie vote, the chairman has the power to cast an additional or deciding vote. Thus, although there is an equal number of labor and shareholder members on the board, there is not parity. (The unions claim that parity is also destroyed because one of the labor representatives must be an executive or a leading employee who they claim will always vote with the shareholder representatives on important issues.) The supervisory board elects the members of the management board by majority vote, including a vote by the chairman if necessary. One member of the management board must be designated as the labor director, but his appointment does not have to be approved by the labor members as is the case under the 1951 law (see figure 5-1).

Following passage of the 1976 law, twenty-nine employers' associations and nine large companies challenged its constitutionality in the courts, claiming that it infringed on the fundamental constitutional rights to own property and to freely operate a business. However, on March 1, 1979, the West German Supreme Court upheld the new law, finding that it did not violate the constitutional rights of owners and managers.

As indicated earlier, the 1951 law was sponsored by the Christian Democratic party. The DGB hoped to have the provisions of that law (which included parity, union officials on the boards, and approval of the labor director by the labor members of the board) extended from coal, iron, and steel to the whole economy. When the CPD refused to sponsor such an extension and instead passed the 1952 law which did not contain these three provisions, the DGB moved its support from the CPD to the SPD.[17] Since 1952, the DGB has pressured the SPD to revise the 1952 law which originally applied to all companies with more than 500 employees (it now applies only to companies with 500, but not more than 2,000 employees). The 1976 law, although meeting some of the DGB's demands, such as providing for union officials on the boards and increasing to one-half the number of labor representatives, falls short of the 1951 law in that: it does not provide parity; it includes representation of "leading employees"; there is no neutral chairman; the labor director does not have to be approved by the labor members of the board; and it applies only to companies with over 2,000 employees, leaving the small companies still under the provisions of the 1952 act.

Although West German management has strongly opposed the extension of the provisions of the 1951 act to the rest of West German industry, it has found that labor representation on the supervisory board as practiced to date has not prevented management from functioning effectively, and indeed, has had certain advantages. In a system where unions do not negotiate with companies, labor representation on the board has provided an avenue of communication between top management and its employees. In general, the labor members have concentrated on social matters, leaving in management's hands financial and economic matters as well as the selection of executive personnel. Thus, although management has not been allowed to forget the human aspects of problems, its initiative in major matters has not been curtailed. The board room has not become an arena, but instead, informal arrangements have been developed in most companies whereby decisions are worked out in small caucuses beforehand and simply ratified at the formal meetings. Labor membership on the board has contributed to a better understanding of management problems by the leaders of the employees and has been a factor contributing to the excellent record of industrial peace and political stability. Although there have been delays in decision making at times in order to convince the worker members of the merits of management proposals, it is believed that in general the costs of such delays have been offset by the greater employee support once the decision has been accepted.

In 1979, however, some West German managements were concerned as to what would happen under the 1976 law which became operative on June 30, 1978. The DBG unions were dominating the elections, and it was feared that they might also control the action of the employee-elected board members. One of the most significant and, from managements' position, one of the most unexpected developments, was the nomination by the unions and election by the employees of prominent leaders of the international trade union movement to the directorships of some of the leading multinational corporations. Gunter Kopke, secretary of the European Metalworkers' Federation (EMF), was elected to the board of Philips; Herman Rebhan, general secretary of the International Metalworkers' Federation (IMF), to the board of Ford; Werner Thonessen, deputy general secretary of the IMF, to the board of Standard Electric, a subsidiary of International Telephone and Telegraph (ITT); and Charles Levinson, general secretary of the International Federation of Chemical, Energy, and General Workers' Unions (ICEF), to the board of DuPont. Levinson said he would use the board seat to provide "a new source of multinational information and experience" and "to further the organization of DuPont workers into free and independent unions . . . in North America and throughout the world."[18]

## The Works Councils

The works councils are the second major form of worker participation in West Germany. Works councils were established originally by the 1952 Works Constitution Act which was revised in 1972. The present law requires that every plant or office with five employees shall have a council consisting entirely of employees nominated and elected every three years by their fellow employees in a secret election. Both union and non-union employees have the right to vote and to serve on the council. However, leading employees and members of the management board are not permitted to vote or to be council members. The chairman of the council is elected by the council from its own membership.

The size of the council varies with the number of employees in the plant: one member for 5 to 20 employees; 3 members for 21 to 50 employees; and so on, up to 31 members for 9,000 employees; and then 2 more members for each additional 3,000 employees.

The council meets at least once per month. The employer may attend the meeting only if invited by the council or if the meeting is especially convened at his request. At such meetings, the employer may be accompanied by a representative of his employers' association. Union officials may attend council meetings only when invited by one-fourth of the members, and then only in an advisory capacity. A representative of the handicapped workers and a representative of the young workers (under 18 years old) may also attend the meetings of the council.

Council members are paid their regular wages while engaged in council work. In a plant with 300 to 600 employees, the council elects one of its members to full-time council work. The number of full-time councillors increases with the size of the plant up to 11 for 9,001 to 10,000 employees, and then one more for each additional 2,000 employees. In addition, the company must pay each councillor for three weeks of training for each three-year term of office (four weeks during a councillor's first term). The company must also provide the council with office space, furniture, materials, equipment, and secretarial help.

Council members are given protection against action by the employer. The law states that they "shall not be interfered with or obstructed in the discharge of their functions" and "they shall not be put to a disadvantage or given preference because of their activities; the same shall apply to their careers." However, one-fourth of the employees, or the employer, the union, or the works council may petition the labor court to expel a member from the council because of "gross violation of legal duties."

Every calendar quarter, the council is required to report its activities to a general assembly of the employees. The employer is entitled to attend and speak at such meetings and at least once per year, he must report to the assembly on personnel and social matters and on the economic condition of the plant.

The law requires management to work with the council on matters that might affect the well-being of the employees. However, certain issues, such as general wage increases, are reserved for collective bargaining with the union, and the council is not permitted to deal with such matters.

In some areas, management need only inform the council of its actions; in others, it must first consult with the council and seek its advice; and in still others, it may not take action without first reaching an agreement with the council (codetermination). The 1972 law increased the number of issues that must be brought before the council and greatly expanded the area of codetermination (see appendix 5A at the end of this chapter). If the management and the council are unable to reach an agreement that must be codetermined, the council is not free to take strike action, but rather, is bound by the "peace obligation." The law states that "tactics used in labor disputes shall be unlawful between employer and works council" and they "shall abstain from actions which interfere with the progress of work or the peace in a plant." However, either party may refer a matter that is subject to codetermination to a conciliation committee whose decision becomes binding on both of them.

The management and the council may establish a permanent conciliation committee or may establish ad hoc conciliation committees as disputes arise. In either case, the committee must consist of an equal number of members appointed by the council and the employer, plus an impartial chairman agreed upon by both parties. If the parties cannot agree on the impartial chairman or the number of members of the committee, the matter is settled by the labor court. A detailed description of the functions and authority of the works council and the conciliation committee are set forth in appendix 5A.

In a multi-plant company, if the plant works councils desire, they may have a company works council made up of representatives from the plant councils. Likewise, in a multi-company corporation, they may have a corporation council made up of representatives from the company councils.

In West Germany, the works council has been a far more important device for worker participation than labor membership on the supervisory board. The council covers a much broader range of issues, many of which are of immediate concern to the employees, and it has codetermination power which labor board members have only in the coal, iron, and steel companies.

Earlier we pointed out that the West German unions are very weak at the plant level. Although there has been some growth of power by local shop stewards in some companies in West Germany, there is no real counterpart to the strong local union in the United States or the vigorous shop steward movement in Britain. In West Germany, management is under no legal obligation to deal with shop stewards or local union committees and usually refuses to do so. On the other hand, the law does require management to deal with the works council. West German management prefers it this way. It believes it is easier to work with a group of its own employees on local plant and company matters than it would be to work with outside union officials. This does not mean that the unions do not have influence in the works councils. It is estimated that 90% of the councillors are union members.

The works council serves as the major avenue of communication between local plant management and the employees. In a 1966 survey, 88% of the workers indicated that the work of their council had been important to them individually.

The 1972 Works Constitution Act also requires all companies with more than one hundred employees to establish, in addition to the works council, an economics committee. The committee, which consists of three to seven employees of the company, one of whom must be a member of the works council, is appointed by the works council. The employer or his representative must meet once per month with this committee and provide it with economic and financial information concerning the company. Much of the material shared with the economics committee may be confidential. The committee reports back to the council but may not divulge the confidential information. Not only members of the economics committee, but also members of the works council and members of the supervisory board are bound to confidentiality by the law. Breaches of secrecy are punishable by up to one year in prison.

One cannot examine the West German works council legislation without coming to the conclusion that it has established a structure in which management could be deprived not only of its right to make immediate decision, but also its right to make final decision on many very significant issues. In fact, under the law, the final authority has been deposited in the hands of a neutral third party, the chairman of the conciliation committee. In actual company operation, however, this does not appear to have happened. Management reports that with very few exceptions, the works councils have been exceedingly reasonable and cooperative. Management has been able to retain the initiative, and its proposals generally have been accepted once they have been understood by the councillors. At times, it was necessary to delay action until agreement could be reached, but once reached, implementation was easier. As one West German manager remarked, "It now sometimes takes us a little longer to reach an agreement but implementation following agreement is much easier and quicker." Both parties have been exceedingly reluctant to place control in the hands of a third party and, as a result, although the conciliation committee appears important in the legislation, in reality it seldom has been used. However, one wonders if a structure has been built that some day, under different economic conditions and more militant worker leadership, might result in severe restraints on management's ability to manage.

**Profit Sharing and Employee Ownership**

Since 1961 West Germany has had an employee capital accumulation law originally known as the DM 312 law and, since a 1970 revision, known as the DM 624 law because it provides that employees can voluntarily save up to 624 deutshe marks per year free from taxes to which the state adds premiums of 30% for single employees and 50% to 63% for married employees, depending on the size of the family. (The government bonuses are not paid to employees whose incomes exceed 24,000 deutsche marks per year for single employees and 48,000 deutsche marks for married couples.) Moreover, a union is free to negotiate the payment of part or all of the 624 deutsche marks by the company instead of the worker, and some of the labor agreements now provide that the company pays from 50% to 100% of it. The funds are frozen for a period of from five to seven years depending on the provisions of the agreement. In 1976, 15.9 million West German workers, about three-fourths of the working population, were saving an average of 580 deutsche marks per year under the law.

There are five basic methods of savings from which the employee may choose: 1. a regular bank savings account; 2. a building society account; 3. premiums for life insurance; 4. shares in the company at below market prices; or 5. an interest-bearing loan to the company. About 79% of the workers have chosen bank and building society accounts, another 20% life insurance, and only 1% shares and loans to the company. Thus, the law has had no significant effect on the ownership and control of West German industry.

In 1974, the government proposed legislation that would have required companies with a profit of more than 400,000 deutsche marks to contribute up to 10% of the profit to the employees in the form of share capital. The funds, although owned by the individual employees, would have been administered as a joint asset fund by the union and the company. The proposal was totally rejected by industry, and in January, 1976, the economics ministry indicated it was not being pursued. Instead, the government has now proposed expanding the DM 624 law to DM 936 and changing it so as to encourage employees to invest in shares of the company.[19]

# Appendix 5A:
# Functions and Authority
# of the Works Council

## General Duties

The Works Constitutions Act of 1972 (section 80) describes the general duties of the works council as follows:

see that effect is given to acts, ordinances, safety regulations, collective agreements, and work agreements for the benefit of the employees;

make recommendations to the employer for action benefiting the establishment and the staff;

receive suggestions from employees and the youth delegation and negotiate with the employer for their implementation;

promote the rehabilitation of disabled persons and others in particular need of assistance;

prepare and organize the election of a youth delegation and collaborate closely with the said delegation in promoting the interests of the young employees;

promote the employment of elderly workers;

promote the integration of foreign workers in the establishment, and further understanding between them and their colleagues.

## Specific Areas of Codetermination and Consultation

In addition to the general duties described in section 80, the law sets forth the rights and authority of the works council in five specific areas.

1. *Social Matters (section 87).* The law specifically provides the works council with "the right of codetermination" in the following matters:

matters relating to the order by operation of the establishment and the conduct of employees in the establishment;

Quotations of the Works Constitution Act of January 15, 1972, were taken from an English translation of the act published by the International Labor Organization (Legislative Series, 1972—Ger. F.R. 1).

the commencement and termination of the daily working hours, including breaks and the distribution of working hours among the days of the week;

any temporary reduction or extension of the hours normally worked in the establishment;

the time and place for and the form of payment of remuneration;

the establishment of general principles for leave arrangements and the preparation of the leave schedule as well as the fixing of the time at which the leave is to be taken by individual employees, if no agreement is reached between the employer and the employees concerned;

the introduction and use of technical devices designed to monitor the behavior or performance of the employees;

arrangements for the prevention of employment accidents and occupational diseases and for the protection of health on the basis of legislation or safety regulation;

the form, structuring, and administration of social services where scope is limited to the establishment, company, or combine;

the assignment of and notice-to-vacate accommodation that is rented to employees in view of their employment relationship as well as the general fixing of the conditions for the use of such acommodation;

questions related to remuneration arrangements in the establishment, including in particular the establishment of principles of remuneration and the introduction and application of new remuneration methods or modification of existing methods;

the fixing of job and bonus rates and comparable performance-related remuneration, including cash coefficients (that is, prices per time unit);

principles for suggestion schemes in the establishment.

Where no agreement can be reached on any of these twelve matters, the conciliation committee may make an award which takes the place of an agreement by the parties.

2. *Employees' Grievances (section 85).* The law states that "the Works Council shall hear employee grievances and if they appear justified, induce the employer to remedy them." If the employer and the works council cannot agree, the council may appeal to the conciliation committee. The award of the committee shall "take the place of an agreement" between the parties.

3. *The Nature of Jobs and the Work Environment (section 90 and 91).* Management is required to inform and consult with the works council on any plans it might have for the:

construction, alteration, or extension of the works, offices, and other premises,

modification of the technical plant, working process, and operations, or

modification of individual job design, or the way in which work is organized.

The law also requires that management take particular interest in the impact these changes may have on the nature of the work and the demands this work places on employees. In cases where the changes envisioned by management are thought to have adverse effects on individual employees, the works council's rights are upgraded from consultation to codetermination.

4. *Personnel ("Staff") Matters (sections 93-104)*. Works council rights in the formation of personnel policies are a mixture of rights to consultation and codetermination. In some areas, only the right of consultation is guaranteed; in others, there is the implicit right of codetermination in that certain policy changes must be "approved" by the works council. If approval is not forthcoming, then the matter is referred to a conciliation committee in the same way that disputes in areas governed by rights of codetermination are referred to the committee.

Specifically, the law provides:

the works council be informed in all matters related to manpower planning,

the works council may request that all vacancies be filled via internal competitions before new employees are hired,

that guidelines for the recruitment, transfer, regrading, and dismissal of employees shall require works council approval,

that management consult with the works council in the development of vocational training programs,

that the works council shall participate in the decision making regarding the implementation of vocational training programs.

The law gives the works council clear rights of codetermination in the areas of individual personnel permanent or temporary transfers or movements, and in all cases involving the dismissal of employees.

In the case of dismissal of employees, the law states "any notice of dismissal that is given without consulting the works council shall be null and void." The law then goes on to state the grounds on which the works council can object to any dismissal notice and the procedures to be followed in cases where objections to management's actions are lodged.

It is interesting to note that the law allows the works council to take the initiative and request that management dismiss employees who have in the works council's opinion "repeatedly caused serious trouble in the establishment." If management does not dismiss an employee that the works council has so designated, the works council may directly petition the labor courts for a decision in the matter.

5. *Economic Matters (sections 111 and 112).* The law gives the works council certain rights when management decides that "alterations" to the company's business are required. The law defines alterations as being:

reduction of operations in or closure of the whole or important departments of the establishment;

transfer of the whole or important departments of the establishment;

amalgamation with other establishments;

important changes in the organization, purpose, or plan of the establishment;

introduction of entirely new work methods and production processes.

Management is required to inform the works council of any proposed alterations that "may entail substantial prejudice to the staff or a large sector thereof . . ." Where such alterations have a prejudicial effect on the interests of employees, management is required to work out an agreement with the works council as to how the alteration will proceed and how those affected by it will be compensated. Where no agreement can be reached, application can be made to the Land (State) employment office for mediation of the dispute. If no application for mediation is made, or if efforts at mediation fail, then the works council can request that the dispute be referred to the conciliation committee which will first attempt to mediate the differences. If the committee cannot resolve the differences, the committee itself will render an award that is then binding on both sides. If management fails to abide by the conciliation committee's award, the employees who are affected by management's noncompliance can bring suit against the company in the labor court.

## Notes

1. E.C.M. Cullingford, *Trade Unions in West Germany* (Boulder, Colorado: Westview Press, 1977), p. 12.
2. Margaret Stewart, *Trade Unions in Europe* (Epping, Essex, England: Gower Press, 1974), p. 104.

3. Joachim Bergman, and Walther Muller-Jentsh, "The Federal Republic of Germany: Cooperative Unionism and Dual Bargaining System Challenged," in *Worker Militancy and Its Consequences 1965-75*, ed. Solomon Barkin (New York: Praeger Press, 1975), p. 242.

4. Richard J. Willey, "Trade Unions and Political Parties in the Federal Republic of Germany," *Industrial and Labor Relations Review* 28 (1):1974:48.

5. Charles J. Connaghan, *Partnership or Marriage of Convenience* (Ottawa, Canada: Canadian Department of Labor, 1977), p. 22.

6. Seyfarth, Shaw, Fairweather and Geraldson, *Labor Relations and the Law in West Germany and the United States* (Ann Arbor: University of Michigan Press, 1969), p. 52.

7. *Employee Participation and Company Structure* (Luxembourg: Commission of European Communities, 1975), p. 58.

8. Seyfarth et al., *Labor and the Law*, p. 83.

9. "West German Labor Court System: A Review," *European Industrial Relations Review*, No. 37, January 1977, p. 19.

10. Hans Reichel, "Recent Trends in Collective Bargaining in the Federal Republic of Germany," *International Labor Review*, December 1971:485.

11. Cullingford, *Trade Unions in West Germany*, p. 48.

12. Ibid., p. 36.

13. "Proposals for Comprehensive New Labor Code," *European Industrial Relations Review*, No. 50, February, 1978, p. 10.

14. "Operating Costs: Long German Vacations Slated to Get Longer," *Business Europe*, July 23, 1976, p. 235.

15. John Dornberg, "The VW, like Cuckoo Clocks and Cameras Become as Sauerkraut. Once Selling More than a Half Million Units Annually on the U.S. Market," *International Herald Tribune*, April 27, 1976, p. 5.

16. "Equal Opportunities in West Germany: A Progress Report," *European Industrial Relations Review*, No. 40, April, 1977, p. 13.

17. Willey, *Unions and Political Parties*, p. 42.

18. Herbert R. Northrup, "Why Multinational Bargaining Neither Exists Nor is Desirable," *Labor Law Journal*, 29 (6):1978:340.

19. "Employee Capital Sharing in West Germany," *European Industrial Relations Review*, No. 44, August, 1977, p. 2.

# Case 8
# Pickardt-Rhine
# International A.G. (A)

One afternoon in March, 1973, Klaus Müller stood at the window of his office overlooking Berlinerstrasse in Frankfurt. To Müller, it seemed as if the weather that winter had been particularly cold, but from the tone of the telephone call he had just received things might be warming up a bit. Müller was employee affairs manager for Pickardt-Rhine International A.G. (PRIAG), a wholly owned subsidiary of the Scott Food Company, a large American food processing and marketing company headquartered in Chicago, Illinois. Müller had just finished a forty-five-minute telephone conversation with Fritz Kringle, the employee relations manager at PRIAG's vegetable canning plant in Krefeld near Düsseldorf. Kringle had informed Müller that there were rumors of a "wildcat strike" circulating in the plant.

The chairman of the Krefeld Plant works council had met that morning with the plant manager and had demanded an immediate upward adjustment in the salaries of certain white-collar employee groups. He had complained that the salaries of Krefeld white-collar workers were not competitive with what was being paid in the other three food processing plants in the immediate area. After checking with his information sources in the plant, Kringle implied to Müller that a "wildcat strike was not out of the question."

Müller knew that the present contract between PRIAG and the Union of Food, Stimulants, Hotel, and Restaurant Employees (Gewerkschaft, Nahrung, Genuss, Gaststätten—NGG) still had three months to run. In fact, both the company and the union had only begun to outline their strategies for the annual contract negotiations due to begin in May. That such a demand should come so soon before the wage negotiations was unusual. Even more unusual, however, was the fact that the local works council had decided to involve itself in wage level discussions with the company. Under West German law, works councils had no authority to negotiate with the company over wages. Wage levels were a matter for the company and the union to decide. Nonetheless, the works council chairman had asked for an immediate increase of 12.6% for employees in certain job categories. Müller was even more disturbed, however, about the report that there might be a strike at a PRIAG plant—that would be unprecedented.

As he stood at the window, Müller was pondering the steps he should take to handle this situation. He surmised that it would not be long before his boss, Hans Smoller-Halde, the employee relations director, would be calling him for a recommendation. His thought pattern was broken by the buzzing of the telephone:

Yes, Herr Smoller-Halde. I don't know what to make of it either . . . OK,
I'll be right up . . . the Chairman's office . . . OK.

## The Company

PRIAG was a wholly owned subsidiary of the Scott Food Company of
Chicago. Scott Foods had purchased PRIAG from the Pickardt family in
1957. At the time of the acquisition, PRIAG was involved only in the canning and processing of a limited number of fruits and vegetables. Although
the company's product line was small in size, the PRIAG brand name enjoyed an excellent reputation with West German, Dutch, and Belgian con-
sumers. In fact, it was primarily the PRIAG brand image that Scott Foods
was interested in acquiring. Once the acquisition was complete, the U.S.
parent moved rapidly to expand the PRIAG product line. In the first ten
years after the acquisition, PRIAG introduced many new product lines, and
as a result, PRIAG's sales grew from 250 million deutsche marks in 1957 to
just over 1.0 billion deutsche marks in 1967.

After 1967, the product expansion effort subsided somewhat, and
PRIAG's top management began to concentrate on increasing the efficiency
of their operations and the productivity of the work force. One of the first
steps taken in this regard was the launching of a major production modernization program. All of the company's older production facilities were
either modernized or closed. Between 1968 and 1971, the company opened
three new, highly automated food processing facilities. The plant at Krefeld
was one of these new plants.

Throughout this period of modernization, the company's growth in sales
and earnings continued so that by 1972, year-end sales stood at just over 1.5
billion deutsche marks with a pre-tax profit of 180 million deutsche marks.
By 1973, PRIAG was one of the five largest food companies in West
Germany.

## Company Organization

At the corporate level, the company was organized along functional lines.
The directors of the six functional departments (marketing, production,
procurement, finance, research, and personnel and social affairs) reported
to the PRIAG general manager. The six department heads and the general
manager formed the company's management board. (See exhibit 8a-1 for
the organizational chart of the Frankfurt headquarters.)

The organization of PRIAG operating units was also along functional
lines. The managers of all production units reported to the director of the
production department, while managers of sales and distribution units reported to the head of the marketing department at Frankfurt. The staff

departments (finance, procurement, and personnel) had most of their personnel concentrated in Frankfurt. Staff in the operating units was kept to a minimum.

The seven processing and canning plants were also organized along functional lines, with all functional managers reporting to the plant manager. (See exhibit 8a-2 for the organizational structure at the Krefeld plant, which is typical of other PRIAG plants.) When asked about the relationship between staff personnel in operating units and the staff at the headquarters, one company executive said that "an informal, dotted-line relationship exists," but he added that the local staff was always directly responsible to the local line manager.

PRIAG employed 7,600 people who were scattered among fifteen locations in West Germany. Approximately 65% of the 7,600 employees were involved in production or production-related activities, 20% in marketing and distribution, and the remainder in staff organizations.

## The PRIAG Boards

At the highest level, PRIAG had the two-tiered board system (that is, a management board and a supervisory board) found throughout West German industry. Under the provisions of the Works Constitution Act of 1952, employees in most West German companies were given representation on their company's supervisory board. The employee representatives, who comprised one-third of the board membership, were not selected by the union or the works council, but were elected directly by the employees in a secret ballot. PRIAG's supervisory board was made up of six members. In management's opinion, the two employee representatives had always been reasonable, intelligent individuals who discharged their responsibilities in a diligent manner.

One of the major tasks of the supervisory board was the selection of the company's management board which at PRIAG was made up of seven top managers (see exhibit 8a-1). Members of the management board were elected by a majority vote of the supervisory board. Once elected to the management board, the new member was given a five-year employment contract with the company. Under the terms of the joint-stock corporation law, the supervisory board could remove any member from the management board although this had never happened at PRIAG.

## Union and Employee Relations

Unionized employees at PRIAG were represented by the NGG. The NGG was one of the sixteen unions in the Deutsche Gewerkschaftsbund (DGB), the trade union federation in West Germany that represented 7 million West

**Exhibit 8a-1**
**Organizational Chart of Pickardt-Rhine International A.G.**

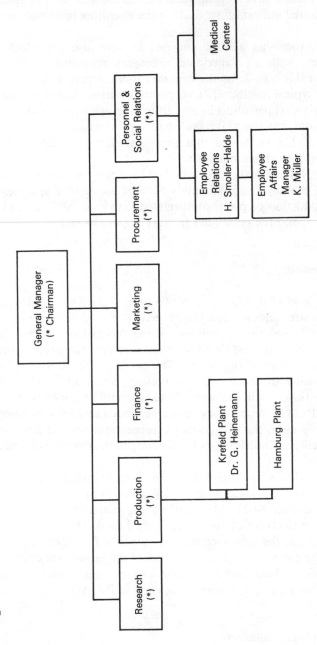

Note: Asterisk indicates members of management board.
The Employee relations department maintained a "dotted line" relationship with employee relations managers at all PRIAG plants.

**Exhibit 8a-2**
**Organizational Chart of Krefeld Plant**

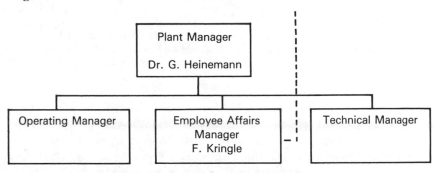

Note: "Dotted-line" relationship to Employee Relations Department of Frankfurt.

German workers. Not all PRIAG employees were members of the NGG, although PRIAG allowed all employees to enjoy the benefits the union was able to secure for its own members.

In the seven plants, union membership was very high, with approximately 80% of all blue-collar and approximately 50% of all white-collar employees being union members. The percentage of union members among PRIAG's white-collar work force varied at the other operating locations, but was considerably less than the 50% represented by the union at the plants. Unionization of white-collar employees was lowest at the Frankfurt headquarters, where less than 1% of the employees were union members.

Unlike most West German companies, PRIAG did not negotiate its labor agreements through an employers' association. PRIAG negotiated its collective bargaining agreements directly with the NGG. Relations between the NGG and PRIAG's management had always been good. A company official spoke with some pride when he said:

> We have never lost a day's work because of a strike. Relations with our employees have been characterized by cooperation, not confrontation. We have always tried very hard to maintain good communications with our workers, and we have always found the union and employee representatives to be reasonable in their dealings with the company.

> Recently, the people at the Chicago office started a big Employee Relations Program. It's interesting to note that we found the things they suggested we had already been doing for more than five years.

Another company executive commented on the company's relationship with the head of the NGG by saying:

> Herr Engles is an intelligent man who knows his business. He's been negotiating with this company for many years. He consistently drives a hard bargain for the workers in his union, but we have always found him to be reasonable in formulating the union's demands and in negotiating with the company.

The labor contract between PRIAG and the NGG was negotiated each year in May and was effective for 12 months beginning in June. Under the terms of the contract, all jobs at PRIAG (both blue- and white-collar) below a certain level were placed in one of fifteen job categories. All jobs were assigned a category irregardless of whether or not the employees in those jobs were union members. All blue-collar employees in job categories 1-8 and all white-collar employees in job categories A-F had their minimum wages set by the terms of the contract. Examples of personnel in job category F, the highest white-collar job category covered by the union contract, would be: a foreman of a workshop, a plant shift leader, or a junior sales representative (sales trainee). The company also had three white-collar job categories above those covered by the contract and below the rank of "leading employee." Personnel in job categories G-I were not represented by the union, but by the company's works councils.

For each job category, the company and the union negotiated a "tariff minima" or minimum wage which the company was required to pay an employee in the category. The company was free to pay any employee at a rate above the established minimum, and in some cases did; however, like most companies that negotiated their contracts directly with the union, PRIAG tried to keep its payroll near the minimums set by the contract.

The question of fitting individual employees into specific job categories was not a matter for negotiation with the union. Placement of present employees in new categories or new employees in existing categories was a matter of "codetermination" between the company management and the works council of the operating unit involved. The actual salary paid any employee was a matter for management alone to decide as long as the salary met the prescribed minimum set by the contract for the job category to which the employee had been assigned.

Any salary increases for an individual or group of individuals were solely a management prerogative and not a matter for codetermination with the works council. In fact, under the law governing the management-works council relationship, the works council had no authority in the area of wage increases. Under West German law, only the union could negotiate wage increases and then only increases in the tariff minima. This is not to say that West German companies had not negotiated "across the board" or overall increases in all employees' actual wages at times, but under the West German labor law, management was not forced to negotiate with either the union or the works council increases in the actual wages paid to company employees.

## The Works Councils

Under West German law, any employer with more than five employees was required to have a works council. Members of the works council served a three-year term and were elected by a secret ballot in which all employees above 18 years of age and below the rank of leading employee had one vote.

Management was required to consult with the works council on all matters that affected the well-being of employees. In many instances, company policies and programs were matters for codetermination, that is, both the works council and the management were required to reach agreement on the policy before it went into effect. If the parties were unable to reach an agreement, then the matter could be referred to a conciliation committee which was composed of an equal number of members appointed by the employer and the works council, plus an independent chairman acceptable to both parties. (If the parties were unable to agree on a chairman, one was appointed by the labor court.) A majority award of the conciliation committee had the same legal standing as an agreement between the parties.

PRIAG operated from fifteen locations in West Germany, and so, the company had fifteen local works councils representing its employees. In addition to these fifteen local works councils, there was also a corporate works council which was composed of one or two representatives from each of the local works councils. The job of the corporate works council was to represent the interests of all PRIAG employees on matters of corporate-wide policy.

Management officials at PRIAG were of the opinion that the works councils had proved to be a very valuable consultation device between management and the employees, providing an excellent avenue of communication both upward and downward in the organization. They were proud of the relationship that they had developed with the works councils and through them with the employees.

One company official referred to the manner in which a dispute over the pension plan had been handled as an indication of this good relationship:

> We recently reached agreement with the Corporate Works Council on a rather important pension plan administration issue. As you know, in Germany pension plans (up to now) are not an area for bargaining with the union. The company is free to decide how much money will be set aside each year for pensions. The labor law does stipulate, however, that works

councils have rights of co-determination in how the pension monies are administered and how they are to be distributed.

We recently re-vamped the PRIAG pension plan and in our discussions with the Corporate Works Council we had a small problem over the definition of "hardship cases." The Works Council wanted hardship cases to be co-determinated between themselves and management. We asked, what if we can't agree on what should be done in some specific case? Well, the Works Council thought it over and came back to us with their solution. If agreement could not be reached between management and the Works Council on how to interpret the meaning of "hardship case" as it applied in some particular context, rather than submit the dispute to the arbitration by a conciliation committee (as is required in the law), the Works Council would agree to leave the final decision up to the Management Board.

## The Krefeld Plant

Situated in West Germany on the west bank of the Rhine, the Krefeld plant was one of four food processing plants in the north Rhine area. Heins Food Products A.G. had a plant in Mülheim. Fischer Foods operated a facility near Oberhausen, and Eurofoods had a plant near Köln.

When PRIAG began production at the Krefeld plant in 1970, the company encountered some difficulty in finding sufficient numbers of trained personnel in the local area. With three other food processors operating in the immediate area and with the West German economy growing rapidly, labor was in short supply. To staff the facility at Krefeld, PRIAG was able to persuade certain key personnel to transfer from its plants elsewhere in West Germany. However, the bulk of the 1,450 jobs at Krefeld were filled from the local labor pool. Many employees were obtained from other industries in the area, but PRIAG was able to induce many others away from Heins, Fischer, and Eurofoods by offering wages at levels above those then prevailing in the local labor market.

Because the short labor supply required PRIAG to pay wages to its Krefeld employees that were well above wages paid in other parts of West Germany, and because of other special circumstances surrounding the start-up of the plant, PRIAG negotiated a separate labor contract with the NGG. This special and separate labor contract was renegotiated again in 1971, but after that, the employees at Krefeld were covered under the nationwide collective bargaining agreement between PRIAG and NGG. (Heins and Fischer negotiated a labor contract for all their workers directly with the NGG. Because the Eurofoods plant was the only operation the company had in West Germany, Eurofoods negotiated their labor contract through an employers' association. Regardless of how these four contracts were negotiated, they were all negotiated with the same union, the NGG.)

In the years that immediately followed the start-up of the plant, the local labor market, indeed the labor market throughout West Germany, tightened. In the early 1970s, unemployment in West Germany was less than 1%, and there were over 2 million foreign workers employed in West German industry. Faced with these conditions, PRIAG was forced to continue paying the substantial wage premiums it had initially offered to Krefeld employees. In 1973, the average premium paid to employees at Krefeld was 20% above the tariff minima set forth in the PRIAG labor contract.

## The Krefeld Works Council

Over the years, the PRIAG's management at the Frankfurt headquarters had come to believe that it had developed an efficient, loyal work force at Krefeld. Relations between the plant management and the Krefeld works council appeared to be good. One company official stated:

> Despite the fact that most of the employees at Krefeld were new to the company, they rapidly developed an esprit de corps. The plant in which they were working was one of the newest, most modern and efficient in the world. The workers at Krefeld were proud of their facility and I think they were proud to be working for PRIAG.

When asked to comment on the works council at Krefeld, another company official who managed the relationship between headquarters and all the PRIAG works councils said:

> There have been some difficulties in getting the workers together at Krefeld. The work force was drawn from workers in two provinces and traditionally people from these provinces have not worked together. You might say they were a little "provincial" in their outlook.

> The leadership of the works council has not always been the best. The chairman, Otto Schmidt, tries very hard to do a good job, but he's not what you would call a "natural leader," and he seems to have trouble getting all the workers together. He's a bit too emotional, not left-wing or radical, just a little erratic at times. As a result, I sometimes think that the workforce is poorly informed on some issues. I don't mean to imply that the relationship between the company and the Krefeld works council is not good, just that things could be better.

## The 1973-1974 Contract Negotiations

It was the custom in West Germany for officials of the union and the employees they represent to meet several months prior to the expiration date of the labor contract to discuss the terms of the upcoming negotiations. As the representatives of the employees, union officials felt obliged to elicit from the employees their objectives for the coming year. The union leaders also believed that having first consulted with the membership, their position was strengthened in the subsequent collective bargaining with the company.

Such a meeting between the leadership of the NGG and the union leaders in all of PRIAG's operations was held in mid-March, 1973. The stated purpose of the meeting was for the union to learn what PRIAG employees wanted from their new labor contract which was due to be negotiated in May.

Apparently, the meeting started normally enough with the union soliciting the views of the delegations from the various plants. When discussion turned to the percentage increase in wages desired by the employees, the meeting took an unexpected turn. When asked what percentage increase in the negotiated tariff minima was desired, Otto Schmidt, the chairman of the Krefeld delegation, shouted: "28%." The chairman of the meeting, a NGG official, chuckled and asked if the Krefeld delegation was serious. However, members of the Krefeld delegation immediately supported their chairman's demand, and the pace and intensity of the discussion subsequently quickened. Twenty-eight percent was very much above the figure that the union leadership expected. Apparently, the members of the other delegations present were also taken aback. Everyone had been thinking in terms of a 8-10% increase in the tariff minima. The Krefeld group was very vocal in their demand even though there seemed to be little support elsewhere for such a high percentage.

Present at the meeting was the leader of the NGG, Herr Engles. As it would be Engles's task to negotiate the new contract with the company, he was asked for his opinion of the Krefeld delegation's remarks. Engles told the chairman of the Krefeld delegation that he was out of line. He said that he was not going to risk his personal reputation as a professional negotiator by asking for 28% and then having to settle for a more reasonable 8-10%. Furthermore, Herr Engles told the Krefeld delegation that he would not subject the NGG to the adverse publicity that would result from such a ridiculous demand.

At this point, Otto Schmidt apparently became very emotional. He complained that his people were being paid a lot less than workers at the other plants near Krefeld. He said that such an increase was necessary to close the gap that had developed in the wage rates. When he insisted that the union demand a 28% increase in the contract's tariff minima, Herr Engles walked out of the meeting.

## The Works Council's Demands to the Plant Manager

News of what had occurred at the NGG union meeting quickly spread around the plant. One morning several days after the meeting, Otto Schmidt walked into the office of the plant manager, Herr Dr. G.

Heinemann, and in his capacity as the chairman of the Krefeld works council demanded that the company make an "on-the-spot correction in the area of wages and salaries" of employees in job categories B-F. The works council chairman said that these increases were warranted because PRIAG wages were not competitive with those of the other food companies in the area. The size of the increases demanded ranged from 12.6% for workers in job category B downward to 5.2% for workers in category F. In addition, the works council demanded that a new job classification plan be implemented. The works council's plan called for the four lowest blue-collar job categories to be replaced by six and that certain adjustments be made to the salaries in these job categories in addition to those requested for purposes of making PRIAG salaries more competitive with the neighboring food processing plants. Dr. Heinemann received the demand and told the works council chairman that he would think it over.

The plant manager then called to the office his employee relations manager, Fritz Kringle, and asked him what was going on. Kringle explained to Dr. Heinemann what had transpired several days earlier at the union meeting and reminded him that the question of noncompetitive wages had been an issue for some time. It had been a topic of discussion at several works council meetings over the last few years and, as Kringle reminded his boss, the topic had been discussed in many of the reports on works council meetings Kringle had submitted to him. Dr. Heinemaan responded:

> Well these demands are ridiculous—they always have been ridiculous. We are paying our people better than Heins, Fischer, and Eurofoods and everyone knows it. Why does the works council insist on raising this issue? I'm tired of all this noncompetitive nonsense. Call Müller in Frankfurt and see what he thinks. And tell Müller I'll be talking to his boss about this problem.

Kringle took the long way back to his office. He stopped several times to talk with employees in the plant and with several members of the works council. It was in these discussions that he got the feeling that the works council members were serious about their demands and that they had informally been discussing what steps they should take if the management did not reply. No one mentioned the word "strike," but Fritz Kringle felt that a strike might have been one of the alternatives the works council had considered.

When he got back to his office, he rang up Müller in Frankfurt to relate the events of the last few hours. Several times during the conversation, Müller asked Kringle what he thought the company should do. He also asked for an assessment of how serious the situation really was. Müller probed:

> Is the works council really serious or is this just another case of Schmidt just letting off some steam? You know his pride may have been hurt by the

way Engles treated him in that meeting. He may be doing this as a way of regaining some of his self-image as a leader of the works council.

Kringle replied:

I don't know, Herr Müller. It may be as you say, but from the people I've talked to around the plant, it appears as if Schmidt may have a stronger backing than you estimate. You know . . .

Kringle hesitated a moment. He wondered if it would be proper to inter-ject that in his opinion the problem had been brewing for quite some time, and that he had warned his boss about it on several occasions. Should he air the plant's "dirty linen" with the employee relations manager at head-quarters?

"I know what?" asked Müller.

Kringle decided that now was not the time to hold back:

"Well, you must know that this issue has been simmering on the back burner for over a year now."

Surprised, Müller responded:

It has? I thought that the first time this dissatisfaction surfaced was at the union meeting several days ago. I have posed several questions about that meeting in a letter I mailed yesterday. All right, well let's get all the facts out now, we have a decision to make.

# Pickardt-Rhine
# International A.G. (B)

The evening of April 2, 1973, Klaus Müller, employee affairs manager at the Frankfurt headquarters of Pickardt-Rhine International A.G., had to run to catch the 6:45 P.M. inter-city train from Düsseldorf to Frankfurt. As he settled into the seat, Müller began to reflect on the meetings he had held that day with the management and leaders of the works council at PRIAG's food processing plant at Krefeld. Müller had gone to Krefeld to investigate the background of a problem that had arisen concerning wages paid to white-collar employees at the plant. Several days earlier, Müller had been informed by the employee relations manager at Krefeld that there were rumors of a wildcat strike at the plant if certain demands of the works council were not met. In a subsequent meeting held in the Frankfurt office of PRIAG's management board chairman, Müller had been charged with finding a solution to the problems at Krefeld.

As the train pulled out of the Köln Hauptbahnhof, Müller began writing his report of the day's events. The meeting at Krefeld was attended by Dr. G. Heinemann, Krefeld plant manager; Fritz Kringle, employee relations manager at the plant; Otto Schmidt, chairman of the Krefeld works council and Walter Bogden, deputy chairman of the works council. Müller was the sole representative of the Frankfurt headquarters. The meeting that morning started with Schmidt outlining what the works council saw as the basis for the problem. The works council believed that:

1. the minimum wages specified in the Krefeld labor contract (the tariff minima) were considerably below those paid at the three other food processing plants in the immediate area;

2. many new employees at Krefeld were being hired on at wage levels above those of employees who had been at Krefeld several years;

3. the tariff minima should be increased to the level of actual wages paid by the company.

The works council chairman produced what he called "documented evidence" that what he said was true. Schmidt showed the management group copies of tariff schedules he had obtained from the works councils at Heins Food Products, Fischer Foods, and Eurofoods. As it was not clear to Müller how the works council, based on this evidence, had reached its conclusion, Müller said he would need some time to study the data the works council had compiled.

Schmidt and Bogden went on to say that they had indications that certain white-collar employees at Krefeld in lower job categories were being paid actual wages that were below those paid to PRIAG employees in similar jobs at other locations in West Germany. The management group was led to believe that the cause of this problem was that these employees' job descriptions had been misclassified and, therefore, the works council was preparing a new plan for job categories for the whole plant which could be negotiated at the same time the tariff schedules were negotiated with the unions.

Management accepted Schmidt's arguments without substantive comment, although on several occasions Müller was distressed by the way Dr. Heinemann reacted to certain of Schmidt's assertions. In three or four instances, Heinemann had interrupted Schmidt saying, "that's just not true" or "your facts are wrong." Müller had hoped that this meeting would help diffuse the situation by giving Schmidt and Bogden a chance to air their case. As the meeting adjourned for lunch, Müller thought that the works council representatives had had the opportunity to do just that, but Heinemann's interjections did not seem to help. Kringle had been silent during most of the morning. He seemed to defer his comments until he had an opportunity to see how Dr. Heinemann was reacting.

The management group lunched alone, and in the privacy of an executive dining room, they discussed individual reactions to the works council's presentation. Heinemann was incredulous about some of Schmidt's assertions. He knew that wages at Krefeld were at least on a par with those of other plants in the immediate area, and he just could not understand how Schmidt had reached some of the conclusions he had. Kringle reminded him of the "evidence" presented and said that there might be some basis for a misunderstanding.

Müller went on to say that because the processes and products of the other three plants were not identical to those at Krefeld, the other companies probably had organized the work of their employees in different manners. This would result in different job descriptions even though the titles used for specific jobs might be very similar to those used at Krefeld. If this were true, direct job-to-job comparisons of the tariff schedules could mislead the works council into believing that PRIAG wages were below those of the company's competition.

About halfway through the main course, Müller suggested that they begin to formulate a strategy for dealing with the works council's complaints. During the morning meeting, Müller had told Schmidt and Bogden that he was sure they could work out something that would be acceptable to both sides. In less than an hour, Müller and the other two managers would again be sitting across the table from the leadership of the Krefeld works council. If Müller was going to be successful in quickly diffusing the situation at Krefeld, he would have to do it in the next several hours.

# Pickardt-Rhine
# International A.G. (C)

By the time lunch was over, Müller, Kringle, and Heinemann had reached a consensus on how to approach the afternoon session with the leaders of the works council. At the afternoon meeting, Müller proposed the following to Schmidt and Bogden:

1.  Management wanted to divide the issues raised by the works council and deal with the problems separately.

2.  First, the company would look into the apparent "misclassification" of certain jobs and if the classifications were wrong, Müller was certain that agreement could be reached between management and trade union on appropriate reclassifications.

3.  Second, on the issue of salary discrepancies between employees in similar positions within PRIAG, Müller stated that the works council was probably mistaken. Wages at the Krefeld plant were way above those paid at other locations because of the shortage of trained local labor; but, this too would be studied by the company.

4.  Third, on the issue of PRIAG paying its Krefeld employees at rates below the neighboring companies, Müller proposed that a comprehensive study of the tariffs and actual wages of the three other firms in the area would be undertaken. The works council was reminded, however, that direct comparisons were probably misleading because of probable differences in job descriptions of the various companies. The company would seek to identify jobs in other plants that were comparable to those at Krefeld, and if it was found that PRIAG employees were underpaid, the company would agree to raise wages to a level that equalled the average paid by the other firms.

5.  The proposed studies would be completed within two months and results reported back to the Krefeld works council.

6.  Müller agreed that the adoption of a new job classification plan for blue-collar workers could be discussed in the upcoming union negotiations.

Müller and the other two managers were pleasantly surprised when the works council leaders posed no objections to Müller's plan. After some general discussion of other more routine problems, management and the two employee representatives thanked each other for the opportunity to discuss their differences and the meeting was adjourned.

Müller had little time to discuss the results of the meeting with Heinemann and Kringle before he hurried off for his train back to Frankfurt.

As the train pulled into Frankfurt station, Müller was just finishing the draft of his report. In the taxi on the way home, he felt confident that the current situation at Krefeld had diffused, at least for the moment. The study he had proposed would not be easy—it would require the cooperation of management at three of PRIAG's competitors. But as Müller thought it over, it was probably the only thing that PRIAG could do. The company valued its relationship with its work force and their works council representatives and would spare no expense to keep the relationship on a sound basis.

For the short term the problem was solved, the apparent crisis over; but, as he walked up the driveway to his house, Klaus Müller was thinking about the root causes of the current problem and what the company might do to prevent such a situation from arising again.

# Case 9
# Fischer Electric A.G.

By the winter of 1974-1975, it was apparent that the West German economy was headed for what some economists had predicted would be the most serious economic recession since the end of World War II. As Kurt Glauber, general manager of the small motors and generators division of Fischer Electric A.G., finished reading the preliminary operating reports of his division for the first two months of 1975, he was forced to conclude that the sales slump the division had recently experienced was growing worse. The preliminary operating reports made it clear that he would soon be required to reach a decision on how best to reduce the division's output. Glauber had watched the sales of his division move steadily downward over the last six months. Faced with steadily rising inventories, two months ago he had taken steps to reduce output, but given present sales levels and the gloomy forecasts emanating from the staff economists at the Fischer's headquarters, more decisive action was needed, and soon.

The small motors and generators (SMG) division was one of six operating divisions of Fischer Electric A.G., a large West German producer of electric generators, motors, and other electrical equipment. In 1974, the SMG division had operated at a sales level of 550 million deutsche marks. What had Herr Glauber so concerned was that when projected on a quarterly basis, the preliminary reports showed that the division's sales were running 48% below last year's figures. To meet present sales levels, the division needed to operate at only 40% of its capacity. Inventories stood at 9.1 months at current sales volume and 4.6 months at the sales level forecasted in the division's operating budget. If the current sales volumes held through the end of the first quarter, the preliminary reports indicated that the division would sustain a loss from operations of close to 8 million deutsche marks in the first quarter of 1975. (See exhibit 9-1 for sales and profit figures for the first quarter in 1973 through the fourth quarter in 1975.)

Glauber had come to the conclusion that to prevent the operating loss from deteriorating further, he would have to take steps to dramatically reduce output. To do so would necessitate a temporary reduction in manpower of at least 30%. Facilities for the storage of inventory were already near capacity, so the length of the reduction would depend on the return of sales to normal levels. As no one knew how long the recession would last, Glauber had no way of knowing how long he would be forced to operate at the reduced level of output.

After first consulting with his operating managers and divisional staff, Glauber requested a meeting with the senior managers in the employee relations department at Fischer's corporate headquarters near Hamburg. The

**Exhibit 9-1**
**Summary of Sales and Profits in the Small Motors and Generators Division**
*(in million Deutsche marks)*

|                  | 1973  |      | 1974  |       |       | 1975  |
|                  | QIV   | QI   | QII   | QIII  | QIV   | QI    |
|------------------|-------|------|-------|-------|-------|-------|
| Quarterly sales  | 132.5 | 144.0| 153.0 | 157.0 | 95.5  | 69.0  |
| Quarterly profits| 5.1   | 6.6  | 6.1   | 3.2   | (4.9) | (8.3) |
| Annual sales     | 498.5 |      |       |       | 550   |       |
| Annual profits   | 19.5  |      |       |       | 11.0  |       |

Note: *Q* stands for quarter; the roman numeral following it shows the first, second, third, or fourth quarter. The data in parentheses indicate losses.

question he would pose to the corporate headquarters' personnel management group was how he should proceed in reducing his labor force output over the next three months.

## The Company

Fischer Electric A.G. was a large multinational corporation that had worldwide sales in 1974 of over 5 billion deutsche marks. The company's traditional product lines included heavy electrical equipment of the type used by public utilities, large electrical motors and generators used primarily in industrial applications, marine generators, electric train engines, and chemical batteries. In recent years, the company had diversified its product line through the acquisition of companies that produced small motors and generators primarily for the automotive industry and a company that manufactured electric appliances for use in the home. Fischer, its subsidiaries, and affiliates conducted substantial business outside West Germany. In 1974, Fischer's consolidated foreign sales stood at nearly 200 million deutsche marks. Around the world, Fischer owned or had an equity interest in over seventy-five companies which operated in eighteen countries.

Within West Germany itself, Fischer operated twenty-three companies. Within the parent company, there were six operating divisions organized along functional lines. Most of the manufacturing operations of the parent company were carried on at a large industrial complex near Hamburg and from three other locations within West Germany. The three plants of the SMG division were located near Lüneburg, about 75 kilometers southeast of the main complex at Hamburg.

## The Small Motors and Generators Division

The principal product lines of the SMG division were electrical motors and generators used primarily by the automotive industry. The SMG division traditionally sold about 45% of its output to industrial customers outside West Germany, primarily to other nations in the EEC, the United States, and Brazil.

The division employed 5,600 workers at its three plants near Lüneburg. As division general manager, Glauber was responsible for the division's sales and marketing and distribution efforts in West Germany and the EEC. Sales outside the EEC were handled by Fischer's international sales division. While most of Fischer's businesses were organized more along functional lines, the SMG division which was the result of a 1967 acquisition of a small, specialized company, was much more decentralized. Rather than disrupt what was seen at the time as a successful operating organization, Fischer's top management had decided not to integrate the existing SMG organization into Fischer's functional structure.

## Union and Employee Relations at Fischer Electric

Workers at Fischer Electric were represented by several unions, the most important of which was the electrical workers' union (EWU). Over 85% of all unionized employees belonged to the EWU—the remainder (primarily white-collar employees, scientists, and engineers), were represented by several much smaller unions and professional associations. Not all of the Fischer work force was unionized, but a large percentage of the blue-collar production workers did belong to the EWU.

Like most companies in West German industry, Fischer negotiated its labor contract through an employers' association. Fischer belonged to the electrical industry employers' association, and each year the association conducted the collective bargaining sessions on behalf of all its members. In this way, Fischer was spared direct confrontation with the EWU and, for the most part, Fischer's relationship with EWU leadership had been good.

Far more important from the company's perspective was the relationship with the work force itself. Relations between workers and management were maintained through a variety of channels, the most important of which were: worker representatives on the supervisory board; the company's works councils; and what at Fischer had come to be called a group of *vertrauensleute* or "men of confidence."

## Employee Representation on Fischer's Supervisory Board

At the highest level, the company had the two-tier board system found throughout West German industry. Under the provisions of the Works Constitution Act of 1952, workers in West German industry were permitted representation on the company's board of directors. These worker representatives were not selected by the union or the works council; rather, they were elected directly by the employees by a secret ballot. Worker representatives comprised one-third of the total board membership. In companies having a three-member board, the single employee representative was required to be an hourly paid employee. In companies having a six-member board, one of the worker representatives was required to be an hourly paid employee; the other, a salaried employee.

Fischer's supervisory board had six members, but the company was preparing to expand the board to twelve seats to accommodate an anticipated change in the law. Under the proposed new law, labor and capital would be equally represented. On the new twelve-seat board would be six directors elected by employees.

When asked about the company's experience with employee representatives on the supervisory board and how the management viewed the recent changes in the law, one senior company official explained:

> We think that having two employee representatives on our board has had some very positive effects on the company. First of all, it gives the employees a feeling that they have real input to the policy-making process. Second, it is an effective channel of communication for both upward and downward information exchange.

> Our experience has been that the employee representatives have been very reasonable in their approach and conscientious in discharging their responsibilities. We have no real reservations about expanding the number of employee representatives on the board. We foresee no real problems developing from it. We have gotten along very well for over twenty years with worker participation in board-level decision making. We know how to handle it, but more importantly, perhaps, our workers know what the responsibility entails and how important rational decision making is to the long-term success of the enterprise.

**The Works Council**

All West German employers with more than twenty employees were required by law to have a works council. The works council was composed of employees (not management) who were elected to three-year terms in a secret ballot in which each employee had one vote. The task of the works council was to assist management in the operation of the enterprise. The primary area of responsibility for the works council was in employee relations and personnel policy. However, the works council also had important duties in the economic management of the enterprise as well.

The Works Constitution Act of 1972 which spelled out the rights and duties of works councils, specifically stated that certain matters of policy had to be codetermined between management and the works council.

Codetermination required consensus between management and works council before any policies or company actions that affected employees could be taken. While labor contracts and wage rates were set through negotiations with the union, the works council had rights of consultation and/or codetermination in areas such as working hours, vacations, administration of benefit plans, job classifications, hiring and firing of employees, and substantive changes in the work routine.

Workers at each of Fischer's operating plants were represented by a works council. In addition, there was a corporate works council at the Hamburg headquarters which represented all Fischer employees. The corporate works council was composed of two members from each of the local works councils.

It had been the long standing policy of Fischer's senior management to actively support the operation and functioning of the company's works councils. One senior company official when commenting on this policy said:

> We have always sought to maintain the best possible relationship with our works councils. It is our policy to inform them as clearly and as openly as possible on all matters which concern our employees. We involve the works council as early as possible in the decision-making process. We have found that by doing so we have always been able to work things out to our mutual satisfaction before actual crises arise. Every week the chairman and deputy chairman of Fischer's works council meet with the top employee relations manager in the company to discuss social and political matters.
>
> Proof of the effectiveness of our policy is the fact that we have not had a strike, slowdown, walkout, or any form of work stoppage in over fifty years. We value our relationship with our employees—we're all members of the "Fischer family"—and we will go to any length to maintain that relationship.

Another Fischer manager added:

> We need a strong stable works council. It helps us tremendously in working with our employees. To insure we have capable people on the works council, we spend millions of deutsche marks a year on works council education programs.

The company did have a substantial program aimed at increasing the professional abilities of works council members. Each year, each works council member was offered the opportunity to attend programs given by company officials in such areas as accounting, financial management, labor law, social development, psychology, and human relations. The purpose of these programs was to educate the works council members in areas that would not only help them to fulfill their responsibilities on the works councils, but would also help them to increase their appreciation of the tasks of management as well.

## The Vertrauensleute

In every plant each year, every fifty to one hundred workers elected what were known as "men of confidence." These men were not representatives of the union, although at Fischer, 80% of the *vertrauensleute* were members of trade unions. The function of the men of confidence was to act as a liaison between the individual employee and the works council. At Fischer, because of the size of the organization and the heavy workload of works council members, it was sometimes difficult for individual employees to have their opinions heard by the council. It was equally difficult sometimes for the works council members to have a good feeling for the mood of the work force on certain issues. The *vertrauensleute* filled the gap—in the words of one company official, they were the "ears of the employees" and the "eyes of the works council." In cases of disputes, the men of confidence acted as the mediators between individual employees and the works council. They also served the function at times as an intermediary between individual employees and the company personnel office or between employees and line management. Like members of the works councils, the men of confidence also received training from the company. They regularly attended special courses in labor law and received training in human relations and leadership skills.

At Fischer, the system of the *vertrauensleute* was in existence before the union began representing the employees. In recent years, the union had tried to get people whose first loyalty was to the union elected to positions of *vertrauensleute*, but had failed. The Fischer system was probably unique in West German companies of its size because the union had not been able to influence the selection of the men of confidence. In other industries, men of confidence often had their first loyalty to the union; at Fischer, the *vertrauensleute* was loyal first to his constituency, then to the company, and only then to the union.

## The Origin of the SMG Division's
## Current Problems

The rapid decline in the SMG division's sales and profits was due to several factors acting in concert. First, about 40% of Fischer's export sales had traditionally been sold directly to automotive manufacturers in the United States. In 1974, the U.S. automobile industry was experiencing major reductions in sales of new models. Fischer's sales to the United States continued at near normal levels until the U.S. manufacturers decided to drastically reduce their output. When Ford, GM, and Chrysler (major Fischer customers) all announced assembly plant closings, Fischer's sales in the U.S. market dropped to near zero.

Shortly thereafter, European automobile manufacturers began to experience similar difficulties. Fischer's sales to the West German automobile industry and sales to automotive manufacturers in other EEC countries dropped, as production cutbacks were announced. The impact on Fischer was further increased when in addition to cutting back production, the automotive industry also attempted to reduce their stocks of automotive parts. It was the combination of the recession in the United States and the production cutbacks in Europe that produced the dramatic drop in the SMG division's sales and profits.

**Actions Already Taken**

As sales and profits had continued to decline in the fourth quarter of 1974, Glauber and the SMG works council had taken several steps to reduce the division's output and cut costs while at the same time trying to minimize the impact of the cutbacks on the Lüneburg work force. Everyone agreed that the Christmas season was a bad time to consider laying off workers, and so, Glauber had taken what steps he could to cut output and labor costs short of actual release of employees. During December, January, and February, SMG management with the approval of the works council had taken the following actions:

1. stopped hiring new employees;

2. reduced work for outside subcontractors and assigned idle workers to fill in for subcontractor personnel;

3. reduced overtime hours and, finally, eliminated all overtime operations;

4. tightened up on discipline; strictly enforcing work rules and terminating employees who did not comply;

5. transferred some personnel to other divisions that were not as badly affected by the recession;

6. offered early retirement to those employees near retirement age; and,

7. asked all personnel who had saved up vacation time from previous years to take their accrued vacation leave.

**The Next Steps**

The actions Glauber had taken in the three previous months eased the problem somewhat, but by mid-March, it was apparent that other more drastic steps would have to be taken if the division was to be saved from substantial financial losses. As Glauber and his staff prepared for the meeting with the Hamburg headquarter's personnel group, they were considering taking one or more of the following actions:

1. ask that all division personnel take their annual 1975 vacations in late March and April as opposed to during the summer months which was the custom in West Germany,

2. reduce the work week by about 30% for all personnel,

3. dismiss 25-30% of the division's work force.

Glauber knew that whatever was done to ease the current crisis would have to be approved by the local works council. Before raising these alternatives with the SMG works council, Glauber thought it best to first discuss the situation with the headquarters' personnel management group. The three alternatives were presented to the headquarters' group and the following analysis of the alternatives emerged from the meeting.

*Forced Early Vacation Leave.* Forcing all employees to take their annual vacations early in the year was obviously the most palatable of the three alternatives for both management and labor. Although early vacations posed some problems for the work force, especially those with children in school, it seemed preferable to shortened hours or mass dismissals. What concerned both the divisional and headquarters' management, however, was the fact that there was really no way of knowing how long the recession would last. Forcing vacations to be taken in late March and April would allow output to be cut by almost 60-75% for a six-week period and, thus, help eliminate some of the overstocks of inventory. But, by the middle of May production would have to be increased again, or Glauber would face once more the situation of having idle workers in the SMG plants.

Aside from the financial effects of the reduction in output, Glauber indicated in the meeting that he was also concerned for the psychological effects idling the plant was having on his work force. The production cutbacks already taken had caused many workers to be without work. Supervisors were now having to ask that machines be cleaned several times a day and that the plant floors be swept three times a day just to keep workers from standing around with nothing to do. The morale of the work force was steadily declining, and if after the vacation the same "make work" routines had to be adopted, Glauber was uncertain about the long-term effects this would have on the work force.

Since the labor contract provided that an employee on vacation would receive his regular pay plus a 30% bonus, forced early leave would do nothing to reduce or even postpone labor costs. As a result, this first alternative would help the division financially only by cutting material costs and inventory carrying charges. Management knew that there would be certain costs attached to idling the plant while the SMG work force was on vacation, and Glauber had asked his engineering and accounting departments to prepare a cost analysis of this alternative. Although the analysis was not yet complete, the preliminary estimates indicated that the income statement would not be materially improved if forced early leave was adopted.

*Reduced Work Hours.* Shortening the work week by as much as 30% appeared to offer a more viable solution to the problem. The division could operate on shortened hours for an indefinite period, if necessary. Labor costs could be cut considerably and at the same time the financial impact on the work force could be lessened if the company could meet the necessary qualifications for a government unemployment compensation program.

The key variable in the adoption of this alternative would be securing the approval of the works council. If the works council agreed, the company could obtain permission from the federal labor office to make application for the insurance benefits. Application for the insurance programs required a long and involved legal process where detailed plans for the short-hours program had to be explained and justified. If accepted by the labor office, the insurance fund would pay each employee 60% of the salary lost due to shortened hours. The law required that every employee receive at least 90% of his regular salary during periods of short hours. If the payment from the insurance fund plus the employees' wages received from the company under shortened hours did not amount to 90% of his regular salary, then the company was required to make up the difference.

The average employee at Fischer earned 2,800 deutsche marks per month. If the division shortened the work week by 30%, then the average cut in pay received from the company would amount to DM 840. The insurance fund would pay the employee 60% of this figure, or DM 504. Thus, the average employee would receive DM 504 from the fund plus 70% of his usual earnings or DM 1,960 for a total of DM 2,464. As 90% of the employees' regular salary (DM 2,800) was DM 2,520, the company would be required to pay an additional DM 56 to the average employee. The company's total labor costs for the average employee would be thereby reduced from DM 2,800 to DM 2,016, a savings of 28%. The total savings in labor costs to the company would amount to over DM 4,390,000 per month.

Also to be considered, however, were the costs of closing down redundant production processes and other expenses that would result from the slowdown in operations. Based on rough calculations of the costs, the management group estimated that the net effect on the income statement would be to reduce the division's loss by approximately DM 2,500,000 per month if current sales levels could be maintained. Given the rate at which the division's operating losses were mounting, a reduction of this magnitude would certainly be welcomed.

Shortened hours had its disadvantages as well. First, the process for gaining labor office approval was long and complicated. The company would have to prepare detailed economic analyses and justifications for its action; and then, the documents would have to circulate through several layers within the bureaucracy of the labor office. The whole process could take ten to twelve weeks.

Second, if the division was forced to continue shortened hours for a long period of time, the risk was run that many of the most capable production employees might grow tired of sustaining a 10% cut in their wages and seek employment elsewhere. Although a long recession would certainly increase unemployment throughout the West German economy, highly trained and skilled technicians of the type employed in many SMG operations would almost be certain to find better employment situations if they had ample opportunity to look. If the best people in the SMG work force left to find better paying jobs, then the division might be hard pressed to replace these workers once the demand for SMG products allowed production to return to normal levels. Loss of key people could perhaps be reduced if the division adopted the third alternative, the dismissal of part of the work force.

## Dismissal of 25-30% of the SMG Work Force

Dismissal of SMG employees was a difficult alternative to consider, yet one that management knew must be discussed. Clearly, the financial difficulties posed by the current recession might eventually necessitate this type of action. The recession in the United States had gone on for almost three years, and if the European economies were in for an economic downturn of anywhere near that length, dismissal of part of the SMG work force seemed to be the best alternative from the financial point of view. Immediate costs of this action would be high, as employees released would have to receive some sort of severance allowance if management had any hope of getting the proposal through the works council and winning the approval of the labor office. The costs in terms of employee morale might also be high. It had been many years since Fischer had been forced to terminate a large number of employees. Management felt that much of the goodwill that existed between the company and its work force was due to the fact that employment with Fischer was seen by most workers as a very secure means of livelihood.

Aside from the long-term financial savings that would accrue from dismissal of part of the work force, this alternative appeared to have another advantage from management's perspective. Over the past four or five years, the West German economy had been booming and the SMG division's business had grown remarkably. During this time, the work force had been greatly expanded, but due to the shortage of labor that accompanied the boom, some of the employees SMG had hired in the last few years were not as skilled or competent as the company might have desired. For the most part, their performance had been adequate, and their productivity acceptable, and until now, the company had no compelling reason to "weed out" the marginal performers in the work force. The present crisis offered such an opportunity. The fat which had accumulated on the SMG organization in the last few years might now be reduced. Employees whose performance had been only marginal could be released, while the company retained the most highly skilled members of the work force. Whereas the company ran the risk of losing some of its best workers if the alternative of shortened hours was adopted, dismissal of part of the work force removed such risk. Those who survived the reduction in force would remain at full salary, and, therefore, not be tempted to seek better employment elsewhere.

Winning approval of the works council would no doubt be difficult and perhaps the long-term effects on employee morale adverse; nonetheless, a mass dismissal was a sure way to move the division out of its current difficulties. Should the return to normal levels of production be long in coming, this alternative was probably the best way to reduce the impact of the slowdown on those employees who remained.

Another serious disadvantage posed by the dismissal alternative would result if the slowdown was only temporary in nature. Of course, management had no way of knowing, and the economic forecasts in SMG markets were not bright, but if normal sales levels were to resume in six to nine months, the division would face the problem of increasing the size of work force to normal levels. This would require hiring and training of a subtantial number of employees. Productivity of new production employees was certain to be below that of even the marginal performers now on the work force, and so, the return to current levels of operating efficiency would take some time.

**The Meeting with the SMG Divsion's
Works Council**

About three days after Glauber and his staff met with the top personnel and employee relations managers at Fischer's headquarters, he requested a meeting with the leadership of the SMG works council. At that meeting, Glauber told the works council representative what steps the company was considering taking to reduce the output of the SMG division, and he presented the results of the analysis made by the management group several days before. Glauber reiterated that none of the alternatives was attractive and that serious disruptions in the family life of some or all employees were bound to occur regardless of what action was taken. He told the works council leaders that as much as he disliked having to reduce output, it had to be done. If the division was to survive the financial consequences of reducing its production output, then some action must be taken to reduce costs, especially labor costs.

Glauber said that forced early vacation was a short-term solution; if adopted, the company would be placed in a "wait-and-see" position. If improved sales were not forthcoming in the three week periods each half of the work force was out, then at the end of six weeks, they would be faced with a choice of short hours or dismissal. Glauber counseled the works council leaders to take the long-range view. He said, "All of our jobs depend upon the financial stability of this division. If we fail to take the proper course of action in this matter, we will certainly lose one way or another."

Glauber closed the meeting by asking for the advice and help of the works council. He made available to the works council the economic analyses that had been prepared on each alternative. He requested that the works council think the problem through and meet again with him within a week.

### The Works Council's Reaction

Five days after the meeting between Glauber and the leadership of the SMG works council, the chairman of the works council requested a meeting in Glauber's office. At that meeting, Glauber was informed that the works council would accept either the forced early vacation or the shortened hours, but not both. The works council chairman told Glauber that asking for both forced vacation and then shortened hours was more than the work force would accept. He stated also that they refused to even consider the alternative of mass dismissal. However, Glauber was of the opinion that the position of the works council in the long run might be somewhat more flexible than the chairman's immediate statements indicated.

### The Decision to be Made

With the reactions of his works council in hand, Glauber went again to the headquarters' personnel group. Up until that time, the discussion had been more or less "informal." Management had only been "considering" alternatives and had asked the works council for its "advice." For management, the task now became one of deciding what course or courses of action it should take to reduce the labor force at the SMG division and how management's decision would be formally proposed to the works council.

A complete review of the legal, social, political, and strategic implications of the alternatives was in order. The decisions made in the case of SMG might become the basis for similar actions in other divisions. In his discussions with the headquarters' staff, Glauber had learned that his division's problems were not unique. Although other divisions were not, as yet, as seriously affected by the economic recession, all indications were that the sales decline that had started in SMG product lines the previous fall, was now beginning to occur in other Fischer divisions. The way in which the SMG division reduced its labor output might well set a precedent that would have to be followed throughout the Fischer organization.

# 6 Labor Relations in Sweden

## Introduction

The population of Sweden in 1978 was 8.3 million, the smallest of all the countries in this study. During the period 1970-1978, Swedish population increased only 3%, a rate of increase higher than that of Britain or West Germany, but considerably below the rate in the other countries (see table A-1).*

The gross national product of Sweden in 1976 was $74 billion, which was the lowest of all the countries. However, the gross national product per person was $9,030—the highest of all seven countries. Moreover, the gross national product per person during the 1970-1976 period grew at an annual rate of 2.1% which, although a smaller growth rate than that of France or the Netherlands, was larger than that of the other countries studied (see table A-2).

Consumer prices in Sweden during the period 1970-1978 increased 98% which was lower than in Great Britain, France, or Italy but higher than in West Germany, the United States, or the Netherlands (see table A-3). During the same period, 1970-1978, unemployment in Sweden averaged only 2.1%—equal to the rate in West Germany and lower than the rate in any of the other countries, including the United States, where the rate was almost three times as high (see table A-4).

The average hourly compensation for production workers in manufacturing in Sweden in 1978 was $11.43, which was approximately equal to the compensation of Dutch workers but was higher than that of workers in any of the other countries, including the United States. During the period 1970-1978, compensation for Swedish workers rose 243% in terms of U.S. dollars which was higher than in the United States and Great Britain but lower than in the other countries. In terms of local purchasing power, Sweden's worker compensation increased 51% during the 1970-1978 period which also was higher than in the United States and Great Britain but lower than in the other European countries (see table A-5).

Output in manufacturing in Sweden increased on an average of 3.9% per year during the period 1960-1978 but only 1.3% per year during 1970-1978. The 1970-1978 rate of increase was lower than in all the other

---

*Tables A-1 through A-13 referred to in this chapter are in the statistical appendix at the end of the book.

233

countries except Great Britain (see table A-6). Productivity as measured in output per hour in manufacturing increased 5.6% per year during 1960-1978 and 2.9% per year during the 1970-1978 period. In the 1970-1978 period, only the United States and Great Britain had lower average yearly increases in productivity (see table A-7).

Unit labor costs in terms of Swedish currency increased 5.8% per year during the 1960-1978 period and 12.0% per year during 1970-1978 (see table A-8). In terms of U.S. dollars, the increases in unit labor costs were 7.0% per year during 1960-1978 and 14.2% per year during the 1970-1978 period. During 1970-1978, the increase in unit labor costs was higher than in all other countries except the Netherlands and was more than twice the increase of that in the United States (see table A-9).

## The Union Movement

### Structure

The Swedish labor movement is split into three confederations: the Swedish Confederation of Trade Unions (LO) for blue-collar workers; the Central Organization of Salaried Employees (TCO) for white-collar workers; and the Confederation of Professional Associations (SACO) for professional employees. Although during the 1970s the three confederations have moved closer together, and in 1975 there were attempts by the LO and TCO to coordinate their bargaining efforts, there appears to be little likelihood of amalgamation in the near future.[1] The major barrier to consolidation is the difference over wage policy. The LO's solidarity wage policy, which will be discussed later, is in sharp conflict with the TCO's and SACO's goal of maintaining broad wage differentials.

1. *LO.* At the top of the Swedish labor movement for blue-collar workers is the Swedish Confederation of Trade Unions, which was founded in 1898. The LO has twenty-five affiliated national unions with a membership of over two million blue-collar workers. This sector of the Swedish labor movement is highly centralized; the *LO* has much more power and authority than does the TUC in Great Britain or the AFL-CIO in the United States. The LO has the authority to: require an affiliate to accept into membership all workers who desire to join; determine the internal structure of a union; settle demarcation disputes between unions; make economy-wide agreements with the employers' confederation (SAF) which are binding on the unions and their members; set the guidelines within which the unions must negotiate their industry agreements; and participate in industry negotiations.[2] Much time and effort of the LO staff is spent in research and the development of proposals for collective bargaining and legislation. Its economic research group, under the leadership of Dr. Gosta Rehn and Dr. Rudolph Meidner, has strongly influenced not only the union movement's

attitudes, but also the government's policies and programs.[3] The LO is also very active in training and educational activities. Finally, it carries on extensive lobbying work for social and labor legislation and represents its constituency on numerous government boards and agencies.

2. *TCO*. The Central Organization of Salaried Employees was formed in 1944 by unions of salaried employees which at that time already had as members 30% to 40% of the salaried workers of Sweden. Following 1944, membership grew rapidly and the TCO now has over one million members in twenty-two unions. It has a separate council (TCO-S) for employees of the national government and a separate council (TCO-K) for employees of municipalities. Within the TCO, there is considerably less centralized control than in the LO.

3. *SACO*. The Confederation of Professional Associations was formed in 1947 by organizations representing doctors, pharmacists, and other professional groups. The SACO now has approximately 170,000 members in twenty-five unions. In 1975, the National Federation of Government Officers (SO), which consists largely of military officers and high-salaried employees of the railroads and post office, merged with the SACO. In the SACO, there has been less centralization of authority than in either the LO or TCO. In 1973, the SACO joined with the TCO in forming the Private Salaried Employees' Association (PTK) in order to represent more effectively their members in private industry.

Because of the power and authority that is concentrated in the three confederations, especially in the LO, it would be easy to underestimate the importance of the national unions which are key units in the Swedish union structure. It is in the national unions that the employees have membership and to which they pay their union dues. Moreover, the labor agreements in each industry are negotiated and signed by representatives of the national unions, albeit within guidelines established by the confederations.

There are 25 national unions in the LO, 22 in the TCO, and 25 in the SACO. The LO affiliates originally were craft unions. However, as early as 1912, the LO became committed to industrial unionism and since then has developed its structure in that direction. As a result, today all but a few of the LO affiliates are industrial unions.[4] Such is not the case with the TCO, and especially with the SACO, where the craft type of union predominates.

In recent years, the number of national unions has been greatly decreased by amalgamation. In the last fifteen years, the number of LO affiliates has dropped from 40 to 25, with the result that the remaining national unions are larger, stronger, and more capable of performing their functions effectively.

The high degree of centralization in the Swedish union movement has been especially evident at the local level. The local units have been under the control of the national unions, with little power and authority to take independent action. Moreover, the emphasis of the labor movement until recently has been to achieve national and industry advances while paying slight attention to local plant and individual employee problems. The responsibility to total society has tended to override local worker issues.[5] It is reported that, as a result, there has been growing discontent among the work force with the functioning of the unions at the local level.[6] However, the recent legislation, which will be discussed later, greatly strengthens the role of the union at the work place and gives considerable authority to the local union representatives. Under this new legislation, the 12,000 factory clubs of the LO unions will probably become a much more significant part of the Swedish union structure.

## Employees' Right to Join Unions

As early as 1906, the employers' association (SAF) reached an agreement with the LO which gave blue-collar workers the right to join unions and guaranteed that they would not be discriminated against for doing so. However, management strongly opposed the unionization of white-collar and professional workers, and the agreement was not extended to cover them. Protection for these latter employees was not achieved until 1936 when the Act on the Right of Association and Collective Bargaining provided that no one could be discriminated against because he had participated in legal union activities. In 1976, paragraphs 7 and 8 of the Act on Codetermination at Work reconfirmed the right of employees "to belong to an organization of employees—to take advantage of that membership, and to work for the organization or in order to establish an organization."[7]

## Union Membership

Union membership is higher in Sweden than in any of the other Western European countries or, indeed, in any of the free nations of the world (see table A-11). It is estimated that 95% of the blue-collar workers, 75% of the white-collar workers, and 60% of the professional workers are union members.

Although the LO is still the major union organization, both the TCO and the SACO have been growing more rapidly in recent years. Since 1960, the growth rates have been LO—23%, TCO—124%, and SACO—151%. In the long run, the TCO and the SACO will have greater potential memberships because of the increase in the percentage of white-collar and professional employees in the work force. It is expected that by 1980, they will equal the number of blue-collar workers.[8]

*Closed Shop and Check-Off*

The high degree of unionization has been achieved without compulsory membership. There are no closed-shop or union-shop agreements in Sweden. Article 32 of the SAF requires all its affiliated employers to include the following statement in all labor agreements: "The employer is entitled to employ workers whether they are organized or not. The right of association shall be left inviolate on both sides." The LO also has rejected all proposals that would oblige management to employ only union members. Finally, when the metalworkers' union sought to avoid an open-shop commitment in its contracts, the labor court ruled that employers had a legal right to hire non-union workers regardless of the wording of the agreement.[9] However, the check-off is legal in Sweden, management has not strongly opposed it, and it is very widespread.

*Ideology*

Contrary to widespread opinions abroad, Sweden's basic industry is still 90% privately owned.[10] The unions have not pushed for government ownership but rather, for economic growth, full employment, and greatly expanded social welfare under capitalism. In the late 1930s, the union movement recognized that any increases in wages and benefits for the workers were dependent upon increases in productivity. As a result, the unions and management found a meeting ground in their efforts to increase efficiency under capitalism.[11] The motto became "make a bigger cake so there will be more to share." In 1973, Arne Geijer, the retiring chairman of the LO, stated "You must see to it that industry can flourish in order that you can secure substantial wage increases and social benefits."

*Politics*

The LO and its affiliated unions are closely allied to the Social Democratic party (SAP). Local branches, but not the LO or the national unions, may affiliate with the SAP. Approximately 60% of LO members are also SAP members (30% is a result of the branch affiliation).[12] Individual members have the right to contract out of branch affiliation, but only 1% have done so. On the other hand, neither the TCO nor the SACO have formal ties with the SAP, and indeed both, especially the SACO, represent a source of strength for the more right-wing parties.[13]

Prior to 1976, the SAP was the party in power for forty-four years. The

SAP and the LO have considered themselves two wings of the same labor movement with constant interchange of personnel and many joint meetings to agree on policies and strategy. Some union officials have been SAP members of parliament. However, the blue-collar group has been decreasing as a percentage of the total work force, and as a result the SAP has found it necessary in recent years to broaden its appeal.[14]

### The Solidarity Wage Policy

One of the major goals of the LO has been to decrease wage differentials. As a result, the LO has pushed for rapidly raising low wages and narrowing the wage spread. Where low wages have been a result of the inability of the company or the industry to pay higher wages, the LO has favored the elimination of such companies and industries, and the movement of employees to a more favorable area of the economy.[15] The SAP has cooperated with labor market policies, which has encouraged and supported greater labor mobility. The policy has been successful in pancaking the wage structure of the LO workers.[16] According to the LO's research department, the spread in average hourly earnings between contract areas decreased from 30% in 1960 to 13% in 1976. In the past, the TCO and the SACO have opposed the solidarity wage policy, but more recently, the TCO leadership appears to favor it.

### Financial Status and Business Activities

The main source of income of the Swedish trade unions is the dues of their members. Although the size of membership dues varies considerably from union to union, it averages about 1% of gross wages. The national unions have set aside large amounts in their "conflict funds." The LO unions have about 1,500 million kronor and the TCO unions about 750 million kronor in such funds. However, since industrial conflict has been unusual in recent years, the assets of the unions have tended to increase.

Swedish unions, like West German unions, have become important owners of businesses and employers of labor. The LO owns and operates *Aftonbladet*, Sweden's second largest newspaper, and many of the provincial newspapers are owned or partly owned by unions. The LO and the TCO each own large blocks of stock in RESO, one of Sweden's largest travel agencies. The unions also have major interests in housing developments, construction companies, and insurance companies.[17]

**Employers' Associations**

The SAF was founded in 1902 as a counterbalance to the LO. The SAF has 38 affiliated employers' associations which represent 26,000 member firms, employing over 1.3 million workers. Thus, over 40% of the total Swedish work force are employed in companies affiliated with the SAF.

In addition to the SAF, there are several independent employers' associations in the private sector, such as the Swedish Shipowners' Association and the Cooperative Labor Negotiating Association (KFO) and also two important public sector employers' associations, the National Collective Bargaining Office (SAV) and the Bargaining Organization for Swedish State-Owned Enterprises (SFO).

In 1936, the Act on the Right of Association and Collective Bargaining recognized the right of employers to join and be active in employers' associations. This right was reaffirmed in 1976 in the Act on Codetermination at Work, which provides in paragraph 7 that employers have the right "to belong to an organization of employers . . . to take advantage of that membership, and to work for the organization or in order to establish an organization."[18]

During its first twenty-five years, the SAF was concerned almost exclusively with wage negotiations, but in more recent years, it has expanded its activities to include labor market and social welfare policies, national economic planning, education, training, and research.[19] The SAF like the LO, has strong authority over its affiliates, including the following rights: 1. to be present at all negotiations; 2. to approve all labor agreements; 3. to require members to refuse to negotiate during wildcat strikes; and 4. to require members to support their fellow employers by lockouts.[20] During 1978, the SAF levied sizeable fines against twenty member companies, including Volvo, Saab-Scania, and Bofors for giving workers pay raises in excess of the industry labor agreements. All the money was paid into SAF's anti-strike fund from which the association provides financial aid to employers during strikes.

**Collective Bargaining**

In 1906, the SAF reached an agreement with the LO to recognize and bargain with unions that represented blue-collar employees. At that time, employers refused to grant the same recognition to white-collar and professional unions. However, in 1936, the Act on the Right of Association and Collective Bargaining guaranteed recognition rights to white-collar and professional as well as blue-collar employees.[21] In 1976, this right to negotiate was confirmed in the Act on Codetermination at Work which provides in paragraph 10 that "an organization of employees shall have a right to negotiate with an employer on any matter relating to the relationship between the employer and any member of the organization who is or has been employed by that employer."

*Levels and Scope of Bargaining*

Negotiations between representatives of labor and management in Sweden have been conducted at three different levels: economy-wide, between a union confederation and the SAF; industry-wide, between a national union and an industry employers' association; and locally, between a factory club and company management.

1. *LO-SAF Negotiations.* Until 1944, when the TCO was formed, economy-wide negotiations were carried on exclusively between the LO and the SAF. Ever since 1944, the LO and the SAF have generally set the patterns that were followed later by SAF negotiations with the TCO and the SACO. However, in 1971, the LO, fearing that the TCO and the SACO would attempt to get improved settlements, refused to sign an agreement with the SAF until the terms of the TCO and SACO contracts were concluded.

In the past, many issues concerning basic rights of management and labor as well as procedural matters, which have been the subject of legislation in other countries, have been settled in Sweden by LO-SAF negotiations. In December, 1906, in the famous "December compromise," the SAF and LO agreed that:

1. blue-collar employees had the right to join unions and management would not discriminate against employees for being active in unions,
2. management would recognize and bargain with unions,
3. management would retain its prerogatives within the plant, including the right to hire non-union employees and to dismiss employees for cause.

In 1938, in the "basic agreement," which was modified in 1947 and again in 1948, the LO and SAF agreed to:

1. ban certain unfair labor practices by both management and labor,
2. establish uniform negotiating procedures,
3. accept the peace obligation as a part of all labor agreements, and
4. establish general rules regarding layoffs and dismissals.

Since 1938, the LO and SAF have concluded a series of cooperative agreements which include the following:

1942    the Industrial Safety Agreement (revised in 1951 and 1976)

1944    the Vocational Training Agreement (revised in 1957)

1946    the Works Council Agreement (revised in 1958 and 1966)
        (cancelled in 1976 by the LO in favor of legislation)

1948    the Works Study Agreement

1967    the Occupational Health Service Agreement

1973    the Rationalization Agreement

In addition to the December compromise, the basic agreement, and the cooperative agreements, since 1956 the LO and SAF have been negotiating so-called frame agreements every two or three years. The frame agreements set the wage cost guidelines within which the national unions and the industry employers' association are free to negotiate. Although the early frame agreements simply set the wage cost limits, the scope of LO-SAF bargaining has expanded to include more and more specific issues. A recent negotiation considered, among other things, pensions, sick benefits, income for transferred workers, termination notice, leaves of absence, overtime pay, vacation scheduling, and part-time work conditions. Central negotiations have become involved increasingly with the way the wage cost increase is to be allocated. As a result, the frame agreements have become longer and longer and the scope for industry bargaining has become more and more limited.

2. *Industry Negotiations*. Within the guidelines established by the LO-SAF frame agreement, each of the industry employers' associations negotiates an industry-wide agreement with a national union. With the expansion of the contents of the frame agreements to cover not only wage cost limits, but also many specific benefits, the scope of industry bargaining has been limited. There is disagreement regarding the extent of the limitations. One authority has stated that "there is now very little scope for deviation in the industry-wide agreements; they are nothing more than adaptations of the model."[22] However, the director of the SAF in 1973 wrote that "collective bargaining in Sweden is still basically a decentralized affair which in practice leaves a good deal of room for the negotiation of agreements both at the level of the industry and in individual firms."[23]

3. *Local Negotiations*. At the lowest level of collective bargaining in Sweden, negotiations occur between the local union factory club and the local company management. In the past, negotiations at this level were involved primarily with adjusting the industry agreement to local conditions, job evaluations, incentive rates, and other local issues that were not covered by the industry agreement. The director of the SAF cites the following as major questions that have been solved at the local level: the status of the local union's representative; employer cooperation in dues collection; and

wages payable to employees reassigned to other jobs.[24] It is clear that the scope of bargaining at this level in Sweden has been quite narrow. However, under the recent legislation the scope of bargaining at the local area has been expanded.

## Shop Stewards

The Shop Steward Act (1974) provides that a shop steward duly appointed by the local union:

1. is protected against dismissal because of his union activity,
2. is guaranteed against inferior pay or working conditions during and immediately following his term of office,
3. must be given access to all employees represented by him,
4. must be provided with a room or suitable space to carry on his union work,
5. must be given priority regarding continued employment (if the union so desires),
6. must be paid at his normal rate for union business at the work place and to attend union courses that are of importance to conditions at the work place.

The law sets no limit on the number of shop stewards, but rather leaves this to negotiation. In some small companies, they constitute as much as 10% of the work force. The union is given priority of interpretation of the Shop Steward Act. In case of disagreement, the union's interpretation must be applied pending settlement by the labor court.

## Conciliation and Mediation

The Law on Mediation of Labor Disputes (1920) established a central mediation office and eight mediation districts, each with a government-appointed mediator. If an impasse is reached in contract negotiations, the parties must notify the mediation service at least seven days before a strike or lockout may be undertaken. The mediator usually requests the parties to postpone any industrial action, and the parties almost without exception comply with his request, although they are not required by law to do so. The mediator tries to help the parties come to an agreement. However, the mediator cannot force the parties to reach an agreement. After the seven days' notice, the union is free to strike and the company is free to lock out. The 1920 mediation law was replaced by a section of the 1976 Act on Codetermination at Work. However, the basic provisions of the new law with respect to mediation are the same as those of the 1920 law.[25]

*Labor Agreements*

Collective agreements, which are negotiated in each industry by the employers' associations and the national industry unions, are legally binding on the organizations and their members. The agreements usually run for a period of from one to three years and, during that period, any disagreement regarding the meaning or application of the contract must be settled without resort to a strike or lockout. Instead, the law specifies the following three-step dispute procedure which the parties must use:

1. negotiation at the company level,
2. negotiation at the industry level,
3. appeal to the labor court (or to arbitration, if the parties agree).

The decisions of the labor court are final and binding.[26]

*Prior Right to Interpret Agreement*

Until 1976, management possessed the prior right of interpretation of all aspects of a labor agreement. In other words, management had the authority to place its interpretation into effect, even though the union argued that such action constituted a violation of the agreement. The union, of course, had the right to appeal such action through the three steps of the appeal procedure. The labor court had the authority to make the final interpretation but, until it did so, management's interpretation remained in effect.

However, in 1976, the Act on Codetermination at Work (paragraphs 32-38) removed from management and gave to the union the prior right of interpretation of an agreement with respect to the following matters:

1. codetermination provisions,
2. provisions concerning disciplinary measures, and
3. a worker's duty to perform certain work.

If the employer disagrees with the union's interpretation on any of these matters, he may seek a reversal by the labor court, provided he initiates such action within ten days after negotiations have been concluded with the union. If the court finds that the union's interpretation of the agreement was erroneous and the union "lacked good reason for its point of view," it must order it to compensate the employer for any losses he may have sustained.

*The Labor Court*

The labor court, which was established in 1928 by a Conservative government, is composed of sixteen judges: four, including the chairman, are representatives of neither labor nor management; six are nominated by labor; and six are nominated by management. It was hoped that the tripartite nature of the court and the fact that the majority of its members are from labor and management would cause its decisions to be more acceptable to the parties. In recent years, 40% of the cases have been settled by conciliation.

The court was established primarily to settle disputes concerning the meaning and application of labor agreements. As explained earlier, the 1928 law prohibited strikes or lockouts during the life of a contract to settle a dispute over its meaning, and substituted instead a three-step procedure ending with a final and binding decision by the labor court. However, several recent laws have greatly expanded the jurisdiction of the court, with the result that contract interpretation cases now make up less than one-half of all its cases.[27] In 1978, 30% of cases involved dismissal cases under the 1974 Employment Protection Act, and another 30% involved interpretation and application of the 1976 Act on Codetermination at Work. Most of the decisions under the latter legislation concerned three provisions of the act: section 11, which states that employers must negotiate before making major changes; section 19, which makes it obligatory for a company to disclose information; and section 38, which gives unions the veto power over subcontracting. The total case load of the court has increased from an average of 85 per year in the early seventies to 367 in 1977.

*Strikes and Lockouts*

Reference has already been made to the fact that labor agreements are legally binding, and strikes or lockouts as a result of disagreements over their meaning are prohibited. The 1976 Act on Codetermination at Work does provide, however, that during the term of a contract, management must negotiate regarding matters to be codetermined and, failure to reach an agreement on same, releases the union from its obligation not to strike.

A labor agreement usually runs for two or three years, and when it terminates, the union is free to strike and management is free to lock out. (Since 1965, even civil servants—with few exceptions—have the right to strike.) However, a one-week notice must be given before a strike or lockout may occur, during which time the negotiations are led by government mediators. In 1941, the LO adopted the "double veto" on strikes. It requires that before a strike may be called, it must be approved by the executive board of the national union and the secretariat of the LO.

Until recently, the amount of money that could be awarded to an employer to compensate for losses suffered as a result of an illegal strike was limited by law to 200 kronor ($48) per employee. That limitation has since been removed and the labor court is now free to assess higher damages. In most of the cases since the change in the law, the court has not assessed more than the 200 kronor. However, in one famous case in which the employees engaged in an unofficial strike action for two months, the court awarded the employer damages of 600 kronor ($144) per employee.

Over the years, losses resulting from strikes and lockouts in Sweden have been remarkably low (see table A-12). During the ten-year period 1967-1976, the loss per employee per year was less than 4/100 of a day, which was lower than in any of the other countries in this study except the Netherlands and West Germany. On only one occasion in recent years has the government prohibited strike aciton. In 1971, rail traffic was halted because of a strike by local and federal government employees who were members of the SACO and SO. In addition, the military officers were threatened with a lockout. Parliament passed a special law extending the original contracts of those employees for six months, thus making strike or lockout action illegal during that cooling off period.


**The Legislation of the Seventies**

Prior to the seventies, labor and management in Sweden were proud of the fact that many issues in labor relations, which had been the subject of legislation in many other countries, had been settled by collective bargaining between the LO and SAF. Instead of a large body of labor law, there were the December compromise, the basic agreement, the cooperative agreement, and the frame agreements. Since 1970, however, Swedish labor has placed more emphasis on achieving its goals through legislation. The result has been a series of labor laws which include the following:

| 1973 | Employee-Director Act (revised 1976) |
|------|--------------------------------------|
| 1974 | Workers' Protection Act Amendments (original Act, 1949) |
| 1974 | Security of Employment Act (revised 1976) |
| 1974 | Promotion of Employment Act (revised 1975) |
| 1974 | Act Concerning the Status of Shop Stewards (revised 1975, 1976) |
| 1974 | Act on Litigation in Labor Disputes (revised 1975, 1976) |
| 1976 | Act on Codetermination at Work |
| 1976 | Public Employment Act |
| 1977 | Vacation Act |

The indications are that Swedish unions will continue their push for more labor legislation. Commenting on the 1976 legislation, Ake Bouvin, chief legal officer of the Swedish Ministry of Labor, stated in 1977 that "the two new enactments do not mark the end of the reform legislation."[28]

The effect of this new legislation on collective bargaining varies with the level of bargaining. The scope of bargaining at the top between the SAF and the LO has been considerably narrowed. On the other hand, the scope of bargaining at the company and plant levels has been greatly widened by forcing negotiation on several issues that were formerly decided unilaterally by management. Although the full effects of the legislation are not yet clear,[29] two results are evident: management's authority has been considerably reduced, and major protection and benefits for workers have been achieved directly through legislation.

### The Decrease in Management Authority

Prior to the legislation of the seventies, Swedish management possessed great unilateral power and authority at the company and plant levels. This authority had its bases in three sources: the management rights clause which was incorporated in the labor agreement of every SAF affiliated company; the legal right of prior interpretation of the labor agreement; and the legal right to initiate changes unilaterally on matters not covered by the labor agreement. Each of these sources of power has been either weakened or eliminated by the new legislation.

Until the new legislation became effective, the SAF constitution required member employers to include the following management rights clause in all their labor agreements:

> Reserving the observance of other rules in the agreement the employer is entitled to direct and distribute the work, to hire and dismiss workers at will and to employ workers whether they are organized or not.

The LO had agreed to accept this provision in the December compromise in 1906. In 1932, when the metalworkers' union refused to agree to it, the labor court ruled that even without such a contract clause, management enjoyed these prerogatives as rights that were inherent in the legal foundation of the nation. Thus, at the local level, unions and employees were able to secure adjustments only at the employer's discretion. Many employers, of course, used this power with care, recognizing that abuse would result in demand for its elimination. Nevertheless, management did possess strong unilateral authority at the shop-floor level.

The new legislation has not eliminated the employer's right to hire union or non-union workers. However, the other parts of the management rights clause have been superseded by specific legislation that deprives management of the authority to unilaterally direct and distribute the work and to dismiss workers at will. The clause is no longer a requirement of SAF affiliation and has been removed from the labor agreements.

Earlier in this chapter, the curtailment of management's right of prior interpretation of labor agreements was discussed. However, some of the new legislation also gives the unions prior right of interpretation with respect to the meaning of legislation itself. For example, the Act Concerning the Status of Shop Stewards (1974) provides that the opinion of the union regarding the proper interpretation of the act is to apply pending the settlement of the dispute by the labor court.[30] The Workers Protection Act (1974) also gives priority of interpretation to the union.[31]

Paragraph 11 of the Act on Codetermination at Work (1976) provides that before an employer decides "on an important alteration to his activity" or "on important alterations on work or employment conditions," he must negotiate with the local union and, if agreement is not reached at that stage, with the central union. Only if urgent reasons so necessitate may an employer implement a major decision before he has negotiated with the union. In paragraph 38, the act deals specifically with subcontracting and provides that before a company may engage in a major new type of subcontracting, it must negotiate the matter with the local organization of employees and, if no agreement is reached there, with the central organization. If the central organization is of the opinion that the proposed subcontracting violates the law or the labor agreement, or is in conflict with what is generally approved practice, it has the power of veto and the company may not proceed with the subcontracting. However, the employer may then appeal the matter to the labor court which may override the veto if it finds the union "lacks good reason for its point of view," and may order compensation to the employer for any losses he may have suffered as a result of the union's erroneous position.

## Legislated Employee Protection and Benefits

### Dismissals

The Security of Employment Act (1974) removes the discharge of an employee from the area of management rights and provides instead that management must show "reasonable grounds" for dismissal. Reasonable grounds is not defined in the act but is determined by the labor court to which the discharged employee may appeal. Trade union activity, illness, and reduced capacity of a worker to do the job are not reasonable grounds. The employer is expected to have given the employee a prior warning at least one month before notification of discharge and to have made an attempt to help him correct his deficiencies by transfer and other means. Only if incompatibility is conclusively established is the discharge likely to be upheld by the labor court.

1. *Notification* must be given prior to discharge and the employee may demand reasons in writing. The period of notification during which the employee must be paid varies with age as follows:

| minimum | 1 month |
|---|---|
| over 25 years old | 2 months |
| over 30 years old | 3 months |
| over 35 years old | 4 months |
| over 40 years old | 5 months |
| over 45 years old | 6 months |

2. *Consultation* may be demanded by the union or the employee regarding his discharge, in which case management must agree to discuss the matter.

3. *Reinstatement and Damages.* If the labor court determines that there was not "reasonable grounds" for discharge, it will order that "formal damages" be paid to the worker and the union for the injury sustained, and will request that the employer reinstate the worker. The employer may refuse reinstatement, but if he does so, he can be ordered by the court to pay the following damages in addition to the "formal damages," depending upon the length of employment of the worker:

| less than 5 years | 16 months' pay |
|---|---|
| 5 years to 10 years | 24 months' pay |
| 10 years or more | 32 months' pay |

However, these amounts may be increased if the employee is over 45 years old. For example, an employee age 60 with 10 years or more of service may receive 50% more than the amounts listed, up to a maximum of 48 months' pay.

## Redundancies

The Security of Employment Act provides that an employer must show reasonable grounds for cutbacks of employment. It is expected that the employer will try other measures, such as transfers, natural reductions, and successive closures before moving to permanent dismissals.

Unless there is an agreement to the contrary with the union, employees within each operational unit must be terminated according to the total length of service with the employer. Where length of service is equal, age becomes the determining factor. However, union representatives, whose duties are of importance, should be assured continuing employment. If new jobs become available at the plant, employees who have been laid off have the right to such jobs in order of their seniority for a period of one year.

Notification or severance pay must be given in cases of redundancy in the same amount as in cases of discharge (see previous section) and must vary with age from one month for an employee under 25 years old, to six months for an employee over 45.

If the labor court determines the redundancy is invalid, the employer is expected to provide the employee with continued employment. If he refuses to do so, the court may order damages such as may be ordered in unfair discharge cases (see previous section) which vary with the length of service and age of the employee from 16 months' pay for a worker under age 45 who had been employed less than 5 years, to 48 months' pay for a worker age 60 or over who had been employed for 10 years or more.

Under the Promotion of Employment Act, an employer must notify the county labor board of dismissal of five or more employees as soon as possible but in any event:

two months before dismissal if 5 to 24 workers are involved,

four months before dismissal if 25 to 100 workers are involved,

six months before dismissal if over 100 workers are involved.

The notice must contain the number of employees, date of dismissal, and after consultation with the union, the names of the employees. In case of a major cutback, the employer must consult with the union, the county labor board, and the municipality to try to arrange the cutback in such a way as to minimize the harm to the workers dismissed. Failure to give the required notice can result in a fine equal to 100 to 500 kronor per week per employee and an order from the labor market board to defer the dismissals.

*Vacation and Vacation Pay*

The Vacation Act of 1977 (effective April 1, 1978) provides a minimum of 5 weeks (25 days) of vacation for all employees, an increase of 1 week over the previous law (1963). The vacation year is from April 1 to March 31 and employees receive as vacation pay 12% of the pay they received in the year prior to April 1. In calculating earnings for vacation pay, the vacation pay of the prior year is not counted. However, days lost from work for the following reasons are counted as if they had been worked: layoffs, illness up to 180 days, maternity leave up to 120 days (180 days for a single mother), training (including trade union training) up to 180 days, military training up to 60 days, and civil defense service up to 60 days. There is no vacation bonus in addition to the regular vacation pay. If an employee is entitled to more than 20 days vacation, he may save up the days over 20 and take them anytime during the next 5 years. If an employee is not entitled to the full 25 days of vacation pay, he may opt to work the unpaid days.

The time of vacation is a matter that must be negotiated if the union so desires. If it is not negotiated, the employer must consult with the employee, but if no agreement can be reached with the employee, the employer may decide. However, at least 4 weeks of vacation must be during June, July, or August, unless agreement is reached to the contrary. The employer must notify the employee of his vacation time at least two months in advance. An employee who is terminated before he receives his vacation must be paid the vacation pay he has accumulated.[32]

### Maternity Leave with Pay

Sweden has the most liberal maternity pay plan in the world. Moreover, it has pioneered in making maternity leave with pay available to fathers as well as to mothers. Under the 1976 legislation, the total length of maternity leave was expanded to nine months, with eight months at 90% of pay and one month at a minimum of approximately 6 US dollars per day. Any part of the leave can be taken by the father instead of the mother. (The original paternity leave provision became effective in 1974 under a law that provided only six months of leave.) Although mothers still take the great majority of the leave time, the share taken by fathers increased from 2.4% in 1974 to 7.5% in 1976. In 1977, the time taken by fathers increased to 42 days compared with 26 days in 1976.[33]

### Equal Pay and Equal Opportunities

Women make up about 42% of the Swedish work force, which is a higher percentage than in most of the Western European countries. Women's pay has been lower than men's pay and continues to be so, although the gap has been decreasing. Women's pay under the LO contracts increased from 70% of men's wages in 1960 to 84% in 1974.[34]

In 1972, the government appointed an Advisory Council on Equality between Men and Women which in 1976 was replaced by the parliamentary

Equality Committee. In the past, these two agencies have attempted to bring about equality by a voluntary approach. In the summer of 1978, the committee proposed equality legislation modeled after the equal opportunities directive of the EEC, but in addition, proposed affirmative action on the part of employers. The law proposed also the naming of a special ombudsman to see that the purposes of the law were carried out.[35]

In 1979, the Swedish parliament passed the Equal Treatment in Working Life Act which became effective January 1, 1980. The new act, however, was much weaker than the proposal of the Equality Committee. It does not require that employers take affirmative action and does not establish an ombudsman or a separate enforcement agency of any kind. The Social Democrats, who were largely responsible for the weakening of the legislation, contended that sex discrimination can be more effectively eliminated through collective agreements.

## Absenteeism

Swedish industry is plagued with extremely high rates of absenteeism. A study by the SAF of absenteeism as a result of reported sickness in 1973 showed Swedish industry with an average rate of 10% which was the highest in Western Europe and far above the U.S. rate of 4% and the Japanese rate of 3% (see table A-13). It is estimated that the average rate has now increased to 12%. Some large Swedish companies have reported much higher rates. In 1974, Gotaverren reported 22%, Volvo 12% for men and 19% for women, and SKF 18% for men and 30% for women.

One major cause of such unusually high absentee rates is believed to be the very liberal sick pay benefits. Under Swedish law, when an employee reports ill, he is entitled to 90% of his regular wages, beginning with the first day of the illness. Thus, the decision not to go to work is made at very little economic cost to the absent employee.

## Worker Participation

### Works Councils

Works councils were originally established in Swedish plants as a result of a cooperative agreement between the LO and SAF in 1946. The agreement had several amendments, including one in 1966 that expanded the scope of the councils to include employment and manpower matters, and one in 1975 that gave the councils the right to review company financial information. The agreement applied to companies with fifty or more employees. The councils were joint management-employee bodies with one-half of the representatives from management and one-half from the union ranks in the plant. Thus, the works councils existed within the union system, not outside it as in West Germany and Holland. The works councils were purely consultative; they had no powers of codetermination.

With the passage of the Act on Codetermination at Work in 1976, the LO cancelled the cooperative agreement on works councils that it had had with the SAF since 1946. The new law, which became effective January 1, 1977, does not set forth the details of the structure, scope, or authority of works councils, but instead, provides that the parties shall determine these matters through collective bargaining. However, the unions are free to resort to a strike (even during the life of a contract) if the parties fail to reach "an agreement on the right of joint regulation." The results of this aspect of the new law will not be clear until the employers' organization and the unions have completed their negotiations.

*Worker Representation on the Board*

An Employee-Director Act was passed in 1973, and after three years of experimentation was amended and confirmed in 1976. The law now applies to all companies with twenty-five or more employees. It provides that two employee representatives and two alternates (the alternates have the right to attend board meetings but not to vote) shall be appointed to the company board by the local union which represents a majority of the employees. It is worth noting that there is no two-tier board system as in West Germany and also that employee board membership is closely tied to the union movement. The employee representatives constitute a minority of the board membership. They can always be outvoted by the shareholder representatives.

Before serving on a board, an employee representative is required to attend a four-week training course which is financed by the government. Employee representatives are excluded from participation in industrial relations or collective bargaining matters when such items have to be considered by the board.

**Profit Sharing and Employee Ownership**

One of the most hotly debated issues in Swedish labor relations today is the LO's proposal for profit sharing. The LO's interest in this area is closely related to its decision to pursue a solidarity wage policy rather than an ability-to-pay wage policy. One of the goals of the former is to achieve equal pay for similar work in every industry regardless of the differences in efficiencies between the industries. Under the latter, efficient industries would pay higher wage rates and inefficient industries would be subsidized by lower wage rates. The LO believes that the solidarity wage plan has been good for Swedish workers because, by causing inefficient industries to be unprofitable, it has eliminated them and, by allowing efficient industries to be highly profitable, it has enabled them to expand production and employment. In the LO's opinion, the solidarity wage policy has been more effective in moving Swedish workers to more efficient industries and, therefore, increasing the general standard of living, than could have been accomplished by the wage spread of an ability-to-pay wage policy.

However, the LO believes it is unfair that the expanded assets of the efficient industries should accrue entirely to the owners of those industries. Instead, it argues that the workers who have forgone the higher earnings, which an ability-to-pay wage policy would have made available to them, should share in the profits. As a result, in 1971, the LO asked Dr. Rudolph Meidner, its chief economist, to develop a plan to correct this inequity.

In 1975, the LO published its first profit-sharing plan which has come to be known as the Meidner plan. Since then, although the details of the plan have been revised, its basic characteristics have remained unchanged as follows: workers of a company would be entitled to a certain share of its profits; however, the company would retain the cash for reinvestment and issue new shares of equal value; the shares would not be issued to individual workers but instead to a workers' fund; voting of the shares would be controlled largely through the unions. The most recent LO proposal which was published in February, 1978, provides that: a company with over 500 employees (except a commerical bank, a consumer cooperative, or a publicly owned company) would pay 20% of its net profits in the form of shares into a workers' fund; employees of the company would have the right to vote 20% of the shares in the fund, but 80% would be voted by a board of no less than 300 members representing the various unions in the county where the company is located.

Swedish employers are strongly opposed to the Meidner plan which they claim would give the unions control over major Swedish industry within a relatively short period of time. They argue that it would result in a conflict of interest within the union movement which would destroy collective bargaining as it is now practiced because the unions would represent both labor and owners at the bargaining table. As an alternative, an industry task force chaired by Erland Waldenstrom, a leading Swedish industrialist, has proposed voluntary profit sharing and savings plans for individual employees.

**Notes**

1. Lennart Forseback, *Industrial Relations and Employment in Sweden* Stockholm: The Swedish Institute, 1976, p. 65.

2. Jack Barbash, *Trade Unions and National Economic Policy* (Baltimore: John Hopkins Press, 1972), p. 20.

3. Ibid., pp. 8-13.

4. Forseback, *Industrial Relations*, p. 24.

5. Casten Van Otter, "Sweden: Labor Reformism Shapes the System," in *Worker Militancy and Its Consequences 1965-75, ed. Solomon Barkin (New York: Praeger Press, 1975), p. 208.*

6. *Barbash, Trade Unions, p. 21.*

7. *Toward Democracy at the Workplace* (Stockholm: Ministry of Labor, 1977), p. 20.

8. Van Otter, "Sweden: Labor Reformism," p. 219.

9. Ibid., p. 202.

10. Ibid., p. 196.

11. Walter Korpi, *Industrial Relations in Sweden* (Stockholm: Swedish Institute for Social Research, 1975), p. 25.

12. Barbash, *Trade Unions*, p. 23.

13. Ibid., p. 35.

14. Van Otter, "Sweden: Labor Reformism," p. 200.

15. Barbash, *Trade Unions*, p. 11.

16. Derek Robinson, *Solidaristic Wage Policy in Sweden* (Paris: Organization for Economic Cooperation and Development, 1974), p. 33.

17. Forseback, *Industrial Relations*, p. 37.

18. *Toward Democracy*, p. 20.

19. Forseback, *Industrial Relations*, p. 22.

20. Barbash, *Trade Unions*, p. 25.

21. Forseback, *Industrial Relations*, p. 20.

22. Gosta Edgren, "Trends in Bargaining for Remuneration," *New Perspectives in Collective Bargaining*, OECD Manpower and Social Affairs Directorate, 1969, p. 58.

23. Gunnar Hoberg, "Recent Trends in Collective Bargaining in Sweden," *Collective Bargaining in Industrialized Market Economies*, (Geneva: International Labor Office, 1973), p. 343.

24. Hoberg, "Recent Trends," p. 344.

25. Forseback, *Industrial Relations*, p. 45.

26. Hoberg, "Recent Trends," p. 344.

27. Forseback, *Industrial Relations*, p. 48.

28. Ake Bouvin, "New Swedish Legislation on Democracy at the Workplace," *International Labor Review* 115,(2):1977:3.

29. Bouvin, "Swedish Legislation," p. 17.

30. *Swedish Laws on Security of Employment, Status of Shop Stewards, Litigation in Labour Disputes* (Stockholm: Ministry of Labor, 1977), p. 27.

31. Forseback, *Industrial Relations*, p. 117.

32. "New Swedish Vacation Leave Act," *European Industrial Relations Review*, No. 44, August 1977, p. 4.

33. "Swedish Promotion Blitz Tries to Lure Dads into the Nursery," *International Herald Tribune*, Paris, April 21, 1978, p. 6.

34. Foresback, *Industrial Relations*, p. 81.

35. "Sweden: Anti-Discrimination Proposals Outlined," *European Industrial Relations Review*, 54, June 1978, p. 5.

# Case 10
# Dagens Nyheters AB

At 6:30 P.M. on Friday, October 1, 1976, Gustaf Douglas, president and chief executive officer of Dagens Nyheters AB, and Rolf Österberg, executive vice president, sat in Douglas's office waiting for the sandwiches and coffee they had ordered for dinner. Both men were tired from their day's work. Since noon, Mr. Österberg had been negotiating with two of the company's unions. At 6 P.M., Mr. Österberg had left the meeting with the union leaders when it became apparent that the two sides had reached an impasse.

While they were waiting, Österberg recapped for Douglas how the meeting had ended.

> By 5:45 it was obvious that we were getting nowhere. For almost six hours we went around and around on the same issue. Finally, I said to Ring (president of the Graphical Workers' Union) that management would accept the limitations on the use of the CRT terminals by the editorial department that he and the journalists had agreed to, but we would do so only if the limitations were renegotiable at the end of the first year of the new system's operation.
>
> Ring's response to me was, "There can be no time limit on the life of this agreement." I told him that, in that case, there would simply be no agreement, that we couldn't spend millions of Kroner on a new system and have its potential effectiveness so dramatically reduced before it was even placed in operation.
>
> Ring's reply was, "Well, Rolf, you know what will happen!" And with that I excused myself from the meeting. I think that Ring is ready to call a strike.

## Company Background

Dagens Nyheters AB was founded as a newspaper publishing company in Stockholm in 1864. Although the company over the years had greatly expanded both the size and scope of its operations, the mainstay of its business continued to be in newspaper publishing. In 1967, the Dagens Nyheters groups of companies was organized into five semi-autonmous operating divisions:

*Dagens Nyheter* (The Daily News), a morning daily newspaper;

*Expressen* (The Express), an evening daily tabloid newspaper;

the Newspaper Production Division;

257

the Financial Administration Group; and

Sevenska Filmindustri (Swedish Film Industries); a group of companies involved in the production and distribution of motion pictures.

It was company policy to allow each of the divisions to operate with considerable autonomy. Each division was headed by a general manager who was responsible for the administration and financial results of his operations. The two newspapers and Svenska Filmindustri (SF) were given complete journalistic and artistic freedom.

In 1975, the net consolidated income from operations was 836.6 million kroner;[1] The company's stock was publicly traded, although a majority of the shares were held by one family.

### Dagens Nyheter

Since 1942, *Dagens Nyheter* had been the largest morning newspaper in Sweden. It concentrated on reporting national and international news and on presenting the local news of the Swedish capital. The paper had traditionally been independent of political party affiliations. The management believed that because of the paper's policy of non-party alignment and its thorough analysis of important social issues and because of its high readership within the ranks of Sweden's decision makers, *Dagens Nyheter* "had played a leading role in Swedish public opinion making for many decades." One company official made the analogy, "*Dagens Nyheter* is *The New York Times* of Sweden."

The paper's average daily circulation was 460,000 copies, 70% of which were sold in the Stockholm area. Roughly 75% of the total circulation was sold through subscriptions. According to a recent market survey, *Dagens Nyheter* was read in 56% of all households in the Greater Stockholm area.

The newspaper's major competition came from Stockholm's other morning daily, *Svenska Dag Bladet*, which had a national circulation of approximately 160,000 copies. The editorial policies of *Svenska Dag Bladet* were closely aligned with the political philosophy of the Conservative party.

In 1975, *Dagens Nyheter* had the highest advertising volume of any newspaper in the country. Advertising revenues in that year amounted to over 309 million kronor. Management saw a direct relationship between the paper's prominent position as an advertising medium and its high penetration in households in the Stockholm area. See exhibit 10a-1 for a summary of *Dagens Nyheter's* circulation and revenue data.

### Expressen

The company's evening newspaper, *Expressen*, was founded in 1944. At that time, a tabloid daily was something new to the Swedish newspaper

**Exhibit 10a-1**
**Circulation and Revenue data for** *Dagens Nyheter*

|  | 1971 | 1972 | 1973 | 1974 | 1975 |
|---|---|---|---|---|---|
| *Circulation* | | *(thousands of papers)* | | | |
| Weekdays | 435 | 435 | 441 | 447 | 443 |
| Sundays | 525 | 529 | 534 | 535 | 527 |
| Average | 448 | 449 | 455 | 460 | 456 |
| *Sales Revenue* | | *(Skr 000)* | | | |
| Newspapers | 71,896 | 82,189 | 88,941 | 102,174 | 121,706 |
| Advertising | 161,645 | 174,782 | 199,561 | 252,258 | 309,534 |
| Total | 233,541 | 256,971 | 288,502 | 354,432 | 431,240 |

industry, and the paper enjoyed almost immediate success. By 1959, *Expressen* had become the largest newspaper published in Sweden. Its average circulation in 1975 was 577,000 copies. Like *Dagens Nyheter, Expressen* was not affiliated with any political party and its editorial policies were free from management influence.

The major difference between the two papers was in their circulation patterns and their methods of distribution. *Expressen's* readership was more evenly spread throughout the country, and its circulation revenues were generated solely through newsstand sales at 1,600 locations throughout Sweden.

The average circulation figures concealed wide fluctuations in copies sold. During 1975, daily sales varied between 700,000 and 500,000 copies. These variations were attributed to the uneven flow of news, and necessitated more flexible production and distribution systems than required by the morning paper. Despite these fluctuations in the number of copies sold, management believed that *Expressen* was less prone to fluctuations in gross annual revenues because advertising sales accounted for only one-third of total revenues.

Market penetration of *Expressen* varied between 3% and 30%, depending on location. Its wide distribution and fairly constant penetration ratios made *Expressen* a desirable national advertising medium. The paper was considered the leading medium for the advertisement of new consumer products. See exhibit 10a-2 for a summary of *Expressen* circulation and revenue data.

**The Newspaper Production Division**

Dagens Nyheters AB operated its own newspaper production facilities in Stockholm and Jönköping; in addition, the company also rented printing capacity in Malmö. *Dagens Nyheter* was printed only in Stockholm, while *Expressen* was printed in all three locations.

**Exhibit 10a-2**
**Circulation and Revenue Data for** *Expressen*

|  | 1971 | 1972 | 1973 | 1974 | 1975 |
|---|---|---|---|---|---|
| *Circulation* | | *(thousands of copies)* | | | |
| Weekdays | 610 | 586 | 592 | 575 | 566 |
| Sundays | 674 | 653 | 664 | 646 | 624 |
| Holidays | 750 | 758 | 737 | 738 | 733 |
| Average | 621 | 599 | 605 | 587 | 577 |
| *Sales Revenue* | | *(Skr 000)* | | | |
| Newspapers | 108,774 | 124,739 | 125,764 | 152,183 | 172,470 |
| Advertising | 56,740 | 61,425 | 67,258 | 75,431 | 87,428 |
| Total | 165,514 | 186,164 | 193,022 | 227,614 | 259,898 |

Management believed that the efficient utilization of its capital-intensive press equipment was extremely important. The company's utilization of its printing capacity was quite good when compared with that of other major European newspapers even though only half of the press equipment was utilized in double shifts. To improve capacity utilization, the company published on a regular basis special supplements to the morning paper. Every week, *Dagens Nyheter* carried a suburban Stockholm supplement, and on Saturdays, the paper included a weekly entertainment guide for the Stockholm area entitled "On The Town."

In recent years, the company had explored the possibility of utilizing its excess production capacity through co-production agreements with other newspapers; however, these efforts had been fruitless. In 1976, negotiations over co-production with *Aftonbladet*, another evening newspaper, were concluded unsuccessfully when the Swedish Confederation of Trade Unions (LO), which owns *Aftonbladet*, refused to agree to the proposal. Management of Dagens Nyheters termed the LO's position on the matter "unwise from the viewpoint of press policy and national economic interest." Management continued to believe, however, that cooperation between publishing companies in the area of technical production could be an important means of countering the recent sharp increase in newspaper product costs.

In management's view, probably more important that the issues surrounding capacity utilization was the question of rapidly increasing labor costs. Despite the considerable capital investment in printing machinery and equipment, labor and personnel costs still accounted for just under 50% of total production costs. In recent years, payroll costs had risen sharply. In 1975, wages for the company were 17.8% higher than they had been in the previous year. Even more dramatic increases had occurred in the areas of payroll taxes, pension costs, and employee insurance benefits. Between

1974 and 1975, these costs had risen 41%, and in 1975 they constituted 12.6% of total production costs.

## Recent Diversification Attempts

Because revenues in the newspaper industry were especially sensitive to economic fluctuations, most newspaper publishers liked to maintain sizeable reserves of relatively liquid assets. The inflationary trends of the 1960s and early 1970s caused Dagens Nyheters's management to pay special attention to protecting the purchasing power of its liquid asset reserves. In 1973, the company organized the Financial Administration Group to supervise the investment of surplus capital in equity securities of other companies and to plan and implement the diversification of the company's business activities. Shortly thereafter, the company purchased a substantial equity position in a major Swedish insurance company. By 1975, Dagens Nyheters also owned a large number of shares of Holmens Bruk AG, the largest manufacturer of newsprint in Europe. The first real diversification attempt came in 1974 when the company bought the group of companies that composed the Svenska Filmindustri. In addition to the production of motion pictures, SF operated the largest film processing laboratory in Scandanavia and owned a chain of 110 movie theaters.

In 1975, the Dagens Nyheters group became involved in the transportation industry. With the large trucking fleet used primarily for the delivery of *Expressen*, the company started a trucking operation which served a nationwide route structure on a daily basis. In the same year, Dagens Nyheters also began an automotive spare parts business through its wholly-owned subsidiary Tidexpress Motor AB.

Despite the company's attempts to diversify its business activities, the newspaper operations still accounted for over 85% of all revenues and 58% of profit during 1975. Recent declines in the profitability of the newspaper operations had not been offset by comparable profit increases in other areas. Exhibit 10a-3 shows the profitability of the major business activities in two recent years.

Despite the encouraging profit increase shown by the SF group of companies and the encouraging beginning of the two new companies, management believed that the only long-term solution to the serious decline in the total operating profit was to improve the performance of the newspaper operations.

## Labor Relations at Dagens Nyheters

Approximately 80% of Dagens Nyheters's 3,200 employees were members of labor unions. White-collar employees, journalists, supervisors, and

**Exhibit 10a-3**
**Divisional Profit Summary**
*(Skr millions, before taxes)*

| Source of Profit | 1974 | | 1975 | |
|---|---|---|---|---|
| | *Profit* | *% of total* | *Profit* | *% of total* |
| Newspapers operations | 36.2 | 76.5 | 22.2 | 57.8 |
| Financial operations | 4.0 | 8.5 | 4.1 | 10.7 |
| Svenska Filmindustri companies | 6.1 | 12.9 | 10.1 | 26.3 |
| Transportation and other activities | 1.0 | 2.1 | 2.0 | 5.2 |
| Total Consolidated Profit | 47.3 | 100.0 | 38.4 | 100.0 |

production workers were each represented by separate unions. The percentage of employees in each of these categories who had joined their respective unions was high, approaching 100% for all but the white-collar union where union members constituted only 65% of the white-collar work force. Each of the company's local or "house" unions was affiliated with a national industrial or craft union which was in turn affiliated with one of the large national labor union federations.

The largest and by far the most powerful union at Dagens Nyheters was the graphical workers' union. In 1972, all production workers at both newspapers were organized into this single union. Prior to that, there had been three separate trade unions representing typographers, lithographers, and bookbinders. When the three unions were combined, they also brought into the new graphics union all the company's truck drivers, carpenters, maintenance men, and other blue-collar employees in trades unrelated to newspaper printing. In all, the graphics union represented over 1,100 employees, or roughly one-third of the company's work force. The national graphical workers' union was affiliated with Sweden's largest labor federation, the LO (*Lands-organisationen*).

The journalists at Dagens Nyheters were organized into two "clubs,"[2] one at *Dagens Nyheter* and one at *Expressen*. Both of these clubs, which had a combined membership of 650 journalists, were associated with the Stockholm Union of Journalists which in turn, was affiliated with the Tjänstemännes Centralorganisation (TCO).

The white-collar employees' union, the youngest of the company's unions, had just over seven hundred members. Unionization of white-collar workers was a recent phenomenon in Sweden which accounted for the relatively low percentage of union members in the white-collar group. Union leaders were making serious efforts to increase the number of people in their union and had gone so far as to suggest that the union's right to organize extended to all white-collar employees below the president of the company. The national white-collar union was affiliated with the TCO.

The one hundred supervisors at Dagens Nyheters were all members of the supervisors' union. Almost all of the supervisors were involved in production of the paper, and so most of them had formerly been members of the graphics union. The supervisors' union was also affiliated with the TCO.

## Works Council

Aside from the unions, the most important avenue for employee-management communications was the company works council. At Dagens Nyheters, employees from all the company's operations (except SF) were represented on one works council. The council had twenty members—ten chosen from management and ten chosen by the five labor unions. The labor seats on the council were divided among the unions according to the relative size of their membership.

In 1976, the Dagens Nyheters's works council had three representatives from the graphics union, two each from the two journalist clubs, two from the white-collar union, and one from the supervisors' union. Each union's board elected its representatives. The union boards were elected directly by the employees once a year.

The chairmanship of the works council rotated between the president of the company, Mr. Douglas, and the senior representative from the graphics union, usually Mr. Sture Ring. Meetings were scheduled six or seven times per year during which management would inform the council of important actions they contemplated taking in the future. The works council handled policy issues affecting all employees. Union disputes with the company were not discussed in the council. Disputes between individual workers and their managers were also handled through the union structure.

Although the works council had no decision-making authority and traditionally had acted only in an advisory capacity, it was unusual for management to fail to consider the council's views on important matters. Should the council oppose a management proposal, it was common that a compromise would be worked out before any action was taken. One member of senior management remarked:

> In practice our works council codetermines policy with management. We bring everything of any potential importance to the employees before the works council for discussion. This includes key management appointments as well. Before Mr. Douglas joined the company as president he met with the workers' representatives on the works council.

Mr. Rolf Österberg, executive vice-president, commented further on the Dagens Nyheters works council:

I think we are moving in the right direction by including the works council in the policy making process, but it's a big job keeping them informed. I spend at least 60% of my time preparing for or in meetings with the works council and the union leadership. It takes a lot of time to convince them that some of our planned actions are correct, but once they are in agreement, it is much easier to get things done.

## Workers Representation on the Company's Board

A 1973 Swedish law provided that company employees be permitted to elect two members to the company's board of directors. At Dagens Nyheters, however, employees were not represented on the company's board of directors because the graphics union opposed it. The union's opposition was based on its contention that: the employees should elect 50% of the board's members; that worker representatives should be released from the legal requirement to maintain confidentiality; and that worker representatives should not be subject to the legal liabilities of board members as set forth in Swedish corporate law.

Although Dagens Nyheters's employees were not represented on the board of directors, it was management's policy that before important decisions were made, the works council would have an opportunity to express its views. If the council opposed the proposed action, management would usually work out a compromise with the council before asking the board for a decision.

## Industrial Peace in the
## Swedish Newspaper Industry

Industrial relations in the Swedish newspaper industry were somewhat different than in most other Swedish industries. Since the 1950s, a system of "peace agreements" between the publishers and the newspaper unions had been in effect. These peace agreements were based on the philosophy that a free press was vital in the functioning of a democratic society and that it should not be threatened by anything, including strikes. The agreements called for compulsory and binding arbitration in cases where contract terms could not be settled through collective bargaining. As strikes were not permitted while matters were under arbitration, the unions had given up their right to strike.

In 1975, the newspaper publishers' association was able to extend the peace agreements to include unions of companies under contract to deliver newspapers and newspaper supplies. Agreements with the teamsters' union stipulated that if they should call a national strike, deliveries of newsprint and other vital supplies would continue and newspaper delivery truck drivers and paper-carriers would be kept on the job.

### Current Problems in Newspaper Production

To improve the profitability of newspaper production, management believed that the time had come for the company to make substantial changes in the newspaper production process which would permit a reduction in the work force. In recent years, the company had been unable to keep revenues rising as fast as costs. Throughout the 1960s, management had concentrated on increasing the volume output to counteract the effects the steady reduction in gross margin was having on overall profit. By the early 1970s however, it became apparent that the company's two newspapers were rapidly approaching the point where there was little growth left in their readership and advertising markets.

In the future, total newspaper readership would not grow much faster than the general growth rate of the population. When coupled with the fact that management believed that both newspapers had just about reached their peak levels of market penetration, the outlook for substantial gains in total circulation was not promising. The company's ability to raise revenues by continuously raising the price of the newspapers it published was also in question. Management believed that subscribers and single-issue buyers were beginning to ask themselves if a daily newspaper was really worth the price they were being asked to pay.

Advertisers were in a similar position. *Dagens Nyheter* and *Expressen* had many advertisers who were feeling the same economic pressures that the newspapers were experiencing. In 1975, the Swedish economy had begun to recover from the worldwide business recession, and this positive business trend had had a favorable impact on advertising revenues. However, the inflation that had accompanied the recovery was increasing costs of all businesses in Sweden. In their efforts to reduce their costs, many Swedish companies were taking a much harder look at the level of their advertising expenditures.

In analyzing the company's ability to continuously raise the price of advertising space, management had to consider the effective cost to advertisers of alternative media. There were limits to the price of newspaper advertising space which were in large part determined by the prices charged by competing advertising mediums. Increasing the average ratio of advertisements to copy in each edition of the papers was not seen as a viable alternative because the company desired to maintain the quality standards of the papers.

Based on these considerations, management believed that over the next ten-year period the gross margin from newspaper operations would continue to be squeezed. With prospects for volume growth dim, the profitability of newspaper operations would almost certainly decline unless as management put it, "something could be done to break the cost curve" in newspaper production operations. Adoption of a new production technology was seen as the only viable long-term solution to this problem.

## Technological Innovation in
## Newspaper Production

To reduce the effects that spiraling increases in wages and personnel expenses were having on the profitability of the newspaper operations and to increase the company's ability to adjust production output to meet demand variations caused by seasonal and business-cycle fluctuations, Dagens Nyheters began in the early 1970s to study the feasibility of employing new technological processes in its newspaper production operations. Recent advances in the application of computer technology to the printing process had made it possible for newspaper publishers to radically modify their production process. Some people in the printing industry had referred to the new technology as the most dramatic change in the printing process since Gutenberg invented movable type in the fifteenth century.

In 1971, management formed a group to study the computerization of the processing of classified advertisements. However, because of the opposition to the proposal voiced by the managers in the classified ad department, the project was dropped before it really got underway.

Shortly after he joined the company in 1972, Rolf Österberg asked the company's four labor unions to designate representatives to a committee he was forming to study the introduction of new technology. Also asked to participate on the committee for new technology were members of middle management, process technicians, and computer experts.

By the fall of 1972, general agreement had been reached that Dagens Nyheters should undertake a more detailed study of the new technology in four basic areas: photo composition, the computerization of the classified ad department, the introduction of a computer-based display system for the processing of editorial material, and the selection of new printing techniques.

The committee's report was more an agreement on general direction in which the company should move rather than a detailed action plan. The committee suggested that task forces be formed to study each of the four areas on technological change and recommended that these task forces initially be composed of only professional people. Mr. Österberg commented on these recommendations:

The technicians and other professionals on the Committee thought they should be allowed to concentrate on the technical aspects of the systems' development. They felt that union representatives on each of the task forces would complicate the working environment. They wanted to work on the technical aspects first, and when they finished, they would then present their conclusions to the unions.

The unions agreed to this arrangement, but put a six-month time limit on their non-participation. However, they did request that they be allowed to observe the task forces as they worked out the technical details. They said they didn't want to participate, only to observe. Their rationale was that they wanted to become familiar with the technical aspects of the proposed systems. I'm sure they also wanted to search out the negotiating issues while the planning was underway.

Task force members, many of them union members, said they didn't want the unions involved at all. Top management overruled their objections, and in the end, each of the task forces we created had observers from the union.

Early in 1973, two task forces began working on the computerization of the classified ad department and the adoption of photo composition. Later in the year, a group was created to study the alternative new printing media. The task forces worked separately for a year at which time they each presented reports to the committee on new technology.

During their initial studies, each of the task forces concluded that there was the potential for problems to arise in the area of job definitions and in determining new boundaries between the various unions. The search for potential solutions, however, was put aside until the technical aspects of the new systems could be mastered.

The task forces' attempts to consider the technicial aspects first were apparently complicated by the presence of union observers. One task force leader described the problems he had had with the union observers:

They didn't insist on actually participating in the work, but they complicated our work by always asking questions that sometimes required quite detailed technical explanations. They took nothing for granted, and I got the feeling they sometimes doubted the professional competence of my team's members. It seems as if they were forever running off to union meetings and coming back with requests for reports on this or that topic. They criticized, but they didn't contribute. Even though they said they were only going to observe, it seemed to me as if they began negotiating right away to change the technical specifications of the systems we were designing. When we wouldn't change things to suit their desires, they would run up to the twenty-second floor[3] asking for new agreements which weren't always good.

Mrs. Ingrid Welin, assistant to the president, commented on the conflicts between the task forces and the union members:

The task forces naturally approached the problems from a very technical point of view, but they gradually were forced to adopt their technical solutions to the very real personnel problems which the new technology was bound to create. We had very rational goals which had to be modified because of the human issues that were involved. The dedicated professionals in the task forces were often very disturbed by the "irrational" changes that they had to make. One task force member complained to me that the union people were always talking about meaningful jobs for their people, but they weren't at all concerned about whether or not the irrational changes were destroying the professional pride of task force participants.

During 1974, the task forces presented their preliminary findings to the full committee on new technology. After the initial reports were received by the committee, the unions requested that they have the opportunity to discuss with management the problems they knew were associated with the task force recommendations. Union leaders complained that because the work of the task forces had been done so quickly they had not had adequate opportunity to study the proposals or discuss their implications. They proposed that task force work be slowed or halted until they had the opportunity to discuss the proposals in detail in the executive committee of the works council.

Management accepted the unions' request for a full discussion of the issue by the works council executive committee, but insisted that the task forces' investigation and planning must continue on schedule.

**Issues Raised in the Works
Council Executive Committee**

In late 1974, the executive committee of the Dagens Nyheters's works council held a series of meetings to discuss the labor unions' views of the changes proposed by the task forces. From the outset, none of Dagens Nyheters's five unions opposed the adoption of the new production and information-handling processes; however, they were deeply concerned with the effects these changes might have on the company's employees.

The concerns voiced by the union presidents centered on three major issues:

employment security for those whose jobs were threatened by the automation of certain processes;

the effects of the new technology on job satisfaction of certain groups of employees, particularly those in the graphics union;

the potential jurisdictional disputes between the unions which were almost certain to result from the modifications of job descriptions and the organization changes required by the implementation of the new technology.

Approximately 200 jobs would be eliminated by the adoption of the new technology. Of these, roughly 150 redundancies would result from changes in the operations of the composing room where the manpower requirements would drop from the current level of 400 to around 250 employees. Fifty jobs would be eliminated in the printing shop where new techniques would be employed in the production of printing plates. The graphical workers' union would be hardest hit by the technological innovations. Approximately 185 jobs currently held by graphics union members would be eliminated. The supervisors' union stood to lose the remaining 15 positions.

The president of the graphics union was justifiably concerned about the job security of his workers. The average age of those employees whose jobs would be eliminated was between 40 and 45 years. All were skilled craftsmen who would find it difficult to train themselves for other occupations. Employment with other newspapers in jobs similar to those they now held was not seen as a viable alternative, because sooner or later, other newspapers were bound to introduce technological changes similar to those now being adopted by Dagens Nyheters.

Early in the discussions of the executive committee, the union presidents received management's assurances that no employee would be terminated until suitable work for him could be found. Management promised that the company would attempt to find positions for redundant employees in other areas of the production operations and to assist those whom they could not place internally with finding jobs in other companies. Should those employees require retraining to enter a new job or profession, management stipulated that the cost of such training would be at the company's expense and that their normal salaries would be paid while they were being retrained.

Although management's attitude on the handling of redundant personnel was reassuring to union leaders, they nonetheless were of the opinion that no employee should be forced to take a new job at Dagens Nyheters or elsewhere that the employee did not want. The employee, they believed, should have the final say about his future work.

The president of the graphics union, Mr. Sture Ring, spoke to the executive committee on several occasions about the need to insure that the jobs his people would have after the changes were made would be "meaningful." He said that the lithographers, stereotypers, and other printing tradesmen in his union were "craftsmen" in the true sense of the word. In other trades, machines had replaced the craft of the tradesman, but Ring maintained that in the the printing trades this was not so. Graphics workers still required a great deal of skill to operate their machines properly. They took great pride in their skill and in their profession. Mr. Ring was afraid that the new technology would do to his profession what automation had previously done to so many others. He was afraid that the craftsmen in his union would become nothing more than machine operators where the quality of their work would no longer be a function of their skill, but would be controlled by the program that operated the computer. "We accept the technology, we accept the change, but my people must have meaningful work. They must be able to have pride in what they have produced," stated Ring.

Potentially the most difficult problem for management was the jurisdictional disputes between the unions which had begun to surface during the executive committee's meetings. These disputes were caused by the changes in the organization of work and by the creation of new job descriptions.

For example, the most expeditious way of processing classified advertisements received by mail appeared to be having the ads received by the classified ad department and having the proper information fed into the computer via the CRT terminals located in the ad department. When the graphics union protested that this would result in the white-collar union employees in the ad department taking work from graphics workers who had traditionally handled the classified ads received by mail, it was decided that mailed-in ads would go to the composing room where they would be processed by graphics workers. But, this raised another issue. Under the old system, the white-collar union employees had first processed the administrative and accounting data on mailed-in classified ads before sending the text of the ad to the composing room for typesetting. The new system eliminated the need for handling the ads twice. A single CRT terminal operator could input both the administrative data and the text of the ad at the same time. The white-collar union argued that it had jurisdiction over the processing of administrative and accounting data, while the graphics union argued that it rightly had jurisdiction over employees involved in production of the newspaper. Accounting data and production data (the text) would be kept separate by the computer program, but the problem remained as to which union's employees should be allowed to input the data into the computer.

A similar dispute arose over who should maintain the computers and where they should be located. White-collar union officials claimed that computer programming and maintenance was historically a white-collar function. The graphics union countered by saying that computers used in production operations should be controlled by the production workers (graphics) union.

Another dispute arose over the right of the graphics union to control the input of data, but this one involved a conflict with the journalists' unions. The specifications of the visual display system proposed for the editorial department called for the journalists to type their stories directly into the CRT terminal. After being edited (also on the CRT terminal), the stories could then be fed electronically directly into the photo composer, thereby eliminating the need for handling of all the information by the composing room personnel. It was possible that the bulk of each day's newspaper would be handled in this manner. The graphics union argued that the journalist was now performing a graphic worker's function, that is, the inputing of data used to produce the newspapers. The journalists' union felt that for the editorial staff, the full advantages of the new system could only be realized if they were allowed to input their news articles themselves. Once all the editorial copy was in the system, it seemed illogical to have the people in the composing room put it in again.

As the discussions within the executive committee continued, it became obvious to all concerned that to resolve the jurisdictional disputes that had arisen, direct negotiations between the unions involved would be necessary. The timetable for the introduction of new systems which the task forces had worked out called for the computerization of the classified ad department to begin in early 1976. During late 1976 and 1977, the company would install and check out the new photocomposition equipment for the composing room and the new plate-making equipment in the printing plant. The final step in the transition to the new technology, the installation of the computer system for the editorial department, was not scheduled to begin until late 1977. If the company was to keep the implementation of the new systems on schedule, the first jurisdictional dispute that had to be settled was that between the graphics union and the white-collar union. The conflict between the journalists and the graphics union could be settled at a later date.

## The Negotiations between the Graphics and the White-Collar Unions

Rolf Österberg described how the negotiations began:

> In the fall of 1974, the border disputes really began to be quite evident. None of the unions were against the technical developments, none opposed the purchase of new equipment—the big problem was the jurisdictional disputes between the unions. The first dispute we had to settle was the one between the white-collar union and the graphics union, but I foresaw a problem which might disrupt the timetable for implementation of the new system.
>
> The president of the graphics union, Mr. Ring, is a good negotiator—he has a knack for picking the issues he wants to fight about. He doesn't waste

time squabbling over minor points; he always gets right to the heart of the matter. On the other hand, the white-collar union leaders have a tendency to get bogged down in negotiating the minor details; this is probably because their union is only five years old, and they don't have the negotiating experience that Ring and his people have.

I knew that if we started the negotiation off at the local level that we'd waste a lot of time dealing with relatively unimportant details—the time we spent negotiating trivial points would probably cause delays in the implementation of the classified ad system. Therefore, I decided that it might speed things up if a settlement could be reached between the unions at the national level on the broad guidelines for the local before we actually sat down to talk in-house.

Unfortunately, the two local unions began to talk before I could get the national unions involved. I went ahead anyway and called privately on both national unions. I suggested that they might want to work out a parallel national solution for use not only in our newspaper, but in others which would be adopting the new technology sooner or later.

Evidently the two national unions started negotiating in secret and during the process they kept in touch with me. As needed, I supplied them with the employer's point of view.

In February, 1976, the national white-collar union and the national graphics workers' union reached agreement on a framework for local negotiations. While these negotiations had been going on in private, the two local unions at Dagens Nyheters had also been trying to reach an agreement. Apparently, the leadership of the national white-collar union had kept its local leadership informed of the existence and progress of the national talks; however, the national leadership of the graphics union had not.

One day in early March, 1976, shortly after the national negotiations between the two unions had been concluded (but before the agreement was made public), a copy of the synopsis of the agreement "found its way into the Dagens Nyheters building." Mr. Österberg described what followed:

The people in the graphics union got hold of it (the synopsis) and immediately called a meeting of the union board. At this meeting the union leadership decided that they would first, misinterpret the purpose of the national agreement; and second, they would quietly spread their misinterpretation around the composing room. They put the word out that the national union had decided everything behind their backs and in the process sold out their jobs. Then they went home.

At 11 P.M. the night of March 5, 1976, the graphics workers in the Dagens Nyheters composing room started a sit-down strike in protest over the agreement their union had reached with the national white-collar workers' union. The spokesman for the union told management that they would not go back to work until the president of their national union came to the building to discuss their objections to the agreement he had negotiated with the white-collar union.

After several phone calls around Stockholm, it was determined that the national union president was out of town on business and could not be reached. In the meantime, management had made attempts to persuade the graphics workers to end their illegal strike by returning to their jobs. Mr. Ring told management that the only solution was a complete renegotiation of the entire dispute. The sit-down continued until 3 A.M. When it became obvious that the president of the national union could not come to the Dagens Nyheters building, Ring instructed his people to return to work. As he did so, he implied to management that until there was a locally negotiated settlement, the paper would experience a slowdown in its production process.

*Dagens Nyheter* appeared the next day, but only in Stockholm and then only with a sixteen-page edition.[4] The first edition (meant for national distribution) could not be published in time. It was the first time in the history of the newspaper that an edition of *Dagens Nyheter* failed to appear.

The next day, management informed Mr. Ring that the strike the previous evening had been illegal and that the paper was preparing to sue his union for damages.[5] Ring explained that the sit-down was not a strike against the company, but rather, a protest against the actions of his national union. After some discussion, he agreed to pay the fines that would almost certainly have been imposed by the labor court, on the condition that management start local negotiations between the graphics and white-collar unions immediately.

Mr. Österberg commented on Ring's decision and on the negotiations that subsequently took place:

> While the strike was unfortunate, I was very pleased with the sensible attitude Ring showed when it was over. I think he displayed a great deal of maturity in agreeing to the settlement.

> As agreed, we went forward with the local negotiations. We wanted to get the matter settled as quickly as possible for we were on a very tight time schedule as far as the classified system was concerned.

> Ring's threat of a slowdown was very real. Since January we hadn't hired any replacements for people who had left the composing room because we wanted to keep the eventual number of people we had to place elsewhere to a minimum. At the same time the volume of production work had been going up because advertising sales were reflecting a general improvement in the economy. We also had started the retraining program for people who could operate the photo composition equipment, and so, these people were not available to work full time at their regular jobs. In short, we had more work and fewer people to handle it. Even before the strike the paper began to run late in getting out of the printing plant. Late papers mean lost sales at the newsstands and angry subscribers. We really couldn't allow a slowdown to complicate an already critical capacity problem in the composing room. The first relief we had in sight for the composing room work load was getting the classified ad system up and operating, so the local negotiations between the graphics and white-collar workers took on great importance to management.

To speed up the negotiating process, management persuaded the graphics and white-collar unions to meet with management away from the company's offices. A hotel in the archipelago near Stockholm was rented for a week as the site of the negotiation. Mr. Österberg continued with his description of the negotiations:

We started on Monday at noon. By Wednesday it looked as if everything was settled. A really positive factor in moving things along so quickly was the fact that the white-collar union brought with them one of their national negotiators. This young man did a very good job—he was very courageous in that he didn't clear everything he was doing with the national leadership. The biggest concession he made to Ring, and the thing that gave us all hope that by Wednesday night there would be an agreement, was offering the graphics union the option of doing the maintenance programming on the software which controlled the classified ad system.

Ring had insisted all along that his people should have a place in the operation of the computer systems. When the white-collar union gave in on the question of programmers, Ring was very happy and he immediately ordered the hotel staff to prepare a big dinner that evening to celebrate. The dinner was scheduled for nine o'clock.

By nine o'clock however, we were in the middle of a major crisis. Earlier in the evening it became apparent that Ring had misunderstood what "maintenance programming" entailed. He thought that his people would be fully-fledged systems programmers. This communications problem caused the agreement to come apart. Ring thought he had been cheated.

Because the dinner had been prepared we ate it anyway, but it wasn't a pleasant evening. After dinner we negotiated on into the night—union to union with management trying to work things out.

By nine A.M. on Thursday, Ring came to see me and said his group was over-tired and that they could not go on. One man had become over-wrought and had collapsed. He had to be taken to the hospital.

So we stopped everything for several hours, and started the negotiations again Thursday afternoon. By four o'clock Friday morning, it was settled. We signed the agreement Friday. Once the agreement was signed we were all very happy, very relieved. Everyone had worked so hard. When it was finished there was great elation.

In the end Ring's union got what they wanted. The white-collar union agreed that the systems programming functions would be shared and that several members of the graphics union would be trained as systems programmers.

The agreement reached between the two unions allowed us to continue the implementation of the classified ad system, although the timetable for the systems introduction had to be revised.

Following the negotiations Mr. Ring told us that the "slowdown was over" and that his people would "work very hard again."

## The Demand for Negotiations with the Journalists' Union

Despite the assurances management had received following the successful conclusions of the white-collar/graphics union negotiations, by May the paper again began to appear late with increasing regularity. When Mr. Österberg discussed the problem with Mr. Ring, he was told that the negotiations that the graphics union had been having with the journalists had not been progressing very well and that Ring was anxious to reach an agreement with the journalists as quickly as possible. Mr. Österberg recalled that he had told Mr. Ring that an agreement between his union and the journalists was not nearly as pressing as the agreement with the white-collar union had been. Mr. Österberg said:

> I told Ring that the editorial system was number five on the priority list of things we had to get done. The installation of the system wasn't scheduled to begin until 1977, and so there was plenty of time for his union to discuss the jurisdictional issues with the journalists' club. I told him we really didn't have the time or manpower to get into those negotiations at that time. I promised Ring that we wouldn't do anything—we wouldn't even do any more planning for the editorial system—unless I checked with him and until he had worked things out with the journalists.

> He wouldn't accept that. He told me, "If we wait, we know that there are weaker graphical unions (at other newspapers) and that you as president of the newspapers employers' association[6] will work solutions for the other papers which are better for management. You will surround us with other agreements and then we will fail. We want to settle it now."

## Negotiations between the Journalists and the Graphics Union

In the early summer of 1976, management agreed to Mr. Ring's request and invited the journalists and the graphics unions to negotiations at a hotel in the Stockholm archipelago. The date of the negotiations was set for early August. Mr. Österberg recalls how the negotiations started:

> We proposed that the two journalists' clubs negotiate as a team. The others present would be Ring's union and observers from the white-collar union and the supervisors' union. As in the other negotiation, management would be in the middle working to bring the two sides together. Our suggestions were accepted and one Monday early in August we went again to the archipelago.

> Things started with the graphics union making a proposal. Ring said that all the CRT terminals should be located in the composing room, and he insisted that all the editorial input had to be done by members of the graphics union. He allowed that for late news and internal communications, maybe five to ten CRTs could be put in the editorial department, but that everyone of them had to be separately justified and negotiated.

Ring was basing his arguments on an agreement which had been made between the national journalists and graphics unions in 1972. This agreement concerned how the new techniques should be handled between the editorial and production departments.

It was a very poorly worded agreement. In one place it said, "The manning of CRTs used in graphic production should be under the jurisdiction of the graphical workers' union. CRTs needed in other departments should be manned by journalists in journalists' clubs."

The language was so vague that it could be interpreted that *all* CRTs as we intended to use them at Dagens Nyheters should be manned by members of the graphics union. And that's exactly the way Ring wanted the national agreement to be interpreted. The journalists objected to this very strongly as did management. By putting all the CRTs in the composing room we would lose many of the advantages that the new system offered.

After an inconclusive discussion of the graphics union's proposal, management briefly withdrew from the negotiations for several hours to prepare their own written interpretation of the 1972 agreement between the two national unions. In this position, management maintained that the editorial department should be equipped with CRTs, that editorial staff should be allowed direct access to the computer, and that the journalists themselves should input their news articles. There would also be sufficient numbers of CRTs located in the composing room so that the text of editorial material that was not time-sensitive could be placed into the system by the composing room staff. By "non-time sensitive," management meant feature articles, material for weekly supplements, and the like.

When management presented its interpretation of the 1972 agreement, the graphics union leaders became very upset. They accused management of trying to wreck the agreement that had already been made between the two national unions. Even though the implementation of the editorial system as outlined in management's proposal would result in the elimination of only twenty jobs, the graphics union appeared unwilling to yield from its original proposal.

For the next two days, the journalists and Mr. Ring negotiated alone. Mr. Österberg recalled:

We (management) just sat by and did not participate. After two days Ring came to me and said he couldn't talk to the journalists any more. He said he couldn't even bring himself to sit in the same room with them. He was very upset.

It took another whole day to calm everyone down, and by then it was obvious that we had reached a major impasse. Instead of calling the negotiations off, we decided that we would adjourn them and go back to Stockholm.

Several days after we got back we had a meeting to try to summarize what the problems were. It was at this meeting that Ring told us he would like to go away again with the journalists for another week of talks without management being there.

We agreed and several weeks later Ring and the journalists went off to talk again. This time they came back with an agreement, but we just couldn't believe what the journalists had agreed to. The agreement they had reached was almost identical to Ring's original proposal.

When they got back they just handed me the agreement and said, "Here, we've agreed to this, now you sign it for management." I told them that we would look it over and that we would want to discuss it with them.

## Management's Reaction to the Agreement

In management's view, the agreement reached between the journalists' club and Mr. Ring's union was unacceptable. Management's major objections centered on the limitation of the use of CRT terminals by the editorial department and on the fact that the way the agreement was worded these limitations would remain in effect forever, that is, they would not be subject to renegotiation at a later date. Mr. Österberg summed up management's position:

> The agreement stated that journalists could use CRT terminals for input of data to the photo composer only the last 45 minutes before the final deadline for finishing the paste-up. Even then they could only input a maximum of 10,000 characters. This all but eliminated most of the significant benefits we hoped to achieve. These limitations were worded in such a way that once the agreement went into effect they could not be changed. The journalists had totally capitulated to Ring's demands. Stephen Teste and the other journalist club leaders were just no match for an old professional like Ring.

For several weeks following receipt of the agreement, management discussed alternative courses of action. The situation had been complicated by the fact that the two unions had reached an agreement that management was forced to oppose. One Dagens Nyheters manager described the situation by saying, "We were put in a position where we had to fight the journalists' battle for them after they had already surrendered."

Management believed that they had to fight either the limitations on the use of CRT terminals by the editorial department or the absence of a time limit on the life of the agreement. Mr. Österberg described management reasoning:

> We thought we would be stronger if we chose only one point to argue about. We decided to put all our chips on the issue of a time limit. If we could force a time limit on the agreed restrictions then we could renegotiate later. We felt we could live with the restrictions for a while anyway. It would take at least a year to have the system fully operational and so we went back to the unions with a proposal that we would accept their agreement, but only if the limitations were open for renegotiation one year after the system was finally installed. After that first year we hoped that mystery

would be taken out of the new technology and the graphics union would not be so afraid of it. Also, it would be two years before we had to renegotiate the issue and by then several other newspapers would have negotiated deals with their local unions. I was confident that these other agreements would contain no such restrictions.

The negotiations between management and the two unions started at noon on Friday, October 1, 1976. Management agreed to accept the 45-minute/10,000 character limitations, but only for a period of twelve months after the new system was fully installed. At that time, the limitations would cease, and they would have to be renegotiated. These new negotiations were to be undertaken without any preconditions made by either side.

The graphics union's response to management's proposal was simple. Mr. Ring said, "There can be no time limit of the life of the agreement."

Mr. Österberg's reply was equally straightforward. "Then there shall be no agreement," he said.

After several minutes of silence Mr. Ring looked at Österberg and said, "Well Rolf, you know what will happen."

Mr. Österberg believed that Ring was threatening either a strike or a severe slowdown in the production operation. He thought that the strike was the more likely of the two outcomes. Mr. Österberg recalled:

> We had been soft with Ring in the past and I'm sure he thought we would give in now. I wasn't sure what we would do, so I excused myself and walked out. I then went up to Gustav's office where I told him what had happened.

## The Meeting of the Newspaper Department Managers

At 7:30 Friday evening, the managers of all department of *Dagens Nyheter* and *Expressen* met with Mr. Douglas, Mr. Österberg, and other senior executives of the company. When Mr. Österberg had finished filling them in on the day's events, Mr. Douglas asked the group what alternatives it thought should be considered.

After much discussion, three alternative courses of action emerged. The company could maintain its present negotiating stance and refuse to accept the ad infinitum limitations on the editorial system. Mr. Österberg maintained that if this were the position that was taken, then the company should be prepared to take a strike. Although the strike would be illegal and the company could sue the union for damages, the maximum award it could expect was around 220,000 kronor. The financial vice-president estimated that a strike would cost the newspaper roughly one million kronor per day in lost revenue. Also, to be considered was the longer-term effects a long strike would have on advertising and subscription revenues. Many advertisers would immediately shift their retail advertising business to the papers' competitors. If the strike went on for several weeks, subscribers would also begin to defect to competing publications.

The second alternative involved capitulation. Although sentiment in the meeting appeared to run against giving-in, Douglas thought that the alternative should be explored. Were the benefits of the CRT system really worth taking a strike? How much flexibility would actually be lost, how great were the opportunity cost-savings that would have to be forgone? Management of the editorial departments of both newspapers were adamant in their support for the system. Although the savings in manpower in the composing room was only twenty jobs, the system gave the editorial staff a great deal of flexibility, especially when it came to getting late-breaking news into the newspaper. The editors were unanimous in their opposition to giving in to Ring's demands.

The third alternative involved a modification of management's present position and a continuation of the talks. Some present at the meeting thought that instead of pushing for a one-year limit, they might consider offering Ring a compromise: a two-, three- or five-year limit. By sticking to the concept of a definite time limit, management would not be seen as giving in to the union's demand. A longer limit also allowed Ring the chance to appear as if he had won something in the bargaining. Management would lose certain of the system's benefit, but not forever; and, a costly strike could be avoided. Mr. Österberg and others present opposed this solution. Österberg was of the opinion that clear lines had already been drawn between the two sides. He said that the first one to move away from its present position would probably be forced eventually to accept the other side's demands. He didn't think that Ring would accept a compromise if offered. Österberg felt that Ring would perceive an offer of a two-year or longer time limit as a weakening of management's resolve. Österberg said: "If he sees us weakening he won't move a centimeter from his present position. He will press even harder in hopes of forcing us to give even more."

After a thorough discussion of all alternatives, it became clear to Mr. Douglas that should he decide to force the issue and should a strike result, he would have the support of his management group. Mr. Douglas was pleased to know that the editors of both *Dagens Nyheter* and *Expressen* were willing to have a showdown with the union on the issue of the editorial system. It was usually the case that editors of newspapers were more committed to having their papers published than they were to winning confrontations with labor unions. The willingness of the editorial group to accept a strike was surprising.

By 10:00 P.M., the management group thought it had exhausted the supply of plausible alternatives. It had received word that Ring and other union leaders were still in the building. From the composing room manager came the report that although they were slightly behind schedule, the situation there was normal. By 1:00 A.M., the last few pages of Saturday's paper would be ready to be sent to the printing plant. The press run on pages completed earlier in the day had already begun, and so, it appeared as if the situation at the printing plant was normal as well.

It was significant that Ring was still in the building. On a normal day he would have left for home by 6:00 or 7:00 P.M. Ring's continued presence signaled that the graphics union did not want to wait until Monday morning for management's reply.

In the next hour or so a decision had to be reached.

**Notes**

1. Income of the Financial Administration Group was not included in operating income. In 1975, the net gain from financial operations amounted to SKr. 5.9 million.

2. The journalists' union was called a club (*journalistklubb*).

3. Dagens Nyheters's top management had its offices on the twenty-second floor.

4. The paper was normally sixty-six pages.

5. Swedish labor law allowed employers to sue unions for damages resulting from illegal strike actions; however, the law limited the liability of the unions at 200 kronor for each employee involved in the strike.

6. Mr. Österberg was president of the Swedish newspaper employers' association.

## Case Appendix
## Excerpts from
## Interviews with
## Union Leaders at
## Dagens Nyheters AB

**Graphical Workers' Union**

Mr. Sture Ring, age 45, was president of the graphics union at Dagens Nyheters and had been employed by the company for twenty years. He had worked as a hand composer before becoming the union president. Mr. Ring was a Maoist Communist. He had been a member of the Communist party in Sweden all his adult life and was one of the organizers of the Maoist faction.

The management of the company had high respect for Mr. Ring's intelligence, his leadership qualities, and his skills as a negotiator. He was considered by management to be astute, articulate, and very tough-minded. He was described as being "much more radical" in his philosophy than his constituents; however, "smart enough to keep his personal politics out of his union business." Mr. Ring was asked for the position of his union on the technological changes that were taking place at Dagens Nyheters. He replied:

> When we realized how dramatic the changes would be and how these changes would affect the workers, we had a very long discussion of principles among the union people. Although the typographers and lithographers are very conservative craftsmen we reached the conclusion that it would be wrong to try to stop the technological change.
>
> I remember an example from Marx. In the nineteenth century people working at machines tried to wreck the machines. Marx says it is not the machines you should look at, but the production conditions. So, you should not try to change the technology. The important thing for us is to try to control the new technology and in that way we can take care of the workers.
>
> The main question is to get meaningful jobs in the new technique [the new technique of reproducing the paper]. Typographers and lithographers for a long time have had great self-confidence. This comes from knowing that they are skilled craftsmen. They know a great deal about the whole production process, and now they have control over the whole production process.

Mr. Ring compared what he was trying to do for his union members with what he had seen of similar technological changes in the United States.[1]

I found the solution in the United States very bad. The agreements they
have there are bad. They have "lifetime guarantees" of work which are in
reality guarantees for about ten years. For these guarantees the unions
have let management do whatever they want with the new technology.
The agreements are wrong because the typographers and lithographers
aren't controlling or shaping their own development. For example, we
could see that in some newspapers people were just standing around with
nothing to do. Management paid them to do nothing. This is very demor-
alizing.

We made a visit to the Big Six[2] where we met David Crockett. I was critical
of Mr. Crockett and said that we in Swedish unions wanted to be in the
process of creating meaningful jobs for our members. We wanted to have a
say in the creation of the process.

Mr. Crockett told us that, "We don't buy machines, that's management's
job. We're only interested in wages." Mr. Crockett then said he was
disturbed that union people were traveling with management.

I criticized them for taking a very hard stand, and for accepting the bogus
jobs. After they did that, they found that they were surrounded by the new
technology and they didn't have control of it.

At the same time that we are fighting with management here, we are of
course fighting our own fight and in a much more sophisticated way than
they did in New York. I told the people at the Big Six that we have taken
a different position from theirs, and because of it we are much stronger.
Our stronger position doesn't let management play out their cards.
Mr. Österberg knows we use our strength when we need to use it.

In our discussions on the new technology we always speak of three basic
principles:

> we don't want to build barriers to the new technology,
>
> the union wants to get meaningful jobs,
>
> the union wants a guarantee that people will not be laid off.

If the need arises to replace people with the new technology and to
transfer them to new jobs, then the man who is to be transferred should
have the last word. Management shouldn't be able to just put him in a
new job.

In our discussions on the new technique we want to have our opinion
given to management before something is decided. The union doesn't say
"yes" to any new technique, but we are positive and want to discuss it.

Mr. Ring commented on the current problems in the discussions over
the implementation of the technological change.

> We are now coming to some problems in moving to the new technique and
> in where we make the borders for the new jobs [new job descriptions and
> which union the people in those descriptions will belong to.].

In a newspaper there are two sides to the operation—the editorial side and the production side. Before the separation between jobs on the two sides were distinct. The new technology with OCRs, [optical character readers] display terminals, and computers confuses the old lines between the jobs and the categories of work.

For us, we just want to draw lines between the editorial staff, the office workers, and the production people.

*Dagens Nyheter* is the first newspaper which has been able to reach agreements between white-collar workers and journalists. These agreements are very interesting.

Regarding the agreement with the office workers—it was very complicated to start with because the central unions of the office workers and the graphics workers reached an agreement without us even knowing it. We struck against our central union. It sounds strange that workers in a union would strike against their own union, but we sat down here until the national leaders came down to see us.

The national leaders of the union came and told us that they would void the national agreement and after that we could have local negotiations.

There are laws against wildcat strikes in this country and before the local negotiations started the company threatened to take our strike to the labor court to make the union pay the fines. But, we made a deal. We said that if you take us to court the whole union will have to go to court, and we weren't striking against the company, but against the union. We said we would pay the fines for those who struck if the company would start the local negotiations. So we paid 200 kronor for each member, and it was worth the price because the negotiations started and we got a better agreement.

The next step was to draw the line between the graphics (production) workers and the journalists (editorial staff). We first tried to make an agreement with the journalists, but we finally had to go to the company.

The final negotiations with the journalists was on three occasions—the last session for twenty-four hours. We were very proud to make an agreement with the journalists because they have many different opinions from our own.

## *Dagens Nyheter*'s *Journalistklubb*

The journalist union of Dagens Nyheters was led by Mr. Stephan Teste. Mr. Teste was 32 years of age and had worked for Dagens Nyheters eight years. He had been union president since 1974. He was asked the question, "How does the new technological change affect your members?"

From our point of view it's not so bad. We have no threat of job loss and there's no loss of skill. As we see it, all newspapers are having economic problems now—especially the smaller ones—and if we don't have this new technology these papers may go out of business.

We talked with the graphics union for two years before we brought the management in. Then we all went out together to the archipelago to find a solution. The journalists want the new techniques, but for the graphics union it's tough—they stand to lose so much. It's difficult to make agreements about emotional issues.

## Commercial White-Collar Workers' Union

Mr. Michael Frey, age 53, had been president of the white-collar union for two years. Prior to that, he had worked as a librarian in the computer department. Mr. Frey joined Dagens Nyheters in 1970. He was asked, "How has the technological change affected your members?"

We are very positive toward the change. As we see it, it's the only way for the paper to carry on. If we do not adopt the new technology the paper does not have a long future. So, from the beginning we believed that the new technology should be forced through.

The source of problems is that with the computer technique the boundaries of jobs are different than before. The jobs of some white-collar workers and some graphical workers are now combined.

On paper it's now all settled, but we don't know how it will work in practice.

In principle, all administrative work should belong to white-collar workers and all process-related work to the graphics union. But now that we will have the computer, it's difficult to decide which part of the computer work should be done by graphics and which part by the white-collar people.

We gave the graphics people a chance to come into computer work—including maintenance programming. The graphical people have a dying trade. They needed help—part of the help came from the company. The management promised that no one would lose their job—and part came from us.

(Mr. Österberg interjected at this point, "Mike's union stepped out of former principles to make a solution possible.")

The graphics union said they didn't want just maintenance programmers, but fully fledged programmers. They said that was the only way for them to keep up with the computer technology. We eventually said okay.

From our perspective, computerization will affect more jobs in the future. Use of the computer will spread to other areas of the company. So for our people it's a chance to increase the scope of our jobs. We can't be blind to technological advances.

Our interest is that this house shall exist.

**Notes**

1. In 1975, Dagens Nyheters arranged for five management and fifteen union representatives to visit several American newspapers that had already installed computerized production systems.

2. The Big Six refers to the headquarters of the six large printing unions in New York City.

# Case 11
# Homeland
# Manufacturing
# Company

## The Company

Homeland is a producer of communication systems and equipment, electronics and electrotechnical equipment, consumer goods, and takes part in distribution. It is among Scandinavia's major business enterprises and has been in operation for more than fifty years. The company also ranks among the largest foreign owned enterprises in Scandinavia with some four thousand employees in various plants and offices throughout the country. Sales in 1975 were $235 million, net profit after tax $10 million, and net assets $125 million. The government is one of the company's main customers.

## Labor Relations

### Trade Unions and Employers' Associations

The labor movement in Scandinavia is highly centralized through the Federation of Trade Unions (LO) with a large number of affiliated national unions, the largest of which is the iron and metal workers' union. Approximately 50% of Scandinavian workers are represented by unions. The employers are represented by the Employers' Confederation (EC), which also has a large number of affiliated national employers' associations. Although there are differences between the various Scandinavian countries, the basic employee-employer relationship is the same.

### The Basic Agreement

In the 1930s, the LO and the Employers' Confederation negotiated the basic agreement, which with alterations and amendments has remained in effect. Part A of the basic agreement provides among other things that:

1. employers and employees have the right to organize freely,
2. where a collective agreement is in force, no work stoppage or other labor dispute will occur,
3. shop stewards will be elected by the organized employees and be recognized by the employer,

4. employers or workers can engage in sympathetic strikes or lockouts in support of other lawful conflicts, provided the consent of the Employers' Confederation and LO is given,
5. a labor contract must be ratified by a secret written ballot of all the organized workers who would be covered by it,
6. the employer will check off union dues.

## Works Councils

Part B of the basic Labor agreement was entitled Cooperation. Under it the Employers' Confederation and LO agreed the works councils would be established in every enterprise with one hundred or more employees. The management appointed five representatives to the council and the employees had five representatives. Three of the employee representatives were elected by blue-collar workers, one by the supervisors, and one by the technical and office employees. The works council met at least once per month. It was a purely advisory and informative body that had no codetermination rights. The agreement stated that "its main task shall be through cooperation to work for the most efficient production possible and for the well-being of everybody working in the undertaking." It is worth noting that many matters, including works councils, which were covered by legislation in many other countries, were here established through the basic agreement.

## Industry Agreements

Although there were a few major companies that negotiated labor contracts directly with the national unions, the great majority of enterprises were covered by contracts negotiated by their industry employers' association. The LO had taken increasing control over these negotiations. A national union had to obtain LO approval of: its desire to terminate an agreement, its list of demands, its wish to strike, and its settlement terms. Wages, hours, and certain other economic matters were reserved for collective bargaining. Works councils were not permitted to deal in these areas.

## Corporate Assemblies and Board Representation

Early in the seventies, the government adopted an amendment to the Joint-Stock Companies' Act which provided for employee representation in company decisions through two devices: corporate assemblies and employee members on the board. Under the law, a stock company with more than two hundred employees had to establish a corporate assembly. The assembly would have from ten to fifteen members. Two-thirds of the members would be elected by the shareholders and one-third would consist of employees elected by employees. The corporate assembly had final decision in a limited number of major company matters. Furthermore, the assembly appointed all members to the board of the company. If one-third of the assembly so desired, election to the board had to be by proportional representation which meant that employees could secure up to one-third of the representatives on the board.

*Few Strikes and Higher Real Wages*

Under the labor relations system, there had been very few strikes, and real wages had gone up rapidly. The remarkably low incidence of strikes in recent years is shown in exhibit 11-1. Between 1952 and 1965, real wages increased 50% and between 1965 nd 1972, increased another 29%.

**Labor Relations at the Company**

Approximately 70% of the company's 4,000 employees were members of the unions. The iron and metalworkers' union with 1,000 company members was by far the largest. There were, however, three other unions for hourly paid workers: the installers' union with 250 members, the electricians' union with 40 members, and a small union with 15 members. In addition, there were two supervisory unions (one inside and one outside the LO), two technician unions (one inside and one outside the LO), a clerical union (LO), and an engineers' union (outside LO).

**Exhibit 11-1**
**Strikes**

|  | Number of Stoppages | Number of Employees Involved | Working Days Lost |
|---|---|---|---|
| 1964 | 3 | 230 | 1,310 |
| 1965 | 7 | 591 | 8,927 |
| 1966 | 7 | 1,392 | 5,207 |
| 1967 | 7 | 436 | 4,720 |
| 1968 | 6 | 486 | 13,514 |
| 1969 | 4 | 824 | 21,636 |
| 1970 | 15 | 3,133 | 47,204 |
| 1971 | 10 | 2,519 | 9,105 |
| 1972 | 9 | 1,185 | 12,402 |
| 1973 | 12 | 2,380 | 11,382 |

Unlike the great majority of companies, Homeland did not negotiate through an employers' association but instead bargained directly with the iron and metalworkers and the other nine unions. The company and its unions, however, had agreed to be bound by the provisions of the EC-LO basic agreement.

Although none of the company union contracts provided for a closed shop, management encouraged union membership and had agreed (through the EC-LO basic agreement) to the check-off of union dues. The chief personnel officer of the company stated "it is company policy that employees should be represented by a union. We prefer to talk to the employees through their elected representatives."

Relations between the management and the unions had been excellent. There had been only one strike in the last thirty years. In 1974, a small group of outside installers struck for fifteen weeks before agreement was reached with the help of a mediator. However, during the fifteen weeks, all the other employees continued to work. Over the years, the company and the unions had been able to settle all differences of contract interpretation and application without outside help. Neither the company nor the unions had ever referred an issue to the labor court.

Although the LO was closely tied to the Socialist party, there appeared to be little sentiment among the company's employees for nationalization of their company. The chief steward of the metalworkers' union stated that "we are not interested in government ownership. We don't think that would be to our advantage. However, we would like to see a majority of the shares in the hands of nationals."

**Employee Participation**

The management was strongly committed to employee participation. As one executive stated "our interest is to have every employee recognized as a human being whose opinions should be heard before decisions are made." In addition to the union structure, there were four other major devices through which employees could and did influence management decisions: the works councils, the milieu board, the corporate assembly and board membership.

1. *Works Councils* were first set up in the company's plants in 1932. They were composed of an equal number of representatives of employees and management—five each. The councils were purely advisory. They had no right to veto any action by management. However, they had become an extremely important communication and consultative device on local plant matters. Management made every effort to secure approval of the council in

a plant before taking any action that would significantly affect the employees. Although a considerable amount of executive time was consumed in the council meetings, management was thoroughly convinced that it was time well spent. Once a council had understood and approved a plan of action, implementation was made much easier.

2. *Milieu Board*. Some years ago, the workers in the company's main plant had become concerned regarding management goals as they affected employees. As a result, management had decided to try to write up its goals with the help of the employees who were asked to review, criticize, and make suggestions. One of the major areas that was explored was the working environment. Certain goals regarding heat, noise, air, and other physical and psychological conditions were established. The company then formed a three-man milieu board consisting of the company doctor, the welfare officer, and the chief steward. The function of the board was to make a diagnosis in each department to determine the differences between the goals and the actual conditions and then to order such changes as would bring the conditions into line with the goals. The company set aside one million dollars for the operation of the committee. Both the management and the employees were impressed with the results. One executive stated: "we thought we would be spending all this money on welfare—pure luxury—but it hasn't turned out that way. In addition to much better employee morale, 90% of the money spent is returned in increased efficiency." A union official, when asked if more money should be allocated to the board, stated, "no, they have ample funds for the present. You see it takes time to do these things. But they are doing a terrific job."

When the company decided recently to build a new plant in an undeveloped area, the milieu board was heavily involved from the beginning so as to "design the facilities around the human environment rather than just a production process."

3. *Corporate Assembly*. Under the law, the company had to establish a corporate assembly which consisted of fifteen members, one-third of whom were elected by the employees and two-thirds by the shareholders. The five employee representatives were elected by proportional representation with the result that three were from the LO union employees. In addition to the regular members, each major plant was entitled to an observer. All the members and observers, including the ten elected by the shareholders, were employees of the company. This condition appeared to be unique. The assembly had final decision power over substantial investments and major rationalizations and reorganization measures. It had to approve the major accounting statement, including the dividend payment. It also elected the members of the board. Under a proportional

representation arrangement, up to one-third of the board members were elected by the employee representatives of the assembly.

4. *Board Membership.* The company had an eight-man board consisting of:

The former managing director, chairman

The current managing director

The retired manager of a large industrial enterprise

The retired technical director

An outside lawyer

An outside businessman, director of a metal company

An employee representative

An employee representative

The two employee representatives had been elected to the board in 1973 by the employee representatives of the corporate assembly. Both were employed as regular workers. One was a mechanic in the production maintenance department and the other was a skilled worker in the rectifier plant. In politics, both were to the left of the Labor party.

In order to enable the employee members to be more effective participants on the board, the managing director arranged pre-meeting discussions with them a day or two prior to each board meeting. At these meetings, the managing director carefully explained financial, technical, and other matters in his report (usually twenty or thirty pages) that might be difficult for the workers to understand. He invited them to raise any questions that they might have. It was felt that these sessions had proved to be very valuable to management as well as to the employee representatives.

The first year, there were no serious differences of opinion on the board. However, in 1974 a dispute arose over the payment of the yearly employee bonus. For many years, the company had paid a bonus of $300 to $400 per year depending on the profits of the divisions. Since one of the plants had been running at a loss for several years, the majority of the board was of the opinion that the employees at that division should not receive a bonus. However, the employee representatives argued strongly that every worker should receive a bonus, depending only on the profitability of the entire company. Nevertheless, the majority of the board (6 to 2) voted not to recommend a bonus for the divison employees, and the assembly followed their recommendation. The first year or two, the employee representatives did not find their job on the board very exciting. There were few major issues in which they became strongly involved.

## The Dividend Issue

About 75% of the stock of the company was owned by a foreign company. The other 25% was held by a bank and a local insurance company. However, the 25% owned by the local companies was preferred stock with a fixed 9% dividend. Thus, only the foreign company held common stock on which the dividends could be varied. It was a stated policy of the parent company that "as a general rule, subsidiaries (should) retain approximately 50% of their net profits." Stated another way, it was the policy that 50% of net profit of subsidiaries should be paid out in dividends to the parent company.

Prior to 1973 when the employee representatives came on the board the company had been paying considerably less than 50% of its profits in dividends. At one time it had paid less than 20% and it was in the process of moving toward 50%. The 1973 dividend of $3 million was between 30 and 35%. In 1974, the board approved an increase to $3.5 million, which was between 35 and 40% of net profits. The employee representatives who were new to the board at the time did not raise any serious objections.

For 1975, management proposed that the dividend be increased from $3.5 million to $4 million which was about 40% of net profits. The six members of the board elected by the shareholder representatives favored the proposal as reasonable under the circumstances, although they probably would not have approved a sharper increase. However, the two employee representatives registered strong disapproval.

The employee representatives argued that: all the profits were made locally by nationals and, therefore, it was not just to be sending such a large percentage of them out of the country; the parent company had not invested new funds for many years, so the drain was entirely one way; the funds could be used very efficiently locally to expand the company, create jobs, and increase employee productivity and income; there was a special need of these funds currently to provide jobs and income for employees who were laid off at the division which was still in trouble. Their appeal to the other board members emphasized nationalism and was highly emotional. Management replied that the parent company as the major shareowner had the legal right to take dividends out of the company, that this was common practice everywhere, that a 40-50% dividend was not unreasonable, and that there was not a one-way flow since the company owed its present favorable position to open access to know-how in technical, manufacturing, and management areas from the parent company and all its subsidiaries. However, the employee representatives were not persuaded by these arguments. Although management had sufficient votes to force through the dividend increase, it was decided that action should be postponed and the matter given further consideration.

The managing director informed the president of the parent company, who paid a personal visit to the company to confer with him and other management representatives of the company. After lengthy discussion, it was agreed that they should not use their power to force through the higher dividend payment but instead should try to work out a compromise. One possibility was to pay the higher dividend with the understanding that the parent company would immediately reinvest an amount equal to the .5 million dollar increase over the 1974 dividend. When this proposal was given to the employee representatives, they accepted it as a compromise to settle the immediate stalemate but not as a precedent for future years. The board then voted to recommend to the corporate assembly the increased dividend payment. The assembly approved it and it was paid to the parent company which then reinvested .5 million dollars in the local company.

In December, 1976, the managing director met with the employee representatives and informed them that it was his intention to propose a dividend payment for 1976 slightly higher than the 40% that was paid in 1975. The employee representatives replied that they would oppose his proposal and intended to discuss in detail the whole matter of dividend payments. The managing director recognized that the publicity arising from the 1975 settlement had resulted in considerable public and employee support for the position of the employee representatives. However, he was of the opinion that the increase in the dividend was reasonable and clearly in line with parent company policy. Should he force it through despite their opposition, or should he seek a compromise again? What if they should refuse a compromise or even demand a decrease in the dividend? He knew that headquarters would be seeking his advice, not only on how to deal immediately with what appeared now to be a perennial problem, but also on a long-run strategy to cope with it.

# 7

## Labor Relations in the United States

### Introduction

The population of the United States in 1978 was 219 million which was between three and four times the population of the largest Western European country, West Germany. Moreover, during the 1970-1977 period, population in the United States grew 6.7%, a greater increase than in all countries in this study except the Netherlands (see table A-1).*

The gross national product of the United States in 1976 was $1,695 billion—more than three times as high as the gross national product of West Germany, which had the highest in Western Europe. The gross national product per person in the United States in 1976 was $7,880, lower than in Sweden but higher than in any of the other European countries. However, during the period 1970-1976, the gross national product per person in the United States grew at only 1.7% per year which was lower than in all countries except Great Britain (see table A-2).

Consumer prices in the United States during the period 1970-1978 rose 68%, the smallest increase of all countries except West Germany (see table A-3). However, the unemployment rate in the United States during the same period averaged 6.2%, which was three times as high as the West German rate and higher than the rate in any of the six European countries in the study (see table A-4).

The average hourly compensation for production workers in manufacturing in the United States in 1978 was $9.43—lower than in the Netherlands, Sweden, or West Germany but higher than in Great Britain, Italy, or France. During the period 1970-1978, the average hourly compensation increased 92% in the United States which was at a considerably lower rate than in any of the European countries. In terms of local purchasing power, worker compensation in the United States increased only 14% during the 1970-1978 period which was also considerably lower than the increase in all the other countries (see table A-5).

Output in manufacturing in the United States increased an average of 3.8% per year during the period 1960-1978 and 2.6% per year during 1970-1978. During the longer period, 1960-1978, the U.S. annual increase in output was lower than that of all countries except Great Britain. However,

---

*Tables A-1 through A-13 referred to in this chapter are in the statistical appendix at the end of the book.

295

in the more recent period, 1970-1978, the rate of increase in the United States exceeded that of all countries except France and Italy (see table A-6). Productivity in the United States, as measured by percentage change in output per hour in manufacturing, increased 2.6% per year during 1960-1978 and 2.4% during the 1970-1978 period. Its rate of productivity increase was the lowest of all countries during the longer period, 1960-1978, and was lower than all except Great Britain during 1970-1978 (see table A-7).

Unit labor costs in the United States in terms of U.S. dollars increased 3.6% per year during the 1960-1978 period and 6.1% per year during 1970-1978. In terms of local currencies, unit labor costs increased less than in all European countries in the 1960-1978 period and less than in all except West Germany during 1970-1978 (see table A-8). In terms of U.S. dollars, the increase in unit labor costs was considerably smaller in the United States than in all the European countries, during both 1960-1978 and 1970-1978. In the period 1970-1978 the unit labor cost increases per year in terms of U.S. dollars in the Netherlands, Sweden, West Germany, and France were each more than double the increase in the United States (see table A-9).

## The Union Movement

### Membership

There are 173 unions in the United States. In 1978, these unions had a membership of 20.2 million U.S. employees, which was 19.7% of the total labor force.[1] This percentage had declined steadily since 1953 when it had reached a peak of 25.5%.[2] The percentage of unionization is lower in the United States than in any of the six European countries included in this study (see table A-11).

Some of the U.S. unions are quite small craft organizations, but the majority of the union membership is in large industrial unions. The membership in the three largest unions in 1978 were: teamsters (IBT)—1.9 million, automobile workers (UAW)—1.5 million, and steelworkers (USWA)—1.3 million. Most of the unions are affiliated with the AFL-CIO. The AFL-CIO is concerned primarily with lobbying, public relations, and union jurisdiction. It does not engage in collective bargaining. The AFL-CIO is a loose confederation in which the national unions maintain a high degree of autonomy.

### The Closed Shop

The closed shop, which is defined in American law as a condition where employees must join the union before they may be hired, is illegal.[3]

However, a union shop, which is defined as a condition where employees must join the union (or at least offer to pay union dues) after they are hired, is legal in all but twenty states. In the twenty states that have so-called right-to-work laws, no one may be forced to join a union or pay union dues.[4] In the other thirty states, many of the labor agreements contain a union-shop clause. The check-off of union dues is also very common in U.S. labor contracts. Union dues vary. In the automobile industry, they are 2% of pay and in 1975 averaged $11 per employee per month.

*Ideology*

U.S. unions are economically and politically very conservative. They support the capitalist free-enterprise system and are strongly opposed to communism and socialism. Communist and socialist influence in the unions has been insignificant since the late forties.

*Politics*

There is no labor party. The Democratic party usually receives the support of the majority of the unions, but there are exceptions. The teamsters' union and the construction unions supported the Republican party in 1972. It is illegal for unions to contribute directly to a political campaign, but they do so indirectly by collecting money from their members through political education funds. They also contribute staff and facilities during campaigns. In the 1976 campaign, President Carter received strong union support.

*Local Unions*

The local plant union organization is very important in the United States.[5] Contract bargaining is usually carried on at the local or company level rather than at the national union level. Moreover, employee grievances that arise during the life of the contract are negotiated with management representatives at least at the first level by local shop stewards elected by the employees.

**Employee Rights**

The basic labor relation law covering the private sector in the United States is the 1935 National Labor Relations Act (*NLRA*). It was modified by the Taft-Hartley Act (1947) and the Landrum Griffin Act (1959). Under this legislation, workers have the right to join and be active in unions and must not be discharged or discriminated against by management for such activity.[6]

If an employee feels he has been discharged or discriminated against because of union activity, he may appeal to the National Labor Relations Board (NLRB). If the board finds such discrimination, it will order the employer to discontinue such discrimination and to make the employee whole for any losses he may have suffered. Employees who have been unjustly discharged are reinstated to their jobs and given back-pay plus 6% interest. In 1978, the NLRB awarded back-pay totalling $13.4 million to 8,623 employees.[7]

Supervisors, including first-line supervisors if they possess authority over employees, are not protected under the NLRA.[8] Thus, an employer is free to discharge a foreman who supports or joins a union. Likewise, an employer may refuse to bargain with a union regarding the wages and other working conditions of foremen. It is not illegal for foremen to develop unions, but they have no protection against action that the employer may take. As a result, very few foremen are represented by unions. Instead, they are considered to be part of the management team and usually represent management in the first step of the grievance procedure. Thus, the management level above which employees are not represented in unions is much lower in the United States than in Western Europe, where union membership often includes not only foremen but also much higher management people. Likewise, unionization of nonmanagement white-collar workers in the United States is quite low (only 10 or 11%) compared with Western Europe. During a strike of the manual workers, the white-collar workers, supervisors, and managers in a U.S. company may enter the plant and temporarily man the equipment. (Sit-down and slowdown strikes are illegal.) In highly automated industries, such as electric power, gas, telephone, oil refining, and chemicals, the result has been that management has been able to operate the plant despite a walkout of all the manual workers. In these industries, union strike power has been greatly reduced.

## Union Recognition

An employer does not have to bargain with a union unless the majority of the workers want the union to represent them. The NLRB will hold a secret election in a plant if 30% of workers indicate they want an election by signing union cards.[9] Workers always have the chance to vote for "no union" as well as for one or more unions. If the majority who vote do not favor a union, the employer does not have to bargain with any union and there cannot be another election for one year. If the majority who vote want a union, the union is certified as the bargaining agent by the NLRB and the employer must bargain with that union. The certified union is the exclusive bargaining agent, which means that the employer does not have to bargain with any other union for the employees in that bargaining unit. In turn, the certified union must represent all the employees in good faith whether or not they are union members.[10] In 1978, the NLRB held 7,433 certification elections. The unions won 48% of these elections.[11]

## Employer Rights

An American employer is free to speak out against and actively oppose unionization of his workers. However, the employer must not engage in espionage and is not permitted to give or promise anything to the employees for not unionizing or deprive or threaten to deprive them of anything if they do unionize.[12] Managements in the United States frequently carry on very vigorous anti-union campaigns, and it is unusual for a U.S. employer to recognize and bargain with a union unless ordered to do so by the NLRB following an election in which the majority of the workers voted for the union. European managers are often surprised by the very strong anti-union policies and programs of many U.S. companies. Some of the factors that account for the difference in the European and U.S. attitude are:

1. U.S. management becomes more directly involved in collective bargaining because negotiations are at the company or plant level;
2. the scope of collective bargaining, that is, the issues covered in negotiations, are much more extensive in the United States;
3. the curtailment of management rights through collective bargaining is more severe in the United States; and
4. if 50% of the workers in a U.S. plant can be convinced to vote "no union," management does not have to recognize or deal with any union.

## Contract Negotiations

If a union wins the election, the law requires that the employer and the certified union must "bargain in good faith" with respect to "wages, hours, and other conditions of employment." Either the union or the company may appeal to the NLRB and eventually to the federal courts if it is convinced the other party is not bargaining in good faith. The NLRB and the courts have had difficulty in determining what constitutes good-faith bargaining.[13] Likewise, the NLRB and the courts have had the task of deciding what items Congress intended to include in the phrase "wages, hours, and other conditions of employment" or, in other words, the things that a party must bargain about if the other party so wishes.[14]

As indicated, contract negotiations usually cover a particular plant or a particular company. Thus, General Motors, Ford, and Chrysler each negotiate separate contracts with the United Automobile Workers' Union. There are exceptions, however, where the basic contract terms are negotiated by the industry, such as in the steel industry. There are no contract negotiations between the AFL-CIO and industry in general.

As indicated, the scope of bargaining is much broader in the United States than in Western Europe. Unlike European labor agreements, U.S. agreements usually include:

actual wages rates, not just minimum rates;

many benefit plans, such as supplementary retirement pay, length of vacation, vacation pay, holidays and holiday pay, supplementary unemployment benefits, and sick pay;

extensive provisions concerning local plants and individual worker matters, such as discipline and discharge, promotions, demotions, layoffs, seniority rights, and plant safety;

grievance procedure; and

arbitration procedure.

If a large company, such as General Motors, bargains on a national scale with its unions, the national contract is usually supplemented by local agreements negotiated at the various plants by the locals of the union. Because of the broad scope of bargaining and the local as well as national agreements, the pages of contracts covering an employee may be quite large. For example, an employee in the Baltimore plant of General Motors in 1973 was covered by the national basic agreement (336 pages), several national benefit agreements (253 pages), and a local agreement (94 pages), for a total of 683 pages. Although most labor agreements are not as long as the General Motors-UAW contract, it is not unusual for them to be more than 100 pages.

U.S. labor contracts are usually for three years but may be shorter or longer. Once a contract has been signed, there cannot be an election to eliminate or replace the union for the period of the contract if it runs for three years or less. When the contract runs out, or at the end of three years, whichever is shorter, if 30% of the workers sign a petition, a new election will be held by the NLRB. In 1978, the NLRB conducted 807 such decertification elections. The unions won 213 of these elections involving 19,671 employees and lost 594 elections involving 19,884 employees.[15]

## Grievance and Arbitration Procedures

In the United States, a labor agreement is a legally enforceable contract.[16] Moreover, with very few exceptions, the labor agreements contain no-strike, no-lockout provisions. The company and the union agree that instead of resorting to their economic power during the life of the agreement, they will settle all disputes regarding its meaning and application by referring the issues to arbitration for final and binding decisions. These contract provisions are enforceable in the federal courts. Thus, during the life of an agreement (usually three years), the union is not free to strike and the employer is not free to lock out the employees.

Under the terms of U.S. labor agreements, management reserves the right of administrative initiative, that is, management has the right to make immediate decisions which must be carried out by the employee unless his health or safety is endangered. However, if the employee or the union believes that a company decision violates the labor agreement, a complaint or grievance may be filed. The grievance procedure consists of three or four steps, with each step involving a discussion by a higher level of company and union officials. Most disagreements are settled by the parties in the earlier steps of the procedure.[17]

However, if the grievance steps are exhausted without an agreement having been reached, the union can appeal the matter to arbitration. The arbitrator is selected by the company and the union, who share equally in the cost of the arbitration process. This is voluntary arbitration in the sense that the company and the union are not required by law to include it in their labor contracts. It is compulsory arbitration, however, in the sense that once it is included in the contract, it must be used instead of strike action. The arbitrator's awards are final and binding and will be enforced by the federal courts.[18]The number of arbitration awards has been increasing each year, and in 1976 was estimated to have been 10,000.

**Strikes and Lockouts**

If a labor agreement terminates and the union and management are unable to reach a new agreement, the union is free to strike and the company is free to lock out the employees until a settlement is reached. (This applies only to the private sector. Strikes by government employees are illegal.) The government maintains a corps of competent mediators who try to help the parties if they reach an impasse. However, the mediators have no power to force them to reach an agreement.[19] There is no compulsory arbitration or other types of compulsory settlement by the government. The President does have the power under the National Labor Relations Act to seek a court injunction to delay a strike or a lockout for eighty days, if it would create a national emergency.

Days lost per year per 1,000 workers in strikes in the United States during the ten-year period 1967-1976 were 593, which was higher than in any of European countries in this study except Italy (see table A-12). In fact, losses caused by strikes were 16 to 20 times as high as in Sweden, West Germany, or the Netherlands. However, it is easy to place too much emphasis on these differences. Actual losses caused by strikes in the United States have been an insignificant percentage of total work time, and that percentage has been decreasing over the years. During the 1967-1970 period, it averaged only 1/4 of 1%. In comparing it to the Dutch, West German, or Swedish experience, it is like saying 26 grains of sand are much larger than 1 or 2 grains of sand. Neither is a significant amount. It is true that the strike statistics record only the direct losses, and in some instances, there may be additional losses at the work places of both suppliers and customers of the struck plant. On the other hand, the statistics assume that there are no offsetting factors, such as less absenteeism, more overtime work, and fewer days of normal layoff following a strike. As a matter of fact, because of these compensating factors, a strike may result in no loss of production over the long run. It is very unlikely that fewer cars have been produced in the United States as a result of the strikes that have occurred in the automobile industry from time to time. Thus, the strike statistics tend to exaggerate the long-run effects on production. In the United States, losses in production caused by unemployment or absenteeism or even coffee breaks have been much more significant than losses caused by strikes.

## Absenteeism

Absenteeism in industry in the United States is at the lowest level of all countries in this study. The Swedish employers' association estimated that sickness absenteeism in U.S. industry in 1973 was only 4% compared with 10% in Sweden (see table A-13). The lower level in the United States appears to be a result of several factors: less liberal sick pay programs and policies; a much higher unemployment rate; and greater ability on the part of U.S. management to check on and discipline employees for unexcused absences.

## Worker Participation

In the United States, there has been little or no interest on the part of employees, unions, or political parties in promoting employee participation through works councils or worker representation on boards of directors. The lack of interest in works councils is a result of the fact that unions are already very active in representing workers' needs at the shop-floor level. Works councils are looked upon as competitive non-union organizations not unlike the old "company unions" that were made illegal by the NLRA in 1935. The lack of interest in worker representation on boards of directors also flows from the structure of U.S. bargaining. In most cases, the union bargains directly with the company rather than with a trade association as is usually the case in Europe. Thus, workers and unions feel that they already have a means of directly influencing company policies. Moreover, they fear that board membership could very well result in conflicts of interest. Thomas R. Donahue, executive assistant to the president of AFL-CIO, has stated that the American labor movement prefers to seek its gains through collective bargaining rather than as members of the boards of directors.[20]

## Notes

1. *Labor Union and Employee Association Membership—1978*, (News Release: Aug. 31, 1978), Bureau of Labor Statistics, Washington, p. 5.

2. Bureau of Labor Statistics, *Handbook of Labor Statistics 1978* (Washington: U.S. Government Printing Office, 1978), p. 507.

3. Benjamin J. Taylor, and Fred Whitney, *Labor Relations Law*, 2nd ed. (Englewood Cliffs, N.J.: Prentice-Hall, 1975), p. 321.

4. Thomas R. Haggard, *Compulsory Unionism, the NLRB, and the Courts* (Philadelphia: University of Pennsylvania Press, 1977), p. 172.

5. Arthur Sloane, and Fred Whitney, *Labor Relations* (Englewood Cliffs, N.J.: Prentice-Hall, 1977), pp. 178-80.

6. Charles J. Morris, *The Developing Labor Law* (Washington: Bureau of National Affairs, 1971), pp. 63-134.

7. National Labor Relations Board, *Forty-Third Annual Report* (Washington: U.S. Government Printing Office, 1978), p. 12.

8. Taylor, and Whitney *Labor Relations Law*, p. 303.

9. Morris, *Developing Labor*, p. 155.

10. Ibid., pp. 726-56.

11. National Labor Relations Board, *Annual Report*, p. 15.

12. Morris, *Developing Labor*, pp. 72-77.

13. Russell A. Smith, Leroy S. Merrifield, and Donald P. Rothschild, *Collective Bargaining and Labor Arbitration* (New York: Bobbs-Merrill, 1970) pp. 67-80.

14. Ibid., pp. 72-74.

15. National Labor Relations Board, *Annual Report*, p. 15.

16. Smith, Merrifield, and Rothschild, *Collective Bargaining*, p. 88.

17. Sloane, and Whitney, *Labor Relations*, p. 220.

18. Frank Elkouri, and Edna Asper Elkouri, *How Arbitration Works* (Washington: Bureau of National Affairs, 1973), pp. 26-46.

19. Daniel Quinn Mills, *Labor Management Relations* (New York: McGraw-Hill, 1978), p. 189.

20. Thomas R. Donahue, "The Future of Collective Bargaining," *AFL-CIO Free Trade Union News*, Washington, September 1976, p. 1.

# Case 12
# First National Bank
# of Lake City

On a Monday afternoon, Wynn Evans, president of the First National Bank of Lake City, received a formal notice from the National Labor Relations Board (NLRB) that an election would be held at the bank's offices thirty days hence to determine if the employees wished to be represented by the International Metalworkers' Union (IMU). Evans arranged for a meeting to be held the following afternoon with the bank's labor attorney, Francis Grant, and a group of its executives, including Paul Blanton, vice-president of personnel. Evans indicated that at the meeting the action taken so far by the bank and the union would be reviewed and he would welcome recommendations concerning what further action, if any, management should take during the thirty days remaining before the election.

Lake City, located in a north-central state, had a population of approximately 70,000 which had remained relatively stable during the last ten years. The economy of the community was completely dependent upon one large plant, an automotive parts plant, which was owned by one of the big three of the auto industry. When auto production was high, the Lake City economy was high and vice versa.

During the mid-thirties, Lake City had had some turbulent labor strife as representatives from the national headquarters of the International Metalworkers' Union tried to organize the workers in the local plant. In the late thirties, however, the automobile company had signed a national agreement with the IMU which included the Lake City plant. Moreover, since 1956 the agreement had included a union shop clause which required all workers at the plant to be members of the union. The IMU had been successful also in organizing a number of machine shops and other types of small plants in the area. The IMU was very active in local politics. Lake City was sometimes described as "a union town."

Most of the employees of the bank had relatives who worked at the auto plant and were members of the IMU. In fact, some of the bank's employees were closely related to the local IMU leaders. The IMU had made several unsuccessful attempts to organize the white-collar workers at the auto plant. Four years ago, it had been successful in organizing the maintenance workers at one of the smaller banks. However, unionization at that bank had not spread to the tellers and the other white-collar employees, and none of the employees in the other banks of the community was organized.

One group of professional employees in the community was represented by a union—the schoolteachers. Most of the grade-school and high-school teachers in Lake City had been members of the National Education Association (NEA) for many years. However, until the sixties the NEA had been a purely professional society that opposed collective bargaining. In the late sixties the NEA, pressed by the success of a rival organization, the American Federation of Teachers which was an affiliate of the AFL-CIO and which had negotiated sizeable wage increases for teachers in some of the major cities, decided to support collective bargaining by its local groups. The business community of Lake City was surprised and disturbed when some of the local teachers who were members of the NEA began to organize for bargaining purposes under the protection of the State Public Employees Relations Act. They were even more surprised when in an election the teachers voted to have the NEA serve as their bargaining agent.

Following the election, the school board and representatives of the NEA entered into collective bargaining. It was six months before agreement was reached on the first labor contract. It was generally agreed that the teachers had secured sizeable economic gains as a result of unionization and bargaining.

The First National was the oldest and largest commercial bank in the Lake City community. It had assets of approximately 300 million dollars which was twice the size of the next largest of the other six commercial banks in the area. Founded in 1892, First National had remained a single-unit bank until about ten years ago, when it had begun an expansion program by merger with and acquisition of several smaller banks in nearby communities. As a result, by now it had eighteen offices, including two that had been opened recently in newly developed suburban shopping areas.

Although the First National was the largest financial institution in the area, it was not the salary pacesetter in the community or even in the banking sector. First National salaries were generally 10% to 20% below those for comparable jobs at the auto plant, and one or two of the smaller banks had somewhat higher salary scales than the First. However, the First seldom lost employees to other banks although recently there had been some movement of younger employees to the auto plant. This had been especially true of men and women whom the First had trained in data processing.

Everyone at the bank except the maintenance employees was on salary. The bank had a formal salary evaluation program in which there were ten classifications, each with a maximum and a minimum rate. The maximum of the range varied from 13% above the minimum for the lowest level classification to 30% above for the highest level classification. Within the ranges, increases were granted each year entirely on merit. All increases whether as a result of a change of job or merit evaluation became effective January 1 of each year. If an employee was promoted during the year, he received the new job title immediately, but his salary frequently was not changed until January 1. Management was of the opinion that its somewhat lower salary scale was more than made up by its excellent working conditions, its job security, and its liberal profit-sharing plan.

The First National was looked upon by the employees as a prestigious place to work. The offices were clean and pleasant and the atmosphere was congenial and unhurried. Most of the employees were proud to say that they worked at the First National. The established work week was 38 hours during a five-day period. However, most employees averaged only 35 hours. For work between 38 and 40 hours, employees received additional compensation at straight-time rates. Beyond 40 hours per week, a rate of time and one-half was paid.

The bank was also viewed as a place where employees without college education, especially men, could rise to important positions. Practically all of the bank's employees, including all but two of its top officers, had terminated their formal education upon graduation from the local high schools. After entering the First, many of them had attended American Institute of Banking (AIB) courses at night which the bank encouraged and financed. A job at the First represented an avenue for dependable young men without college educations to become eventually important leaders in the community.

Jobs at the First were valued also because of their security. Employees were never laid off and discharge for poor work or offensive conduct was extremely rare. Once a person was hired, he or she could count on a regular pay check for the rest of life. In the past, this job security had been very important in a community where the major industry was known for heavy overtime one year and heavy layoff the next. However, in recent years the advantage of working at the bank in this respect, compared to working at the auto plant, had largely disappeared as the union in the fifties and early sixties negotiated supplementary unemployment benefits (SUB) and in 1967 topped off its drive for income security by negotiating a Guaranteed Annual Income (GAI) which replaced the SUB. Under the GAI, employees at the auto plant with seven years of service were guaranteed 95% of their take-home pay for a period of 52 weeks. (Employees with less than seven years of service received the 95% guarantee, but for a lesser number of weeks.) Moreover, employees who were discharged at the auto plant could usually count on strong support from the union, including carrying the issue to the last step of the grievance machinery which was arbitration by a neutral third party. One of the union leaders was quoted as saying: "Discharge is the capital punishment of labor relations so we almost always walk the last mile with them."

The management was of the opinion that its profit-sharing plan was highly valued and appreciated especially by its older employees. All employees became eligible for profit sharing after two years of employment and percentage-of-salary participation was equal for everyone, including officers. Under the plan, the bank contributed an amount each year that was equal to 7.5% of its net operating income after customary reserves and dividends. The amount was then divided by the combined yearly salaries of the plan participants, and that percentage was applied to each employee's base annual salary to determine his or her amount. During the twenty years that the plan had been in effect, it had never paid less than 10% of salaries and in recent years it had approached the 15% limit set on such plans by the Internal Revenue Service. However, the payments from the profit-sharing plan were not immediately available to a participant, but instead were held in a trust fund that earned income until the employee left the employment of the bank either as a result of quitting or as a result of retirement at age 65. At retirement at 65, the employee received 100% of the balance in his account. Employees who left the bank before 65 received less than the full amount depending upon the number of years they had been in the plan. It became 50% vested after 5 years and then increased 10% each year, becoming fully vested at the end of 10 years. The plan did permit employees to withdraw any amount in their balance that exceeded two and one-half times their annual salary. Likewise, if an employee died, the entire amount in his account was paid to his estate. The First National was the only bank in the Lake City area that had a profit-sharing plan in effect. The International Metalworkers' Union had tried to negotiate a profit-sharing plan with the auto company, but had not been successful. None of the other smaller industrial and commercial firms in the area had profit-sharing plans.

In addition to the profit-sharing plan, the bank had also a death benefit plan, a pension plan, and a salary continuation plan. The death benefit plan was intended to supplement the amount that the employee's family or estate would have received at his death from the profit-sharing plan. It paid $3,000 to employees whose salary was $5,000 or less, and dropped down in $500 units for each $200 increase in salary, so that it paid nothing for salaries over $6,200.

The bank's pension plan required an employee to have 15 years of service to be eligible for benefits. Retirement was mandatory at age 65. Early retirement was possible at age 55. However, in the case of early retirement, benefit payments were decreased on an actuarial basis unless the employee opted to have his payments begin at age 65. The plan provided also for payments at any age after 15 years of service in case of total and permanent disability.

Determining one's pension benefit under the plan was a complicated matter. It involved three separate calculations. Most of the employees had difficulty understanding it, although the bank had prepared and published a booklet that explained it with examples.

Benefits under the pension plan were not as liberal as those provided under the union contract at the auto plant, especially for the lower-paid employees and for those who wished to retire early. However, they were as good or better than those paid by any of the other banks in the area. In fact, two of the other banks had no pension plans. Management was of the opinion that the pension plan and the profit-sharing plan had to be considered as a package and that when this was done, the retirement benefits compared well even with those of the auto company.

The bank's salary continuance program, which became effective for employees immediately following the ninety-day probationary period, provided one full week of sick pay during the first year and six full weeks of sick pay per calendar year thereafter. The six weeks were not cumulative. The weekly paycheck was decreased for any day of absence other than those covered by the salary continuation program.

The bank's vacation plan provided two weeks of paid vacation after one year of service, and three weeks after fifteen years of service. It was identical with the vacation plans of the other banks in the area, but not as good as the vacation plan at the auto plant. The bank also paid for six holidays, which was the same as the number of paid holidays at the other banks in the area, but only about half the number at the auto plant.

The bank also permitted employees to borrow at reduced interest rates on mortgages, car loans, and personal loans. On mortgage loans, for example, the rate was reduced by .25%, thus enabling an employee to save a considerable amount of interest cost over the purchase period of his property.

The bank also enrolled all of its employees in the American Institute of Banking. The AIB conducted night courses in Lake City in bank accounting and numerous other subjects. The employees of the First National could attend without cost. Approximately 25% of the employees took one or more courses each year.

Conspicuous by its absence in the bank's benefit package was an employer-paid hospital and medical care program. Such a program had been discussed by the management with Blue Cross-Blue Shield and several insurance companies, and on several occasions proposals had been presented to the board. However, each time they had been turned down because of the vigorous opposition of Mr. Fred Savage. Savage, who was in his late seventies and controlled the largest block of stock in the bank, felt very strongly on the issue. It was his sincere belief that the good of the country would be served best if each person paid his own medical and hospital bills. He was able to bring enough pressure to bear on the president and the other members of the board to prevent adoption of any employer-paid hospital and medical plan.

The bank did work out a group plan with Blue Cross-Blue Shield to be paid for entirely by the employees. Individual rates varied form $25 to $48 per month depending on the type of coverage. The bank agreed to deduct the amounts from the paychecks if employees so desired. The great majority of the employees participated in the group coverage and many of those who did not were covered elsewhere because their husbands or wives worked in other firms that provided free family coverage.

The First National was the only bank in the area that did not have a hospital-medical plan that was entirely or partially paid by the employer. At the auto plant, the union had negotiated a very liberal hospital-medical plan, the cost of which was born entirely by the company. Many of the other industrial and retail firms in the area also had plans in which the employer paid all or part of the costs.

The first indication of union activity at the bank occurred one Sunday morning. John Mason, a guard at the main office discovered that IMU membership cards had been distributed to the various teller stations on the first floor, the desks in the bookkeeping department on the second floor, at the switchboard, and in the ladies' lounge. Mason reported the matter to his superior who in turn reported it to Paul Blanton, vice-president of personnel. Blanton discussed the matter with the bank's attorney, Francis Grant, and upon his advice it was decided to collect and hold the cards.

On Monday morning, Wynn S. Evans, president of the bank, called Blanton to his office. Evans, who was scheduled to retire in less than a year, had been president for fifteen years. He had spent his entire working career with the bank. Starting out as a clerk immediately after graduation from Lake City High School, he had worked his way up through the ranks to his present position. He had good reason to be proud of the progress that had been made at the bank during his presidency. From a single office, it had expanded to the point where it now had seventeen branch offices. Total assets and profits had increased far more rapidly than at any other bank in the area.

Blanton showed the cards to Evans and told him where they had been found. Blanton said that he and the other members of management with whom he had talked had no idea who might have been responsible for distributing them. Evans did not appear to be disturbed. Blanton was surprised when he said "Paul, I don't think we should get too excited about this. After all, in a place like Lake City, I suppose its inevitable that we will eventually have to deal with a union. Let's keep it all low key."

Management never was able to determine who was responsible for the distribution of the cards, and the only action that was taken was to tighten security. Four months passed by without any outward indication of further union activity, and management came to feel that the card distribution incident could be dismissed as the act of a single disgruntled employee. Supervisors who were in close touch with the employees who worked for them reported no evidence of any organizing activity. Then one Monday morning, a number of employees reported to their supervisors that they had received a letter from the IMU addressed to their homes. It was soon learned that the letter had been sent to all of the employees. Evidently, one of the employees had provided the union with a runoff of the names and addresses from the computer. The letter read as follows:

TO THE EMPLOYEES OF FIRST NATIONAL BANK OF LAKE CITY

A considerable number of your co-workers have shown an extreme interest in the desire to unite for the good of all the First National Bank employees in Lake City and area branches.

You have the right by law from the National Labor Relations Act to self-organize to form, join, or assist labor organizations for the purpose of collective bargaining. This is exactly what your co-workers are attempting to do.

In order to petition the National Labor Relations Board (NLRB) for an election, we must have a sufficient number of the enclosed cards—signed! These signed cards are held in strict confidence and no one but a staff member of IMU or a field representative from the NLRB will see these cards.

No initiation fees or monthly dues are payable until an NLRB election is won. This is accomplished by each of you voting by secret ballot to accept IMU as your collective bargaining representative along with a committee of employees of your own choosing.

The professional employees of banking institutions are long overdue in exercising their right to self-organize. You must realize that you are way behind professional employees pertaining to wages, vacations, pensions, paid hospitalization, and accident and sickness insurance.

In just a few short years of self-organizing, professional teachers of America have made substantial gains in all of the aforementioned benefits. You have that same privilege guaranteed by federal law. For your own benefit, take the first step as your fellow co-workers have and sign the enclosed card, which is held in strict confidence, and return it to IMU, Box 72, Lake City.

An extra card is enclosed for any of your fellow employees who wish to sign cards but did not receive a copy of this letter.

IMU Organizing Committee

One of the employees gave Blanton his copy of the letter which Blanton took to the president's office. Evans read it and discussed it by phone with attorney Grant. Evans then scheduled a 1:00 P.M. meeting of the top management people and attorney Grant to discuss the matter. At the meeting, Grant explained that the union would have to get 30% of the employees to sign membership cards before the NLRB would hold an election. He said, however, that it was his experience that the IMU would not ask for an election unless it had at least 60 or 70% of the employees signed up. Among those present at the meeting, surprise was expressed that the union felt it had enough interest among the employees to warrant sending out the letter. On the other hand, there was a belief that only a very small number of the employees were involved and that the union had no chance of getting 30% to sign cards. It was agreed that for the time being, management would take no special action except to gather as much information as possible. Blanton was appointed by the president to serve as clearinghouse for any facts or rumors that became known to any of them.

Approximately one month after the union's first letter, it addressed a second letter to the employees which read in part as follows:

> Your response to our first letter was very encouraging. As a result an informative meeting will be held next Thursday evening at the Lake City Hotel at 8:00 P.M.
>
> We will tell you what we believe we can gain through collective bargaining and will answer any questions you may have.

The meeting was held as scheduled and management learned that between 75 and 100 of the bank's 350 employees had attended. The group was made up largely of employees from bookkeeping, personal loan, and main office tellers, although there were some from other department and from some of the branch offices. It was reported that not all those who attended appeared to be in sympathy with unionization.

Although salaries, individual grievances, and other matters were talked about at the meeting, the discussion centered around two major topics: 1. the pension and profit-sharing plans, and 2. the lack of an employer-paid hospital-medical plan. Several of the older employees spoke favorably about the pension and profit-sharing plan and indicated that they were fearful that the bank might decrease the pension benefits and eliminate profit sharing if it had to bargain with the union. The union representatives assured the employees that the union would never agree to changes in the pension and profit-sharing plans that would be to the detriment of the employees. Instead they said that the union would insist that the employees receive even better pensions and a larger share of the profits, too much of which, they declared, now went to the owners and the management.

The issue that seemed to be of most concern to the majority of the employees at the meeting was the lack of an employer-paid hospitalization-medical plan. The union leaders played up this issue. They said they found it hard to believe that in this day and age a major bank like First National could be so little interested in its employees' welfare as to refuse to cover them with hospital-medical insurance. They pointed out that several of the smaller banks in the community did provide their employees with such insurance. They showed the employees a copy of the employer-paid plan that the union had negotiated for the employees at the auto plant. They also referred to a number of other contracts that the union had negotiated with other companies in the Lake City area all of which contained employer-paid hospital-medical plans. They said they knew of no contract that the IMU had negotiated in recent years in which it had not secured an employer-paid plan, and they assured the employees that if they chose the IMU as their bargaining agent, the union would insist that the bank foot the entire bill for a good hospital-medical insurance plan. One of the union representatives stated that the value of his benefit alone would more than make up the cost of the union dues.

As the reports of the union meeting filtered in to Blanton, he became convinced that the bank was facing a serious unionization threat. Blanton had been appointed as vice-president of personnel about ten months earlier. Prior to that time, the personnel function had been handled by an officer of the bank who had other major functions. Blanton had had no prior training or experience in personnel work. Among the bank officers he was relatively young both in age and service, having been hired only five years earlier. Prior to coming with the First, he had worked with one of the big Chicago banks. At the First, he had served as vice-president of mortgages and manager of a branch before becoming vice-president of personnel.

Blanton proposed to Evans and the other officers that the bank should engage in an active campaign to convince employees not to join the Union. Attorney Grant urged a very aggressive campaign, including a series of letters by President Evans and a meeting of all the employees. It was decided that Blanton should meet in small groups with the employees. Attorney Grant cautioned Blanton to be careful not to promise the employees anything as a result of not becoming unionized or to threaten them with anything if they did. "If you promise them anything or threaten them with anything the NLRB could find us guilty of an unfair labor practice and might even order us to bargain with them on the basis of their signed cards without ordering an election—assuming they have a majority of the employees signed up," Grant warned.

Blanton discovered that the employees were primarily interested in discussing the bank's wage and benefit policies, of which to his surprise most of them had very little knowledge and appreciation. (The bank had never developed an employees' handbook or a pamphlet explaining the various benefit plans.) The newer employees seemed to be better informed than many of the older employees because at the employment interview the policies and plans were explained. Blanton believed that the meetings were helpful, but came away from some of them with a conviction that there was a sizeable group that really wanted the union.

In several areas, Blanton felt that he got a very cool reception. One of these was the data processing center. The center had been set up in the bank's main office building six years earlier. In addition to the bank's work, it did some outside work for customers. Although a few of the bank's former employees had moved into jobs in the data center, the great majority of the thirty workers there were new employees. It was the only area in the bank that was on shift work. The twelve keypunch operators were on two fixed shifts, and the computer operators were on three rotating shifts. Blanton had the impression that the employees here looked upon themselves as a group apart with very little loyalty to the bank. "Their loyalty," he said, "is first to the equipment, then to the system, and only after that to the bank. They are a lot closer to the data processing people at the auto company and other companies and banks in the area than they are to employees in the other departments here at the First." During the six years of its operation, there had been a considerably higher turnover of employees in this division than elsewhere in the bank except in the personal loan department. Blanton felt that the bank to a considerable extent served as a training school for employees in data processing who once trained, moved to the auto company or in some cases even to out-of-town companies and banks.

Blanton divided the data-processing employees into four meeting groups. At each of these meetings, the question of wage rates for similar jobs at the auto company was raised by the employees. They seemed to be very well informed. Blanton admitted that the bank's rates were not as high as those paid by the auto company, but said that in some cases this was a result of the fact that there was a difference in the skill requirements of the jobs. Moreover, he said that if they took into account the whole pay package including the profit-sharing plan, he believed the pay was as good or better at the bank. However, Blanton left the meetings with the feeling that the employees were unconvinced. He was of the opinion that all of the data-processing employees were interested in the union and many of them were strongly interested.

Another area where the reception was quite cool was the consumer loans department in the main office. This division of the bank had been unusually successful compared with similar divisions in the other banks in the community, primarily because of the ability and drive of Frank Lockard who had become vice-president of consumer loans ten years earlier. Blanton was aware that, although Lockard's performance in terms of profit to the bank was outstanding, he lacked skill and understanding in dealing with employees. In the short time that Blanton had been vice-president of personnel, several of the thirty-five employees from consumer loans had discussed with him actions by Lockard that they believed to be very unfair and autocratic. On one occasion, a female employee complained that she had been demoted from an interviewer to a loan teller without any explanation or warning. Lockard had simply attached a note to her time card which said, "As of today you will work as a teller instead of an interviewer." Turnover in this department was higher than anywhere else in the bank including the data center. In the past year, 35% of the employees had quit or transferred to jobs elsewhere in the bank. Blanton had discussed the problem with President Evans and had recommended that some action be taken. Evans had replied, "I know Frank has problems with people, but with his performance on loans I think we'll just have to live with his people problems." Blanton came away from the meetings with the consumer loan groups convinced that 100% of them favored the union.

When Blanton returned to his office from one of the meetings, Harold Newton, vice-president of branch operations, was waiting for him. Newton reported to him that a number of the branch office employees had informed him that the three assistant auditors were engaging in union organizing activities in the branch offices. At the time, the bank was in the process of converting its savings accounts to the computer. As part of the conversion program, meetings were scheduled at all branch offices during which the "internal auditors" as they were called, explained the new system. According to Newton's informants, the auditors spent only about fifteen minutes explaining the computer printouts and the remainder of the two-hour session talking about the advantages of having a union. At the end of the meetings, they had passed out union membership cards. By the time Newton received the information, meetings had already been held by the auditors at about half of the branches. Newton called off the other meetings.

The news that the assistant auditors were engaging in union organizing activities came as a surprise and a shock to the officers of the bank who had always considered them as part of the management team. It was agreed that Newton and the cashier should meet with the auditor and the three assistant auditors. At the meeting, the assistants admitted that they favored a union and had been trying to get other employees to join. Following the meeting, Newton discussed the matter with Attorney Grant who said it was his opinion that the assistant auditors were a part of management and, therefore, that union activity by them was not protected under the National Labor Relations Act. Newton then recommended to President Evans that the three assistant auditors be discharged. However, Evans was of the opinion that the discharge of all three of the internal auditors would raise serious questions in the community regarding the integrity and soundness of the bank. As a result, no disciplinary action was taken. The meetings at the other branch offices were rescheduled at times when Newton could be in attendance, and the assistant auditors limited their discussions to an explanation and discussion of the printouts.

Two weeks following the union meeting at Lake City Hotel, Robert Marple, the international representative of the IMU, called on Attorney Grant and informed him that 80% of all the bank's employees had signed up with the union. He offered to produce the signed cards for signature comparison. Grant informed him that he would prefer not to see the cards, but had "an honest doubt" that the union really represented the majority of the employees. Marple then informed Grant that the union would petition the National Labor Relations Board to hold a representation election.

One week after informing the bank's council that it had a majority of its employees signed up and wished to bargain for a contract, the union sent another letter to the employees which read as follows:

### TO THE EMPLOYEES OF FIRST NATIONAL BANK OF
### LAKE CITY—6/2/72

For the benefit of the employees who were unable to attend our last meeting, I would like to point out the major question that arose during the meeting and that is of the current profit-sharing pension program.

There is absolutely *no* way that you can jeopardize this benefit or any other benefits that you presently enjoy by self-organizing. Your pension program is currently available to all employees of the bank including some twenty (20) or so officers who are not eligible by law to join with you in a collective bargaining agreement.

The monies in this program have been set aside for pension benefits and your employer has already received a tax exemption by meeting Internal Revenue Service requirements. The pension money which has been set aside cannot be used for anything else but pension benefits. Furthermore, the federal law forbids your employers from reducing any of your present benefits for the reason you chose to self-organize.

Organizing can improve on benefits in two ways. First, eliminate those not in the bargaining unit who take a lion's share from the fund, the second, negotiate higher benefits for those in the bargaining unit.

Unfortunately, a few employees at the First National honestly believe they can gain more on their own. Take a good look at these individuals and see where this has led them. What have they gained? Even your employer is distrustful of them. However, he would use them to his advantage. What happens when they are no longer useful to him? In unity there is strength and in strength and unity there are rewards at the bargaining table with the employer.

                                        Robert Marple
                                        IMU International Representative

It was decided that President Evans should reply to the union. Evans's letter to the employees read as follows:

### TO: ALL EMPLOYEES—6/7/72

I understand each of you received a letter signed by an international representative of the IMU, which states as follows:

"Unfortunately, a few employees at the First National Bank honestly believe they can gain more on their own. Take a good look at these individuals and see where this had led them. What have they gained? Even your employer is distrustful of them. However, he would use them to his advantage. What happens when they are no longer useful to him? In unity there is strength and in strength and unity there are rewards at the bargaining table with the employer."

The statement that we are distrustful of any of our employees is absolutely and unqualifiedly false and untrue. If we were distrustful of an employee, he or she would not be working for us.

You have the right to deal with us directly without the intervention of a union on any matter, both with respect to either present benefits or the consideration of any new or additional benefits.

It has certainly not been necessary in the past to have a union intervening on your behalf and we would hope that our past record would indicate that a union is neither needed nor necessary in considering future benefits.

The letter states that we would use employees so long as they are advantageous to us and asks what happens when they are no longer useful to us. All of our employees are valued by us and are useful to us. We do not *use* any of you in the manner suggested in this letter.

In fact, these statements are outrageous and show to what lengths this union will go to get you to sign cards.

We wish to make it perfectly clear, however, that you have the right to join a union. You have just as much right not to join. No union can guarantee you economic benefits. If a union wins an election, the bank is not required to sign any contract that it feels is not in its best interest.

In their letter, the union refers to our profit-sharing plan. Both our pension and profit-sharing plans are purely voluntary on the part of the bank and, as you know, both are totally paid for by the bank. We hope to continue them, but there is nothing in the law to require us to do so if we feel economic considerations warrant a change. If you vote in favor of a union, all of these items are subject to negotiation.

I trust that each of you will give all these matters your serious consideration.

Wynn S. Evans<br>President

Two weeks after sending out its first letter to its employees regarding the union-organizing drive, the bank filed with the Internal Revenue Service a request to institute a hospital-medical plan, the costs of which would be paid entirely by the bank. (Mr. Fred Savage, a major stockholder and influential director of the bank, who had successfully opposed such plans in the past had died eight months earlier.) Following the filing, announcements were sent to all department heads, supervisors, and branch managers informing them that the bank was instituting a free hospital-medical plan subject to approval by the necessary government agencies. No letter was sent directly to the employees on the hospital-medical plan at this time, but they were informed about it by their supervisors.

Two weeks after the bank announced its intention to assume the cost of a hospital-medical insurance plan, the union filed a petition with the NLRB requesting a representation election. At the same time, the union filed an Unfair Labor Practices (ULP) charge against the bank, claiming that the promise to institute a hospital-medical plan paid by the employer was for the purpose of avoiding unionization. The charge as filed by the union with the NLRB read a follows:

> The above-named employer, by its officers, agents and representatives, has, by establishing a hospitalization plan for employees and their dependents and other acts and conduct, interfered with, restrained and coerced its employees in the exercise of the rights guaranteed in Section 7 of the Act.

As a result of the filing of the ULP charge, the NLRB held in abeyance the union's request for a representation election.

Four weeks following the filing by the union, a hearing on the ULP charge was held before an officer of the NLRB. The company produced witnesses and correspondence to show that work on the hospital-medical plan had been undertaken before the bank was aware that the union was attempting to organize its employees. Attorney Grant argued that if the bank had not proceeded to develop the plan and try to place it into effect according to its original schedule, then indeed the bank would have been guilty of unfair labor practices. He requested that the hearing officer find that the union's charge was without merit.

One month later, the bank received a notice from the NLRB that the union had withdrawn the ULP charges. The president then addressed a letter to all the employees informing them that the new hospital-medical plan would become effective in two months.

At about this same time, three employees at the bank's main office were observed (by a supervisor in a part of the bank other than where they worked) handing out union membership cards to other employees during working hours. The officers of the bank were surprised when they learned that one of the employees was Esther Douglas, who had an excellent record of employment with the bank for the last 29 years. A review of personnel record showed the following facts:

> unmarried and supports her mother; hired 29 years ago as a clerk upon recommendation of Wynn Evans who attended same church; excellent attendance record; very good ratings by her supervisors; interested in advancement, took AIB courses at night and worked hard; advanced over time to better and better jobs; eight year ago placed in charge of General Ledger Bookkeeping which required her to bring together all the data from the main office and the branches and deliver it to the President by noon each day; two years ago Bank computerized the General Ledger and Esther was moved to the Savings Department where she maintained controls over various matters; Savings Department job was important and Bank maintained her prior salary; President still called upon her for data from time to time, but not every day; two months ago as a result of computerization of

the Savings Department Esther was moved to the job of Collection Clerk with no decrease in salary; works with two other Collection Clerks who receive considerably less pay; still has desk at back of main floor but no reason for President to see or talk to her now.

Two of the vice-presidents discussed the incident with Esther. She admitted that she had passed out the cards and urged employees to join the union. She agreed with the officers that it was not fair to the bank for her to do this during working time and assured them that she would not do it again. Attorney Grant recommended that Esther and the other two employees who were observed passing out the cards be discharged. However, President Evans decided that it was better not to take any disciplinary action other than a warning. Esther continued to be interested in the union, but limited her activities to non-working time.

Two weeks following the withdrawal by the union of the ULP charge, the NLRB informed the bank that it was proceeding with the union's request for a representation election. The bank refused to follow the informal procedure, but instead requested a formal hearing.

At the hearing, which was held a month later, the matter of the employees who should be included in the bargaining unit and therefore would be eligible to vote was discussed. Much to the surprise of management, the union did not ask to have the watchman and the other building and maintenance employees included in the unit. Management was happy to go along with their exclusion. Management argued also for the exclusion of the secretaries of the president and the personnel vice-president on the grounds that they had access to confidential material. The union agreed to their exclusion. The greatest difference of opinion developed regarding supervisory employees. The National Labor Relation Act defines, the term "supervisory" and provides that they do not have to be included in the bargaining unit. Some of the employees whom the bank had given the title of supervisor did not meet the requirements as set forth in the act. The bank argued that most of the branch manager, the assistant branch managers, and the purchasing agent should be included in the unit, but that the auditor and the assistant auditors should not be included. After discussing the content of these jobs, it was agreed that three of the branch managers, three of the assistant branch managers, the three assistant auditors, and the purchasing agent should be included and the others excluded. However, the election was delayed because the bank challenged the validity of the union's signature cards and moved that the election petition be dismissed.

Following the hearing, the union sent another letter to the employees explaining the delay and assuring the employees regarding the profit-sharing plan. Two weeks later, the hearing officer denied the bank's motion to dismiss, and his decision was approved by the regional director of the NLRB. The bank then filed a petition for review with the NLRB which was denied two weeks later. The regional director of the NLRB then set a date for the election and sent formal notices to the bank and the union. The date was approximately one month later, and almost exactly five months after the union had filed for an election. It was also a few days after the new hospital-medical plan became effective.

On the Monday afternoon on which the bank received the notice of the election date, Paul Blanton, vice-president of personnel, discussed the matter briefly with Wynn Evans, president. They agreed it would be wise to have a meeting the next afternoon with their labor lawyer, Francis Grant, and the other executives of the bank in order to plan management's strategy and tactics during the thirty days that remained before the election. Evans informed Blanton that he would expect him to present a tentative plan of action which could form the basis for discussion and final decision.

# Case 13
# Wilson Distributors
# Company (A)

On October 24, 1974, Mr. Donald Wilson, vice-president of personnel and labor relations of Wilson Distributors Company, was faced with the problem of deciding what action, if any, to take against a company truck driver, Thomas Boling. Boling had been hired by the company approximately six years earlier. He had worked for about one month as a delivery truck driver and then had been transferred to the warehouse where he had worked for approximately one year. At the end of that period, he had bid for and received another delivery truck driver job which he still held. The job consisted of transporting the company's products from the warehouse to the customers.

Recently, the company had been informed by two of its customers and several of its competitors' salesmen that Boling was offering to sell company merchandise to customers on his delivery route at prices far below the regular prices quoted by the company's salesmen. After reviewing the evidence presented to him by company officials, Wilson was convinced that Boling was guilty of this offense. He wondered what he should do about it.

**Background**

The Wilson Distributors Company was a family-owned wholesale distributor to lumber dealers of windows, doors, and related products. It was started in 1904 and in 1974 operated three warehouses, with overall sales of $15 million. Its main office and largest warehouse (sales of $8 million) were located in Chicago. Initially, Wilson was a retailer, then moved into wholesale distribution, and then into manufacturing, mainly through assembly. In recent years, company officials had decided to limit their operations to wholesale distribution because of the high labor costs they had incurred as a manufacturer. By 1974, incidental manufacturing operations, such as the glazing of purchased glass and the finishing of various pieces of lumber, were a very minor part of overall activity in each warehouse.

The company employed 300 people of whom 175 were in Chicago, including 55 shop personnel (of whom 30 were assemblers), 83 employees in warehousing and shipping (including 18 drivers), and 12 salesmen (classified as office personnel). All non-supervisory warehouse and shop employees belonged to the carpenters union, which had won bargaining rights in 1948. In the last five years, the level of employment had remained constant. There had been no layoffs or terminations because of lack of work, and only four disciplinary discharges. The union had appealed only one of the discharges to arbitration, and in that case the company's action had been upheld by the arbitrator.

Since the company's primary activity was distribution of assembled products, the Chicago warehouse was usually full of merchandise. As orders were received, they were recorded on order forms which were forwarded to the appropriate departments for processing. When the materials for a particular order were ready for delivery, they were collected at the shipping dock. The shippers were responsible for what was then loaded onto each truck. Normally, the driver who was to make the deliveries then backed up his truck to the loading platform and the shippers loaded it. Occasionally, the truck driver assisted the shipper. Sometimes there were no shippers immediately available, and the driver was trusted to load his own truck. Once the truck was loaded, the driver delivered the materials to the company's lumberyard customer. Under a company policy begun about eight years ago, employees who owned their own homes could purchase a limited amount of company materials at reduced cost for use in their homes. With the exception of these personal purchases, all the materials were delivered from the warehouse in company trucks to the lumberyard companies.

## The Pilferage Problem

In the latter part of 1972, management heard through numerous rumors and reports that merchandise was leaving the Chicago warehouse without accompanying order forms. When the annual physical inventory check was concluded in December, company executives discovered that they had suffered inventory losses of approximately $40,000.

Management was of the opinion that such a large loss could not have been a result of errors in shipments. Likewise, it was convinced that it was not the result of thieves breaking in from the outside because the warehouse was completely surrounded by a high fence and guards were on duty constantly. The company concluded that some of its drivers and warehousemen were colluding to steal and resell company goods.

The reports from customers and competitors regarding Boling were not the first that the company had had concerning attempts of its drivers to sell its merchandise at low prices. In one earlier case, a customer had reported that a driver had offered to sell merchandise to his yardman at ridiculously low prices. The customer had claimed that he had threatened his yardman with dismissal if he bought any of the "stolen merchandise." In another earlier case, a customer had reported that a driver had approached him directly and had offered to sell him company products "for cash" at very low prices. In still another earlier incident, it had been reported that one of the drivers had had business cards printed with his own name and that of a fictitious company through which he proposed to sell merchandise at below normal prices. Although management investigated all of these earlier cases, it did not believe that it had sufficient evidence to move against the suspected employees. The company tried rotating employees among the various delivery routes in order to make it difficult for those who were suspected of selling to build up regular customers. This procedure, however, was discontinued because it worked against the company's desire to build long-term good relationships between the drivers and the customers.

## The Company Hires a Security Consultant

Further checks in the spring of 1973 indicated that the inventory losses were continuing. That summer, an employee confirmed management's impressions that the pilferage was the result of collusion between some of the drivers and some of the warehouse workers. As a result, late that summer, the company hired Security Advisers Associates (SAA), a firm that specialized in company security matters, to conduct a complete investigation and make recommendations. SAA's study, which included a review of company policies and security practices, was made known to all personnel. As a part of the study, a number of employees were interviewed. As the study began, R. Steven Wilson, Jr., president of Wilson Distributors, sent the following letter to the company's supervisory personnel:

> In recent inventories we have found the actual count of certain items of stock to be quite a bit lower than our stock records showed that we should have.
>
> We did not follow this up at the time, as we felt the shortages were possibly due to clerical differences in our stock records. Recently, however, we have checked several of these items that have been consistently short and we find that shortages also exist in the first eight months of this year.
>
> Of course our stock material is no different than cash. We have periodic audits made of our books and records in the office, which is good business practice, but up to now we have not followed a similar audit approach in the warehouse.
>
> The continued existence of the above condition, added to information received from the outside that our material is being sold by some employees at ridiculously low prices, brings us to the point where we must take action.
>
> We have, therefore, engaged Security Advisers Associates, investigative consultants, to make a security survey.

By November of 1973, the consultants concluded their study. Some of the changes that they recommended to management to stop the illegal disappearance of materials were as follows:

1. Start checking the truck loading process on a random basis;
2. Install a guard house at the gates and a procedure for checking materials entering and leaving;
3. Institute pre-hiring checks on all prospective employees;
4. Arrange for a larger loading area on the shipping platform so that when goods are left on the platform to await loading, there is no confusion about which truck they are for, and so that supervisors can be sure no extra materials are being placed on trucks;
5. Check the shipping operations during the lunch-hour break;
6. Make it an ironclad rule that a trucker may not load his truck.

Company officials put the first three of these suggestions into effect, but decided not to implement the rest. They agreed that the loading area was too small and confused and thus comparatively easy for pilferage, but felt it would be too costly to enlarge it significantly. Similarly, they chose not to prohibit any driver from loading his own truck, even though there were no available shippers, although they recognized certain security problems. Management also decided against checking the shippping area during the noon hour. They did not consider this a serious security problem since there was usually a lot of activity at the warehouse during the lunch hour, and someone trying to steal materials was likely to be seen by another employee or a commercial visitor.

**The Walsh Discharge**

In September 1974, company officials uncovered a serious shortage of one of their products. This product was one that had also been disappearing in large quantities in the two previous years, so management believed that the pilferage problem was continuing. Early in October, the manager of one of the company's lumberyard customers notified the Wilson management that one of its driver, Anthony Walsh, had delivered some company materials to one of the lumberyard employees. This lumberyard was on Walsh's regular route, but he had not been scheduled to make any stops there that day. The materials were transferred to a private garage in another part of the city the next day, Saturday. Shortly thereafter, local police entered the garage with a search warrant and recovered stolen company material worth approximately $1,000. Company officials examined the stolen material and found that the boxes had been marked for a company customer on another route, but the order numbers that had been written beside the customer's name were fictitious. A local handwriting specialist, who had frequently given expert testimony in court, was retained by the company, and she was able to match the handwriting on the box with that of one of the company's warehousemen, Jack Blake.

While company officials immediately discharged Walsh, they decided not to take any immediate action against Blake. They wanted to be positive before they confronted him and they also hoped to discover first whether others in the warehouse had colluded to steal company property.

No court action was initiated against Walsh. The lumberyard manager did not want to be identified as the informer. He indicated that although one of his employees had agreed to take material stolen from Wilson, the employee was a trusted one of the lumberyard, and one they did not wish to antagonize. Management believed civil action against Walsh would be fruitless without the lumberyard manager's testimony.

About two weeks later, Blake purchased some company materials for his own use, and then told his supervisor he was leaving work early to take his wife and baby to the hospital. Management asked their security consultants to follow him and they traced him to a bar where he was observed transferring the materials to another man's car. After remaining at the bar for several hours, Blake left and went to another bar where he worked evenings. He remained there for his night job. Management suspended Blake for three days for lying as to the reason he had to leave work and for breaking company rules by giving to another person the material that he had purchased at low rates for his own use.

When they told him of his suspension, company officials also questioned him about the stolen material they had uncovered, and said that they had good reason to believe that he was involved. They told him about the results of the handwriting analysis they had performed, and urged him to admit he had colluded to steal the materials. He denied stealing the material and refused to implicate others. When Blake did not report back to work after his three-day suspension, he was fired. Neither Walsh, Blake, nor the union entered a grievance.

**The Case Against Boling**

Throughout the early part of October, 1974, John Wilson, vice-president of sales, had been receiving information from the salesmen of other companies that Wilson drivers were again selling company goods at unusually low prices. On the morning of October 14, a customer told him that the company's truck driver, Thomas Boling, had offered to sell company merchandise below cost to one of the employees of the customer. Accompanied by a representative of SAA, Wilson visited the customer's place of business. Both the customer and his employee told them that Boling had offered to sell the employee merchandise at about half price.

Also on October 14, Alan Conway, treasurer and credit manager of the company, received a call from another customer claiming that the company's regular driver, Boling, had offered to sell him company merchandise at a substantial discount. Three days later, another SAA investigator interviewed this customer. The customer positively identified Boling from a photograph taken by SAA consultants and repeated that Boling had approached him with an offer of merchandise at half price. In his report of this interview to the Wilson management, the SAA consultant stated that he was sure the customer was telling the truth.

On the morning of October 24, Donald Wilson was becoming increasingly concerned about Boling's actions. Although Wilson believed that some of the other drivers had been stealing company property for some time, he thought that Boling's approaches to customers had been very amateurish, and probably were his first attempts. Wilson realized also that the company had no direct evidence that Boling had actually stolen company property but only that he had attempted to find buyers for such material. On the other hand, Wilson felt that strong action against Boling, if successful, would serve as a forceful deterrent against the other drivers who were engaging in dishonest activities but against whom the company had been unable to secure any substantial evidence. Wilson read the section of the labor agreement on discipline and discharge and wondered what action he should take. The section of the agreement read:

Article VI Miscellaneous

It is agreed that the Employer has retained the usual management rights and that the right to manage the Employer's business and direct the working force is vested exclusively in the management of the Employer, which right shall include, but shall not be limited to, the right (except insofar as limited herein) to suspend, discharge, or otherwise discipline for just cause; to transfer or layoff because of lack of work or for other legitimate reasons; to plan, direct and control its operations; and to change methods, processes, equipment or facilities; provided, however, that this will not be used for the purposes of discrimination against any employee or to avoid any of the provisions of this agreement or the obligation to bargain collectively concerning changed wages, hours, or working conditions.

# Wilson Distributors Company (B)

At 8:45 A.M. on the morning of October 24, Donald Wilson called Boling to the office of Jerry Cooper, superintendent of the plant. In Cooper's presence, Wilson told Boling that he had received reports from customers that he, Boling, had approached them and had offered to sell the company's merchandise at much lower than standard prices. Boling strongly denied that he had made such solicitations, asked who was responsible for the accusations, and demanded the right to confront them. Wilson refused to divulge the customers' names, but said the he was convinced the reports were true and that, therefore, he had no choice but to discharge Boling immediately.

Boling then contacted the shop steward who called the union's business agent, Hank Rich. Rich, the steward, and Boling went to Cooper's office and Rich talked with Cooper. No agreement was reached at this meeting. The company insisted that it had sufficient evidence to prove that Boling had solicited customers to sell merchandise at far below regular prices and that it considered his action cause for discharge. The union vigorously dissented, and argued that the evidence against Boling was hearsay inasmuch as it involved unnamed persons, unnamed places, and unnamed times. Furthermore, they pointed out that Boling denied all charges against him, and that prior to his discharge he had never been disciplined or reprimanded. Management agreed that Boling's previous record was good, but repeated that he had offered to sell merchandise below cost, and that this action constituted "just cause" for discharge. When further attempts to settle the issue were unsuccessful, the union demanded arbitration.

Following the union's demand for arbitration, the company contacted the two customers who had made the accusations against Boling and asked them if they would be willing to appear and testify at the arbitration hearing. Both customers refused to do so, saying that they would not have informed the company if they thought it would handle the matter so as to get them involved in arbitration or court proceedings. They appeared genuinely fearful and resentful. The company knew that it could ask the arbitrator to subpoena the two customers and thus force them to appear and to testify. It hestitated to take such action, however, because it valued the business of these customers and feared also that forcing them to testify might result in loss of goodwill among other customers as it became known throughout the trade. The company officials and the SAA consultants who had talked with the two customers remained convinced that the latter had told the truth. These company officials and the SAA representatives were prepared to testify regarding what the customers had said. Wilson wondered what action he should take.

# Wilson Distributors Company (C)

The arbitration hearing was held January 6. Two company executives and three SAA investigators testified for management. None of the company's customers was present or testified. The union's only witness was the grievant, Thomas Boling.

The arbitrator found that: 1. the charge against Boling of soliciting customers and offering to sell them company merchandise at a heavy discount, if proved, would have been a sufficiently serious offense to have constituted "just cause" for discharge; 2. the very serious nature of the accusation (which implied that Boling was guilty of or contemplated either theft or the receiving of stolen goods) and the strong penalty that conviction would carry with it required a high "quantum of evidence" to sustain a judgment of proof beyond a reasonable doubt; 3. the testimony by company officials and SAA investigators constituted only hearsay evidence, and the absence of any testimony by the customers denied Boling an opportunity to confront directly or cross-examine the men who had accused him, and did not allow the arbitrator to hear their story directly and evaluate their credibility. This resulted in a lack of due process which could not be considered as demonstrating proof beyond a reasonable doubt. Boling was ordered reinstated with full seniority and benefit rights restored and was granted full back-pay for the wages he would have received if he had not been discharged, minus any earnings that he received from other employment during that period.

# 8 Transnational Labor Relations

## Multinational Conglomerates versus National Industrial Unions

A multinational company (MNC) may be defined as a business enterprise with production facilities in more than one country. In recent years, the number of MNCs and the percentage of output controlled by them in the noncommunist world have increased very rapidly. It has been estimated that by 1970, there were 490 large MNCs in the manufacturing and extractive industries.[1] The total production controlled by MNCs increased from 8% in 1950, to 17% in 1967, to 22% in 1974.[2]

Most of the MNCs have production facilities in a large number of countries. A recent study of 391 MNCs found that only 22% had subsidiaries in fewer than 6 countries, whereas 23% had subsidiaries in 6 to 10 nations, 37% had them in 11 to 30 countries, and 18% had them in more than 20 countries.[3] Moreover, the majority of MNCs that operate plants in Western Europe do not have their headquarters there. Approximately 50% of the MNCs are headquartered in the United States and another 15% in Japan, compared with 30% in Western Europe.[4]

The great majority of MNCs cross over not only national boundaries, but also industry boundaries. In other words, they are not only multinational, but also multi-industry or conglomerate organizations. There are some important exceptions, such as IBM and the automobile companies, which confine themselves to narrow product lines but, as Vernon has noted, most MNCs "operate in many product lines."[5] For example, International Telephones and Telegraph (ITT) one of the major MNCs, has subsidiaries in thirteen different industries in the United States alone.[6]

Unlike the MNCs, unions (almost without exception) are limited to a particular country. A French union has membership only in France, a Swedish union only in Sweden, and so on. Even the unions in the United States that use the term *international* in their names, such as the International Brotherhood of Teamsters or the International Association of Machinists, do not have members outside the United States and Canada.

Moreover, most of the unions are also industrial unions, that is, their membership is limited to a particular industry. (However, in United States and Great Britain there are also some craft and general unions.) In West Germany, for example, the sixteen affiliates of the DGB are all industrial unions, each confined to a particular industrial segment of the economy. The West German chemical workers' union covers the chemical industry, the West German printers' union, the publishing industry, and so on.

It is because of this difference in structure—the unions are limited to one industry and one nation, whereas the MNCs are multi-industry and multinational—that the union leaders view the growth of MNCs as a serious threat to the economic power of their organizations. A union, being industrial and national, can bring its economic power to bear only upon the plants in one industry in one nation. An MNC, however, has plants in more than one nation and usually in a number of industries. As a result, strike action by a union can shut down only a part, frequently a small part, of the total production facilities of an MNC. Therefore, the economic pressure that a union can exert on an MNC is much less than it could exert if the company's operations were limited to one industry in one nation.

## The Threat to Union Bargaining Power

Union leaders see the following characteristics of an MNC as the bases for the threat to union bargaining power: formidable financial resources; alternative sources of supply; ability to move production facilties to other countries; superior knowledge and expertise in labor relations; a remote locus of authority; and production facilities in many industries.

Union leaders point out that the large MNCs possess formidable worldwide financial resources which they can and do make available to any subsidiary that may become engaged in a struggle with a national union.[7] Although a strike may cause heavy financial losses in a particular national subsidiary, the MNC usually is in a much better position than the subsidiary to absorb such losses. In fact, in many such situations, the MNC would be able to continue to show an overall profit despite the shutdown of its facilities in a particular country. This is particularly true of those MNCs which have production facilities in a large number of countries and, as indicated earlier in this chapter, over half of the large MNCs have subsidiaries in more than ten countries.

In the case of a strike, an MNC may be able to continue to supply its customers from plants in other countries. Production in the plants elsewhere in the world may simply be increased to fill the gap caused by the shutdown in a particular country. The union leaders believe that some MNCs have adopted a definite policy of "dual sourcing" whereby they have alternative sources of products or components in different countries in order to reduce the impact of a strike by any national union.[8] A Conference Board study released in 1975 supports this fear. The study states that "some management officers do have such a consideration in mind."[9]

The labor leaders believe also that the ability of a national union to take a hard stand in bargaining is reduced by the power of an MNC to move its production facilities to another country or to engage in an "investment strike" which in the long run would have the same effect.[10] Under an investment strike, the MNC, although not closing the plant, would refuse to invest additional funds in it with the result that eventually its equipment would become obsolete and economically noncompetitive. Professor Blanpain believes that the investment strike poses a greater danger to unions than the immediate moving of a plant.[11] As Professor Vernon points out in his study of MNCs, "money as a rule is a fungible resource . . . capable of being used anywhere in the system."[12] In deciding where to invest its available funds, an MNC would be expected to take into account the labor costs and labor climate at each of its subsidiaries.

Union leaders claim that MNCs are able to hire, and make available to the managements of their subsidiaries, advisors and counselors on labor relations who have special expertise in the area. Moreover, the MNCs, the labor leaders say, can afford to gather information and make special studies that a union may find too costly to duplicate.

Bargaining with a subsidiary of an MNC is made more difficult, the union leaders contend, because of the union's inability to deal directly with the people on the management side who make the final decisions on major labor issues. Although most MNCs claim that authority in labor relations matters rests entirely with the local management of the subsidiary, union leaders do not believe this is true. The union leaders are of the opinion that final authority on issues that really matter, rests with the headquarter management of the MNC and is exercised "beyond the reach of the trade union concerned."[13]

Finally, union leaders see their bargaining power weakened also because of the conglomerate nature of most MNCs. As pointed out earlier, most unions not only are limited to one nation, but also are limited within the nation to a particular industry. As a result, a union strike against an MNC subsidiary may be able to stop the MNC's production in that particular industry, but not in other subsidiary plants which may be a part of other industries in the country where the union is located. Thus, when an MNC is also a conglomerate, as is true of most MNCs, the unions which are not only national in scope but also industrial in structure feel their bargaining power squeezed from two directions.

**Labor's Response—International**
**Trade Secretariats**

As indicated earlier, the membership of a union is limited to the employees within a particular country. As a result, although unions in several countries may represent the employees of a particlar MNC, no one union has the authority to bargain internationally for all of the employees of the MNC. For example, the United Automobile Workers' Union represents Ford employees in the United States, and IG Metall represents Ford employees in West Germany. In several other countries, other unions represent Ford employees. However, none of these unions has the authority to represent Ford employees on an international basis.

Long before the union leaders had recognized the MNCs as a threat, they had developed a group of international organizations that tied together on a worldwide basis the national unions in a particular trade or industry. These organizations, which are known as International Trade Secretariats (ITS), are now sixteen in number:[14]

International Federation of Building and Wood Workers (IFBWW)

International Federation of Chemical and General Workers' Unions (ICF)

International Federation of Commercial, Clerical, and Technical Employees (known as FIET, for its French title, Federation Internationale des Employes et des Techniciens)

Universal Alliance of Diamond Workers (UADW)

International Secretariat of Entertainment Trade Unions (ISETU)

International Union of Food and Allied Workers' Associations (IUF)

International Graphical Federation (IGF)

International Metalworkers' Federation (IMF)

Miners' International Federation (MIF)

International Federation of Petroleum and Chemical Workers (IFPCW)

International Federation of Plantation, Agricultural, and Allied Workers (IFPAAW)

Public Services International (PSI)

International Federation of Free Teachers' Unions (IFFTU)

Postal, Telegraph, and Telephone International (PTTI)

International Textile, Garment, and Leather Workers' Federation (ITGLWF)

International Transport Workers' Federation (ITF)

In addition to the ITSs, there have been established in Europe several subsidiary European trade federations in such industries as metalworking, food, transport, chemical, and textile. The most active of these multinational European union organizations has been the European Metalworkers' Federation (EMF) which claims to represent five million workers in the EEC countries. The EMF works very closely with the world secretariat of the metalworkers, the International Metalworkers' Federation.

Each ITS is made up of affiliates that consist of national unions in a particular trade or industry. For example, in 1977, the IUF was made up of 158 affiliated national unions in 61 countries, with a total membership of about 2.2 million. The ITSs, most of which are headquarterd in Geneva, are very loose federations in which the affiliates retain complete autonomy. Finances of the ITSs are quite limited. In 1977, one ITS taxed each of its affiliates one Swiss franc ($.60) per member per year. As a result, their staffs are small and their programs are not very extensive.

In order to meet the threat to their power posed by the multinational corporations, the unions have been turning increasingly to their ITSs. Gunter Kopke, secretary general of the European Metalworkers' Federation, has stated that although the main reason for creating the first international labor organization in the last century was to achieve international solidarity, and in the fifties, to establish worldwide labor standards, in recent years the emphasis has shifted to meeting the power of the MNCs.[15]

Because the ITSs are structured along trade or industry lines, they have been recognized by union leaders as the international organizations through which the national industrial unions might attempt to develop international bargaining power vis-à-vis certain MNCs. To return to the Ford Motor Company example, British, French, West German, and many other automobile workers' unions throughout the world for many years have been affiliated with one of the major ITSs, the International Metalworkers' Federation. It was natural, therefore, for the leaders of the automobile unions throughout the world to turn to the IMF as the vehicle through which they might develop international bargaining power with the Ford Motor Company. It should be noted, however, that because the ITSs are built along industry lines, they do not provide the unions with the ideal structure to deal with multi-industry MNCs, such as ITT.

### The International Trade Secretariats' Aid and Support for National Unions

The ITSs recognize that their future depends on their ability to help their affiliated national unions be more effective in dealing with the MNCs. With this in mind, the ITSs have developed both a short-run and a long-run strategy. The short-run strategy consists of providing immediate aid and support to national unions that are currently engaged in conflicts with MNCs. The long-run strategy involves a planned step-by-step program of cooperative and coordinative action among the various national unions representing the employees of a particular MNC, with the ultimate goal of transnational bargaining.

In order to implement the short-run strategy, the ITSs have developed an arsenal of weapons which include: research and information; advice and counsel; training of union leaders; publicity; support messages; messages to managements and governments; headquarters national union intervention; refusal to perform "struck work" or additional overtime; sympathy strikes; boycotts; and financial help.

In a study published in 1976, the International Labor Organization (ILO) reported that "a virtually universal concern expressed by the unions . . . was the lack of information on multinational companies."[16] The ITSs view the development and dissemination of such information as one of their basic functions. They gather, analyze, and publish for their affiliates information concerning the financial condition and business activities of the various MNCs that operate in their industries as well as data on the wages, benefits, working conditions, and other labor relations matters at the various subsidiaries of the MNCs. At least two of the ITSs have computerized the material. The IMF has data banks at the United Automobile Workers' Union headquarters in Detroit and at IG Metall headquarters in Frankfort. The ICF has data banks with the United Chemical Workers' Union in Akron, Ohio and with IG Chemie-Papier-Keramik in West Germany.[17] Several managements of MNCs have expressed to the author their surprise at the extent and accuracy of the information regarding their companies that has been supplied by the ITSs to their affiliated unions.[18] The comparative data on wages, benefits, and working conditions have proved to be especially valuable to some of the affiliated unions when bargaining with subsidiaries of the MNCs.

The ITSs are prepared also to offer expert advice and counsel to their affiliates on labor relations problems. Most frequently, this is accomplished by letters, telegraphs, or telephone conversations with headquarters. But at times, the ITSs have sent consultants and advisors into the field to aid an affiliate. For example, when a union in Peru, affiliated with the IUF, became involved in a strike with a subsidiary of a European-based MNC, the IUF dispatched its Latin American secretary to Peru to help the union.

Some of the ITSs, including IMF and ICF, have conducted seminars at headquarters and in the field to enable national union leaders to be more effective in dealing with MNCs. One such series of seminars was conducted by the IMF in Latin American countries with emphasis on the Philips and General Electric companies. The participants in the seminar were provided with worldwide information concerning the companies and were coached on how to bargain more effectively with them.[19]

When conflicts have occurred between unions and MNCs, the ITSs have been effective in giving them wide publicity. Some of the general secretaries, especially Charles Levinson of the ICF, are very adept at making statements and preparing press releases which newspapers and other media are prepared to use. Since most MNCs are very sensitive to any kind of adverse publicity, this weapon at times has proved to be quite effective.

When an affiliated union becomes involved in a struggle with an MNC, the ITS urges its worldwide affiliates to send telegrams expressing support and solidarity. Such messages are most effective when they come from unions in other subsidiaries of the same multinational company. A former United Automobile Workers' Union representative has written that the impact of such messages should not be underestimated. "At a strike rally," he states, "particularly in an undeveloped country where the union may be weak and struggling for recognition, a message of this type from other unionized company workers thousands of miles away packs a punch for worker morale."[20]

In addition to messages of support to the union and its members, the ITS will send a telegram or a letter to the management of the company on behalf of all its affiliates, criticizing the management because of the treatment being accorded the local union and its members. The ITS will also urge its member unions, especially those in the company's plants in other countries, to express their dissatisfaction with the way the company is dealing with the dispute. Such critical messages are usually given wide publicity. An ILO study in 1976 found this to be one of the most widely used actions by ITSs and their affiliates.[21]

The ITS also may urge the national union that represents the employees in the MNC's home country to complain to headquarters management regarding the manner in which the local management of a subsidiary is dealing with a union in another country. For example, when General Motors announced that it was closing its plant at Bienne, Switzerland, the IMF alerted the automobile workers' union in the United States and requested its help. As a result, the vice-president of the UAW in charge of the General Motors department wrote a strong letter to the chairman of the board of the company asking the company to reconsider its action. In 1973, when a series of strikes and lockouts at SKF's Madrid plant resulted in the dismissal of sixty Spanish workers, the IMF affiliate in Sweden (SKF's headquarters is in Sweden) protested vigorously to the home management, and all but four of the dismissed employees were reinstated. In its 1976 study, the ILO stated that although "it is difficult to estimate the direct outcome or effect of these types of interventions by unions with their own managements on behalf of unions in another country—this is one of the tools or weapons most extensively used by unions when difficulties occur in one of several plants of a multinational" and "is certain to continue to be an important part of union and management relations in multinational enterprises."[22]

An ITS may urge its affiliates to refuse to do work that has been transferred from an MNC's struck plant in another country. Likewise, the affiliates may be urged not to work overtime, to hamper the MNC's efforts to make up the production lost as a result of a strike elsewhere. In 1970, the ICF asked its affiliates in the United Kingdom, West Germany, Belgium, and Turkey to refuse overtime at Pirelli plants because it was believed that the additional production would be used to offset the loss being suffered by the company as a result of a strike at its Italian plant.[23] The ILO has reported in a survey that a very large majority of trade unionists have indicated that they would support a request to refuse to work on any "struck" production or to perform additional overtime work where an MNC was attempting to transfer work because of labor difficulties.[24]

The sympathy strike has not been used very extensively by the ITSs and their affiliates. It is reported that workers in a Nabisco plant in Italy did stage a one-hour sympathy strike to support a strike against the company in the United States.[25] Likewise, when one of the European airlines was struck by the transport workers in the United States, unions in several of the major European airports did stage short sympathy strikes. However, the automobile councils of the IMF, as a matter of policy, do not ask affiliated unions to engage in sympathy strikes. One of the automobile union leaders has stated, "In addition to the possible legal obstacles, no one should lightly ask a worker to give up even a half-hour's pay on behalf of strikers in a different nation."[26] On the other hand, the ILO has reported that several European union leaders say they would recommend strike action to support a stoppage against an MNC in another country.[27] The strong legal restraints in effect against sympathy strikes in many countries limit the viability of this device. It is worth noting, however, that the United Nations eminent persons' report in 1973 recommended the easing of government restrictions on sympathy strikes where MNCs are involved, and the European Trade Union Confederation in its 1977 action program on multinational companies urged that sympathy strikes and boycotts be made legal within each defined economic sector whenever an international trade union organization called for such a strike.

Boycotting MNC products that are items in labor disputes has been urged by some ITSs and their affiliates. In 1976, the ICF asked its members to boycott products made by rubber companies in the United States, and at an earlier date, the ICF asked its members to boycott the products of American Cyanimid. The ITGLWF asked its worldwide affiliates to join in the boycott of the products of the Farah Company and the JP Stevens Company as a result of labor struggles at those companies' plants in the United States. Perhaps the most famous boycott in recent years has been that called by the IFPAAW which urged its affiliates everywhere to boycott California grapes in order to support the efforts of Cesar Chavez to organize the migrant Mexican farmworkers in California.

Financial aid by the ITSs to unions engaged in struggles with MNCs does not appear to have been very significant. As indicated earlier, the ITSs are not well financed. There is no indication that any ITS has a strike fund which would compare in size to the strike funds of some of the large American and European unions. However, some ITSs have diverted some of their funds to weak and struggling unions. Also, through the ITSs, some of the financially strong unions have contributed to the strike funds of weaker unions.[28]

## The International Trade Secretariat's Goal: Transnational Bargaining

In the long run, the ITSs envisage themselves as playing a much more important role in international labor relations than simply supplying aid to national unions through the devices just discussed. They see themselves eventually as the vehicles through which the various national unions representing employees of a particular MNC will combine their power and coordinate their actions so as to present a united front in bargaining with that MNC. Norris Willat, who made a study of the sixteen active ITSs, concluded that each has the same well-defined, long-range program which it hopes to accomplish with each of the MNCs in its industry. The ultimate goal of the program is transnational bargaining.[29] The elements of the program in the chronological order in which the ITSs hope to achieve them are:

1. research and information
2. company conference
3. company council
4. company-wide union-management discussions
5. coordinated bargaining
6. transnational bargaining

We have already discussed research as one of the devices which ITSs employ to provide aid for national unions that are bargaining separately with MNCs. Research plays a vital role also in the long-run strategy of ITSs. It is the foundation upon which everything else rests. The same data that can be useful to a national union in bargaining separately with an MNC can also be essential to effective multinational bargaining. Thus, research serves both the immediate and the long-run goals of the ITSs.

The second step in the ITS long-range program in relation to a particular MNC is the calling of a company conference. National unions that represent employees of the MNC throughout the free world are invited to help plan the agenda and to send delegates. The purpose of the conference is to: build understanding and solidarity among the national unions; share information and knowledge; discuss means of fuller cooperation; and plan how they may meet more effectively the threat to their bargaining power that is posed by the MNC. For example, in 1972 the IUF convened the first "Nestle World Conference" in Geneva which was attended by forty-three delegates from sixteen different countries. The IUF has convened a number of other conferences of national union representatives from other MNCs. Many of the other ITSs have convened similar company conferences.

During the first company conference, a permanent company council is usually established to carry on the work of the conference and to plan future conferences. For example, during the first Nestle World Conference, a Nestle permanent council made up of delegates from eleven countries under the chairmanship of the Swiss delegate was established and was given the following tasks:

1.   to contact the management of Nestle on international questions or at the request of affiliates

2.   to call future Nestle conferences

3.   to follow up on decisions of the conference.

Similar councils have been established by ITSs for many of the MNCs, including the major automobile companies, General Electric, Westinghouse, Philips, Brown Boveri, ICI, Rhone-Poulenc, Dunlop-Pirelli, Ciba Geigy, Michelin, Hilton, Unilever, and W.R. Grace. Industry councils have also been established by ITSs in a number of industries, including bauxite mining, copper mining, tobacco, aerospace, and electronics.

The fourth phase of the ITS program is to request a meeting with central management of the MNC to discuss problems of mutual interest. If a company council has been formed, the request may come from the council which is made up of union leaders who represent employees of the MNC. Most MNC managements, fearing that such a meeting is a step in the direction of transnational bargaining, have turned down such requests, stating that within their organization, labor matters are delegated entirely to local national management which deals directly with the national unions. Where the MNC managements have refused to cooperate, the ITSs have not been able to force them to meet. However, some MNC managements, such as those at Philips, Fokker-VFW, Nestle, and Continental Can, have agreed to such meetings. After the first meetings, even these managements have been reluctant to agree to future meetings. As a result, the ITSs have been largely frustrated in their attempts to make progress in this phase of their program.

An intermediate goal of the ITS is to achieve cooperative support among unions while they are bargaining separate national contracts with a multinational firm in the industry. In the spring of 1969, when five different national unions affiliated with the chemical workers' secretariat (ICF) entered into separate negotiations with St. Gobain, the ICF arranged a meeting of these five and other affiliated unions that represented St. Gobain employees. As a result of the meeting, all the affiliated unions pledged to give financial aid to strikers and to ban compensating overtime in non-struck plants. Moreover, the West German union agreed to continue pressuring the company even if it reached a favorable settlement, and the U.S. union postponed its strike for two weeks so that it and the Italian union could threaten a simultaneous stoppage. As a result, the ICF claimed that the company granted concessions to all five affiliates, concessions which none of them could have achieved separately.

The ultimate goal of each ITS is to bargain transnational contracts with each of the multinational companies within its industry. Gunter Kopke, secretary general of the European Metalworkers' Federation, stated in 1974 that "the EMF is preparing the ground for transnational bargaining on a very large scale in Europe."[30] That same year, Norris Willat, after studying the programs of the sixteen active ITSs, concluded, "However far away it may be, they have all set their sights on stage 3, when the numerous affiliates at all the subsidiaries of an MNC (multinational corporation) will time their demands on management to coincide, thus presenting it with a worldwide united front of labor."[31]

**Barriers to the International Trade Secretariats' Progress**

Although the ITSs have developed interesting short-range and long-range programs to counteract the bargaining power of the MNCs, progress in implementation has been very slow. The major difficulties or barriers that have prevented the ITSs from achieving their goals are: the good wages, fringe benefits, and working conditions at MNCs; the strong resistance from MNC managements; the conflicts within the labor movement; and the differing laws and customs.

In general, MNCs have the reputation of paying higher wages, offering superior fringe benefits, and providing better working conditions than non-MNC companies in the same country. This condition was confirmed by an ILO study in 1973.[32] It is true, however, that MNCs often pay lower wages in one country than in another country for the same type of work. International labor leaders have used this fact to urge employees and unions to join in an international effort to obtain more uniform rates. However, the labor leaders have never been able to show that MNCs pay less than non-MNCs in the same country. In fact, the opposite is usually true. Northrup has stated that the lack of interest on the part of employees is one of the most important barriers preventing the ITSs from achieving their goals.[33] The recognition on the part of MNC employees that they are receiving wages, benefits, and working conditions as good as, or better than, the workers in non-MNC companies in their country is perhaps the factor that has made it most difficult for the ITSs to mobilize the workers and their national unions against the MNCs.

Managements of the MNCs strongly oppose the programs developed by the ITSs. They see these programs, if successful, not only as decreasing management's bargaining power vis-à-vis the unions, but also as interfering with management's freedom to make important business decisions. They argue also that transnational bargaining would further complicate labor relations by adding an additional level of collective bargaining on top of those which already exist.[34] As a result, most MNC managements have refused to meet with ITS representatives. They believe such meetings would only increase the prestige of the ITS leadership and move it one step further toward its goal of transnational bargaining, which MNC managements strongly oppose. In the half-dozen or so instances where managements have agreed to meet with the ITS representatives, the results have not been very fruitful. In most cases, management has insisted on a very narrow agenda and has refused to continue the dialogue after the first one or two meetings.

Conflicts within the labor movement have made it difficult for the ITSs to mount united campaigns against the MNCs. The international trade union movement is not homogeneous. There are major differences of religion and ideology within the movement which tend to fragment it. For example, the major ITS in the metalworking industry, the International Metalworkers' Federation, will not accept the major union groups in France and Italy into membership because such unions are dominated by Communists. On the other hand, the small Christian union movement operates its own separate group of ITSs.[35]

Even where there are no important differences of ideology or religion, unions may find themselves with conflicting economic interests when attempting to deal with MNC problems. The decision of an MNC to move production of a major item from one country to another may be viewed quite differently by the two unions involved. For example, it is reported that in 1971, when Henry Ford was being castigated by British unions for saying that the labor climate in that country might prevent further investment there by the Ford Motor Company, a group of Dutch businessmen urged him to consider transferring his investment funds to their country, and no Dutch union leader spoke out against such a transfer.[36]

The national unions, although recognizing the need for international solidarity in dealing with MNCs, have been unwilling to give much authority to the ITSs. As previously noted, the ITSs are weak confederations in which the power remains with the affiliated national unions. Within the various countries, the national unions have opposed the loss of power to central labor organizations such as the TUC, AFL-CIO, or DGB. They oppose even more vigorously the loss of power to an international organization such as an ITS. Also, most of the unions have plenty of problems within their own countries, and the struggle of another union with an MNC in another country may seem too remote to warrant the expenditure of scarce resources which are badly needed at home. Finally, it has been pointed out that language differences are much more of a barrier between union leaders than between managers in an MNC.[37]

Even where national union leaders may be prepared to take action through an ITS to meet the threat of an MNC, they are likely to be frustrated by differing laws, customs, and practices in the labor relations area. There is, as yet, no international law that requires MNCs to recognize and bargain with international representatives of unions. If an MNC refuses to negotiate with an ITS, there is no international legislation that can be invoked to force it to do so.

Each country has its own system of labor legislation, and even within the European Economic Community, there has been little in the way of harmonization of such laws to date. Often the laws make it difficult for unions to offer effective help when a union in another country is struggling with an MNC. Sympathetic actions such as strikes, boycotts, or even refusal to work overtime, or refusal to work on "struck work" may be illegal. In this respect, it is significant that although Dutch and West German union leaders indicated in a 1976 ILO survey that they would favor refusal to work on "struck work" and refusal to work additional overtime when unions at the same company's plant in another country were on strike, they thought it possible that legal restraints in their own country might block such solidarity assistance.[38] In the United States, the prevalence of no-strike contract provisions, often lasting for three years, plus the legal enforceability of such contracts, greatly limit the possibility of industrial action by American unions to aid unions that might be engaged in a conflict abroad with the same MNC. Finally, the structure of bargaining within a country may make it very difficult to move to transnational bargaining with an MNC. For example, in West Germany, most labor contracts are negotiated between an employers' association and a union. It is unlikely that West German companies or even West German unions would be willing to abandon association bargaining in favor of transnational MNC bargaining.

As a result of such resistance factors, the advance of the ITSs toward transnational bargaining has been slow, and now appears to be stymied. In only a few instances has an ITS moved to item four (union-management discussions) in the six-point program discussed earlier in this chapter. In some situations, there has been retrogression. MNC managements that have met with ITS representatives are now refusing further meetings. Although Levinson claims that ITSs frequently have been successful in achieving results for affiliated unions that the unions could not have achieved alone,[39] Northrup and Rowan, who have reviewed many of the instances where ITSs have intervened, refute Levinson's claim. They contend that the ICF and other ITSs have been strong on publicity but very weak on results.[40]

## The Threat to Union Political Power

We have noted in earlier chapters that the labor movements in the European countries possess and exercise strong political power and influence. European unions have relied heavily upon this power to gain recognition for themselves as institutions and to gain benefits for the employees whom they represent. Compared to labor unions in the United States, the dependence of the European unions on political power has been much greater and the dependence on economic or bargaining power much less.

The unions now see their political power as well as their economic power threatened by the MNCs. As stated earlier, the MNCs have the power of the "investment strike," that is, they can refuse to invest or to reinvest in countries where they consider labor or social legislation to be unfavorable. As a result, MNCs are in a position to exert strong pressure on a national government. The pressure exerted by the MNCs may be contrary to the pressure being exerted by the country's labor movement. The labor leaders see this countervailing force of the MNCs as a threat to their ability to achieve their goals through political action.[41]

## The Union Response in the Political Arena

The union attack against the MNCs in the political arena has been developed not only to meet the growing political power of the MNCs, but also to counterbalance the strength of the MNCs compared to the unions in the economic arena. Professor Blanpain has pointed out that because the unions are weak at the bargaining table, they have been forced to move to the political arena.[42] The union political attack has been developed along two lines: 1. the sponsoring of national legislation aimed at restricting MNC power, and 2. the support of control and regulation of MNCs by international political institutions.

## Restrictive National Legislation

The major MNCs have their headquarters in countries where the union movements have considerable political power. As a result, some of the national union organizations, such as the AFL-CIO in the United States and the LO in Sweden, have acted to restrain and control the power of the MNCs through legislation within the headquarters nations. In most cases, the goal of the unions has been to prevent the export of jobs by MNC investment policies, but the action has not been limited to that issue. The AFL-CIO has lobbied strongly for changes in the tax laws which would make it less profitable for U.S.-based MNCs to invest abroad. In addition, it has supported legislation that would give the President authority to regulate the flow abroad of funds or technology when employment in the United States might be decreased by such action.[43] In Sweden in 1973, the national metal union demanded legislation that would give "decisive influence" to "community and wage earner groups" over major decisions by MNCs.[44] Under pressure from the labor movement, the Swedish Department of Industry in 1974 issued "Guidelines for Permits for Swedish Investments Abroad" which state that the government should assume the task of preventing investments abroad that would be detrimental to the Swedish economy. Finally, the Swedish labor movement was successful in getting a social code added to the government's investment guarantee program which specifies that to qualify for such guarantees, an MNC must agree to "recognize trade unions, . . . enter into collective bargaining according to the host country's rules," and "give the union notice of layoffs and facilitate the adjustment of workers laid off."[45] However, the attempts by the American, Swedish, and other labor movements to restrain and control the power of the MNCs through national legislation have not been very effective. The legislation sponsored by the AFL-CIO has not been enacted, and in Sweden, very few of the MNCs have sought guarantees of investments in countries where the guidelines would have been meaningful. Other labor movements have been no more successful in their attempts to influence the decisions of MNCs through national legislation.

## Regulation of Multinational Companies by International Organizations

The trade unions are exerting their political influence to try to obtain international regulation of the MNCs through three types of international institutions. First, they are making use of their own international and European trade union federations, such as the International Confederation of Free Trade Unions (ICFTU) and the European Trade Union Confederation (ETUC). Both of these organizations are composed of representatives of national trade union bodies, such as the TUC of Great Britain and the DGB of West Germany. The unions are also pushing strongly for MNC regulation within the International Labor Organization, which is a tripartite organization with representatives of governments and managements as well as of unions. Finally, the unions are exerting pressure through their respective governments on the international organizations, such as the European Economic Community, the Organization for Economic Cooperation and Development (OECD), and the United Nations (UN) in which only governments are represented.

The International Confederation of Free Trade Unions, which is headquartered in Brussels, was established in 1949. Its members are national confederations of trade unions, such as the TUC of Great Britain and the DGB of West Germany. The AFL-CIO was an active participant in the formation of the organization but withdrew in 1969. The ICFTU has no power to regulate or control MNCs. However, as the leading international organization of free trade unions (the Communist unions are members of another organization—the World Federation of Trade Unions), it does serve as a forum for discussion of policies and strategies to be followed in dealing with the MNC problem and also as a strong lobbying force with those international organizations which could undertake regulation and control.

Following a number of years of study of the MNC problem and the passage of a resolution in 1971 urging the adoption of international and national standards to regulate MNCs, the ICFTU at its Eleventh Congress in Mexico in 1975 adopted a "multinational charter" which calls for the establishment of a tripartite international agency (similar in structure to the ILO) for the purpose of issuing conventions to regulate MNCs. The conventions would then be adopted by national governments to make them legally enforceable. The charter calls for conventions that, among other things, would permit unions to engage in sympathy strikes to support a union strike against an MNC in another country, and that would require an MNC to: facilitate union organization and representation; supply information to unions; arrange and pay for representatives of all its employees throughout the world to meet together at least three times per year; make no layoffs without prior arrangements for jobs of equivalent income; and meet certain other social obligations. Although willing to support a voluntary code of conduct for MNCs at this time, the ICFTU views such a code "only as a first step toward binding regulations."[46]

The European Trade Union Confederation was formed in 1973 to replace an organization in which only the union confederations from the original six countries of the EEC were represented. The ETUC was expanded to include union confederations in the other Western European countries. The organization now has seventeen affiliated union confederations from fourteen countries. Unlike the ICFTU, the ETUC has admitted the Italian Communist union federation.

The ETUC cooperates with the ICFTU but concerns itself primarily with European labor matters. It works closely with the various agencies of the EEC. For example, in 1976 when the European Commission decided to establish and finance the European Trade Union Institute, the Commission asked the ETUC to prepare the draft statutes for the new organization. The board of the institute will be nominated by the ETUC. The institute will be heavily involved in research and collection of information which could prove very valuable to national unions in their bargaining with MNCs.[47]

In July, 1977, the executive committee of the ETUC adopted a program of action regarding MNCs. Among other things, the action program urges the EEC and its member governments to make possible "sympathetic strikes and boycotts . . . within each defined economic sector, whenever an international trade union organization, having agreed with its member organizations, calls the strike."[48]

The International Labor Organization is a worldwide tripartite organization composed of representatives of government, management, and labor from many nations, including some in Eastern Europe. The United States was a member of the ILO until 1977 when it withdrew. It is expected, however, that the United States will rejoin the ILO at some later date. The ILO issues codes of conduct on labor and social matters. However, the codes are not mandatory for the member nations. They become effective in a nation only when approved by that nation's government. The unions of Western Europe are able to affect the actions of the ILO not only directly, through their own representation, but also indirectly, through their strong influence on the government representatives, because many of the Western European governments are heavily dependent on trade union support.

In November, 1972, the ILO convened in Geneva a meeting on the relationship between multinational corporations and social policy. The meeting was composed of experts drawn from government, management, and labor. The working papers submitted to this meeting were published by the ILO in 1973 "to provide a point of departure for . . . further work."[49] In 1976, the ILO published the results of five studies that dealt with the impact of MNCs on labor relations and employment.[50] In November, 1976, the governing body of the ILO established a committee to draft a "declaration of principles" regarding MNCs. In November, 1977, the draft was approved by the governing body of the ILO. In the labor relations area, it would require MNCs to engage in bona fide collective bargaining (free from fear of discrimination), establish grievance procedures, and adopt employment practices that would assure job security to workers. This ILO code for MNCs, like all other ILO codes, is voluntary and, as a result, its future status is uncertain. However, the director general of the ILO has been directed by the governing body to prepare a statement concerning the follow-up which should be given to the declaration. To date, the ILO's actions appear to have had little direct effect upon the attitudes and policies of the MNCs in the area of labor relations. Although the labor representatives may be expected to continue to push the ILO to take further action in this direction, because of the limitations and obstacles in the ILO structure and procedures, as Kassolow has stated, "it is really impossible to predict when any ILO impact on the multinational question may actually be felt."[51]

The United Nations is a worldwide organization with representatives from most of the nations. Unlike the condition in the ILO, labor is not directly represented in the UN. Instead, the delegates are appointed by their respective governments. Nevertheless, in most of the Western European countries, the unions are so strong politically that they are able to make their influence felt through their government representatives. However, the UN is a large organization, and many of the delegates come from parts of the world where labor's political influence is not very significant. Although the UN is one of the few institutions that is broad enough to deal with the MNCs on a worldwide basis, the composition of the organization, as well as its structure and procedures, make it difficult for it to move effectively in this area.

In 1974, "a group of eminent persons" appointed by the UN to study the MNC problem issued a report which recommends among other things that: unions should have a role in the decision-making process of MNCs at both the local and the international level; unions should be able to bargain jointly with MNCs; unionists from other countries should be allowed free entry into a country at the invitation of the workers of that country to assist them in bargaining with an MNC subsidiary; an international social fund should be established by contributions from MNCs to aid employees who are displaced or laid off as a result of MNC action; unions should be permitted to engage in sympathy strikes where MNCs are involved; and home countries should prevent MNCs from opening plants in countries where worker rights are not respected, unless the MNC agrees to free collective bargaining.[52]

However, it is doubtful that the UN will act to implement the recommendations of its eminent persons' report. In 1974, the UN established a commission on transnational corporations (forty-eight persons) to further study the problem. The international union organizations were very critical of the UN because no union representatives were appointed to the commission.[53] When the UN will adopt a program of regulation of MNCs and to what extent such a program will contain provisions that will meet labor's demands are not clear at this time.

The European Economic Community consists of representatives of the nine Western European nations that constitute the European common market (Belgium, Denmark, France, Ireland, Italy, Luxembourg, the Netherlands, United Kingdom, and West Germany). Thus, geographically the EEC covers a much smaller area than the UN and is probably not large enough to enforce a set of rules for parent companies located outside its territories. On the other hand, the EEC does cover an area where many of the world's MNCs (30%) have their headquarters. Moreover, it is an area in which European unions can exert maximum political pressure. Since European unions have always relied heavily on national legislation to secure many benefits for themselves and their workers, it is natural that in their struggle with the MNCs they should turn to EEC legislation, especially since the use of economic power through the ITSs has not been very effective.

One way in which the EEC is aiding the unions in their struggle with the MNCs is through "harmonization," whereby an attempt is being made through EEC directives to make social legislation the same or similar in all nine countries. The directives of the EEC, unlike the codes of the ILO, are mandatory within the nine-nation area. Harmonization directives have been issued already on many issues including: equal pay for equal work regardless of sex; equal opportunities regardless of sex; maintenance of acquired rights by employees following a merger, consolidation, or takeover; rules governing layoffs and redundancies; and health protection for workers exposed to the chemical VCM. Another directive requiring equal treatment of male and female employees in the social security field was approved in November, 1978, but does not become fully effective until November, 1984. In process at the present time are drafts of other directives covering: protection of employees against loss caused by insolvency of a company or a subsidiary; regulation of shift work; profit sharing and asset formation; and reduced working time.

In 1977, the committee on economic and monetary affairs for the European Parliament issued a working paper on MNCs which in a section entitled "Social Policy and Labor Market Policy" provides that MNCs must:

> Recognize trade unions, workers' bargaining units, direct representatives of the staffs (worker councils), or other duly constituted workers' organizations as contractual partners in negotiations on wage agreements and the fixing of work conditions . . . ;
>
> Afford representatives of the workers the opportunity to hold consultations with management responsible for the policy of the firm;
>
> Inform and consult with workers in good time on matters affecting them;
>
> Give workers an important voice in drawing up labor phase-out plans;
>
> Guarantee retention of pension and other acquired rights [in case of a merger, consolidation or take over;]
>
> [Refrain from transferring work from a struck plant to another plant of the same enterprise] in order to thwart the legitimate and legal objectives of the workers;
>
> [Take steps] to establish the framework for internationally valid collective bargaining agreements.

If the scope of the social harmonization directives is eventually sufficiently broad, these directives could have the same effect on an MNC as a multinational contract negotiated by an ITS covering the nine-county area. For example, a directive on sick pay could mean that an MNC would have to pay the same benefits in each of the nine EEC countries. However, social harmonization is still in its infancy and has not yet begun to deal with such items as sick pay. Moreover, since the EEC is limited to harmonization within the nine-country area, this device could not prevent the MNCs from taking advantage of less liberal social and labor legislation in other parts of the world. In fact, since the goal of harmonization is to bring the social legislation of all the nine countries into line with the country having the most liberal legislation, the effect may well be to encourage MNCs to move production outside the EEC area.

The EEC also has in draft form a statute for a European company (SE) that would enable an MNC operating in several or all of the nine EEC countries to incorporate under a single statute. The draft provides that a European corporation must have a central works council representing "all of its European employees and a two-tier board system with a supervisory board in which one-third of the members would be representatives of the owners, one-third would be representatives of the workers, and one-third would be co-opted by the other two groups." In recommending the draft, the European Parliament stated that economic, social, and political solidarity in Europe is inconceivable without satisfactory participation by the employees in the management of the business.

Finally, the EEC is establishing and financing the European Trade Union Institute "to help the trade union organizations extend the training of trade union members in the European sphere." The board of the institute will consist of members nominated by the ETUC. It will be financed by the EEC with an initial budget of $729,000. The institute will emphasize research and the development of information as well as training.[54] Thus, it is expected that it will become a vehicle for providing unions with comparative information in bargaining with MNCs and for training union leaders in the most effective ways to use such information in their negotiations with MNCs.

### Guidelines of the Organization of Economic Cooperation and Development

The Organization of Economic Cooperation and Development is composed of twenty-four countries with industrialized free-market economies. It includes not only EEC countries, but also other Western European nations and Australia, Canada, Japan, New Zealand, Turkey, and the United States. Thus, it covers a much broader area than the EEC. It is estimated that the OECD nations account for 60% of the world's industrial production, receive 80% of the world's investment, and serve as home countries for over 90% of the world's MNCs.[55]

Membership in the OECD is limited to national governments. Neither management nor labor is directly represented. However, the OECD has established two advisory groups: the Business and Industry Advisory Committee (BIAC) and the Trade Union Advisory Committee (TUAC). Through these two committees, management and labor are able to influence OECD actions.

In June, 1976, the OECD issued a set of guidelines for multinational corporations. In so doing, it became the first international organization (excluding purely labor organizations) to adopt such guidelines. The guidelines deal not only with labor relations, but also with many other matters, including competition, taxation, finance, disclosure, science, and technology. The international business community appeared to be quite happy with the results of the OECD efforts. The guidelines were publicly endorsed by a number of MNCs, including Exxon and Unilever. Labor's reaction was much less favorable. The ICFTU expressed keen disappointment, pointing out that the guidelines placed too much reliance on voluntary acceptance by the MNCs and established no complaints procedure. The Nordic council of Unions petitioned their governments to reopen negotiation to strengthen the guidelines.[56]

Although the guidelines received criticism from labor groups, they do contain many of the provisions regulating MNCs that labor has been trying to get into some kind of international legislation for several years. The section of the guidelines entitled "Employment and Industrial Relations" sets forth the following nine policies that MNCs should follow:

1.  respect the right of their employees to be represented by trade unions and other bona fide organizations of employees, and engage in constructive negotiations, either individually or through employers' associations, with such employee organizations with a view to reaching agreements on employment conditions, which should include provisions for dealing with disputes arising over the interpretation of such agreements, and for ensuring mutually respected rights and responsibilities;

2.  a. provide such facilities to representatives of the employees as may be necessary to assist in the development of effective collective agreements,
    b. provide to representatives of employees information that is needed for meaningful negotiations on conditions of employment;

3.  provide to representatives of employees where this accords with local law and practice, information that enables them to obtain a true and fair view of the performance of the entity or, where appropriate, the enterprise as a whole;

4. observe standards of employment and industrial relations not less favorable than those observed by comparable employers in the host country;

5. in their operations, to the greatest extent practicable, utilize, train, and prepare for upgrading members of the local labor force in cooperation with representatives of their employees and, where appropriate, the relevant governmental authorities;

6. in considering changes in their operations that would have major effects upon the livelihood of their employees, in particular in the case of the closure of an entity involving collective layoffs or dismissals, provide reasonable notice of such changes to representatives of their employees, and where appropriate to the relevant governmental authorities, and cooperate with the employee representatives and appropriate governmental authorities so as to mitigate to the maximum extent practicable adverse effects;

7. implement their employment policies including hiring, discharge, pay, promotion, and training without discrimination unless selectivity in respect of employee characteristics is in furtherance of established governmental policies that specifically promote greater equality of employment opportunity;

8. in the context of bona fide negotiations with representatives of employees on conditions of employment, or while employees are exercising a right to organize, not threaten to utilize a capacity to transfer the whole or part of an operating unit from the country concerned in order to influence unfairly those negotiations or to hinder the exercise of a right to organize;

9. enable authorized representatives of their employees to conduct negotiations on collective bargaining or labor management relations issues with representatives of management who are authorized to take decisions on the matters under negotiation.

In addition to the section devoted specifically to labor relations, two other parts of the guidelines could prove to be valuable to labor. The section entitled "Disclosure of Information" sets forth a list of financial and other data that MNCs should "publish on a regular basis, but at least annually." The availability of such information, if it was not formerly available, should enable unions to bargain more effectively. Finally, paragraph 8 of the introduction provides that the guidelines are addressed to the parent company and/or the local affiliate of an MNC "according to the actual distribution of responsibilities among them on the understanding that they will cooperate and provide assistance to one another as necessary to facilitate observance of the guidelines." This last provision would appear to make it necessary for a parent company to assume responsibility for carrying out the provisions of the guidelines, if because of bankruptcy or for some other reason a national affiliate is unable to do so.

The guidelines are not legally enforceable. It is specifically stated that "the guidelines . . . are recommendations . . . Observance of the guidelines is voluntary and not legally enforceable." It is toward this lack of legal enforceability that the unions have turned most of their criticism. If an MNC does not follow the guidelines, there are no legal sanctions that can be brought to bear against it. The Trade Union Advisory Committee of the OECD believes that the guidelines are only a first step in a process in which eventually the OECD will move to binding regulations of MNCs.[57] However, Theodore Vogelaar, special consultant to the OECD, has stated that "in the present state of our diffused world . . . any attempt to establish a binding code, is, I am afraid, doomed to remain illusory."[58]

Despite the voluntary nature of the guidelines, labor believes they may prove to be very valuable in its struggle with the MNCs.[59] The first case in which labor leaders claimed a major violation of the guidelines involved the Badger Company, a Belgian subsidiary of Raytheon, a U.S.-based MNC. In 1976, Badger discontinued operations and dismissed its employees. Belgian law requires that under these conditions, the company must provide the dismissed employees with sizeable termination payments. However, Badger, which filed for bankruptcy in early 1977, did not possess the funds to make these payments. The Belgian labor leaders then turned to Raytheon, claiming that, under the OECD guidelines, the parent company had an obligation to assume this liability.

When Raytheon refused to pay, the Belgian labor leaders convinced the Belgian government to bring the case before the Committee on International Investments and Multinational Enterprises (CIME) of the OECD. Although the Belgians did not insist that a charge against a specific MNC could be brought before the CIME, they did argue successfully that clarification of the guidelines requires the analysis of specific situations, such as the Badger case. Following debate on the matter, the CIME concluded that, in a situation such as existed in this case, the parent company did have an obligation under the guidelines to assume the cost of the termination payments. Following the committee's decision, Raytheon worked out an agreement with the Belgian labor leaders whereby the parent company did make funds available for termination pay. Professor Blanpain, who has carefully studied and written a book on the Badger case, concluded that the OECD guidelines did play a decisive role in the Badger settlement.[60]

During the first three years of the OECD guidelines, 1976-1979, labor issues clearly occupied the center of the stage. The CIME devoted a large part of its time to discussing the labor provisions. In addition to the Badger case, seventeen other labor matters were presented to the committee. All but three of these were based on actual incidents that had happened in specific MNCs. The MNCs where the incidents occurred were: Raytheon, Massey-Ferguson, Black and Decker, Philips (2 incidents), Poclain, Bendix, Siemens, Warner-Lambert, Litton Industries, ITT, Citibank-Citicorp, Hertz, British American Tobacco Company, and Firestone.[61].

As a result of these many discussions, numerous aspects of the guidelines were "clarified" and one amendment was adopted. Paragraph 8 was amended to prohibit companies from transferring workers from one affiliate to another to act as strike breakers.[62] The discussions also gave much publicity to the guidelines. In addition, they placed considerable pressure on the companies, whose incidents formed the bases for the discussions, to take action consistent with the "clarifications." Although the CIME was quick to assert that the purpose of the discussions was not to judge the behavior of the individual company,[63] they did have that effect. Once the committee had stated its understanding of a particular guideline, the company was under strong public pressure to take action consistent with the "clarification." Thus, by bringing the issues up for discussion, the unions were forcing the CIME to assume a role of policing the guidelines.

## Summary

The MNCs pose a real and growing threat to the power of European labor unions. The threat arises because of the difference in scope and structure of the two types of organizations. An MNC is by definition multinational, and in practice, most of them are conglomerates. A labor union is limited to a particular nation, and in most cases, to a particular industry.

The labor unions have attempted to meet the challenge by building international economic power through International Trade Secretariats which are composed of union affiliates in a particular industry throughout the world. The ITSs have developed programs to offer immediate aid to their affiliates in dealing with MNCs. In addition, the ITSs have developed long-run programs which have transnational bargaining as their ultimate goal. However, the ITSs have had only limited success in their short-run programs, and the long-run programs appear to be completely stymied. From a structural point of view, the ITSs have a serious defect in dealing with most MNCs. The ITSs, although international, are limited to a particular industrial area whereas most MNCs are conglomerates.

The European unions have turned also to political power as a means of meeting the challenge of the MNCs. Through the influence they possess in many of the national governments, they have sought to have the labor relations of MNC regulated and controlled by means of restrictive national legislation and the establishment of rules or guidelines by international organizations: ILO, UN, EEC, and OECD.

The most successful development for the unions in the political arena has been the establishment by the OECD of MNC guidelines which include important provisions on labor relations. By requesting clarification of the guidelines, the unions have been able to bring about discussions and statements by the OECD committee (CIME) regarding labor relations incidents at fifteen different MNCs. Although the CIME has asserted that its purpose was not to judge the behavior of individual companies, the statements of clarification have had that effect. Professor Blanpain has stated that although the OECD guidelines are purely voluntary and the role of the CIME is not that of a court, in time, its clarifications may become part of the generally accepted body of common international law applicable to all MNCs. Whether or not the CIME statements assume such importance in the long run remains to be seen. However, it is clear that in the short run, the European unions have found the OECD guidelines to be a promising device in meeting the threat of the MNCs.

## Notes

1. *Forbes*, July 1, 1974, pp. 39-43.

2. Raymond Vernon, *Storm over the Multinationals* (Cambridge, Ma.: Harvard University Press, 1977), p. 3.

3. Harvard Multinational Enterprise Project.

4. Vernon, *Storm over the Multinationals*, p. 12.

5. Ibid., p. 21.

6. *ITT 1978 Annual Report* (New York).

7. *Multinational Enterprises and Social Policy* International Labor Office, (Geneva: 1973), p. 90.

8. Multinationals in Western Europe: The Industrial Relations Experience (Geneva: International Labor Office, 1976), p. 20.

9. Conference Board, *The Multinational Union Challenges the Multinational Company* (New York: Conference Board, 1975), p. 3.

10. *Multinational Enterprises*, p. 90.

11. R. Blanpain, *The Badger Case (the Netherlands: Kluwer Deventer, 1977), p. 21.*

12. *Vernon, Storm over the Multinationals*, p. 29.

13. *Multinational Enterprises*, p. 91.

14. Norris Willatt, *Multinational Unions* (London: Financial Times Ltd., 1974), p. 7.

15. Gunter Kopke, "Union Responses in Continental Europe," in *Bargaining without Boundaries*, by Robert J. Flanagan, and Arnold R. Weber (Chicago: University of Chicago Press, 1974), p. 207.

16. *Multinationals in Western Europe*, p. 48.

17. Willatt, *Multinational Unions*, p. 23.

18. See Meert International Case.

19. David H. Blake, "Trade Unions and the Challenge of the Multinational Corporation," *The Multinational Corporation*, Annals of the American Academy 403 (1972):43.

20. Burton Bender, "A Labor Response to Multinationals: Coordination of Bargaining Goals," *Monthly Labor Review* 101 (7) 1978:10.

21. *Multinationals in Western Europe*, p. 51.

22. Ibid., p. 62.

23. Willatt, *Multinational Unions*, p. 31.

24. *Multinationals in Western Europe*, p. 51.

25. Willatt, *Multinational Unions*, p. 31.

26. Bender, "Labor Response," p. 10.

27. *Multinationals in Western Europe*, p. 51.

28. Ibid., p. 10.

29. Willatt, *Multinational Unions*, p. 33.

30. Kopke, "Union Responses," p. 215.

31. Willatt, *Multinational Unions*, p. 33.

32. *Multinational Enterprises*, p. 73.

33. Herbert R. Northrup, "Why Multinational Bargaining Neither Exists Nor Is Desirable," *Labor Law Journal*, 28, 6, (1977):339.

34. Ibid., p. 333.

35. Ibid., p. 337.

36. David Blake, "Corporate Structure and International Unionism," *Columbia Journal of World Business* 7, 2 (1972):20.

37. Kopke, "Union Responses," p. 208.

38. Multinationals in Western Europe, p. 51.

39. Charles Levinson, *International Trade Unionism* (London: George Allen and Unwin Ltd., 1972), pp. 112-117 and 132-134.

40. Northrup, "Multinational Bargaining," pp. 331, 339, 340.

41. Vernon, *Storm over the Multinationals*, p. 113.

42. R. Blanpain, "The OECD Guidelines for Multinational Enterprises," *Journal of the Royal Society of Arts* 126, 5262 (1977):328.

43. Everett M. Kassalow, "Regulation and Control of Multinational Corporations: The Labor Aspects," in *Industrial Policies, Foreign Investment and Labor in Asian Countries* (Tokyo: Japan Institute of Labor, 1978), p. 156.

44. Ibid., p. 157.

45. Ibid., p. 159.

46. *Multinational Charter of Trade Union Demands for Legislative Control of Multinational Companies* (Brussels: ICFTU, 1975), p. 26.

47. *European Industrial Relations Review*, no. 35, November 1976, p. 5.

48. *European Industrial Relations Review*, no. 43, July 1977, p. 19.

49. *Multinational Enterprises*.

50. *Multinationals in Western Europe*.

51. Kassalow, "Regulation and Control," p. 171.

52. *The Impact of Multinational Corporations on the Development Process and International Relations* (New York, United Nations Social and Economic Council, 1974), pp. 60-61.

53. Kassalow, "Regulation and Control," p. 174.

54. *European Industrial Relations Review*, no. 35, pp. 5-6.

55. Carl Nisser, and Don Wallace, Jr., "National Treatment for Multinational Enterprises: Will the OECD Governments Meet the Challenge?" *Columbia Journal of World Business* Fall, 1978, p. 14.

56. Kassalow, "Regulation and Control," p. 170.

57. Blanpain, *The Badger Case*, p. 42.

58. From a speech by Vogelaar on December 13, 1976.

59. Paul J. Weinberg, *European Labor and Multinationals* (New York: Praeger Publishers, 1978), p. 94.

60. Blanpain, *The Badger Case*, p. 128.

61. R. Blanpain, *The OECD Guidelines and Labor Relations*, *Badger and Beyond*, A speech delivered in West Germany on July 15, 1979, p. 3.

62. Ibid., p. 9.

63. Ibid., p. 5.

# Case 14
# Belgian Royal Airways

In late November, 1973, Mr. Jacques Martou, vice-president of personnel, was preparing to meet with other top-level executives of Belgian Royal Airways (BRA) to discuss the eleven-week-old strike by BRA employee ground personnel at Boston's Logan International Airport. The Boston dispute was threatening to escalate into a multinational strike action.

As a result of this development, Mr. Dirk Vleeschauwer, vice-president for European operations, had recommended to Mr. Martou that BRA headquarters quickly assume full responsibility of, or at least take a prominent part in, the ongoing negotiations. At issue, in Mr. Martou's opinion, was the company's long-standing policy of conducting all labor negotiations at the local level in the organization. He was concerned about the precedents the company's current actions would set for future union relations.

## Belgian Royal Airways

BRA, headquartered in Brussels, operated a worldwide air system serving 106 airports in 71 countries. In 1972, BRA ranked twelfth among western airlines in the number of passenger air miles flown.

BRA employed about 15,000 persons. This employment figure included about 2,000 flight personnel (pilots, flight engineers, and stewardesses) and about 13,000 ground personnel responsible for maintenance, passenger handling, cargo handling, baggage handling, communications, and commissary.

In Brussels, BRA hired its own personnel to handle all ground functions. At foreign stations, the company often relied on other airlines or independent service organizations to handle portions or all of its ground activities. About 4,000 of BRA's ground personnel was based outside of Belgium; all flight personnel were based in Brussels.

## Labor Relations

BRA's Belgian employees were organized by four unions representing pilots, flight engineers, cabin attendants, and ground personnel (including much of the management staff). The airline bargained with each union separately.

357

BRA ground personnel abroad were represented by many different unions. This arrangement reflected the company's policy of decentralizing labor negotiations to local field management. Mr. Martou described this policy:

> While headquarters here in Brussels handles negotiations with the Belgian unions, the local general manager of a foreign operation is responsible for labor negotiations. Brussel's only input is to establish a maximum value for the overall increase in benefits to be allowed. The particular combination of benefits is a matter for local management to negotiate. We are prepared to counsel our managers on particular problems if requested, but we try to avoid interfering or becoming involved in the actual negotiation process.

Mr. Maurice Haas, personnel manager for field operations, explained the reasons for BRA's decentralized policy:

> It would be impossible for someone at headquarters to be fully familiar with local labor laws and customs in all the countries where we operate. Unions in different countries have very different goals and employ different tactics in dealing with management. For example, the peculiar adversary role of labor unions in the United States is not common to the Continent.
>
> Moreover, labor relations must necessarily involve many informal and implicit understandings which cannot possibly be spelled out in a contract. Since local managers are constantly interacting with the local unions, they are better placed than headquarters people to negotiate in the best interests of BRA.

**Situation in Boston**

BRA in Boston had employed its own personnel to handle all ground activities except for commissary, which had been contracted to an independent service organization. The Transportation Workers' Union (TWU) had successfully organized BRA's ground personnel at Logan Airport when the airline first begain operations there in early 1950s. Separate contracts were negotiated for maintenance, communications, passenger handling, and cargo and baggage handling personnel.

According to BRA management, TWU Local 509, the bargaining agent for BRA's 310 Boston ground personnel, had repeatedly pressed during the 1960s to increase the benefits received by the relatively unskilled cargo and baggage handlers[1] so that they would be more in line with those accorded to the more highly skilled maintenance and communications personnel. Management had resisted these pressures, warning the union that such increases would make the company's cargo handling uneconomical. Despite this resistance, labor costs for cargo handling had mounted to the point where management judged them to be out of line and excessive. Mr. Haas complained that the union had over the years negotiated work rules leading to widespread featherbedding[2] in cargo handling. The average pay per worker for BRA handlers was about equal to that for other airlines operating in Boston.

In mid-1972, Mr. Andre Deschamps, BRA's general manager for Boston,[3] proposed to BRA headquarters that the company's cargo- and baggage-handling operation in Boston be subcontracted as of January 1, 1973, following termination of the current union contracts. This decision was taken following an abortive attempt in late 1971 to have the union agree to changes in the work rules. According to Mr. Deschamps' plan, the sixty-five BRA handlers would be terminated with severance pay.

Corporate management agreed to the move, although it recognized the possibility of a strike over the issue. Mr. Haas remarked:

> We foresaw the likelihood of a strike in November when our decision to close the baggage- and cargo-handling operations would be made known to the unions. In our estimation, such a strike, if called, would not last more than three weeks. Our reasoning was that the strike for cargo and baggage handlers would not be popular with our other workers at Boston and that the union would not have sufficient funds to support a lengthy walkout. The first year's savings from subcontracting this work would easily equal our loss of cargo business during such a strike.[4]

**The Boston Strike**

At the opening bargaining session in November, 1972, the U.S. lawyer who normally conducted the actual negotiations for Mr. Deschamps informed the union that the sole company demand was to discontinue the cargo- and baggage-handling operations. Severance pay would be given to the employees affected by this action in accordance with the terms of the existing contract.

Union leaders of Local 509 refused to discuss any of the new contracts so long as the company insisted on closing down the handling operations. After two unproductive days of bargaining, the issue was sent to the national mediation board which appointed a federal mediator to handle the case.[5]

By mid-July, 1973, it was apparent that all attempts at mediation had failed, and the case was returned to the national mediation board which immediately offered to arbitrate the matter. BRA accepted the offer, but the union refused.

On September 1, 1973, after a thirty-day cooling-off period, TWU Local 509 called a strike of all BRA ground personnel at Boston. Picket lines at the airport and full-page advertisements in the local newspapers

urged the public not to fly BRA in view of the allegedly unfair treatment of
its U.S. workers.

BRA supervisory personnel and staff, working to keep the airline functioning, were able to handle passenger baggage. The picket lines, however,
prevented the company from receiving and handling cargo, and BRA had to
forego this business at Boston for the duration of the strike.

BRA ground employees in Los Angeles, including passenger handling,
baggage handling, and communications personnel, struck for less than a
week in support of the Boston union. During this action, a number of
employees resigned from the union to continue working. In Chicago, where
BRA employed only a small number of people in passenger and baggage
handling, no problems were encountered. In Boston, however, numerous
acts of violence were directed against managers and staff who continued to
work. These included telephone threats, a bomb explosion in a manager's
car, and physical attacks on personnel crossing the picket lines.


**Reverberations Abroad**

Shortly after the strike began, local TWU union leaders, believing that they
could not apply sufficient pressure on BRA in Boston alone, called on the
international TWU[6] leadership for aid. In response to this plea, Mr. Walter
McKay, a vice-president of the ITWU, was assigned the responsibility of
trying to enlist wider support for the union's demands.

Mr. McKay turned for assistance to the International Transport
Workers' Federation (ITF), the worldwide labor organization in which the
ITWU held membership (the appendix at the end of this case describes the
ITF). Invoking Rule XIV of the ITF constitution[7] ITF to ask its member
unions to boycott BRA operations throughout the world.

On September 27, the assistant general secretary of the ITF held a
meeting of the disputing parties to assess the situation and to see how settlement might be reached.[8] As a result of the discussions, ITF officials concluded that the ITF should not become directly involved in negotiations but
that the ITWU had sufficient cause to seek solidarity support from other
member unions.

Following the meeting, Mr. Haas went to Boston to describe to Mr.
Deschamps what had taken place and to devise new terms that could break
the deadlock. In effect, BRA was willing to increase the severance pay offered and to guarantee work in other departments for baggage and cargo
handlers who did not wish to leave BRA employ.

According to Mr. Haas, the visit had the unintended result of under-
mining Mr. Deschamps's bargaining position with the local. Haas was not
certain whether union officials had concluded that he meant to take over

negotiations or whether they had simply used his visit as a pretext to seek direct contact with a representative from headquarters. Whatever the reason, the effect was to delay negotiations for many days.

In the meantime, Mr. McKay had sent telegrams to all ITF member unions asking for solidarity actions. He subsequently visited union officials connected with BRA's major European operations. Walkouts and picketing of BRA operations took place in Paris and Milan as a result of these appeals.

In view of Mr. McKay's success in enlisting support at Paris and Milan, BRA management in Brussels became worried that the dispute could escalate throughout its worldwide operations. Mr. Martou commented on this point:

> We failed to anticipate the possibility of the Boston strike spreading. We simply did not believe this issue would be of worldwide concern. Apparently the TWU and to some extent the ITF feared the precedent that might be set if we were successful in closing this part of our Boston operations. In their view, if we could close one operation in Boston, there would be nothing to prevent us from closing others there or elsewhere. Moreover, they probably feared that other airlines would soon follow suit. It is now obvious that they perceived a threat against job security.
>
> As a practical matter, BRA can tolerate a total strike in Tokyo or a limited strike in Boston. But if a major strike should occur in Brussels or another key location, we would have major difficulties continuing operations.[9]

## The Company's Tactics and Policy under Review

Mr. Vleeschauwer voiced his belief that the company was making an error in not negotiating from headquarters in the Boston case:

> BRA is on the threshold of experiencing an economically disastrous labor dispute. We cannot afford to wait much longer and continue what have been, thus far, fruitless negotiations. Headquarters must deal directly with the ITWU or even the ITF if necessary to avoid further spreading of the strike.

Concerning the long term, Mr. Vleeschauwer argued that it was becoming increasingly necessary for BRA to centralize its major negotiating efforts around the world:

> Cross-national union collaboration is growing in strength across all industries. Moreover, the movement toward multinational bargaining is not far removed from our industry. In a recent meeting of the ITF, a major portion of the agenda was devoted to the subject.[10] Organizations like IFALPA, ATLAS, and KSSU will further solidarity among pertinent unions.[11]
>
> Once the unions get together, you can be sure that they will demand to deal directly with headquarters . . . unless it serves their purposes to pick off

our overseas offices one by one. The company should be prepared to deal with these new circumstances.

At the very least, headquarters should review all company labor negotiations around the world to prevent concessions which might serve as precedents for union demands against other BRA offices or against other airlines. Moreover, labor negotiations require special skills not found in many of our overseas stations. Nor can we afford to have people with these skills on a permanent basis except at headquarters. As for taking local conditions into account, we often have people at headquarters who know the overseas situation better than the local manager as the result of our personnel rotation practices. In any event, BRA could retain a labor law expert in each locality to assist our headquarters' negotiator with respect to local practices.

In weighing these arguments, Mr. Martou had also to consider the contrary views put forward by several of his colleagues. The latter, believing the Boston dispute to have been exacerbated by headquarters' explicit intrusion in the affair, took the position that BRA should adhere strictly to its policy of negotiating at the local level. Industry experience was not particularly helpful to Mr. Martou in this matter inasmuch as other European airlines were somewhat divided in their bargaining practices.

## Notes

1. Cargo handlers were almost exclusively black or Puerto Rican men.

2. A situation where a company must employ workers to perform tasks that could be handled by others in the work force or tasks that might no longer even exist.

3. Mr. Deschamps, aged 54, had been in the United States twelve years and general manager in Boston for the last six years. Before, he had been a general manager for a BRA station in West Germany.

4. According to management, the independent baggage-handling services were less costly because the small companies involved in performing these services were not burdened with unfavorable work rules.

5. In the United States, the aviation industry was subject to the rules set forth under the Railway Labor Act for all aspects of labor relations. This act specified that either party (company or labor organization) could request the mediation services of the national mediation board if a major dispute involving a new contract would not be settled through normal negotiations. (In mediation, also called conciliation, a government specialist in labor negotiations attempted to assist the two parties to arrive at an agreement.) If mediation were unsuccessful, the national mediation board would offer to provide arbitration. Either party could refuse arbitration. (In arbitration, both parties agreed to be bound by the terms of

an agreement declared by an arbitrator or panel of arbitrators selected by the parties themselves.)

6. Although called international, the ITWU was basically a U.S. organization.

7. Rule XIV of the ITF constitution stated that "affiliated organizations may call upon the ITF for assistance in disputes of major importance."

8. The meeting was attended by Mr. McKay (ITWU), Mr. Haas (BRA), and the chairman of the civil aviation section of the ITF.

9. The Belgian workers were bound by agreement not to strike over issues taking place abroad and not specifically covered in their contracts. In turn, the company could not add extra flights or increase the work load in Belgium to compensate for an overseas strike. Similar agreements were also in effect in Holland and West Germany.

10. International Transport Workers' Federation Ground Staff Conference, November 12 and 13, 1973, Amsterdam. The background paper for the agenda item *Are Airlines Multi-National Companies?* answered the question in the affirmative and called "for ever closer cooperation and strengthened solidarity throughout the whole international free trade union movement if the multi-national challenge is to be adequately met."

11. IFALPA—International Federation of Airline Pilots' Associations. ATLAS and KSSU were organizations joining several airlines for the purpose of purchasing major equipment and of allocating major maintenance tasks to each member. ATLAS consisted of Air France, Alitalia, Lufthansa, and Sabena. KSSU consisted of KLM, SAS, Swissair, and Union Trans Aérienne (France).

# Case Appendix
# The International
# Transport Workers'
# Federation (ITF)

The ITF, founded in 1896, was one of 17 autonomous International Trade Secretariats.[1] By 1973, the ITF comprised more than 300 transport-related member-unions from over 80 countries.

The ITF was organized into nine sections representing railways, road transport, inland navigation, ports and docks, shipping, fisheries, civil aviation, allied industries, and a special section for the promotion of fair practices in the maritime industry. Each section was headed by a full-time official located at ITF headquarters in London.

Among the aims of the ITF were:

> to defend and further internationally the economic and social interests of transport workers and their trade unions . . . to oppose . . . any discrimination based on colour, nationality, sex, race, or creed . . . [and] to promote universal recognition of fundamental trade union rights, and in particular freedom of association and the right to organize and bargain collectively.[2]

Membership in the ITF was open "to all trade unions which have members working in the transport industry, which uphold democratic principles and which are able to operate independent of any outside control." Member unions were expected to accept the obligations imposed on them by the ITF constitution.

The ITF claimed that it had "achieved a large measure of success . . . [in winning] solid gains for its members." This success was possible "because its [ITF's] industrial strength [was] based on the most powerful force in the trade union movement: the spirit of solidarity. No ITF affiliate [had] ever appealed in vain in a trade union cause for the Federation's support."

In practice, the ITF:

> can give highly worthwhile assistance to its affiliates in collective bargaining . . . by responding to specific requests for information from member unions, . . . by supplying comparative data from other countries on wages and working conditions in the relevant transport sector, by producing studies of trends and developments individual branches of the transport industry, and through the regular issue of periodical publications giving news of events concerning transport workers' unions throughout the world and discussing topics of common concern.

> Finally, the Federation can offer its members valuable aid in the settlement of industrial disputes . . . assistance can take many forms: a simple cable

pledging support . . . ; a direct approach from the ITF to employers or government; the use of publicity to stir public opinion on the side of the workers; the provision of an on-the-spot adviser; financial assistance to relieve extreme hardship or the mobilization of sympathetic industrial action by other affiliates which may range from picketing to a full-scale boycott.

## Notes

1. The International Trade Secretariats, which served to affiliate trade unions according to broad industry sectors, were loosely associated to the International Confederation of Free Trade Unions.

2. Quoted sections are taken from an official ITF brochure.

# Case 15
# Meert International

Upon his return from lunch on March 18, 1977, Paul Gemmil, managing director of Meert International, was informed by his secretary that Conrad Kopp, secretary general of the International Electrical Workers' Federation (IEWF), had telephoned from Geneva during his absence and had requested that he return the call. Gemmil was surprised because he knew of no significant labor dispute at any of Meert's subsidiaries. However, he had heard that the IEWF might be interested in resuming discussions with Meert after a break of two and one-half years. If Kopp requested a meeting, Gemmil wondered what his response should be.

### The Company

Meert International with headquarters in Brussels was one of the world's leading producers of electrical and electronics equipment. From an original plant near Antwerp, it had expanded its operations, frequently by acquisition, until in 1977 it had 58 plants in 22 countries and a total of over 100,000 employees including administration and staff.

Meert operated in a highly decentralized fashion. The central organization at Brussels made the major financial decisions regarding allocation of funds, methods of financing, dividends, and such, and the central staff also included experts in production, marketing, research, personnel, and international law who were available to help local managers on request. However, the company was divided into a number of operating subsidiaries, and within each subsidiary, the Brussels management had delegated wide authority with little control from headquarters so long as the operation remained reasonably profitable. The system had worked well. Headquarters' overhead costs were kept very low. Production and profits had expanded rapidly. Meert was proud of the quality of the managers it had developed.

### The International Electrical Workers' Federation

The International Electrical Workers' Federation with headquarters in Geneva, Switzerland, was a loose confederation composed of national unions of electrical and electronics workers. In 1977, it had 165 affiliated unions in 64 countries with aggregate membership of about 3 million. About one-half of the members were in Europe and one-third in North America.

The IEWF was formed in 1902 by a number of the major European electrical workers' unions. Originally, it served primarily as a means of sharing information on wages, employee benefits, labor legislation, and so on. However, from the very beginning it attempted to support new attempts at unionization and to gather funds for unions that faced financial difficulties because of strikes.

Although the basic authority of the IEWF resided in its World Congress which met every four years, the actual work was carried out by the general secretary, Conrad Kopp, and a small administrative staff that worked for him in Geneva. The national affiliated unions jealously guarded their autonomy, and as a result, the IEWF had no control over their activities. It could not order them to strike or take any other action. It could only urge them to offer support to affiliates in need and suggest such action as might be appropriate.

In recent years as a result of the growth of multinational companies, the affiliated unions had shown much greater interest in and support of the IEWF than had been true earlier in its history. General Secretary Kopp had been successful in developing ongoing wage and financial studies of a number of the major companies in the industry. According to the companies, the studies were well done and increasingly sophisticated. They provided the national electrical unions throughout the world with valuable financial, wage, and employee benefit information in each of the companies and between companies. These data were used effectively in contract bargaining.

Under Kopp's leadership, the IEWF had also established company councils which were made up of affiliated unions throughout the world that bargained with a particular company. The council members traded information and offered advice and support to each other. Kopp hoped that through the company councils, the IEWF would be able to meet and talk with the multinational companies regarding the labor problems in their various subsidiaries. However, to date, only one company had agreed to such meetings.

### Relations between Meert and the International Electrical Workers' Federation

Before 1969, the IEWF had made no direct contact with Meert management. In that year, a strike occurred at one of the company's French plants. During the strike, Kopp sent a telegram to Paul Gemmil stating that the French subsidiary was not dealing reasonably with the French unions and suggesting that "it might be desirous for us to consult together in order to bring about a mutually satisfactory settlement." However, the strike in

France was settled by the French management and the French unions the next day, and no further action was taken on Kopp's proposal by the company or the IEWF.

During the succeeding three years, the IEWF undertook an active program to enable it and its affiliates to deal more effectively with the large multinational electrical and electronics companies, including Meert. With the help of its affiliates, it gathered financial, wage, employee benefit, labor contract terms, and other information concerning Meert and its numerous subsidiaries. In 1972, this information was printed in a "confidential report" which the IEWF sent to all of its members. The report was purely factual and contained no criticisms of Meert. The company was impressed with the extent of the information and its accuracy.

Further organizational efforts on the part of the IEWF resulted in the convening of a Meert World Conference in Amsterdam in April 1974 attended by 54 delegates from 19 countries. In addition to pledging the exchange of information and financial and other support to each other, the conference: created the Meert World Council consisting of 13 professional unionists to carry forward the conference's objectives; established a confidential information bulletin to be issued periodically; and drew up a list of specific demands which was sent to Paul Gemmil, along with a request for a meeting to discuss the list and other matters of common interest. The 1974 IEWF Meert World Conference demands for Meert employees in every country were as follows:

1. Full recognition and respect of trade union rights.
2. Advance information to unions on mergers, transfers, closings, rationalizations, layoffs, expansions, new plants, investments, dividends, and such.
3. Elimination of unfair wage policies.
   a. No discrimination between unionized and non-unionized employees.
   b. No differentials because of age, sex, race or nationality.
4. Job security guarantees.
5. Consultation with trade unions before specific decisions affecting work forces of different countries.

After receiving the communication, Gemmil called together his top management group to discuss the conference's request for a meeting with him. Although all agreed that labor matters should be reserved for local negotiations, some were of the opinion that, if a sufficiently narrow agenda could be agreed upon in advance, such a meeting could do no harm and might result in better relations with the individual unions that made up the conference. They pointed out that a few other multinational companies had held such meetings with representatives of ITSs with apparently no undesirable results. Others on the management team opposed such a meeting, arguing that it was the opening wedge that the IEWF would try to use to eventually achieve multinational bargaining, which the nature of the demands clearly indicated was its ultimate goal. They pointed out that, although a few companies had acceded to such requests by their ITSs, most companies had politely refused to do so. It was simpler and easier to draw the line at this point, they contended, than to prevent a gradual movement toward multinational negotiations once discussions were undertaken.

After careful consideration, Gemmil decided that the long-term interest of the company would be served by agreeing to meet with the IEWF. A meeting was arranged for May 21, 1974, at the company's headquarters in Brussels. On that date, Kopp, accompanied by three other members of the Meert World Council, met with Gemmil and three other members of the Meert management.

Gemmil opened the meeting by welcoming Kopp and the other IEWF representatives. He then stated that:

1.  Meert was in favor of unions except where they followed political objectives opposed to free enterprise;
2.  the decentralized structure of Meert did not allow headquarters to deal with working conditions of employees in the affiliated companies.

Kopp replied that the IEWF was not trying to do the job of local unions or interfere with local negotiations, but instead, wanted only to deal with the central management of the company on certain general principles. He said the Meert council was of the opinion that in the past, the company had not made it clear to its subsidiaries that it did expect them to respect union rights, and that it hoped the company would do so in the future. Gemmil replied that he was prepared to make appropriate recommendations to affiliates if this matter should become an issue.

Kopp said the Meert council was also of the opinion that the company had not kept the unions properly informed in advance on such matters as investment programs, plant closures, transfers, mergers and other company actions that would affect employees. Gemmil replied that the company could not give the IEWF and the unions any more information than it provided to its stockholders. He said he would be happy to review the matter with a view to providing such information as could reasonably be given without harming the company. The meeting ended on a friendly note, and Gemmil was of the opinion that the company's best interest had been served by developing this open relationship with the IEWF representatives.

**The Spanish Incident**

In August, 1974, three months after the meeting with the IEWF delegates at headquarters, Meert management announced its decision to construct a plant in Spain in collaboration with a Spanish company. Immediately following the announcement, Gemmil received a letter from Kopp which read in part as follows:

> Through the press we have learned of your intention to build a plant in Spain. According to the news article this plant will make it possible for you to discontinue importing certain Meert products into Spain.
>
> Will you please inform us which Meert plants now export to Spain and will, therefore, be affected by this new plant and what steps will be taken to protect the workers in those plants.
>
> We want to inform you also that IEWF and the entire world labor movement is opposed to the Spanish dictatorship and its attitude toward unions. The legitimate Spanish union leaders are either in jail or in exile. We strongly urge that Meert reconsider its decision to invest in this fascist country and instead use its capital to increase production by free workers represented by free unions.

Gemmil replied to the IEWF letter in part as follows:

> Your information is correct. Meert is planning to construct a plant in Spain. The present plants which will be affected significantly are the Belgian plant at Antwerp and the French plant at Bayonne. The company will take the necessary steps to see that employees in those plants who may be affected will be treated fairly in every way.
>
> The opening of a Spanish plant is something which the company has been forced to do to retain its share of the market in that country. We would have preferred to have continued to supply it from our French and Belgian plants where we already have ample capacity. However, we had no choice. Had we not agreed to build the new plant we would have lost the market to other companies who were willing and anxious to do so.
>
> Since we have had no plant in Spain we have had no actual experience on the social questions in that country. We are of course aware of the political regime which exists there. However, as you know, it has always been our policy not to become involved in the political problems of any country where we operate.

**The Korean Incident**

Meert had a plant in South Korea which not only supplied that country, but also produced sizeable quantities for export. The employees in the Korean plant were represented by the Korean Electrical Workers' Union. In the fall of 1974, the company and the union were not able to reach agreement on a new labor contract and a strike resulted. However, after one week an agreement was reached and work was resumed. The union then demanded that the strikers be paid for the period they had been on strike, claiming discrimination because non-striking workers had been paid. When the management refused, the union workers stopped production and occupied the plant. The management appealed to the government which declared the strike illegal, but the employees disregarded the order and continued to occupy the plant.

The Korean union then appealed to the IEWF which sent a telegram to the Meert management at Brussels, urging it to order the Korean subsidiary to "discontinue its discrimination against the union members." The IEWF also urged its affiliates around the world to appeal to the Meert headquarters and to send financial help to the Korean union. To provide immediate on-the-spot help, the IEWF sent its general secretary for Asia, Mr. Kisaka of Japan, to Korea.

In Korea, Mr. Kisaka requested a meeting with the managing director of the Korean company. A meeting was arranged. However, the managing director refused to negotiate with Kisaka although indicating a willingness to talk with the local union leaders. Kisaka then went to the plant and spoke to the striking workers, promising them support and financial aid. The managing director informed the government of Kisaka's actions, whereupon he was expelled from the country. The strike continued for another week at which time an agreement was reached whereby the employees returned to work but the company did not pay for any time that they had spent on strike.

The IEWF was greatly disturbed by the treatment of its Asian general secretary. It insisted that Meert central management was responsible. Telegrams were sent to the Brussels headquarters not only by IEWF but also by many of its affiliates throughout the world protesting "the company's action in having a legitimate union leader expelled from the country." The company denied any responsibility for the expelling of Kisaka, claiming it was entirely an action of the Korean government which the company had neither suggested nor approved. It stated, however, that management at the Korean plant had its support in refusing to negotiate with Kisaka but instead insisting on local negotiations. It reiterated its position that all labor matters should be negotiated by the local managers and the local unions without interference from either central company management or international union organizations.

Following the Korean incident, the IEWF adopted a very belligerent attitude toward Meert. No more meetings were requested. IEWF studies, publications, and news releases used every opportunity to criticize the company and its activities. Management was of the opinion that any goodwill that may have been generated as a result of the meeting with IEWF representatives in May had been destroyed by the events in the fall in Korea. The IEWF was now engaged in a "cold war" against the company.

## The American Incident

In 1952, Meert had purchased a small electronics company in the United States, the Gener Corporation, with a plant at Waltham, Massachusetts. At time of purchase, Gener had only 300 employees, 85 of whom were white collared, including 55 engineers and technicians. The 160 hourly-paid employees were represented by the Amalgamated Electrical Workers' Union (AEW) which had won a certification election at the plant in 1948.

Following the purchase by Meert, production facilities at Waltham were rapidly expanded, and by 1977, the plant had 1,500 employees, including 1,300 production workers. Relations between the company and the AEW were excellent. There had never been a work stoppage of any kind, and only two grievances had gone to arbitration. In 1966, Gener had agreed to a union-shop clause with the AEW.

In 1968, Meert opened two new U.S. plants, one near Dayton, Ohio and one near San Francisco. Soon after the plants were opened, the AEW won bargaining rights at each of them. In the first negotiations at each plant, the company agreed to a union shop in return for certain concessions made by the union. Union relations at both of these plants were very good. There had been no strikes or work stoppages.

In 1975, Meert purchased Carolina-Southern Electronics, Incorporated (CSE). CSE operated four plants in small towns in the southeastern area of the United States, two in South Carolina, one in Georgia, and one in Mississippi. From its beginning in 1955, CSE had been a non-union operation and, despite active organizing campaigns by the AEW during the seventies, it remained non-union. The union's activity had resulted in elections at one of the South Carolina plants and at the Georgia plant, but in each case, considerably less than one-half of the ballots had been for the AEW (33% in South Carolina; 22% in Georgia).

During the organizing campaigns, CSE management rigorously opposed unionization. It sent letters to the employees' homes, held meetings in the plants addressed by the president and other officers, and trained its supervisors to deal with questions regarding the union. Under American law, the company had the right to oppose unionization so long as it did not discriminate, or threaten the employees, or promise them advantages for not joining the union. Throughout the campaign, the company was careful to stay strictly within the law. Following each of its election defeats, the union filed unfair labor practice charges against the company, but in each case they were dismissed by the National Labor Relations Board.

After the purchase of CSE by Meert, the union appealed to the IEWF for help in organizing CSE. The IEWF responded by asking its affiliated unions to inform Meert of their opposition to CSE's action. As a result, the company received forty-two communications from unions asking it to order the local CSE management to discontinue its anti-union activities and to recognize and bargain with the AEW. From its Geneva office, the IEWF sent a telegram to the managing director of Meert which read in part:

> The local CSE management in the U.S. continues to display extreme hostility to AEW union efforts to represent its employees. This is clearly in violation of what you have informed us is the policy of Meert. We urge you to now implement your policy by ordering the CSE management to discontinue its anti-union activities and to accept the AEW as the representative of its employees.

The IEWF then issued several press releases that condemned the "anti-union action of Meert in its southern U.S. plants." The president and the secretary general of the IEWF also telephoned the company headquarters and requested management to take action.

To all of these communications by the IEWF and its affiliates, the company replied that it was its firm policy and practice that labor relations should be dealt with at the local level by the associated or allied companies that alone had the necessary elements for evaluating the situations. The company refused to intervene in the CSE-AEW dispute.

**Management Reassesses Its Position**

During the winter of 1976-1977, under Gemmil's guidance Meert management gave considerable thought at to how it should meet the IEWF's new belligerent approach. The IEWF was now issuing a "confidential information bulletin" every month. Whereas the early bulletins which were published less frequently were not highly critical of Meert's activities, such was not the case with recent issues. The recent bulletins dealt not only with labor matters, but also with other aspects of the business and generally painted the company in a very unfavorable light. Meert management was continually subject to accusations of bad intentions that were completely untrue. Gemmil wondered if management should disregard the bulletins or respond to them, perhaps by issuing bulletins of its own to its local managers or even to its employees.

The IEWF was now supplying sophisticated information regarding wages, employee benefits, and other personnel information on all Meert subsidiaries to all of its union affiliates throughout the world. It was also advising local union leaders on how to bargain more effectively with local managers. Finally, the local union leaders knew that the IEWF was prepared to launch strong campaigns of financial and other support for any union that became involved in a strike with a Meert subsidiary. Gemmil wondered if the company should be making an effort to train its local managers in labor relations and also to supply experts to advise them during negotiations.

At times, some local managers had taken action in labor relations matters that had been embarrassing to the Meert central management. Although Gemmil was very desirous of preserving local autonomy in labor relations, he wondered if headquarters should be exerting more leadership and guidance at least with respect to general policies in the area.

As the management proceeded to discuss such matters during the early months of 1977, it received copies of the IEWF's January and February "Meert Confidential Bulletins." It was surprised to see that they were much less critical of the management than earlier bulletins. Gemmil also was informed by some friends in Geneva that Kopp had indicated to them that he would not be adverse to meeting with Meert management with the hope of improving relations. Gemmil had decided not to take the initiative, but he wondered what his answer should be if Kopp should propose such a meeting.

# 9

# Some Major Issues in European Labor Relations

As we have studied the literature, discussed labor problems with management and union representatives, and written cases in each of the six European countries covered in this study, certain major issues have emerged. Several of these issues center around the multinational corporations, and we have already considered their impact in the previous chapter. Of the other major issues, we have chosen the following for further analysis in this concluding chapter: 1. employee representation on company boards, 2. works councils, 3. asset formation and employee ownership, 4. dismissals, 5. absenteeism, and 6. women's benefits and rights.

## Employee Representation on Company Boards

It is in West Germany that the important pioneering developments in worker participation have occurred, both at the company level in the form of employee representation on supervisory boards and at the plant level in the form of works councils. It is significant, we believe, that worker participation in West Germany has developed at the two levels of industrial relations where West German unions have not played important roles. Although West German unions have been active politically at the national level and economically (through collective bargaining) at the industry level, there has been little or no union presence at the company and plant levels. As a result, vacuums existed with respect to effective representation of employees at these two lower levels. Worker participation was developed to fill these vacuums.

The company board structure in West Germany is by law two-tiered, consisting of a supervisory board and a management board. The supervisory board has control over broad company policies and also elects the members to the management board. The day-to-day operation of the company is in the hands of the management board. Employees are represented only on the supervisory board.

Employee board representation in West Germany takes place under one of three different laws passed in 1951, 1952, and 1976. The 1951 law applies only to the coal, iron, and steel sector; the 1952 law applies to companies in other industries with from 500 to 2,000 employees; the 1976 law applies to companies in other industries with more than 2,000 employees. The basic differences in the laws concern: 1. parity, 2. union nomination of employee representatives, and 3. selection of the company director of labor. Under the 1951 law in coal, iron, and steel industries, the employee representatives are equal in number and power to the owner representatives. Under the 1952 law, the employees elect only one-third and the owners elect two-thirds of the members of the board. Under the 1976 law, although the employees elect one-half of the board members, parity is not achieved because the chairman, who is an owner representative, has two votes in case of a tie. Under the 1951 law, the union has the right to nominate a majority of the employee representatives, whereas under the 1952 law it has no right to nominate any of them, and under the 1976 law it has the right to nominate only a minority. Under the 1951 law, the company's labor director must be approved by the employee representatives of the board, but under the 1952 and 1976 laws he is selected by a simple majority vote of the board.

At the center of the struggle over changes in employee board representation in West Germany have been the three issues that distinguish the present West German laws as outlined in the previous paragraph. Unions have proposed and management has opposed: 1. parity, that is, that worker representatives should be not only equal in number, but also equal in power to the owner representatives on the supervisory board, 2. an increased union role, whereby employee representatives would be selected through or at least nominated through the union institutions, and 3. a requirement that the director of labor on the management board must be approved by the employee representatives on the supervisory board.

In sponsoring the 1976 employee board representation legislation, the West German unions hoped to achieve these three objectives in all of industry. But the employers strongly resisted these changes and were successful in having the union proposal weakened to the point where the new legislation accomplishes none of them. The unions, of course, were disappointed. Heinz-Oscar Vetter, chief of the DGB, stated that the new law makes a joke of parity.[1] The struggle, however, did not end with the passage of the 1976 legislation. Achievement of the three goals in worker directorships remains an important part of the long-run legislative program of the West German labor movement.

West German companies report that employee board membership has not prevented management from functioning effectively, and indeed, has provided company management with a good avenue of communications with its employees. The West German managers with whom we spoke indicated that the employee representation system has contributed to a much better comprehension of management problems by the leaders of the employees, and in turn, by the employees themselves. It is the general opinion that the time spent by management in educating and dealing with employee board representatives has been time well spent.

During the sixties and early seventies, the West German industrial system with its high gross national product per person and relatively low inflation and unemployment rates became the envy of other countries, both in Europe and elsewhere. It was believed by many that much of the West German success could be attributed to the high degree of industrial peace and cooperation that prevailed in the country and that employee board membership was an important factor contributing to that peace and cooperation. As a result, in the early seventies, several other European countries passed legislation that required employee board representation. Although for more than twenty years employee board representation had been a purely West German phenomena, in the two-year period 1973-1974, four other European countries—Austria, Sweden, Denmark, and Norway—adopted employee board representation plans, and in the Netherlands legislation became effective that gave the Dutch works councils the right to nominate and veto candidates for company supervisory boards. Then in 1975, the European Commission published a revision of its proposed directive which would require adoption of employee board representation plans in all of the countries in the European Economic Community. The Commission also recommended in its proposed statute for a European company that all such companies be required to have employee board participation.

The expansion of employee representation plans to other countries in Europe did not continue after 1974. Since then, no other European country has adopted such plans except Ireland, where in 1977 legislation was enacted that entitles the employees of seven state-owned companies to elect one-third of the board members from candidates nominated by the unions.

The failure of employee board representation plans to continue to be adopted in other European countries has been a result of several factors. First, there has been a growing body of opinion that such plans have not been the basic cause of labor peace in West Germany and increasing doubt concerning their possible effectiveness in countries where the labor relations structure and ideology are quite different from that of West Germany.[2] Second, management organizations and conservative political groups have vigorously opposed employee board representation which they argue would erode the decision-making power of managements and the owners to the detriment of the whole community. Finally, strong opposition has developed from many labor leaders who perceive employee board representation as interfering with the development and maintenance of an effective labor movement.

No employee board representation plans have been adopted in Italy, Belgium, or Switzerland. In Italy and Belgium, they have been vigorously opposed by the left-wing labor unions on the basis of ideology. In Switzerland, a proposed plan was defeated in 1976 in a national referendum. In France, it is generally agreed that the present plan, which allows the works councils to send four observers to board meetings, is completely illusory; but the major French unions, like their Italian and Belgian counterparts, oppose the adoption of an effective employee board representation plan for ideological reasons.

In Great Britain, there was much debate of the issue before and after the publication of the Bullock report in January, 1977. In May, 1978, however, the Labor government issued a White Paper which placed the emphasis on the development of union joint representation councils (JRCs) rather than employee board representation. However, it did provide that after three or four years, if a JRC so desired and the majority of the employees so voted, the company would have to accept employee representatives on its supervisory board. There is no indication that the new Conservative government in Great Britain will support even the watered-down proposal of the former Labor government. Finally, the European Commission has not issued a directive that would force the member countries to adopt an employee representation plan. Now that the West Germans and Dutch have lost their dominance in the European Trade Union Confederation as a result of the expansion of that organization, there will be less pressure on the Commission to issue such a directive or to insist upon employee board representation as an integral part of the European company legislation.[3]

It may be of course, as W.W. Daniel states, that in the long run, the tide of employee board representation as an element of industrial democracy in Europe is irresistible, but as Daniel has said, it appears now that it "will not be realized quickly or easily."[4]

**Works Councils**

A works council is a plant committee (composed of employees, or employees and company representatives) with which the management must consult, and in some cases, reach agreement before taking action on certain matters that affect the workers. After World War II, works councils were established by legislation in a number of European countries: France (1945), Sweden (1946), the Netherlands (1950), West Germany (1952), and Italy (1953). Thus, West Germany, which had a pioneer role in enacting legislation involving workers on company boards, was not the first country to adopt works council legislation. However, over the years works councils have played a much more important role in West Germany than in any of the other countries. The number of employees covered by works councils, the number of employees serving as councillors, the scope of the issues considered by the works councils, and the power of the councils have been greater in West Germany than in any of the other countries in this study. In a study by Bluechen in 1966, 88% of the West German workers stated that the works council in their plant had secured important concessions from management and had been important to them individually in their relations with management.[5]

As indicated earlier, the West German labor movement has not been important at the plant level. While some of the West German unions, such as IG Metall, have made attempts to develop power at the local level, generally such development has not been significant. Under West German law, management is not required to deal with union representatives at the plant level, and in fact, has vigorously opposed any attempt on the part of the unions to force it to do so. On the other hand, the law does require West German management at the plant level to recognize and deal with a works council. As a result, the works council has become the body through which West German workers are represented at the local level. In the other European countries where works councils have been important, the unions have been weak at the local level. By comparison, in Great Britain and the United States where unions have had strong plant organizations, works councils have not developed.

Although works councils have received far less publicity than representation of workers on company boards in West Germany, the former have had more effect than the latter on West Germany employees and on the West German industrial relations system. The number of employees who participate as works councillors is much larger than the number who participate as board representatives, and the number of hours spent on council work is much greater than the number spent on board work. Many of the councillors now spend full time on council matters. Although it is true that the boards sometimes deal with issues that have a profound impact on the employees, the issues covered by the works councils are much more extensive in scope and of more immediate concern to the workers. Moreover, employee representatives are likely to be more knowledgeable about the issues discussed in works council meetings than about many of the items that come before the supervisory board. As a result, participation by employee representatives is more meaningful at the council level. Finally, on a number of issues the works council possesses parity of power with management. In other words, codetermination exists and management cannot take action unless the council agrees. Only in the coal, iron, and steel industries do employee board members have parity of power. In all other industries, they can be outvoted by owner representatives.

The 1972 amendments to the West German Works Constitution Act greatly increased the scope and power of the works council. The number of issues that management must discuss with the council was greatly enlarged, and many issues were moved from consultation to codetermination. On the other hand, the 1976 board representation legislation did not provide the employee representatives with parity of power. In light of these developments, it is expected that the future impact of the works councils will be even more important in comparison with employee board representation.

In the other five European countries in our study, the importance of the works councils varies from being practically non-existent in Great Britain to being very significant in the Netherlands. In Great Britain, there is no law requiring works councils, and although some companies did have them in the past, such organizations have been largely replaced by shop stewards councils which now represent British employees quite effectively at the local level. In France, although a 1945 law, as revised in 1966, required a plant with fifty or more employees to have a works council (comité d'entreprise), a government study in 1975 found that the committees had been set up in less than half of the plants. In Italy during the fifties, the national unions and the national industry association (Confindustria) agreed upon a plan to establish works councils (internal commissions) in each plant. In recent years, however, the commissions have been replaced by union factory councils (CDFs) which engage in local bargaining. In the Netherlands, since the revision of the law in 1971, works councils have been very important and a new law which became effective September 1, 1979, further increases the scope and power of the councils. Swedish works councils became operative in 1946 as a result of an agreement between the national union confederation (LO) and the national employers' association (SAF). In 1966 and again in 1975, the scope of the councils was enlarged. However, in 1976 the LO cancelled the agreement on works councils and opened up the whole matter for collective bargaining. It is expected that the bargaining will result in a continuation of the works council system, but its nature may be altered considerably.

Debate over the future role of works councils continues in the European countries where they have been operating. The debate concerning their future has centered around four topics: 1. the role of management, 2. the role of the union or unions, 3. the scope of issues that management must discuss with the council, and 4. the power of the council, that is, the authority to codetermine with management rather than simply to advise management.

In West Germany and in the Netherlands the works council is composed entirely of employees. However, in Sweden the works council is a joint body, consisting of an equal number of management and employee representatives.

The West German unions have no formal role in the nomination or election of members to the works councils. The employees in each plant draw up lists of candidates from among the employees, and then vote for them in secret elections. Non-union as well as union members can and do serve as councillors. However, a study in 1972 found that 78% of the councillors were union members,[6] and an earlier study found that 98% of the council chairmen were union members.[7]

In Sweden, the employee members of the works council are elected from the union ranks only. In addition, the chairman of the factory union committee is an ex-officio member of the works council. Since 95% of the blue-collar workers in Sweden are union members, very few workers are excluded from council participation. Nevertheless, it is significant that in Sweden the works councils exist within the union system.

In the Netherlands, the unions have the right to propose lists of candidates, but groups of non-union employees may also propose lists. As a result, non-union as well as union members may be elected to the Dutch works councils.

There appears to be no move at present by the West German unions to get formal control over the nomination and election of councillors. In Sweden, the works council system is now the subject of collective bargaining, but it is highly unlikely that the Swedish unions will give up control of the works council election process. In the Netherlands, the 1979 legislation did not change the unions' role in the nomination and election of councillors. Thus, in the three countries in our study where works councils are important, the formal role of the unions is likely to remain as it has been in the past—very weak in West Germany, very strong in Sweden, and somewhere in-between in the Netherlands.

West German works councils are not permitted to deal with certain matters, such as general wage increases and job evaluation schemes, which are reserved for collective bargaining between the union and the trade association. However, as previously indicated, the scope of works council matters has been very broad and was greatly expanded in the 1972 legislation. West German management has objected to this expansion, because it means that management can make fewer and fewer decisions without first consulting with the works council.

In Sweden, the scope of issues under the jurisdiction of the works council was expanded in 1966 and again in 1975. It is possible that the unions will attempt to further expand the scope in the collective bargaining that will replace the old system. Swedish management may be expected to oppose such expansion.

The 1979 Works Council Act in the Netherlands expanded the scope of the councils' work to include: hiring of temporary workers, setting up of new firms, entering into or withdrawing from cooperation with another firm, and seeking advice from outside experts. Dutch management opposed the expansion.

The strongest opposition by management to changes in existing works council laws in West Germany and the Netherlands has concerned the attempt to increase the power of the works councils by moving items from consultation to codetermination. Both the West German and the Dutch laws have provided that management must only consult with the works council on certain items, but must reach an agreement (codetermine) on certain other items. Under consultation, management loses the right unilaterally to make an immediate decision, but may retain the right to make the final decision. However, under codetermination, management loses not only the right to make the immediate decision, but also the right to make the final decision. Under West German law, if the management and works council cannot agree on a matter that is subject to codetermination, the issue may be referred to a conciliation committee on which a neutral party casts the tie-breaking vote. The decision of the conciliation committee is binding on both parties. Under Dutch law, if management and the union cannot reach agreement on a matter that must be codetermined, the issue may be referred to an industry council and, if necessary, to the Minister of Social Affairs for a final decision.

The 1972 amendments in West Germany greatly expanded the area of codetermination. Many items, which prior to that time were subject only to consultation, became subject to codetermination under the new law. As a result, the power of the works council was increased and by the same token, management's decision-making authority was eroded.

Under the 1971 works council law in the Netherlands, codetermination was limited to a small number of items: work rules, pensions, profit-sharing or savings schemes, working hours and holiday arrangements, and safety and health measures. Under the 1979 act, codetermination rights were expended to include: wage scales and remuneration schemes, hiring and dismissal policies, promotion policies, training, personnel rating systems, welfare services, and grievance procedures. Dutch management strongly opposed this loss of decision-making authority.

In Sweden the works councils, which are composed of an equal number of company and employee representatives, have been purely consultative and are likely to remain so. The unions have been more interested in increasing the power of the plant union representatives than in giving the works councils codetermination authority.

## Asset Formation and Employee Ownership

Asset formation accomplished through employee stock ownership, which could result in worker participation in company decision making, is an issue that has been hotly debated by management and labor in Western Europe in recent years. To date, however, no legislation incorporating the provisions of such a plan has been enacted.

As has been indicated in earlier chapters, in West Germany, France, and the Netherlands, laws have been passed that provide for bonus-savings plans or profit-sharing plans. Under the West German law, employees may save tax free up to 624 deutsche marks per year to which government adds a bonus of 30% to 64%, depending on the employee's marital status. Under the French law, companies are required to share profits with employees.

Under the Dutch law, employers, if they wish, may adopt either a bonus-savings plan or a profit-sharing plan for their employees. British companies also may provide savings or profit-sharing plans for their workers, and legislation has been suggested to make such plans more attractive in the tax realm. However, none of the plans contemplates participation by the employees in corporate decision making through stock ownership. In fact, most of the plans do not involve stock ownership, and in the West German plan, which does permit employees to invest their savings in company stocks or bonds, only about 1% have opted to do so.

The French and Italian communist and socialist unions are opposed on the basis of ideology not only to the existing asset formation schemes, but also to any other type of asset formation plan. Both French and Italian labor leaders have condemned such plans as being contrary to the immediate interests of the employees and to the long-run goals of their union organizations.[8] On the other hand, although British, Dutch, West German, and Swedish unions are critical of current plans, they do support a system of asset formation that would: 1. secure its funds through profit sharing rather than worker savings, 2. invest the funds in company stock, and 3. place control of the stock in the unions rather than in the individual workers. The British, Dutch, West German, and Swedish unions see in asset formation, based on these three principles, a device whereby employees through their unions might attain a role, and perhaps eventually a controlling role, in company decision making.

During the 1970s the West German, Swedish, and Dutch union have sponsored legislation in their countries based on the three principles set forth in the previous paragraph. In 1974, the West German unions sponsored a plan that would have required companies to contribute up to 10% of their profits to the employees in the form of stock, which although held individually by the employees, would have been controlled jointly by the union and the company.

In 1973, the Swedish Confederation of Trade Unions published its first version of a proposed asset formation plan, which has become known as the Meidner plan after its author who is an economist for the LO. The most recent version of the Meidner plan provides that Swedish companies would pay 20% of net profits in the form of shares into a workers' fund. Individual employees would have the right to vote 20% of the shares, but a coalition of unions in the area would have the right to vote the other 80%.

In 1964 in the Netherlands, the union federations published a compulsory profit-sharing plan (VAD) which would have established a national fund financed by "excess profits" and managed entirely by union representatives. In 1977, the union proposal was changed to provide that 23% of company profits be used to buy shares, one half of which would go to the workers and one-half of which would be paid to the national pension fund.

In each of the three countries, West Germany, Sweden, and the Netherlands, the asset plans proposed by the unions have met with severe criticism and vigorous opposition from management. As a result, none of the plans has been adopted. In West Germany, the government has moved instead to strengthen the workers' premium savings plan. In Sweden, industry has proposed as an alternative a voluntary profit-sharing and savings plan for individual employees. In the Netherlands, the new government in 1978 proposed a watered-down bill which contains both individual and collective features. Under the new proposal, a 12% tax on company "super profits" would be used to give extra benefits to employees, and an additional 12% tax would be paid into a special fund for pensions to be administered by twelve members nominated by the unions and eight members nominated by the government.

## Dismissals

One of the most significant and dramatic changes in labor relations in Europe in the last ten years has been in the area of dismissal of employees—dismissal of individual employees for alleged misconduct, and dismissal of groups of employees for economic reasons, that is, redundancy.

There was a time when a European employer possessed the unqualified right to discharge an employee for alleged misconduct or to terminate a group of employees that he claimed was redundant. The employer did not have to: consult with the representatives of the employee, prove that the dismissal was reasonable or just, give the employee advance notice, or compensate the employee for the loss of the job. Just as the employee had the right to terminate the employment contract by quitting, the employer had the right to terminate it by dismissing the employee.

However, during the last ten years, in every one of the six European nations that we have studied, legislation has been enacted that has severely curtailed management's rights in this area. The new legislation has been based on the concept of the employee's property right in the job, the notion that since an employee works on a job, he invests his "assets" in it, and that these assets should not be destroyed by the employer unless he has good cause and is willing to compensate the employee for the loss.[9]

In the earlier chapters, we have discussed the current job protection program in effect in each of the six European countries. Although the elements of the legislation differ from country to country, the trend is toward a program that requires management to:

1. demonstrate reasonable cause for the dismissal,
2. specify such causes in writing to the employee,
3. consult with the representatives of the employee before dismissal,

4. provide the employee with a period of notification prior to dismissal,
5. keep the employee at work until the court determines if dismissal is justified,
6. compensate the dismissed employee for the loss of his property rights in the job,
7. reinstate the employee, if he has been dismissed and the court determines the dismissal was not for just cause.

Not all of these seven components are in effect in all six countries. Likewise, in the countries where a particular item is in effect, the requirements under it may vary. For example, prior notification is required in all six countries, but the length of notification varies considerably. Notification reaches a maximum of six months under certain conditions in Sweden and the Netherlands; whereas it is limited to a maximum of twelve weeks in Great Britain. Likewise, the amount of compensation varies but can be as high as 3,000 pounds in Great Britain and forty-eight months of pay in Sweden. In all six countries, management is required to consult with representatives of the employees before action is taken, but in most of the countries, after consultation, management is free to dismiss the employee or employees prior to a court decision on the merits of the case. However, in France, redundancy dismissals may not occur without the approval of the regional department of labor, and in West Germany, the court may order the company to continue to employ the worker or workers until the court decides whether dismissal is reasonable.

Reinstatement of employees who have been found to have been unjustly discharged is still not required in most European countries. Instead, it is contended that compensation for loss of a job is a more desirable and practical solution. However, in at least two of the six countries, reinstatement is now provided in the legislation. The current Italian legislation requires that an employee who has been unjustly discharged must be reinstated as well as be paid damages of at least five months' pay. Effective April 1, 1978, British labor tribunals were given the power to order employers to reinstate employees who had been unfairly discharged. (Prior to that date, the British tribunals could recommend reinstatement but could not order it.)

There is reason to believe that the move to curtail management's rights to dismiss employees and to recognize and protect the property right of employees in their jobs will be continued in the 1980s. Referring to possible developments in the future in this area in Great Britain, Rubenstein has written that while Britain already has moved far in this direction, it is virtually a certainty that the 1980s will see further major improvements.[10]

Employee dismissal is not only an area where advances through national legislation are being made, but also an area where the EEC has been active and will probably continue to be active. In 1975, the European Council adopted a directive (effective in February, 1977) which requires that no company in the European Economic Community may make redundant ten or more employees without proper consultation with workers' representatives and public authorities. In 1976, the European Commission sent to the Concil a preliminary draft on "Protection of Workers in the Event of Individual Dismissals." A final draft on this aspect of job security is expected to come before the Council in the near future. The thrust of EEC action is to bring about harmonization of dismissal policies among all the countries in the European Economic Community.

The effect of the new dismissal legislation is that employees have gained protection, and management has lost authority in a very important area of labor relations. In a case where the company desires to discharge an employee because of inefficiency, poor workmanship, bad conduct, or insubordination, management must now be prepared to prove its case before a labor tribunal or a court. Thus, the worker is given protection against arbitrary or capricious action by management. On the other hand, many European managers are of the opinion that because of the political power of the unions in many of the countries, the deck is stacked against management, and disciplinary discharges are upheld only in those cases where the employee clearly has been guilty of the most serious type of offense. The result, many managers contend, has been a severe decrease in plant discipline which has had serious effects on quality, production, and costs.

As we have stated earlier, in most European countries, management may still discharge an employee and refuse to reinstate him, even though the tribunal or court finds that the discharge was not for just cause. However, management may conclude that the cost of the procedure plus the cost of compensation to the employee is too high to risk. As a result, some employees who management believes should be discharged are permitted to continue to work.

Under the new legislation, management is still free to dismiss redundant employees. However, employees are provided considerable protection and must be given compensation for the loss of their "job assets." As a result, management finds that it now has much less flexibility to adjust to a decrease in demand for its product. At the very time when it needs to cut costs most, management may either have to continue to employ workers whom it does not need or give them sizeable termination payments. As a result, labor has become much less a variable and much more a fixed cost.

## Absenteeism

Absenteeism among workers in Western Europe is very high compared with absenteeism in the United States or Japan. A study by the Swedish employers' association showed that in 1973 sickness absenteeism among industrial workers in Europe ranged from a high of 10% in Sweden to a low of 5% in the United Kingdon, compared with only 4% in the United States and 3% in Japan (see table A-13 in the statistical appendix). It is believed that since 1973 the rate has continued to climb. In each of the European countries in this study, the production loss resulting from absenteeism was many times the loss resulting from strikes. (Compare table A-12 in the statistical appendix with table A-13.) For example, in 1976 in Great Britain, workers lost 350 million man days as a result of "certified sickness" absences compared with 6 million man days as a result of strike action. In France, the Heilbronner report stated that in 1975 time lost as a result of absenteeism was almost one hundred times that lost as a result of strikes.

The high rate of absenteeism is believed to be primarily a result of the very liberal sick-pay plans in effect in most of the European countries. The basic provisions of the sick-pay laws in 1974 in the six countries are shown in table 9-1.

In France and Italy, the sick pay as required by law is heavily supplemented by collective agreements. Under the Italian agreements, it is almost universal practice to pay 100% of earnings for the first three days of absence because of sickness. Moreover, under many Italian agreements, the 100% is extended for a much longer period than the three days. In a survey of twenty Italian companies in 1978, it was found that all twenty had agreed to supplementary sick pay, which most commonly provided employees with

**Table 9-1**
**Sick Pay Provisions**

| Country | Duration of Benefits | Amount of Benefits |
| --- | --- | --- |
| Great Britain | Flat rate benefit limited to 312 days, if less than 156 contributions have been paid; otherwise replaced by invalidity benefit after 168 days entitlement. Earnings-related supplement limited to 156 days. | Flat rate of £ 8.60 per week plus earnings-related benefit at 33-1/3% of earnings between £ 10 and £ 30, and 15% of earnings between £ 30 and £ 42, plus family supplements. |
| France | 12 months over a three-year period. | 50% of earnings, plus family supplements. |
| Italy | 6 months per year. | 50% of earnings, 66 2/3% after 21 days. |
| The Netherlands | 12 months. | 80% of earnings. |
| West Germany | 78 weeks over a three-year period. | 100% of earnings for first 6 weeks, thereafter 80%, plus family supplements. |
| Sweden | Unlimited. | 90% of earnings. |

full pay for the first several months of absence resulting from illness.[11] In France, the mensualization agreements not only provide monthly pay for blue-collar workers, but also extend to them the supplementary sick-pay benefits that formerly were available only to white-collar workers. As a result, the total percentage of earnings received by French workers who are absent because of illness is much higher than the legislative requirement, as set forth in table 9-1.

Waiting periods for benefits under the various basic and supplementary plans either do not exist or are very short. For example, under the West German plan, there is no waiting period, and under the British plan, the waiting period is only three days.

As the sick-pay plans have become more and more liberal, the worker has had less and less economic incentive to work rather than stay home. In Sweden, where sick pay is now 90% of normal pay, one industrialist has stated that, "every worker has to make the decision whether to go to work or not at very little economic cost. One cost of this social reform is absenteeism."[12]

The plans do provide penalties for workers who fake illness, but enforcement has been lax and difficult. Statements from doctors certifying that the employees have been ill seem to be easy to obtain and very difficult not to accept. In Italy, for example, the 1970 labor law prohibits companies from using their own doctors to check alleged employee illnesses. However, in 1978 the Supreme Court in France did rule that before making supplementary sick payments, a company could insist on an examination by a doctor or doctors not employed by the social security system. The Ministry of Labor ruled later, however, that such doctors had to be approved by the company's works council.

It is generally recognized that there is widespread abuse and excessive absenteeism under the plans. The Heilbronner report in France stated that much of the absenteeism was a result of workers taking advantage of the lax controls. It was found, for example, that 40% of the employees who had reported too ill to come to work were not at home when social security inspectors called. In Italy in January, 1979, following a three-hour mid-week stoppage at the Alfa Sud plant in Naples, half of the employees reported sick for the remainder of the week and received sick pay by providing the company with medical certificates.[13]

The cost of this excessive absenteeism is not only the money that is paid out to the absentee workers, but also the cost of hiring, training, and maintaining replacement workers. A Swedish executive has pointed out that in one of his company's 8,000 employee facilities which has an absentee rate of 15%, management has had to take on 1,200 additional employees. "This," he writes, "is inefficient, inflationary and makes planning and managing production difficult. It is also 'lumpy.' Having enough people to cover the peaks means that many are underemployed on days when absenteeism is low."[14]

**Rights and Benefits for Women Employees**

During the last ten years, major changes have been made in the rights and benefits of women employees in all six of the European countries in this study. The governments have moved to provide greater protection and benefits to women by enacting three types of legislation: maternity rights and benefits laws, equal pay laws, and equal opportunity laws.

All six countries now have legislation that provides that a woman employee may not be dismissed because of pregnancy and also must be reemployed without loss of acquired job rights following childbirth. In addition, the legislation provides that for a certain number of weeks before childbirth and a certain number of weeks after childbirth, the woman worker must be given time off with pay. The number of weeks of maternity leave varies from six weeks in Great Britain to nine months in Sweden, and pay varies from 80% in Italy to 100% in the Netherlands and West Germany (see table 9-2).

In addition to paid maternity leave prior to and immediately following confinement, several of the acts provide for leave to take care of the child. The French 1975 law requires that an employer grant an employee an unpaid leave of up to one year after giving birth, with reemployment and acquired job rights guaranteed. Moreover, the French 1977 Parental Leave Act permits either parent to stop work at any time for two years without pay to care for children, with reemployment and acquired job rights guaranteed. Italian law provides for maternity leave at 30% pay for up to six months during a child's first year, plus another six months when a child under three years old is sick. Reemployment and acquired job rights are guaranteed in both situations.

Since 1974, the Swedish law has permitted a father as well as a mother to take time off with pay to care for a young child. As revised in 1976, a total of nine months' parental leave with pay may be taken, eight months at 90% of pay, and one month at about $6 per day. (The nine months include maternity leave prior to childbirth, which, of course, must be taken by the mother.) The percentage of eligible fathers participating in the program has risen rapidly as follows:

| | |
|---|---|
| 1974 | 2.4% |
| 1975 | 5.2% |
| 1976 | 7.5% |
| 1977 | over 10.0%[5] |

The five countries that are part of the European Economic Comunity (Sweden is not a member of the EEC) have been under pressure from the

**Table 9-2**
**Maternity Protection and Benefits Acts in Six Western European Countries**

| Country | Legislation | Protection against Dismissal Resulting from Pregnancy | Reemployment and Protection of Acquired Job Rights | Length of Paid Leave | Pay during Leave as % of Prior Pay |
|---|---|---|---|---|---|
| Great Britain | 1975 Employment Protection Act (as amended) | Yes | Yes, provided worker returns within 29 weeks after child birth | 6 weeks | 90% including social security |
| The Netherlands | Sickness Benefit Act and 1976 Protection Against Discrimination Act | Yes | Yes | 12 weeks | 100% |
| West Germany | 1972 Act for Protection for Women in Employment | Yes | Yes | 14 weeks | 100% |
| France | 1975 Maternity Protection Act (amended July 1978); 1977 Parental Leave Act | Yes | Yes | 16 weeks | 90% |
| Italy | 1971 Act for Protection of Working Mothers | Yes | Yes, job must be held for one year | 20 weeks | 80% |
| Sweden | 1976 Parental Benefits Act | Yes | Yes | 9 months | 90% for first 8 months and about $6/day for ninth month |

EEC to enact and make effective equal pay legislation. The treaty of Rome which established the EEC in 1957 provides in paragraph 119 that, "Each member state shall . . . ensure and subsequently maintain the application of the principle of equal remuneration for equal work as between men and women workers."

In 1975, the European Commission issued a directive to the member countries ordering them to implement the equal pay provisions of paragraph 119, and in 1976 the European Court of Justice issued its first decision on this issue. In 1968, Miss Gabrielle Defrenne had brought a suit against Sabena Airlines claiming that she had been paid less than male workers for the same type of work. Her plea was rejected by the Belgian labor tribunal and on appeal by the Belgian labor court and council of state. She then appealed to the European Court. The European Court ruled that "the principle of equal pay for women as set forth in Article 119 is enforceable . . ."

In West Germany, equal pay has been the law since 1959 when a federal court ruled that the constitution required the same pay for men and women doing the same work. In 1975, new laws requiring equal pay became effective in Great Britain and the Netherlands. (The British law had been passed in 1970 but was not fully effective until 1975.) In Italy, an act implementing the constitutional provision for equal pay became effective in 1977.

Despite such constitutional provisions, legal decisions, and legislative enactments, the European Commission found in late 1978 that its directive ordering equal pay under paragraph 119 of the treaty of Rome "has still not been completely implemented in any of the Member States of the Community." The Commission proposed a European-level meeting of employer and employee organizations to discuss the elimination of indirect discrimination through job classification systems and initiation of infringement proceedings against certain member states before the Court of Justice.[16]

In Sweden, which is not covered by the Commission directive, the move toward equal pay has resulted largely from collective bargaining aided also by a Council on Equality (1972) and later a Parliamentary Equality Committee (1976). In 1979, a new law requiring equal pay was passed, but it was a watered-down version of the original proposal and its effectiveness is much in doubt.

Equal opportunity legislation generally has been more recent than equal pay legislation. For example, equal opportunity legislation in Great Britain was not passed until 1975, five years after the equal pay legislation. The 1975 British Sex Discrimination Act provides that it is unlawful for an employer to discriminate against women in hiring or dismissal or "in the way he affords her access to opportunities for promotion, transfer or training or to any other benefits, facilities or services". In West Germany, the 1972 Works Council Act provides that there shall be no discrimination because of sex, and in Italy the 1977 Anti-Discrimination Act prohibits discrimination because of sex with respect to hiring, training, promotion, and career development.

In December, 1975, the European Council issued an equal opportunity directive which became effective for all EEC countries on July 1, 1978. Article 3 of the directive requires that: "There shall be no discrimination whatsoever between men and women on grounds of sex in the conditions, including selection criteria, for access to all jobs or posts, whatever the sector or branch of activity, at all levels of the professional hierarchy." It is still too soon to determine how effective the directive will be in promoting equality of opportunity for women employees.

In Sweden, the Equal Treatment in Working Life Act, which was enacted in 1979 and became effective January 1, 1980, provides for equal treatment for women in hiring, promotion, and training. However, as stated earlier, the new law is a watered-down version of the original proposal and its effectiveness in bringing about equal pay and equal opportunities is much in doubt.

In November, 1978, the European Council adopted a directive that requires equalization of social security benefits for men and women. The directive applies to retirement, sickness, invalidity, industrial injury, and unemployment benefits. The directive is not immediately effective, but instead, allows the member nations until 1985 to bring their systems into compliance with all its provisions.

In summary, during the last ten years, major progress has been recorded in providing Western European women with maternity rights and benefits. Sweden has surpassed all of the other nations in this respect. Within the countries in the European Community, there are considerable differences in the rights and benefits. This appears to be an area that will lend itself to harmonization by directives of the European Council.

Much progress has been made also in the areas of equal pay and equal opportunities. However, in these areas, especially in the area of equal opportunities, much still remains to be done to implement the national legislation and the directives of the European Commission. A 1978 directive of the European Commission will attempt to bring about equality in social security benefits by 1985.

## Notes

1. Craig R. Whitney, "Labor's Voice Heard in West Germany," *New York Times,* January 25, 1976.

2. P. Brannen, et al., *Worker Directors* (London: Hutchinson of London, 1976), p. 229.

3. Emil Joseph Kirchner, *Trade Unions as a Pressure Group in the European Community* (England: Saxon House, 1977), p. 47.

4. W.W. Daniel, "Industrial Democracy," in *Comparative Industrial Relations in Europe,* by Derek Torrington (London: Associated Business Programs, Ltd., 1978), p. 49.

5. Ivor L. Roberts, "The Works Constitution Acts and Industrial Relations in West Germany, Implications for the United Kingdom." *British Journal of Industrial Relations* 11 (1973): 354.

6. Solomon Barkin, *Worker Militancy and Its Consequences* (New York: Praeger Publishers, 1975), p. 251.

7. Roberts, "Works Constitution Acts," p. 352.

8. Norris Willatt, *Multi-National Unions* (London: Financial Times, Ltd., 1974), p. 40.

9. Michael Rubenstein, "Dismissals and the Law," in *Comparative Industrial Relations in Europe,* by Derek Torrington (London: Associated Business Programs, Ltd., 1978), p. 147.

10. Ibid., p. 149.

11. *European Industrial Relations Review,* No. 55, July-August, 1978, p. 14.

12. Pehr G. Gyllenhammer, *People at Work,* (Reading, Ma.: Addison-Wesley, 1977), p. 148.

13. *European Industrial Relations Review,* No. 63, April 1979, p. 9.

14. Gyllenhammer, *People at Work,* p. 148.

15. "Swedish Promotion Blitz Tries to Lure Dads into the Nursery," *International Herald Tribune,* April 21, 1978, p. 6.

16. *European Industrial Relations Review,* No. 58, November 1978, pp. 5-6.

# Statistical Appendix

**Table A-1**
**Population**
*(at midyear in millions)*

|  | 1970 | 1978 | % Growth 1970-1978 | % Growth 1970-1978 |
|---|---|---|---|---|
| Great Britain | 55.42 | 55.82 | 0.40 | 0.72 |
| France | 50.77 | 53.28 | 2.51 | 4.94 |
| Italy | 53.66 | 56.70 | 3.04 | 5.67 |
| The Netherlands | 13.03 | 13.94 | 0.91 | 6.98 |
| West Germany | 60.71 | 61.31 | 0.60 | 0.99 |
| Sweden | 8.04 | 8.28 | 0.24 | 2.99 |
| United States | 204.88 | 218.55 | 13.67 | 6.67 |

Source: United Nations: *Monthly Bulletin of Statistics*, June, 1979.

**Table A-2**
**Gross National Product**

|  | 1976 (in U.S.) Millions of Dollars) | 1976 Per Capita (in U.S. Dollars) | Annual Real Per Capita % Growth 1970-1976[a] |
|---|---|---|---|
| Great Britain | 233,550 | 4,180 | 1.7 |
| France | 355,960 | 6,730 | 3.3 |
| Italy | 180,650 | 3,220 | 2.0 |
| The Netherlands | 91,610 | 6,650 | 2.6 |
| West Germany | 461,810 | 7,510 | 2.0 |
| Sweden | 74,220 | 9,030 | 2.1 |
| United States | 1,694,900 | 7,880 | 1.7 |

Source: *World Bank Atlas,* 1978.
[a]Adjusted for inflation and exchange rates.

**Table A-3**
**Consumer Price Index**
*(all items)*

|  | 1970[a] | 1971 | 1972 | 1973 | 1974 | 1975 | 1976 | 1977 | 1978 |
|---|---|---|---|---|---|---|---|---|---|
| Great Britain | 100 | 109 | 117 | 128 | 148 | 184 | 215 | 249 | 270 |
| France | 100 | 106 | 112 | 120 | 137 | 153 | 167 | 183 | 200 |
| Italy | 100 | 105 | 111 | 123 | 146 | 171 | 200 | 237 | 265 |
| The Netherlands | 100 | 108 | 116 | 125 | 137 | 151 | 165 | 176 | 183 |
| West Germany | 100 | 105 | 111 | 119 | 127 | 135 | 141 | 146 | 150 |
| Sweden | 100 | 107 | 114 | 122 | 134 | 147 | 162 | 180 | 198 |
| United States | 100 | 104 | 108 | 114 | 127 | 139 | 147 | 156 | 168 |

Source: International Labor Office
[a]1970 = 100

**Table A-4**
**Unemployment Rates**
*(adjusted to U.S. concepts)*

| | 1970 | 1971 | 1972 | 1973 | 1974 | 1975 | 1976 | 1977 | 1978 | Nine-Year Average |
|---|---|---|---|---|---|---|---|---|---|---|
| Great Britain | 3.1 | 3.7 | 4.1 | 2.9 | 2.9 | 4.6 | 5.5 | 6.2 | 6.1 | 4.3% |
| France | 2.6 | 2.8 | 2.9 | 2.7 | 3.0 | 4.3 | 4.7 | 5.0 | 5.4 | 3.7 |
| Italy | 3.1 | 3.1 | 3.6 | 3.4 | 2.8 | 3.2 | 3.6 | 3.4 | 3.5 | 3.3 |
| West Germany | 0.8 | 0.8 | 0.8 | 0.8 | 1.7 | 3.6 | 3.6 | 3.6 | 3.4 | 2.1 |
| Sweden | 1.5 | 2.6 | 2.7 | 2.5 | 2.0 | 1.6 | 1.6 | 1.8 | 2.2 | 2.1 |
| United States | 4.9 | 5.9 | 5.6 | 4.9 | 5.6 | 8.5 | 7.7 | 7.0 | 6.0 | 6.2 |

Source: U.S. Bureau of Labor Statistics

Note: Data for The Netherlands not available.

**Table A-5**

**Average Hourly Compensation for Production Workers in Manufacturing**
*(in U.S. dollars)*

| | 1970 | 1976 | 1977 | 1978 | % Increase 1970-1978 | % Increase in Local Purchasing Power[a] |
|---|---|---|---|---|---|---|
| Great Britain | $1.63 | $3.34 | $ 3.56 | $ 4.58 | 180 | 27 |
| France | 2.05 | 5.58 | 6.23 | 7.69 | 275 | 53 |
| Italy | 1.86 | 5.07 | 5.66 | 6.71 | 261 | 66 |
| The Netherlands | 2.46 | 8.04 | 9.37 | 11.44 | 365 | 52 |
| West Germany | 2.30 | 6.70 | 7.97 | 9.90 | 330 | 58 |
| Sweden | 3.33 | 9.39 | 10.23 | 11.43 | 243 | 51 |
| United States | 4.91 | 7.97 | 8.68 | 9.43 | 92 | 14 |

Source: U.S. Bureau of Labor Statistics and Citibank Estimates

Note: Compensation includes all payments made by employers directly to their employees, before deductions of any kind, plus employer contributions to legally required insurance programs and contractual and other private welfare plans for the benefit of employees.

[a]In real terms in local currency

**Table A-6**
**Output**
*(annual percentage change in output in manufacturing)*

| | 1976 | 1977 | 1978 | 1960-1978 | 1970-1978 |
|---|---|---|---|---|---|
| Great Britain | 1.4 | 1.4 | 0.8 | 2.3 | 0.7 |
| France | 7.5 | 3.5 | 2.5 | 5.7 | 4.4 |
| Italy | 12.6 | 2.2 | 1.7 | 6.2 | 4.1 |
| The Netherlands | 5.4 | 0.9 | N/A | 5.4[a] | 2.3[a] |
| West Germany | 6.8 | 2.9 | 1.7 | 4.6 | 2.5 |
| Sweden | − 1.2 | − 4.8 | − 1.3 | 3.9 | 1.3 |
| United States | 9.5 | 7.3 | 4.8 | 3.8 | 2.6 |

Source: U.S. Bureau of Labor Statistics.

[a]Data relate to period ending 1977.

**Table A-7**
**Productivity**
*(annual percentage change in output per hour in manufacturing)*

|                 | 1976 | 1977  | 1978 | 1960-1978         | 1970-1978         |
|-----------------|------|-------|------|-------------------|-------------------|
| Great Britain   | 3.0  | -1.0  | 1.6  | 3.2               | 1.8               |
| France          | 8.5  | 5.0   | 4.9  | 5.6               | 5.0               |
| Italy           | 8.5  | 1.1   | 2.9  | 6.2               | 4.6               |
| The Netherlands | 9.9  | 3.5   | N/A  | 7.4[a]            | 6.4[a]            |
| West Germany    | 5.9  | 5.4   | 3.7  | 5.5               | 5.4               |
| Sweden          | 0.7  | -0.6  | 5.5  | 5.6               | 2.9               |
| United States   | 4.4  | 3.3   | 1.1  | 2.6               | 2.4               |

Source: U.S. Bureau of Labor Statistics.
[a]Data relate to period ending 1977.

**Table A-8**
**Unit Labor Costs in Local Currencies**
*(annual percentage change in manufacturing)*

|                 | 1976 | 1977  | 1978 | 1960-1978         | 1970-1978         |
|-----------------|------|-------|------|-------------------|-------------------|
| Great Britain   | 14.7 | 11.3  | 15.1 | 7.9               | 15.8              |
| France          | 5.5  | 9.5   | 7.7  | 5.4               | 10.2              |
| Italy           | 10.4 | 17.5  | 10.6 | 8.7               | 16.3              |
| The Netherlands | 1.9  | 4.5   | N/A  | 5.7[a]            | 8.3[a]            |
| West Germany    | 1.3  | 4.1   | 3.4  | 4.7               | 5.9               |
| Sweden          | 18.6 | 12.4  | 7.1  | 5.8               | 12.0              |
| United States   | 3.8  | 5.3   | 7.7  | 3.6               | 6.1               |

Source: U.S. Bureau of Labor Statistics.
[a]Data relate to period ending 1977.

**Table A-9**
**Unit Labor Costs in U.S. Dollars**
*(annual percentage change in manufacturing)*

|                 | 1976  | 1977  | 1978 | 1960-1978         | 1970-1978         |
|-----------------|-------|-------|------|-------------------|-------------------|
| Great Britain   | -6.8  | 7.6   | 26.5 | 5.4               | 10.8              |
| France          | -5.4  | 6.3   | 17.6 | 5.7               | 12.6              |
| Italy           | -13.3 | 10.5  | 15.1 | 7.2               | 10.4              |
| The Netherlands | -2.7  | 12.6  | N/A  | 8.3[a]            | 14.8[a]           |
| West Germany    | -1.2  | 12.8  | 19.7 | 8.8               | 13.5              |
| Sweden          | 12.8  | 9.6   | 6.0  | 7.0               | 14.2              |
| United States   | 3.8   | 5.3   | 7.7  | 3.6               | 6.1               |

Source: U.S. Bureau of Labor Statistics.
[a]Data relate to period ending 1977.

**Table A-10**
**Unemployment Benefit Systems: 1976**

| Country | Benefits as % of Average Earnings | | | Waiting Period (days) | Maximum Duration (weeks) | % of Labor Force Covered |
|---|---|---|---|---|---|---|
| | Single Worker | Married Worker and Two Children | | | | |
| | | Unemployment Benefits | Unemployment Benefits and Family Allowances | | | |
| United States[a] | 50 | 50 | 50 | 7 | 65 | 82 |
| France | | | | | | |
| Regular system | | | | 0 | 52-104[f] | 60 |
| First three months | 56 | 63 | 69-77 | | | |
| Subsequent months | 50 | 57 | 63-71 | | | |
| Supplementary benefits system[b] | 90 | 90 | 96-104 | | | |
| West Germany | 60 | 60 | 66 | 0 | 52 | 77 |
| Great Britain | | | | | | |
| First six months[c] | 38 | 60 | 63 | 3 | 52 | 80 |
| Next six months[c] | 19 | 41 | 44 | | | |
| Italy | | | | | | |
| Flat-rate benefits | 9 | 22 | 22 | 7 | 26 | 51 |
| Earnings-related scheme[d] | 67 | 80 | 80 | 7 | 26 | 51 |
| Sweden[e] | 62-72 | 62-72 | 67-79 | 5 | 60-90[f] | 100 |

Source: U.S. Bureau of Labor Statistics.

[a]System varies with states. Figures are representative of most states.

[b]For workers under age 60 laid off permanently.

[c]Public assistance payments may add substantially more.

[d]Industrial worker at same company for 3 months.

[e]Trade-union systems. Amounts vary with union.

[f]Duration increases with age.

**Table A-11**
**Estimated Union Membership**

|                  | Membership (in millions) | Percentage of Labor Force |
|------------------|--------------------------|---------------------------|
| Great Britain    | 11.9                     | 50                        |
| France           | 3.8                      | 23                        |
| Italy            | 4.3                      | 34                        |
| The Netherlands  | 1.4                      | 40                        |
| West Germany     | 8.6                      | 38                        |
| Sweden           | 2.9                      | 83                        |
| United States    | 20.2                     | 20                        |

Sources: The U.S. figures are from the U.S. Bureau of Labor Statistics. The other figures are from various sources.

**Table A-12**
**Days Lost through Industrial Disputes**
*(per 1,000 employees in non-agricultural industries)*

| | 1967 | 1968 | 1969 | 1970 | 1971 | 1972 | 1973 | 1974 | 1975 | 1976 | Ten-Year Average | Average Days Lost per Employee per Year | Percentage of Estimated Working Time[b] |
|---|---|---|---|---|---|---|---|---|---|---|---|---|---|
| Great Britain | 122 | 207 | 302 | 488 | 625 | 1,102 | 324 | 666 | 269 | 148 | 425.3 | .43 | 0.185 |
| France | 295 | 29 | 150 | 114 | 282 | 237 | 241 | 204 | 237 | 307 | 209.6 | .21 | 0.091 |
| Italy | 683 | 763 | 3,186 | 1,560 | 924 | 1,347 | 1,723 | 1,285 | 1,649 | 1,575 | 1,469.5 | 1.47 | 0.639 |
| The Netherlands | 2 | 4 | 6 | 70 | 26 | 36 | 154 | 2 | a | 4 | 30.4 | .03 | 0.013 |
| West Germany | 19 | 1 | 12 | 4 | 207 | 3 | 26 | 49 | 3 | 26 | 35.0 | .04 | 0.015 |
| Sweden | a | a | 35 | 48 | 250 | 3 | 3 | 16 | 12 | 9 | 37.6 | .04 | 0.016 |
| United States | 649 | 737 | 626 | 956 | 681 | 374 | 373 | 629 | 415 | 485 | 592.5 | .59 | 0.258 |

Source: U.S. Bureau of Labor Statistics (from data gathered from the ILO and national statistical publications).

[a]Less than one day lost per 1,000 employees
[b]Assumes 230 work days per year

**Table A-13**

**Sickness-Absenteeism—Industrial Workers, 1973**

%

| | |
|---|---|
| 10 | |
| 8 | |
| 6 | |
| 4 | |
| 2 | |

Japan
United States
Great Britain
Belgium
West Germany
France
The Netherlands
Italy
Sweden

Source: From a study by the Swedish Employers' Association (SAF). Reprinted by permission of the Swedish Employers' Association.

# Index

# Index

ACAC. *See* Advisory Conciliation and Arbitration Committee

AEW. *See* Amalgamated Electrical Workers' Union

AFL-CIO, 296, 300, 303, 306, 340, 342- 343, 344

AIB. *See* American Institute of Banking

APEX. *See* Association of Professional, Executive, Clerical, and Computer Staff

APO. *See* Labor Placement Law

ASAP (Italy), 90, 91

ASTMS. *See* Association of Scientific, Technical, and Managerial Staffs Union

ATLAS (Air France, Alitalia, Lufthansa, and Sabena), 361, 363

AUEW. *See* Amalgamated Union of Engineering Workers

Ability-to-pay wage policy, 253

Absenteeism, 388-390, 406; France, 56-57, 389; Great Britain, 17-18, 389; Italy, 101-102; Japan, 389; Netherlands, 128; Sweden, 250-251, 389; U.S. 302, 389; West Germany, 185

Act for the Protection of Women (West Germany, 1972), 184

Act for the Protection of Working Mothers (Italy, 1971), 99-100

Act on Codetermination at Work (Sweden, 1976), 236, 239-240, 242, 243, 247, 252

Act on the Right of Association and Collective Bargaining (Sweden, 1936), 236, 239

Adenauer, Konrad, 177

Advisory Conciliation and Arbitration Committee (Great Britain), 32

Advisory Conciliation and Arbitration Service (Great Britain), 6-8, 11, 12-13, 15, 17

Advisory Council on Equality between Men and Women (Sweden), 251

*Aftonbladet* (Sweden), 238, 260

"Agency shop," 175-176

Agnelli, Giovanni, 91

Akzo, 134

Albeda, Willem, 135

Albrecht, M., 122

Alfa Romeo, 97, 104

Alfa Sud, 390

Amalgamated Electrical Workers' Union (U.S.), 373-374

Amalgamated Union of Engineering Workers (Great Britain), 23, 35-44

American Cyanamid, 336

American Federation of Teachers, 306

American Food Products Corporation, 157

American Institute of Banking, 307, 309

Amersfoort Division. *See* Hobbema & Van Rijn, N.V.

Anti-Discrimination Act (Italy, 1977), 99, 394

Anti-strike funds, 239

Arbitration. *See* Conciliation, mediation, and arbitration

Armed forces, unionization of, 121

"Articulated bargaining," 91, 92, 93

Association of Professional, Executive, Clerical, and Computer Staff (Great Britain), 35, 36, 37, 42, 44

Association of Scientific, Technical, and Managerial Staffs Union (Great Britain), 24-44

Austria, 379

Average hourly compensation, 401; France, 45; Great Britain, 1; Italy, 85; Netherlands, 117; Sweden, 233; West Germany, 173

Aviation industry (U.S.), 362

BDA (German national employers' association), 177, 179

BIAC. *See* Business and Industry Advisory Committee
BICC (Great Britain), 20
BLHP (Netherlands), 121
BOC (Great Britain), 20
BRA. *See* Belgian Royal Airways
BSC. *See* British Steel Corporation
Badger Company (Belgium), 351
Bank of Italy, 91
Barclays Bank (Great Britain), 19
Bargaining Organization for Swedish State-Owned Enterprises, 239
Bariclim (Bari Petrochemical Co., Inc.), 105-115
Barre, Prime Minister (France), 56
Barrett, Edward and John, 23
Barrett Cycle Company (Great Britain), 23-33
"Basic agreement" (Sweden, 1938), 240, 287-288, 290
Belgian Royal Airways, 357-363
Belgium, 351, 363, 379, 393
Bendix, 352
Black and Decker, 352
Blake, Jack, 325
Blakey (Barrett Cycle Company), 29, 33
Blanpain, R., 331, 342, 351, 353
Blanton, Paul, 305, 310, 311, 312, 313-314, 315, 320
Blue Cross-Blue Shield, 309-310
Bluechen, 380
Board observer (France), 59
*Bodes* (Dutch union messengers), 120
Bofors (Sweden), 239
Bogden, Walter, 215, 216, 217
Boling, Thomas, 321, 322, 325-326, 327, 328
Bonjour, Robert, 77, 78, 79, 80
Bonus plans, 384, 385; Italy, 96; Netherlands, 133, 384, 385; Sweden, 292; West Germany, 183-184, 195, 384
Boston airport, 357-363
Bottleneck strike, 51
Bouclier Copper Company (France), 75-83
Boulanger, François, 77, 78, 79, 80
Bouvin, Ake, 246

Boycotts, 336, 341, 345, 360
Brandon (CGT), 79, 81
Brandon, Carl, 40, 41, 42
Bratton, John, 31, 32
Brewer, John, 35
Bridlington procedure (Great Britain), 3
British American Tobacco Company, 352
British Steel Corporation, 18
Brown Boveri, 338
Brun, Jean, 80
Bullock report (Great Britain, 1977), 18-19, 380
Burns, George, 31, 33
Bus blockade (Italy), 112-114
Business and Industry Advisory Committee (OECD), 349
*Business Europe*, 101, 184
Butters (Barrett Cycle Company), 29, 30, 33

CAC. *See* Central Arbitration Committee
CBI. *See* Confederation of British Industries
CdF. *See* Charbonnage de France
CDF. (*Consiglio di Fabbrica*). *See* Factory councils
CFDT. *See* Confédération Française Démocratique du Travail
CFTC. *See* Confédération Française des Travailleurs Chretiens
CGC. *See* Confédération Générale des Cadres
CGIL. *See* General Confederation of Italian Labor
CGT. *See* Confédération Générale du Travail
CGT-FO. *See* Confédération Générale du Travail—Force Ouvrière
CIDA. *See* National Confederation for Managers
CIG (Italian central wage guarantee fund), 98
CIME. *See* Committee on International Investments and Multinational Enterprises

CISL. *See* Confederation of Italian Trade Unions

CISNAL. *See* National Confederation of Italian Labor

CNPF. *See Counseil National du Patronat Français*

CNV (Netherlands), 118, 120, 121, 123

CPD. *See* Christian Democratic party (West Germany)

CSE. *See* Carolina-Southern Electronics, Incorporated

Cabot, George, 79, 82

Callaghan, James, 5

Canadian unions, 329

Carli, Guido, 91

Carlson (Barrett Cycle Company), 40, 41

Carmoy, Guy de, 71

Carolina-Southern Electronics, Incorporated, 373-374

Carrefour, 60

Carter, Jimmy, 297

Cassell (CFDT), 79

Category unions: Italy, 87, 91; Netherlands, 119

Catholic church: France, 46, 47, 64, 66; Netherlands, 118, 120, 121, 122

Catholic Republican party (France), 64, 66

Central Arbitration Committee (Great Britain), 7, 8, 11, 12, 32

Central Organization of Salaried Employees (Sweden), 234, 235, 236, 237, 238, 240, 262, 263

Certification elections (U.S.), 298-299, 305, 311-312, 316-317, 319-320, 373

Certification officer (Great Britain), 7

*Charbonnage de France*, 63, 66, 67, 69, 70, 72, 73

Chavez, Cesar, 336

Check-off system for union dues: France, 47; Great Britain, 4; Italy, 89; Netherlands, 120; Sweden, 237, 290; U.S., 297; West Germany, 176

Chicago, 360

Christian Democratic party (Italy), 87, 89, 105

Christian Democratic party (Netherlands), 135

Christian Democratic party (West Germany), 177, 190, 191

Christian union movement, 340

Chrysler, 225, 299

Ciba Geigy, 338

Citibank-Citicorp, 352

Civil service unions, 175

Clegg, Hugh A., 3

Closed shop: France, 47; Great Britain, 4, 37-38, 44; Italy, 88; Netherlands, 120; Sweden, 237; U.S., 296-297; West Germany, 175-176

Coal industry (France), 63

Codetermination and consultation rights, 381, 383-384; France, 57; Italy, 102; Netherlands, 128-131, 169-170, 383-384; Sweden, 252, 288, 290-291; West Germany, 193, 197-200, 208, 209, 210, 223, 383-384

Collective bargaining: France, 48-52; Great Britain, 7-14; Italy, 91-96, 103-104, 106-107; Netherlands, 122-126; Sweden, 239-245; U.S., 297, 299-300, 306; West Germany, 178-181

Collective bargaining, bona fide ("in good faith"), 299, 345

Collective bargaining, "continuous bargaining" (open-ended contracts), 9, 50, 94

Collective bargaining, levels of: France, 48-49; Great Britain, 9-10; Italy, 91-93; Netherlands, 122-125; Sweden, 240-242, 246; and transnational bargaining, 340, 341; U.S., 299; West Germany, 178

Collective bargaining, scope of: France, 49; Sweden, 240-242, 246; U.S., 299, 300; West Germany, 178-179

Collective bargaining, transnational, 337-339

Collective Bargaining Agreement Act (West Germany, 1949, 1952), 176, 177

Collective bargaining agreements. *See* Labor agreements

Collective bargaining and labor legislation: Great Britain, 14-15; Sweden, 246; West Germany, 178, 181-182

*Comité d'establissement* (plant council), 57

Committee on International Investments and Multinational Enterprises (OECD), 351-352, 353

Communists, 281, 340, 344; France, 46, 48, 64, 385; Italy, 87, 89, 90, 105, 344, 385

Company bargaining: France, 49; Great Britain, 9-10; Italy, 92-93; Sweden, 290; U.S., 297, 299

Company board systems: single tripartite, 18-19; two-tier, 19, 103, 131, 160, 185-186, 205, 221, 252, 348, 377. *See also* Worker participation

Company conferences (ITS), 337-338

Company councils (Italy), 93

Company councils (ITS), 338, 368

Company Savings Act (Netherlands, 1965), 133-134

Company Structure Act (Netherlands, 1971), 131, 133

"Company unions" (U.S.), 302

Conciliation, mediation, and arbitration: France, 50; Great Britain, 12-13; Italy, 94; Sweden, 242, 264; U.S., 327, 328, 362n; West Germany, 179, 200

Conciliation committees (West Germany), 193, 195, 198, 200, 209, 210

Condon (ASTMS), 31

*Confagricoltura* (Italy), 90

*Confédération Française Démocratique du Travail*, 46, 48, 53, 64-71, 75, 81

*Confédération Française des Travailleurs Chrétiens*, 46, 47, 53, 66, 67, 75

*Confédération Générale des Cadres* (France), 46, 47, 66, 67, 68-69

*Confédération Générale du Travail* (France), 46, 47, 48, 53, 55, 60, 64-71, 75, 80, 81, 83

*Confédération Générale du Travail—Force Ouvriére* (France), 46-47, 48, 53, 66, 67, 75

Confederation of British Industries, 6, 19

Confederation of Industrial Employers (Italy), 88-106, 382

Confederation of Italian Trade Unions, 87, 88, 105, 109 Confederation of Professional Associations (Sweden), 234, 235, 236, 237, 238, 240, 245

Confederation of Shipbuilding and Engineering Unions (Great Britain), 9

*Confindustria. See* Confederation of Industrial Employers

*Conforcommercio* (Italy), 90

*Conseil National du Patronat Français*, 48, 49, 52, 53

Conservative party (Great Britain), 11, 14, 20, 37

Conservative party (Sweden), 243, 258, 380

Consumer price index, 399; France, 47; Great Britain, 1; Italy, 85; Netherlands, 177; Sweden, 233; U.S., 295; West Germany, 173

Continental Can, 338

"Continuous bargaining" (open-ended contracts): France, 50; Great Britain, 9; Italy, 94

Contract negotiations. *See* Collective bargaining; Labor agreements

Contracts of Employment Act (Great Britain, 1973), 12

Conway, Alan, 326

Cooper, Jerry, 327

Cooperative agreements (Sweden, 1942-1973), 240-241, 251

Corporate assemblies (Sweden), 288-289, 291-292

Cortes, Gaetano, 97

Cost-of-living adjustments. *See* Wage policies

Council of administrators (Italy), 103
Council on Equality (Sweden, 1972), 393
Courts: France, 51; Italy, 95, 97; Netherlands, 125, 126, 131; Sweden, 243-244, 247, 248; U.S., 301; West Germany, 180, 182, 183, 193
Craft unions: Great Britain, 3; Italy, 95; Sweden, 235
Crane, Dwight, 28, 29, 30, 31, 32
Crockett, David, 282

D '66 party (Netherlands), 135
DAG (West Germany white-collar union), 175
DBB (West German civil service union), 175
DGB (*Deutsche Gewerkschaftsbund*). *See* German Confederation of Labor
*Dagens Nyheter* (Sweden), 258
Dagens Nyheters AB (Sweden), 257-285
Daniel, W.W., 380
Dayton, Ohio, 373
Death benefits plans, 308
"December compromise" (Sweden, 1906), 236, 239, 240, 246
Defrenne, Gabrielle, 393
DeGaulle, Charles, 60
*Délégués du personnel* (France), 51
*Délégués syndicaux* (France), 51
Delouvier report (France), 60
Democratic party (U.S.), 297
Denmark, 379
Deschamps, Andre, 359, 360, 362
"Development agreements" (Italy), 104
*Direktie* (Dutch management board), 131
*Dirigenti* (Italian managers), 100-101
Disciplinary actions, 388; Great Britain, 39-44; U.S., 326. *See also* Dismissals
Disclaimer clause, 11, 12

Dismissals, 386-388; France, 54: Great Britain, 15-16, 39-44, 387; Italy, 97, 387; Netherlands, 126, 387; Sweden, 247-248; 387; U.S., 307, 326, 327, 328; West Germany, 182, 199-200, 387. *See also* Redundancies; Severance pay
Dispute procedures. *See* Grievance procedures
Donahue, Thomas R., 303
"Double veto" on strikes, 244
Douglas, Esther, 318-319
Douglas, Gustav, 257, 263, 278, 279
Draftsmen and Allied Technicians Association (Great Britain), 35
"Dual sourcing" policy (MNCs), 330
Dunlop-Pirelli, 338
DuPont, 192

EC. *See* Employers' Confederation
EEC. *See* European Economic Community
EEF. *See* Engineering Employers' Federation
EFI. *See* Europa Food Industries B.V.
EMF. *See* European Metalworkers' Federation
ENI. *See* National Hydrocarbon Corporation
EPA. *See* Employment Protection Act (Great Britain)
ETUC. *See* European Trade Union Confederation
EWU (West German electrical workers' union), 221
Economics committee (West Germany), 194
Economy-wide bargaining, 240-241
Embick, W.R., 39, 40, 41
Employee capital accumulation laws (West Germany), 195, 196
Employee-Director Act (Sweden,1973/1976), 252
Employee representation. *See* Worker participation

Employee rights: Great Britain, 4-5; Sweden, 236; U.S., 297-298

Employee Shareholding Act (France, 1973), 60

Employer rights (U.S.), 299

Employers, punishment of: France, 59; Italy, 97; Sweden, 249; U.S., 298

Employers' associations: France, 48; Great Britain, 5-6; Italy, 90-91; Netherlands, 122; Sweden, 239, 287; West Germany, 177

Employers' Confederation (Sweden), 287-288, 290

Employment agencies, government: Italy, 96-97; Netherlands, 126; West Germany, 200

Employment Protection Act (Great Britain, 1975), 6-8, 10, 11, 12, 15, 16, 17, 32, 43n

Employment Protection Act (Sweden, 1974), 244

Engineering Employers' Federation (Great Britain), 6, 9, 24, 31, 36

Engles (NGG), 208

Equal Opportunities Act (Netherlands, proposed), 128

Equal Opportunities Commission (Great Britain), 17

Equal Opportunity Act (Great Britain, 1975), 17

Equal Pay Act (Great Britain, 1970/ 1975), 16-17, 32

Equal Pay Act (Netherlands, 1975), 127

Equal pay and equal opportunity, 391-394; Great Britain, 16-17, 25-28, 393; Italy, 99, 393, 394; multinational corporations, 347; Netherlands, 127-128, 393; Sweden, 251, 393, 394; West Germany, 184-185, 393-396

Equal Treatment in Working Life Act (Sweden, 1979), 251, 354

Equality Committee (Sweden), 251

Eurofoods, 210, 215

Europa Food Industries B.V. (Netherlands), 157-172

European Coal and Steel Community, 177

European Commission, 103, 344-345, 379, 380, 388, 393

European Council, 387-388, 394

European Court of Justice, 127, 393

European Economic Community: and equal pay-equal opportunity, 127, 184-185, 251, 347, 391-393, 394; member nations, 346; and redundancies, 387-388; transnational labor relations, 333, 341, 344-345, 346-348; and worker participation, 103, 379

European Metalworkers' Federation, 192, 333, 339

European Parliament, 347-348

European Trade Union Confederation, 336, 343, 344-345, 348, 380

European Trade Union Institute, 344-345, 348

Evans, Haydn, 28

Evans, Wynn S., 305, 310-320

*Expressen* (Sweden), 258-259

Exxon, 349

FEN (French teachers' union), 47

FIM (Italy), 88

FIOM (Italy), 88

FLM (Italian metal-mechanical category union), 87, 88, 104

FNDAI. *See* National Federation of Managers of Industrial Enterprises

FNV. *See* Netherlands Trade Union Federation

FO. *See Confédération Générale du Travail—Force Ouvrière*

Factory clubs (Sweden), 236

Factory councils (Italy), 92-93, 95, 103, 106-107, 382

Fair Wages Resolution (Great Britain), 12

Farah Company, 336

"Featherbedding," 359, 362

Federal Vacation Act (West Germany, 1963), 183

Fiat Company, 91, 101, 104

Financial Administration Group (Dagens Nyheters AB), 258, 261)

Fines and punishments, 59, 97, 180, 194
Firestone, 352
First National Bank of Lake City, 305-320
Fischer Electric A.G., 219-231
Fischer Foods, 210, 215
Flextime (Great Britain), 38-39, 44
Fokker-VFW, 338
Ford Motor Company, 11, 192, 225, 299, 332, 333, 340
Foreman: Great Britain, 2, 36; U.S., 298
Foundation of Labor (Netherlands), 123, 124, 133
Frame agreements (Sweden), 241
France, 45-83 (*See also names of individual unions, companies, and political parties*); board observer, 59; *Charbonnage de France*, 63, 66, 67, 69, 70, 72, 73; coal industry, 63; *comité d'establissement*, 57; *délégués du personnel*, 51; *délégués syndicaux*, 51; Delouvier report, 60; economic and labor statistics, 45-46; Employee Shareholding Act (1973), 60; individual employment contract, 49; labor courts, 51; mensualiza-tion, 53, 56, 390; Ministry of Labor, 46, 50, 61, 390; Ministry of Industrial and Scientific Development, 69; Ministry of Industry, 67; National Employment/Unemployment Funds, 70; offenses, types of, 54; overtime, 53; profit-sharing legislation (1959/1967), 59-60; *Salaire Minimum de Croissance*, 52; Social Audit Act (1977), 59; strikes, types of, 51-52; Sudreau Commission, 57, 58-59; Supreme Court, 57, 390; transnational labor relations, 340, 368-369; unions and confederations, 46-47
French Communist party, 46, 48, 64
French communist union, 385
French Socialist party, 48
French socialist union, 385
Frey, Michael, 284

GAI. *See* Guaranteed Annual Income
Geijer, Anne, 237
Gemmil, Paul, 367-375
Gener Corporation (U.S.), 373
General Confederation of Italian Labor, 87, 88, 90, 105, 109
General Electric, 334, 338
General Motors, 225, 299, 300, 335
General union (Great Britain), 3
German Confederation of Labor, 174-180, 190-191, 205, 329-330, 340, 343, 344, 378
Glauber, Kurt, 219-230
Gotaverren, 250
Government employee unions: Nether-lands, 121; Sweden, 245; West Ger-many, 175
Government employees' strikes illegal (U.S.), 301
W.R. Grace, 338
Grand Verger plant. *See* Bouclier Cop-per Company
Grant, Francis, 305, 310-320
Graphical Workers' Union (Sweden), 257, 262-283
Great Britain, 1-44 (*See also names of individual unions, companies, and political parties*); Advisory Concilia-tion and Arbitration Committee, 32; Advisory Conciliation and Arbitra-tion Service, 6-8, 11, 12-13, 15, 17; Bridlington procedure, 3; Bullock report (1977), 18-19, 380; Central Arbitration Committee, 7, 8, 11, 12, 32; certification officer, 7; Con-tracts of Employment Act (1972), 12; disclaimer clause, 11, 12; economic and labor statistics, 1-2; Employment Protection Act (1975), 6-8, 10, 11, 12, 15, 16, 17, 32n, 43n; Equal Opportunities Commission, 17; Equal Opportunity Act (1975), 17; Equal Pay Act (1970/1975), 16-17, 32; Fair Wages Resolution, 12; flextime, 38-39, 44; general union, 3; Industrial Relations Act (1971), 11, 37; industrial relations

Great Britain (cont.)
code of practice, 41n; industrial tribunals, 5, 7, 10, 15-16, 17, 43; Inland Revenue, 20; joint representation councils, 19, 380; labor law reform, 14; labor legislation and agencies, 6-7; multiunionism, 3; parliament, 5; Race Discrimination Act (1976), 17; Redundancy Act (1965), 16; Redundancy Rebate Act (1969), 16; Sex Discrimination Act (1975), 393; Trade Union and Labor Relations Act (1974), 4, 5, 12, 15, 20; transnational labor relations, 340; unions and confederations, 2, 3; wage restraints, 8-9; worker director systems, 18
Grievance procedures: France, 50-51; Great Britain, 10; Italy, 95; Sweden, 243, 244; in transnational bargaining, 345; U.S., 297, 298, 300-301, 307; West Germany, 198
Gross national product, 399; France, 45; Great Britain, 1; Italy, 85; Netherlands, 117; Sweden, 233; U.S., 295; West Germany, 173
Guaranteed Annual Income (U.S.), 307

Haas, Maurice, 358, 359, 360-361, 363n
Hague Protocol, 123
Handicapped, the: Italy, 97; West Germany, 192
Heilbronner, Francois, 56
Heilbronner report, 389, 390
Heinemann, G., 212-218
Heins Food Products A.G. (West Germany), 210, 215
Hertz, 352
Hilton, 338
Hiring procedures (Italy), 96-97
Hobbema & Van Rijn, N.V. (Netherlands), 137-155
Holding companies: Netherlands, 131-132; West Germany, 186
Holmens Bruk AG, 261
Homeland Manufacturing Company (Sweden), 287-294

Hoogovens, 122, 124
Hospital and medical care programs (U.S.), 309-310, 312-313, 317, 318, 320
Hostage-taking (France), 68-69, 73

IBM, 329
IBT. See International Brotherhood of Teamsters
ICEF (International Federation of Chemical, Energy, and General Workers' Unions). See International Federation of Chemical and General Workers' Unions
ICF. See International Federation of Chemical and General Workers' Unions
ICFTU. See International Confederation of Free Trade Unions
ICI, 338
IEPI. See Imperial Electric Products, Inc.
IEWF. See International Electrical Workers' Federation
IFALPA. See International Federation of Airline Pilots' Associations
IFPAAW. See International Federation of Plantation, Agricultural, and Allied Workers
IG Chemie-Papier-Keramik, 334
IG Metall (West Germany), 174-181, 332, 334, 381
ILO. See International Labor Organization
IMF. See International Metalworkers' Federation
IMU. See International Metalworkers' Union
INAM (Italian government sickness insurance agency), 100, 101-102
IRI (Italy), 92
ITF. See International Transport Workers' Federation
ITGLWF. See International Textile, Garment, and Leather Workers' Federation
ITSs. See International Trade Secretariats

ITT. *See* International Telephone and Telegraph

ITWU. *See* International Transportation Workers' Union

IUF. *See* International Union of Food and Allied Workers' Associations

Ideology, 340, 379-380, 385; France, 48; Great Britain, 5; Netherlands, 118, 121-122; Sweden, 237; U.S., 297; West Germany, 176

Imperial Electric Products, Inc., 35

Individual employment contract (France), 49

Industrial Relations Act (Great Britain, 1971), 11, 37

Industrial relations code of practice (Great Britain, 1972), 41

Industrial tribunals (Great Britain), 5, 7, 10, 15-16, 17, 43

Industrial unions: Great Britain, 3; Italy, 87; Sweden, 235; and transnational labor relations, 329-330, 331, 333; U.S., 296; West Germany, 174, 329-330.

Industry councils, 338

Industry-level bargaining: France, 49; Great Britain, 9; Italy, 91-92; Netherlands, 118, 124; Sweden, 241, 288

Information requirements: France, 59; Great Britain, 11; Netherlands, 131, 141-142; Sweden 244; and transnational labor relations, 334, 337, 345, 348, 350, 368, 369, 375; West Germany, 194

Internal commissions. *See* Works councils, Italy

Internal Revenue Service (U.S.), 308, 317

International Association of Machinists, 329

International Brotherhood of Teamsters, 296, 297, 329

International Confederation of Free Trade Unions, 87, 343, 344, 349, 365n

International Electrical Workers' Federation, 367-375

International Federation of Airline Pilots' Associations, 361, 363

International Federation of Chemical and General Workers' Unions, 192, 334, 335, 336, 339, 342

International Federation of Plantation, Agricultural, and Allied Workers, 336

International Labor Organization, 334, 335, 339, 341, 343, 345-346

International Metalworkers' Federation, 192, 333, 334, 335, 340

International Metalworkers' Union (U.S.), 305-318

International Telephone and Telegraph, 192, 329, 333, 352

International Textile, Garment, and Leather Workers' Federation, 332

International Trade Secretariats, 331-342, 352, 365n; list of names, 332

International trade union leaders elected to MNC boards, 191-192

International Transport Workers' Federation, 360, 361, 363n, 364-365

International Transportation Workers' Union, 360, 361, 363

International Union of Food and Allied Workers' Associations, 334, 338

Intersind (Italy), 90, 91, 94

"Investment strike" (MNC), 331, 342

Ireland, 379

Italian Communist party, 87, 89, 90, 105

Italian Communist union, 344, 385

Italy, 85-115 (*See also names of individual unions, companies, and political parties*); Act 604 (1966), 97; Act for the Protection of Working Mothers (1971), 99-100; Anti-Discrimination Act (1977), 99, 394; "articulated bargaining," 91, 92, 93; bonus plans, 96, 101; bus blockade, 122-114; central wage guarantee fund, 98; civil code (1942), 100; *consiglio d'amministrazione*, 103; *consiglio di fabbrica*, 92-93, 95, 103, 106-107, 382; Con-

Italy (cont.)
  stitution (Article 39), 86, 88, 94, 102; courts, 95, 97; "development agreements," 104; *diregenti*, 100-101; economic and labor statistics, 85-86; government employment agency, 96-97; government sickness insurance agency, 100, 101-102; hiring procedures, 96-99; internal commissions, 91, 95, 102-103, 106, 380, 382; labor law (1975), 98; Law 1369 (1960), 98; Ministry of Labor, 86, 94; petroleum industry, 93, 100, 101; Protocol of Intentions, 92; Statute on Workers' Rights (1970), 86, 89, 92, 97, 101, 103, 106; temporary layoffs and short-time work, 98; transnational labor relations, 339, 340, 344; unions and confederations, 87-88; wage escalation clause, 95-96

J & M Construction Company (France), 78, 79-80
JRC. *See* Joint representation councils
Japan, 389
Job classification systems, 393; Sweden, 267, 270; U.S., 306; West Germany, 179, 208, 216, 217
Job security, 388; Sweden, 268, 269; in transnational labor relations, 345, 361; U.S., 307
Johnson (ASTMS), 31, 32
Joint representation councils (Great Britain), 19, 380
Joint Stock Companies Act (Sweden), 288
Journalists "club" (Sweden), 262, 271, 275-277, 283-284
Jurisdictional and demarcation disputes: Great Britain, 3-4, 35-36; Italy, 95; Sweden, 267, 270, 271; West Germany, 174

KFO (Swedish Cooperative Labor Negotiating Association), 239

KLM, 134
KSSU (KLM, SAS, Swissair, and Union Trans Aèrienne), 361
*Kaderledens. See* Shop stewards, Netherlands
Kassolow, Everett M., 346
Kisaka (IEWF), 372
Kok, Wim, 134
Kopke, Gunter, 192, 333, 339
Kopp, Conrad, 367, 368-369, 370, 371, 375
Korean Electrical Workers' Union, 372
Krefeld plant. *See* Pickardt-Rhine International A.G.
Kringle, Fritz, 203, 213-214, 215, 216, 217, 218

LO (*Lands-organisations*). *See* Swedish Confederation of Trade Unions
Labor agreements: France, 49, 50; Great Britain, 11-12; Italy, 94; Netherlands, 125; Sweden, 243; U.S., 300-301; West Germany, 178-180, 210-212
Labor courts: France, 51; Sweden, 243-244, 247, 248; West Germany, 180, 182, 183, 193
Labor Courts Act (West Germany, 1953), 180
Labor legislation: France, 52-56; Great Britain, 14-17; Italy, 96-100; Netherlands, 126-128; Sweden, 245-246, 247-250; transnational labor relations, 341, 342-343; West Germany, 178, 181-185
Labor party (Great Britain), 5, 12, 14, 19, 20, 37, 380
Labor party (Netherlands), 134
Labor Placement Law (Netherlands), 127
Lama, Luciano, 90
Landrum Griffin Act (U.S., 1959), 297
Law on Mediation of Labor Disputes (Sweden, 1920), 242
Lay-offs. *See* Dismissals; Redundancies
"Leading employee" (West Germany), 186-190

Length-of-service bonus (Italy), 101
Levinson, Charles, 192, 335, 341
Liberal party (Great Britain), 20
Limited liability companies (Italy), 103
Litton Industries, 352
Local bargaining: Great Britain, 10; Italy, 106-107; Netherlands, 124-125; Sweden, 241-242; U.S., 297
Local unions; Netherlands, 119; Sweden, 235-236; U.S., 297
Lockard, Frank, 314, 315
Lockout: France, 51, 80; Italy, 94; Sweden, 239, 242, 244-245; U.S., 301-302; West Germany, 181
Logan International Airport (Boston), 357-363
Los Angeles, 360
Lyon (CGT), 83

MNCs. See Multinational corporations
MRP. See Catholic Republican party
M-S Limited (Great Britain), 35-44
McCarthy, W.E.J., 4
McKay, Walter, 360, 361, 363
Mahon, John, 41, 42-43
Management boards: Netherlands, 131, 132, 133; West Germany, 185-186, 205, 210
Mantel agreement (West Germany), 179
Maoism, 281
Marple, Robert, 315-316
Martou, Jacques, 357, 358, 361, 362
Mason, John, 310
Massey-Ferguson, 352
Maternity protection and pay, 391, 392; France, 55-56, 391; Great Britain, 17, 391; Italy, 99-100, 391; Netherlands, 128, 391; Sweden, 250, 391; West Germany, 184, 391
Mediation. See Conciliation, mediation, and arbitration
Meert International, 367-375
Meidner, Rudolph, 234
Meidner plan, 253, 385
Melitta, 178
Mensualization (France), 53, 56, 390

Michelin, 338
Milan, 361
Milieu board (Sweden), 291
Minimum wage: France, 52; West Germany, 178, 179
Minors (Germany), 192
Minot, Jacques, 63, 67, 73
Misconduct, types of (France), 54
Montedison, 104
Monthly salary, 53
Müller, Klaus, 203, 213-214, 215, 216, 217-218
Multinational corporations, 192, 329-355
Multiunionism (Great Britain), 3

NCHP (Netherlands), 121
NCW (Dutch Christian employers' federation), 122, 123
NEA. See National Education Association
NGG (Gewerkschaft, Nahrung, Genuss, Gaststätten). See Union of Food, Stimulants, Hotel, and Restaurant Employees
NKV (Netherlands), 118, 119, 120, 121
NKVW (Netherlands), 122
NLRB. See National Labor Relations Board
NUGMW. See National Union of General and Municipal Workers
NUM. See National Union of Mineworkers
NVV (Netherlands), 118, 119, 120, 121
Nabisco, 336
National Collective Bargaining Office (Sweden), 239
National Confederation for Managers (Italy), 100-101
National Confederation of Italian Labor, 87
National Education Association (U.S.), 306
National Employment Fund (France), 70
National Federation of Government Officers (Sweden), 235, 245

National Federation of Managers of Industrial Enterprises (Italy), 88
National Hydrocarbon Corporation (Italy), 90, 92
National Labor Relations Act (U.S., 1935), 297, 301, 302, 315
National Labor Relations Board (U.S.), 298, 299, 300, 305, 311-320, 374
National Unemployment Fund (France), 70
National Union of General and Municipal Workers (Great Britain), 2, 3
National Union of Mineworkers (Great Britain), 2, 3
National unions: Italy, 382; Netherlands, 118-119; Sweden, 235, 272, 287, 288; and transnational labor relations, 329-330, 331, 333-337, 339, 340-341
National Westminster Bank, 19
Nationalization: France, 63; Great Britain, 5; Netherlands, 121; Sweden, 290; West Germany, 176, 177
Nationwide bargaining: France, 48-49; Italy, 91; Netherlands, 122-124
Nestle, 338
Netherlands, 117-172 (*See also names of individual unions, companies, and political parties*); armed forces unionization, 121; *bodes*, 120; Company Savings Act (1965), 133-134; Company Structure Act (1971), 131, 133; courts, 125, 126, 131; *direktie*, 131; district employment offices, 126; economic and labor statistics, 117-118; Equal Opportunities Act (proposed), 128; Equal Pay Act (1975), 127; Foundation of Labor, 123, 124, 133; Hague Protocol, 123; *kaderledens*, 124-125, 382; Labor Placement Law, 127; Minister of Social Affairs, 125, 130; national

health plan, 128; parliament, 122; profit-sharing plans, 133-135, 385; *raad van commissarissen*, 131; "responsible unionism," 121, 123; Social and Economic Council, 123, 124, 125, 126, 130, 131; Socialist-Humanist (nonconfessional) block, 118, 120, 122; trade commissions, 129-130; transnational labor relations, 340, 341, 363n; union consultation board, 119, 120; union cooperation and amalgamation, 119-120; union leadership, 121; unions and confederations, 118-119; works councils laws, 128-129, 169, 383
Netherlands Trade Union Federation, 118, 119, 120, 121, 123, 129, 131, 133, 134
Newspaper Production Division (Dagens Nyheters AB), 259-261
Newton, Harold, 315
No-strike clauses: France, 50; Italy, 94; U.S., 300-301, 341
Nordic Council of Unions, 349
Northrup, Herbert R., 339, 342
Norway, 379

OECD. *See* Organization for Economic Cooperation and Development
OETV (West German government employees' union), 175
Occupational strike (France), 52
L'Oreal, 60
Organization for Economic Cooperation and Development, 344; MNC guidelines, 348-352, 353; member nations, 348
Organization of Higher Personnel (Dutch EFI), 159, 160
Osterberg, Rolf, 257, 263-279, 284
Output in manufacturing, 401; France, 45; Great Britain, 1; Italy, 85; Netherlands, 117; Sweden, 233-234; U.S., 295-296; West Germany, 173

Overtime ban: Great Britain, 14, 38, 44;
and transnational labor relations,
336, 339, 341

PCF. See French Communist Party
PRIAG. See Pickardt-Rhine International A.G.
PTK. See Private Salaried Employees'
Association
Paris, 361
Parvis (Barrett Cycle Company), 25,
29, 30, 33
Paternal Leave Act (France, 1977), 391
Paternity leave: France, 391; Sweden,
250-251, 391
Patronat. See Conseil National du Patronat Français
"Peace agreements" (Sweden), 264
"Peace obligation" (Germany), 180,
193
Pension plans: U.S., 308-309, 312, 316,
317; West Germany, 209-210
Peru, 334
Petroleum industry (Italy), 93, 100, 101
Philips, 124, 192, 334, 338, 352
Pickardt-Rhine International A.G.,
203-218
Pirelli, 336
Pivari, Alberto, 109-115
Plant-level bargaining: Italy, 93; U.S.,
299
Plural unionism: France, 47; Great
Britain, 3; Italy, 88
Poclain, 352
Police unions: France, 47; West Germany, 175
Political strikes: France, 52; Italy, 95;
West Germany, 180
Politics: France, 48; Great Britain, 5;
Italy, 89-90; Netherlands, 122;
Sweden, 237-238; and transnational
labor relations, 342, 345, 346, 347;
U.S., 297; West Germany, 176-177
Pompidou, Georges, 53, 71
Poncet mine (France), 63-73

Poppins, James, 39-44
Population, 399; France, 45; Great
Britain, 1; Italy, 85; Netherlands,
117; Sweden, 233; U.S., 295; West
Germany, 173
Private Salaried Employees' Association (Sweden), 235
Productivity, 389, 402; France, 45-46;
Great Britain, 1-2; Italy, 85-86;
Sweden, 234; U.S., 296; West Germany, 173-174
Professional unions: Great Britain, 2,
35; Sweden, 234, 235
Profit-sharing and employee ownership, 384-386; France, 59-61, 384,
385; Great Britain, 19-20, 385; Italy,
385; Netherlands, 133-135, 384, 385,
386; Sweden, 252-253, 293-294, 385,
386; U.S., 307, 312, 313, 314, 316,
317; West Germany, 195-196, 384,
385, 386
Promotion of Employment Act (Sweden, 1974/1975), 249
Protection Against Dismissal Act (West
Germany, 1969), 182
Protestants (Netherlands), 118, 120,
121, 122
Protocol of Intentions (Italy), 92
Publilic sector employers' associations
(Sweden), 239

RACAL Electronics, 20
RESO (Swedish travel agency), 238
RO (Dutch union ctation board),
119, 120
RSA (rappresentanze sindicali azienda),
106
Raad van commissarissen. See Supervisory boards, Netherlands
Race Discrimination Act (Great Britain, 1976), 17
Railway Labor Act (U.S.), 362n
Raison, Jacques, 77, 78, 80, 81
Raytheon, 351, 352
Rebhan, Herman, 192

Recognition strikes: Italy, 95; West Germany, 180

Redundancies (*See also* Severance pay): and European Economic Community, 387-388; France, 55, 387; Great Britain, 16, 28-33, 44; Italy, 98, 387; Netherlands, 126-127, 163-168; Sweden, 248-249, 269; West Germany, 183, 228-229

Redundancy Act (Great Britain, 1965), 16

Redundancy Rebate Act (Great Britain, 1969), 16

Regional bargaining: France, 49; Great Britain, 9

Rehn, Gosta, 234

Renault, 49

Republican party (Italy), 87, 105

Republican party (U.S.), 297

"Responsible unionism" (Netherlands), 121, 123

Retirement age, mandatory (Italy), 99, 308

Rhone-Poulenc, 338

Rich, Hank, 327

Right-to-work laws (U.S.), 297

Ring, Sture, 257, 263, 269-283

Rotating strike (France), 51

Rubenstein, Michael, 387

SAA. *See* Security Advisers Associates

SACO. *See* Confederation of Professional Associations

SAF (Swedish employers' confederation), 234, 236, 237, 239, 240-241, 245, 246, 252, 382

SAP. *See* Social Democratic party (Sweden)

SAV. *See* National Collective Bargaining Office

SER. *See* Social and Economic Council

SFO. *See* Bargaining Organization for Swedish State-Owned Enterprises

SKF, 335

SMG (small motors and generators) division. *See* Fischer Electric A.G.

SMIC. *See* Salaire Minimum de Croissance

SO. *See* National Federation of Government Officers

SPD. *See* Social Democratic party (West Germany)

SUB. *See* Supplementary unemployment benefits

Saab-Scania, 239

Sabena Airlines, 393

St. Gobain, 339

*Salaire Minimum de Croissance* (French minimum wage law), 52

Salary continuance program (U.S.), 309

Salary evaluation program, 306-307

San Francisco, 373

Savage, Fred, 309, 317

Savings plans: Netherlands, 133-134, 384, 385; West Germany, 195, 384

Schmidt, Otto, 211, 212-214, 215-216, 217

Scott Food Company, 203, 204

Security Advisers Associates, 323, 326, 327, 328

Security of Employment Act (Sweden, 1974), 247, 248

Severance pay, 387, 388; France, 54; Great Britain, 16, 43n, 44, 387; Italy, 97; Netherlands, 126, 166; Sweden, 248, 249, 387; and transnational labor relations, 351, 359, 360; U.S., 328; West Germany, 182, 183

Sex discrimination. *See* Equal pay and equal opportunity

Sex Discrimination Act (Great Britain, 1975), 393

Shift work: France, 53; U.S., 314

Sick pay: 389-390; France, 53, 56-57, 389-390; Great Britain, 18, 390; Italy, 101-102, 389, 390; Netherlands, 128; Sweden, 250, 390; U.S., 302, 309; West Germany, 185, 390

Shop Steward Act (Sweden, 1974), 242, 247

Shop stewards: France, 51; Great Britain, 11, 39-44, 382; Netherlands, 124-125, 382; Sweden, 242

Siemens, 352

Sit-down strike: France, 52; U.S., 298

Slowdown strike: France, 51; Sweden, 273; U.S., 298

Smoller-Halde, Hans, 203

Social and Economic Council (Netherlands), 123, 124, 125, 126, 130, 131

Soial Audit Act (France, 1977), 59

Social codes, international, 343, 344, 345-346, 347-348

Social Democratic party (Italy), 87 105

Social Democratic party (Sweden), 237-238, 251

Social Democratic party (West Germany), 177, 191

Social security benefits, 394: France, 49; Great Britain, 15

Socialist-Humanist (nonconfessional) block (Netherlands), 118, 120, 122

Socialist party (Sweden), 290

Socialist union (Italy), 385

Solidarity wage policy (Sweden), 238, 252-253

Sonneveldt, Jan, 148, 151, 153

South Korea, 371-373

Spain, 335, 371

Staaterman, Peter, 157, 158, 167, 170, 171, 172

Standard Electric, 192

State level bargaining (West Germany), 178

State Public Employees Relations Act (U.S.), 306

Statute on Workers' Rights (Italy, 1970), 86, 89, 92, 97, 101, 103, 106

JP Stevens Company, 336

Stockholm Union of Journalists, 262

Strike benefits: France, 52; Great Britain, 13; Italy, 94; Netherlands, 126; and transnational labor relations, 337, 359, 368; West Germany, 176, 181

Strike breakers, 352

Strike losses, 389, 405; France, 52; Great Britain, 13; Italy, 95; Netherlands, 125-126; Sweden, 245; U.S., 301-302; West Germany, 181

Strikes: France, 51-52, 68, 69-70, 77-80, 81; Great Britain, 13-14, 24, 26-28, 36, 42-44; Italy, 94-95, 109-110, 111, 112; Netherlands, 123, 125-126; Peru, 334; Sweden, 239, 242, 244-245, 272-273, 278-279, 283, 289, 290; and transnational labor relations, 330, 334, 336, 341, 357, 359-361, 368-369, 372; West Germany, 180-181

Strikes, types of: France, 51-52; Great Britain, 14; Italy, 95; West Germany, 180

"Struck work," 336, 339, 341, 363

Subcontracting: Italy, 98-99, 107-115; Sweden, 244, 247; and transnational labor relations, 359

Subsidies, 71

Sudreau Commission (France), 57, 58-59

Supervisors' unions (Sweden), 263

Supervisory boards: Netherlands, 131, 132, 133, 160-161; West Germany, 185-186, 205, 221-222

Supplementary unemployment benefits (U.S.), 307

Svenska Dag Bladet, 258

Sweden, 233-294 (See also names of individual unions, companies, and political parties); ability-to-pay wage policy, 253; Act on Codetermination at Work (1976), 236, 239-240, 242, 243, 244, 247, 252; Act on the Right of Association and Collective Bargaining (1936), 236, 239; Advisory Council on Equality between Men and Women, 251; Bargaining Organization for Swedish State-Owned Enterprises, 239; "basic agreement" (1938), 240, 287-288, 290; cooperative agreements (1942-1973), 240-241, 251; corporate assemblies, 288-289, 291-292; Council on Equality (1972), 393; "December compromise" (1906), 236, 239, 240, 246; Department of Industry, 343; "double veto" on strikes, 244; economic and labor statistics, 233-234; economy-wide bargaining, 240-241; Employee-Director Act (1973/1976), 252;

Sweden (cont.)
    Employment Protection Act (1974),
    244; Equal Treatment in Working
    Life Act (1979), 251, 394; Equality
    Committee, 251, 393; factory clubs,
    236; Financial Administration
    Group, 258, 261; frame agreements,
    241; iron and metal workers' union,
    287, 289, 296; Joint Stock Com-
    panies Act, 288; *journalistklubb*,
    262, 271, 275-277, 283-284; labor
    courts, 243-244, 247, 248; labor
    laws (1970s), 245; Law on Media-
    tion of Labor Disputes (1920), 242;
    management authority, decrease in,
    246-247; milieu board, 291; Ministry
    of Labor, 246; National Collective
    Bargaining Office, 239; parliament,
    245, 251, 393; paternity leave,
    250-251, 391; "peace agreements,"
    264; prior right to interpret agree-
    ment, 243; Private Salaried
    Employees' Association, 235; Pro-
    motion of Employment Act
    (1974/1975), 249; public sector
    employers' associations, 239; Secur-
    ity of Employment Act (1974), 247,
    248; Shop Steward Act (1974), 242,
    247; solidarity wage policy, 238,
    252-253; supervisors' union, 263;
    technological innovation, 266-271,
    281, 282-284; transnational labor
    relations, 335, 343; unions and con-
    federations, 234-236; unions'
    business activities, 238; Vacation
    Act (1977), 249; Workers' Protec-
    tion Act (1974), 247
Swedish Confederation of Trade
    Unions, 234-246, 251, 252, 253, 260,
    262, 287-288, 289, 290, 343, 382,
    385
Swedish Film Industries, 258, 261
Swedish Shipowners' Association, 239
Switzerland, 379
Sympathy strikes: and transnational la-
    bor relations, 336, 341, 344, 345;
    West Germany, 180

TASS. *See* Technical and Supervisory
    Section (AUEW)
TCo (*Tjänstemännes Centralörganisa-
    tion*). *See* Central Organization of
    Salaried Employees
TGWU. *See* Transport and General
    Workers Union
TUAC. *See* Trade Union Advisory
    Committee (OECD)
TUC. *See* Trades Union Congress
TULRA. *See* Trade Union and Labor
    Relations Act
TWU. *See* Transportation Workers'
    Union
Taft-Hartley Act (1947), 297
Tariff agreement (West Germany),
    178, 179, 208, 211, 215
Teachers unions: France, 47; U.S.,
    305-306
Teamsters union. *See* International
    Brotherhood of Teamsters
Technical and Supervisory Section
    (AUEW), 35, 36, 37, 42
Technological innovation (Sweden),
    266-271, 281, 282-284
Technology, capital, and job transfer,
    343
Teste, Stephen, 277, 283-284
Thatcher, Margaret, 14
Thompson, Alex, 162, 163, 170, 171,
    172
Thonessen, Werner, 192
Tideexpress Motor AB, 261
Trade commissions (Netherlands), 129-
    130
Trade Union Advisory Committee
    (OECD), 349, 351
Trade Union and Labor Relations Act
    (Great Britain, 1974), 4, 5, 12, 15,
    20n
Trades Union Congress (Great Britain),
    3-4, 5, 14, 20, 340, 343, 344
Transnational bargaining, 337-339
Transnational labor relations, 329-355;
    cases, 357-377
Transport and General Workers Union
    (Great Britain), 2, 3, 23

Transportation Workers' Union, 358-360

Treaty of Rome (1957), 184, 393

UAW. *See* United Automobile Workers' Union
UIL. *See* Union of Italian Labor
UILM. (Italy), 88
ULP. *See* Unfair Labor Practices
UNEDIC. *See Union Nationale Interprofessionelle pour l'Emploi dans l'Industrie et le Commerce*
USWA (U.S. steelworkers union), 296
Unemployment compensation, 403; France, 55, 70; Great Britain, 16; Italy, 98; U.S., 307; West Germany, 181, 227
Unemployment rates, 400; France, 45; Great Britain, 1; Italy, 85; Sweden, 233; U.S., 295, 302; West Germany, 173, 211
Unfair Labor Practices, 318, 319
Unilever, 134, 338, 349
Union financial status: France, 47; International Trade Secretariats, 337; Italy, 89; Sweden, 238; West Germany, 176, 181
Union membership, 404; France, 47; Great Britain, 2; Italy, 89; Netherlands, 120-121; Sweden, 236, 290; U.S., 296; West Germany, 175
Union movement: France, 46-48; Great Britain, 2-5; Italy, 86-90; Netherlands, 118-122; Sweden, 234-238; U.S., 296-297; West Germany, 174-177
*Union Nationale Interprofessionelle pour l'Emploi dans l'Industrie et le Commerce* (France), 55, 70
Union of Dutch Conscripts, 121
Union of Food, Stimulants, Hotel, and Restaurant Employees (West Germany), 203, 205-208, 210
Union of Italian Labor, 87, 88, 105, 109
Union recognition: Great Britain, 7-8;
U.S., 298-299; West Germany, 178
Union shop, 297, 305, 373
Union stucture (federations and confederations): France, 46-47; Great Britain, 3; Italy, 87-88; Netherlands, 118-119; Sweden, 234-236, West Germany, 174-175
Unions: adversary role (U.S.), 299, 358; business activities (Sweden), 238; certification elections (U.S.), 298-299, 300, 305, 311, 316-317, 319-320; and multinational corporations, 329-355; and profit-sharing plans, 385; punishment of, 180, 244-245, 247, 280; and worker participation, 377, 378, 379-380; and works councils, 142-143 (Netherlands), 381, 382-383, 384
Unit labor costs, 402; France, 46; Great Britain, 2; Italy, 86; Netherlands, 117-118; Sweden, 234; U.S., 296; West Germany, 174
United Automobile Workers' Union (U.S.), 296, 300, 332, 334, 335
United Chemical Workers' Union (U.S.), 334
United Nations, 336, 344, 346
United States, 295-328 (*See also names of individual unions, companies, and political parties*); automobile industry, 244-225; aviation industry, 362; "company unions," 302; courts, 301; economic and labor statistics, 295-296; employer rights, 299; guaranteed annual income, 307; hospital and medical care programs, 309-310, 312-313, 317, 318, 320; Internal Revenue Service, 308, 317; Landrum Griffin Act (1959), 297; National Labor Relations Act (1935), 297, 301, 302, 315; National Labor Relations Board, 298, 299, 300, 305, 311-320, 374; national mediation board, 359, 362; Railway Labor Act, 362n; right-to-work laws, 297; salary continuance program, 309; salary evaluation pro-

United States (cont.)
gram, 306-307; State Public
Employees Relations Act, 306; Taft-
Hartley Act (1947), 297; teachers
union, 305-306; transnational labor
relations, 329, 332, 335, 336, 339,
341, 342-343, 345, 362n, 373-374;
Unfair Labor Practices, 318, 319;
union certification elections,
298-299, 305, 311-312, 316-317,
319-320, 373; unions' adversary
role, 299, 358

VAD (Dutch compulsory profit shar-
ing), 134-135, 385
VHP. *See* Organization of Higher Per-
sonnel
VNO (Netherlands), 122, 123, 131
VPCW (Netherlands), 122
VW, 184
Vacation Act (Sweden, 1977), 249
Vacations and holidays: Italy, 96, 100;
Sweden, 249-250; U.S., 309; West
Germany, 183-184, 226-227
Van Berkel, Dirk, 137-155
Van Rijn, Derk, 157, 170, 171
Vermeer, Hendrick, 157, 170, 171
Vernon, Raymond, 329, 331
*Vertrauensleute* (West German "men
of confidence"), 224
Vetter, Heinz-Oscar, 378
Viniprix, 60
Vleeschauwer, Dirk, 357, 361-362
Vogelaar, Theodore, 351
Volvo, 239, 250

WAO (Dutch national health plan),
128
WFTU. *See* World Federation of
Trade Unions
Wage policies: France, 53; Great Brit-
ain, 8-9; Italy, 95-96; Sweden, 238,
252-253, 289; U.S., 306-307
Waldenstrom, Erland, 253
Walsh, Anthony, 324-325
Warner-Lambert, 352
Warning strike (France), 51

Welin, Ingrid, 267-268
West Germany, 173-231 (*See also
names of individual unions, companies, and political parties*); Act
for the Protection of Women
(1972), 184; "Agency shop,"
175-176; Bundestag, 177; chemical
workers' union, 180, 330; civil service and government employees'
unions, 175; Collective Bargaining
Agreement Act (1949, 1952), 176,
177; conciliation committees, 193,
195, 198, 200, 209, 210; constitution, 177; economic and labor
statistics, 173-174; economics committee, 194; employee capital accumulation laws, 195, 196; employment agency, 200; Federal Vacation
Act (1963), 183; government level
bargaining, 91; labor courts, 180,
182, 183, 193; labor directors on
company boards, 185-192; "leading
employee," 186-190; mantel agreement, 179; minimum wage, 178,
179; "peace obligation," 180, 193;
Protection Against Dismissal Act
(1969), 182; state level bargaining,
178; tariff agreement, 178, 179, 208,
211, 215; transnational labor relations, 329-330, 339, 341, 363;
unions and confederations, 174-175;
*Vertrauensleute*, 224; Works Constitution Act (1952/1972), 186, 192,
193, 194, 197, 205, 221, 222, 381;
Works Council Act (1972), 184, 393
Westinghouse, 338
Wherry (ASTMS), 31
White-collar workers: France, 47;
Great Britain, 2; Italy, 88, 100-101;
Netherlands, 121; Sweden, 234, 235,
262, 270, 271-274, 284; U.S., 298,
305; West Germany, 175, 203, 207,
208, 215-216
Wildcat strikes: Sweden, 239, 272-273,
283; West Germany, 203, 325
Wilkins (ASTMS), 25, 31
Willat, Norris, 337, 339

Williams and Glyn Bank (Great
Britain), 19
Wilson, Donald, 321, 326, 327
Wilson, John, 325-326
Wilson, R. Steven, Jr., 323
Wilson Distributors Company (U.S.),
321-328
Wisner, Alain, 53
Work-to-the-rule strike: France, 51;
Great Britain, 14, 38, 44
Work week, shortened: Great Britain,
16; Italy, 98; U.S., 307; West Ger-
many, 227-228
Worker director system (Great
Britain), 18
Worker participation, 377-380; France,
57-59, 379-380; Great Britain, 18-19,
380; Italy, 102-104, 106, 379; in
multinational corporations, 348;
Netherlands, 128-133, 143-145;
Sweden, 251-252, 264, 288-289,
290-292, 379; U.S., 302-303; West
Germany, 185-195, 221-222, 377-379
Workers Protection Act (Sweden,
1974), 247

Works Constitution Act (West Germany, 1952/1972), 186, 192, 193,
194, 197, 205, 221, 222, 381
Works Council Act (Netherlands,
1979), 129, 383
Works Council Act (West Germany,
1972), 184, 393
Works Councils, 380-384; France,
57-59, 380, 382; Great Britain, 381,
382; Italy, 91, 95, 102-103, 106,
380, 382; Netherlands, 128-131,
138-155, 160, 169-171, 380, 382,
383-384; Sweden, 251-252, 263-264,
268-271, 288, 290-291, 380, 382-383,
384; U.S., 302, 381; West Germany,
175, 178, 192-195, 197-201, 208-218,
222-224, 229-230, 380-381, 383-384
Works councils: and company boards
Netherlands), 143-145; transnational
labor relations, 348; and unions
(Netherlands), 142-143
World Federation of Trade Unions, 87,
88, 344

# About the Author

**Thomas Kennedy** is professor emeritus of labor relations at the Harvard Business School and visiting professor of labor relations at Babson College. At Harvard, where he taught for twenty-three years, he held the Weatherhead Professorship in Business Administration. In 1971 he received the Salgo Award as the outstanding teacher at the school. Before teaching at Harvard, he was director of labor relations at Atlas Chemical Company (now ICI America). Earlier he taught at The University of Pennsylvania and at Muhlenberg College. He received the A.B degree from Swarthmore College, M.A and Ph.D degrees from The University of Pennsylvania, and the M.A degree from Harvard University.

Professor Kennedy is an active labor arbitrator, hearing forty to fifty cases per year, including disputes under a contract between Eastern Airlines and the Air Line Pilots' Association, in which he is named as a permanent arbitrator. He is a charter member of the National Academy of Arbitrators. He is author of *Effective Labor Arbitration* and *Automation Funds and Displaced Workers*, and coauthor (with Selekman, Fuller, and Baitsell) of *Problems in Labor Relations*.